Culture and Customs of the Baltic States

Culture and Customs of the Baltic States

KEVIN O'CONNOR

Culture and Customs of Europe

GREENWOOD PRESS
Westport, Connecticut • London

Library of Congress Cataloging-in-Publication Data

O'Connor, Kevin, 1967–
   Culture and customs of the Baltic states / by Kevin O'Connor.
     p. cm.— (Culture and customs of Europe)
   Includes bibliographical references and index.
   ISBN 0–313–33125–1 (alk. paper)
   1. Baltic States—Social life and customs. 2. Baltic States—Civilization. I. Title. II.
Series.
DK502.6.O24 2006
947.9—dc22   2005031498

British Library Cataloguing in Publication Data is available.

Library of Congress Catalog Card Number: 2005031498
ISBN: 0–313–33125–1

First published in 2006

Greenwood Press, 88 Post Road West, Westport, CT 06881
An imprint of Greenwood Publishing Group, Inc.
www.greenwood.com

Printed in the United States of America

The paper used in this book complies with the
Permanent Paper Standard issued by the National
Information Standards Organization (Z39.48–1984).

10 9 8 7 6 5 4 3 2 1

Contents

Series Foreword

THE OLD WORLD and the New World have maintained a fluid exchange of people, ideas, innovations, and styles. Even though the United States became the de facto world leader and economic superpower in the wake of a devastated Europe in World War II, Europe has remained for many the standard bearer of Western culture.

Millions of Americans can trace their ancestors to Europe. The United States as we know it was built on waves of European immigration, starting with the English who braved the seas to found the Jamestown Colony in 1607. Bosnian and Albanian immigrants are some of the latest new Americans.

In the Gilded Age of one of our great expatriates, the novelist Henry James, the Grand Tour of Europe was de rigueur for young American men of means, to prepare them for a life of refinement and taste. In a more recent democratic age, scores of American college students have Eurailed their way across Great Britain and the Continent, sampling the fabled capitals and bergs in a mad, great adventure, or have benefited from a semester abroad. For other American vacationers and culture vultures, Europe is the prime destination.

What is the New Europe post–Cold War, post Berlin Wall in a new millennium? Even with the different languages, rhythms, and rituals, Europeans have much in common: they are largely well educated, prosperous, and worldly. They also have similar goals and face common threats and form alliances. With the advent of the European Union, the open borders, and the Euro and considering globalization and the prospect of a homogenized Europe, an updated survey of the region is warranted.

Culture and Customs of Europe features individual volumes on the countries most studied and for which fresh information is in demand from students and other readers. The Series casts a wide net, inclusive of not only the expected countries, such as Spain, France, England, and Germany, but also countries such as Poland and Greece that lie outside Western Europe proper. Each volume is written by a country specialist, with intimate knowledge of the contemporary dynamics of a people and culture. Sustained narrative chapters cover the land, people, and brief history; religion; social customs; gender roles, family, and marriage; literature and media; performing arts and cinema; and art and architecture. The national character and ongoing popular traditions of each country are framed in an historical context and celebrated along with the latest trends and major cultural figures. A country map, chronology, glossary, and evocative photos enhance the text.

The historied and enlightened Europeans will continue to fascinate Americans. Our futures are strongly linked politically, economically, and culturally.

Acknowledgments

THIS BOOK BENEFITED from the help of numerous people. I am greatly indebted to Darius Staliūnas and the Lithuanian Institute of History, whom I thank for providing me with housing, materials, and much stimulating conversation during my brief visit in the spring of 2004. Thank you also to the staff, faculty, and students of Vidzeme Augustskolas, in Latvia where I enjoyed a longer stay in the summer of 2002. With great affection I would like to express my appreciation to the Lapicka family for their extraordinary hospitality in 2002 and for a lovely visit to the Open-Air Ethnographic Museum in Riga on my return visit in 2004. Among my friends and acquaintances from the Baltic states I am especially grateful to Bozena Meckovskaia, with whom I shared the experience of traveling through Estonia. Bozena corrected some of my misperceptions about northeastern Europe and taught me more about the realities of life in Lithuania during the 1990s than any professor could.

That said, I must acknowledge my debt to all those professors who made useful suggestions and saved me from making still more silly errors than the finished product undoubtedly already contains. Thanks especially to Andrejs Plakans of Iowa State University for being kind enough to read the entire manuscript and to Ted Weeks of Southern Illinois University for his comments on various chapters. I am also grateful to Bob Stagg and Phyllis Passafiume for their helpful suggestions on art history, and to Gonzaga University's theater director John Hofland for his comments on chapter 7.

The entire manuscript was written during my first two years at Gonzaga University, where I have been fortunate to join a wonderful department that has kindly accommodated my professional priorities. I am indeed grateful to the university's friendly, efficient, and professional staff, including Michelle Reich, who helped with the index, and Fawn Gass and Diana Lartz, whose mastery of fax and photocopy machines made my life much easier. I would also like to thank Apex Publishing, who saw to it that this book was published without undue delay, and Wendi Schnaufer, my editor at Greenwood Press, for her patience and encouragement—and for allowing me enough latitude so that I could write the book that I wanted to write.

Introduction

SINCE THE BEGINNING of the thirteenth century the region presently inhabited by the Estonian, Latvian, and Lithuanian peoples has been a crossroad between Germanic and Slavic Europe. It has endured German colonization, numerous wars of conquest, and demographic Russification. In light of this seemingly unending series of catastrophes, it is a wonder that the three Baltic countries exist at all and that the cultures and traditions of their peoples have managed to survive. Yet some would argue that it is precisely because of these threats that the Baltic peoples, led by their artists, writers, politicians, clerics, and other cultural figures, have made conscious efforts to sustain many of their oldest and dearest customs and traditions.

Although most Estonians and Latvians view the hundreds of years of German domination as regrettable, they also tend to see this as a period of tutelage that yielded some benefits; there is relatively little questioning of the Germanic and Christian elements that were blended into their cultures. The Balts' relationship with Russia and its culture, however, is often quite different. Moscow's attempts in the past century to demographically Russify, ideologically Sovietize, and forcefully secularize the Baltic region provoked an anti-Russian reaction that persists to this day. Just as there has been relatively only a modest little intermarriage between Estonians and Russians, so has there been blending of their traditions and cultures.

Estonians conceive of themselves as Westerners, as Scandinavians, and above all as Estonians. Numbering less than one million, the Estonian people are protective of the native traditions that are so integral to their collective identity. Lithuanians, although never subject to a German elite, long ago accepted Western Catholicism and many of its traditions and holidays, which they came to regard as their own; these, naturally, have been grafted onto ancient Lithuanian traditions and holidays. Latvia, historically the most Russophile and presently the most ethnically diverse of the three Baltic countries, has the highest rate of intermarriage between Latvians and non-Latvians; but even here, too, what is Latvian is glorified because it is Latvian, and what is Russian is foreign and is for the most part peacefully tolerated.

Imagine a journey through this region little more than one century ago, before the wars and revolutions of the twentieth century, before there were independent countries called Lithuania, Latvia, or Estonia. Embarking from Klaipėda (then Memel), the curious traveler subsequently stops for visits in Kaunas (then Kovno), Vilnius (Wilno to its Polish inhabitants, Vilna to the Jews and Russians), through the Lithuanian and Latvian heartlands to Riga, Valmiera, and Tartu (Dorpat), and after a month or perhaps several he would finally arrive in Tallinn (Reval). If he were German, he would see and hear much that is familiar to him in the port cities of Memel, Riga, and Reval, yet his natural curiosity about the surrounding people and their unusual languages and customs would have him make the acquaintance of Lithuanian peasants near Memel, Latvian shipyard workers in Riga, and Estonian shopkeepers in Reval. In Kovno he would observe two worlds—that of the staunchly Catholic Lithuanian and that of the Yiddish-speaking Jew—existing side by side, almost equally impoverished but rarely intermingling. In Wilno, a third Polish and a fourth Russian world would complete the galaxy of peoples inhabiting this rather quaint, medium-sized city. In the Latvian countryside the traveler would encounter almost nothing but Latvian peasants and their livestock, and in Estonia he would pass a series of German estates surrounded by tidy but meager Estonian farms, until finally reaching Dorpat, the center of a burgeoning Estonian culture.

This world, this multinational mosaic sustained for more than two centuries by the ubiquity (in the port cities, at least) of German *Kultur* and the threat of the Russian imperial knout, no longer exists. The Estonians, Latvians, and Lithuanians remain, and they are the masters of their own countries and destinies. The Baltic Germans who dominated much of the region permanently abandoned it in 1939; the Jews of Lithuania and Latvia were murdered shortly afterward; while the large Russian-speaking communities who remain in the region today often feel like strangers in what was until fairly recently a vastly larger, Russian-dominated enterprise. Much has been lost over the past century, but much has survived as well. This book explores what remains, and more specifically what has been consciously preserved and developed in the cultures and traditions of modern Estonia, Latvia, and Lithuania. It is about their religions, their music, their literature, their art, and their architecture. It attempts to describe how the Baltic peoples live when they are not working, how they prepare for and celebrate their holidays, and what they eat and drink when doing so.

Understanding of the past is shaped by the needs of the present just as the present is shaped by the struggles and triumphs of the past. Thus, in exploring the traditions and customs of the Baltic peoples, this book pays much attention to history. The Estonians, Latvians, and Lithuanians themselves would have it no other way, as they view their contemporary cultures in the broader context of their own histories and their struggles to shape their own national identities, to create their own national literatures, and to sustain their own independent national states.

The observant visitor to the region today can see that the theater, music, literature, and art of the Baltic countries are responding to the international trends of the modern (and postmodern) era; in a deeper sense, however, the contemporary developments in the region's cultural life are part of an ongoing conversation about the Balts' understanding of their own histories, destinies, and national identities. To a Lithuanian, it would be preposterous to discuss modern orchestral music or abstract painting without paying due respect to the achievements of Mikalojus Čurlionis a century ago; to a Latvian, any conversation about theater or literature begins with Jānis Rainis, who might be considered the Latvian Shakespeare; and Tallinn, more than any other Baltic city, retains the architectural inheritance of its German masters of old, while the city's skyline is deformed by its dozens of Soviet-era housing projects. Indeed, modern culture in Eastern Europe (or as some prefer, East Central Europe) is not only a product of history, in many ways it is its hostage. Thus, desiring to avoid the sin of presentism, and begging the forgiveness of the reader who might be expecting something different, this book discusses the past as much as it does the present, and often more so.

Chronology

ca. 3000–2000 B.C.E.	Finno-Ugric and proto-Baltic tribes settle on the Baltic shores.
8th–12th centuries	Baltic peoples trade and battle with Vikings and later with Slavic tribes.
1180	First attempt to convert Baltic pagans led by Father Meinhard, a German priest.
1198	Pope Innocent III sanctions the first Baltic crusade.
13th century	Latvia and southern Estonia conquered by Germans. A Livonian state formed.
1201	Riga founded by the Bishop of Livonia, Albert von Buxhoevden of Bremen.
1211	Foundation stone of the Riga Dome laid.
1219	Northern Estonia conquered by the Danes.
1237	Livonian branch of the Teutonic Order established.
1253	Mindaugas crowned the King of Lithuania.
1267	St. Olaf's Church in Tallinn, Estonia, built.

14th century	Lithuanian territory extended southward to the Black Sea.
1316–41	Grand Duke Gediminas rules Lithuania and encourages traders and merchants, including Jews, to settle in the region.
1343–46	Estonian peasant uprising forces Danes to surrender control of northern Estonia to Germans.
1386	Lithuanian prince Jogaila marries into the Polish royal family, thus establishing a nominal union between Lithuania and Poland. Lithuania, Europe's last pagan kingdom, accepts Christianity.
1410	Lithuanian defeat of the Teutonic Knights prevents further German expansion eastward.
1520s	Lutheranism reaches the Baltic region.
1525	In Lübeck, a Lutheran book of common prayers published in Estonian, Livonian, and Latvian. All copies are subsequently destroyed.
1547	First Lithuanian-language book, Martynas Mažvydas's *Catechism,* printed.
1558–83	Russia's Tsar Ivan IV attempts to conquer Livonia, but is checked by Sweden and Poland. The Livonian Confederation is dissolved and most of Livonia is incorporated into Poland-Lithuania.
1561	Sweden acquires Tallinn and surrounding region.
1569	Lithuanian and Polish crowns formally unite to form the Polish-Lithuanian Commonwealth.
1579	Vilnius University established.
1581	Church of St. Anne in Vilnius completed.
1584	Sweden annexes northern Estonia, creating the Duchy of Estland.

1629	Poland forced to cede Livonia to Sweden.
1632	Swedes found Dorpat (Tartu) University in the Duchy of Estland.
1675	First Baltic German newspaper, *Ordinari Post-Zeitung,* published, probably in Tallinn.
1688–94	Ernst Glück translates the Bible into Latvian.
1699	Dissolution of Hanseatic League.
1710	In the Great Northern War (1700–15), Russian Tsar Peter I seizes Estland and Livland (southern Estonia and northern Latvia) from Sweden.
1772–95	Prussia, Austria, and Russia partition Poland. Lithuania and Courland (western Latvia) annexed by Russia.
1803–09	Main building of Tartu University constructed.
1806	Appearance of the first Estonian-language newspaper, *Tarto maa-rahwa Näddali-Leht.*
1816–19	After the Russian defeat of Napoleon, serfdom formally abolished in Estland and Livland. Initially the former serfs do not receive land with their freedom.
1822	Appearance of the first Latvian-language newspaper, *Latviešu Avīzes.*
1824–79	Establishment of literary societies facilitates the formation of distinctive national identities among the Baltic peoples.
1840–60	Agrarian reforms are undertaken in Estland and Livland.
1845–48	Massive conversion of Estonian and Latvian peasants to Russian Orthodoxy.
1849	First Lithuanian-language newspaper, *Keleivis,* published in Königsberg.

1857–61	Estonian national epic *Kalevipoeg* is published by F. R. Kreutzwald.
1861	Lithuanian serfs freed.
1862	Riga Polytechnicum founded by tsarist authorities.
1863	Polish insurrection, aided by Lithuanian peasants. Peasant unrest subsequently breaks out in Livland, Courland, and Estland.
1867–68	Famine followed by the massive emigration of Lithuanians.
1869	First theater performance in Latvian, Ādolfs Alunāns's *Self-Tutored*.
1870	Performance of Lydia Koidula's *The Cousin from Saaremaa* marks the birth of Estonian theater.
1880s–1890s	Russification policies implemented in the Baltic territories.
1888	Latvian national epic *Lāčplēsis* published by Andrējs Pumpurs.
1898–1913	Art Nouveau architecture flourishes in Riga.
1900–09	Lithuanian composer and artist Mikalojus Čiurlionis at his peak.
1905	Revolution in the Russian Empire.
1908–10	First short films produced in the Baltic provinces.
1914–18	World War I; Russia's Baltic territories occupied by German forces.
1917	Russian Tsar Nicholas II abdicates throne in March as the tsarist regime collapses. Russia's new Provisional Government assents to the territorial unification of its Estonian province.
November 1917	Bolsheviks seize power in Russia.

February–March 1918	Russia and Germany agree to peace terms at Brest-Litovsk. Russia must surrender its western territories, including the Baltic provinces. Estonia and Lithuania proclaim independence.
November 1918	Latvia proclaims independence.
1918–20	Baltic states fight the Bolsheviks, White Russian armies, and German and Polish forces to defend their independence. Lithuania loses Vilnius region to newly independent Poland.
1920	Baltic states sign peace treaties with Soviet Russia.
1919–22	Baltic states carry out land reform and introduce democratic constitutions and are admitted to the League of Nations in 1921.
January 1923	Lithuania annexes the Klaipėda (*Ger.* Memel) region, formerly under international control.
December 1924	Communist coup attempt in Estonia fails.
Mid-1920s	First radio broadcasts in the Baltic countries.
December 1925	Premiere of Lithuania's first professional ballet, *Coppélia.*
September 1926	Lithuania signs nonagression and neutrality pact with USSR.
1926–29	Antanas Smetona establishes dictatorship in Lithuania.
1928	Premiere of first Estonian opera, *The Vikings.*
1931	Appearance of first Estonian animated film, *Adventures of Juku the Dog.*
1933	Debut of Lithuanian national opera *Gražina.*
1934	Konstantin Päts and Kārlis Ulmanis establish dictatorships in Estonia and Latvia.
August–September 1939	Nazi-Soviet nonagression pact; secret protocols award the Baltic states to the USSR.

June–August 1940	Baltic states occupied by Soviet troops, then annexed to USSR.
June 1941	Massive deportations of Baltic peoples to Soviet Russia.
1941–44	Nazi occupation of Lithuania, Latvia and Estonia. Nearly the entire Jewish populations of these countries murdered.
1944	Soviet forces reoccupy Baltic states. Westward flight of thousands of Balts continues through 1945.
1944–48	"Forest brothers" resist Soviet occupation. A few bands continue to resist into the mid-1950s.
1944–52	Massive deportation of Estonians, Latvians, and Lithuanians to other Soviet republics, accompanied by industrialization and the first waves of Russian and other Slavic immigrants.
1947	First collective farms established in the Baltic republics. Collectivization completed by 1952.
1949–51	Bloody purge of "bourgeois nationalists" from the Estonian Communist Party.
Mid-1950s	First television broadcasts in the Baltic republics.
1956–64	Nikita Khrushchev's "thaw" loosens ideological restrictions throughout the USSR.
1970s	Nationalist and human rights movements grow in the Baltic republics.
1972	Rioting and demonstrations in Lithuania following the self-immolation of student. First appearance of the dissident publication *Chronicle of the Lithuanian Catholic Church*.
1985	Mikhail Gorbachev named CPSU general secretary and launches reform program.
1987–88	Growth of environmentalist activity in the Baltic republics, which becomes the basis for resurgent nationalist movements.

April–June 1988	Popular Fronts formed in Estonia and Latvia. *Sajūdis* formed in Lithuania.
November 1988–July 1989	Restrictive language laws enacted in the Baltic republics, followed by declarations of sovereignty within the USSR.
August 23, 1989	"Baltic Way" demonstration unites up to two million Balts in protest against the Nazi-Soviet pact of August 1939.
March 1990	Elections to Baltic parliaments. Vytautas Landsbergis selected to head the Lithuanian government. Lithuania declares secession from the USSR.
April–June 1990	Soviet embargo imposed on Lithuania.
January 1991	Soviet paratroopers and KGB units attack the Vilnius television tower.
February–March 1991	Baltic peoples overwhelmingly vote in favor of independence in public referenda.
August 19–21, 1991	Hardline coup in Moscow attempts to depose Gorbachev and fails.
September 6, 1991	USSR formally recognizes independence of Baltic states.
September 17, 1991	United Nations admits Estonia, Latvia, and Lithuania.
November 1991	Baltic Assembly formed.
December 31, 1991	Commonwealth of Independent States (CIS) created to replace the USSR. Baltic states opt not to join.
1992–93	Baltic economies hit bottom: high inflation and unemployment, declining production. New currencies are adopted in each country. New constitutions adopted and elections held. Peak of Russian emigration from Baltic states. Privatization of broadcast media.
September 1993	Pope John Paul II visits the Catholic shrine in Aglona, Latvia.

1994	Baltic economies begin to recover. Baltic states join NATO's Partnership for Peace Program.
August 1994	Russian troop withdrawal from the Baltics completed.
September 28, 1994	Passenger ferry, the *Estonia,* sinks to the bottom of the Baltic Sea; 852 people die.
1995	Baltic Battalion (BALTBAT) established as part of Partnership for Peace program.
January 1995	Free Trade agreement concluded between European Union and Baltic states.
May 1995	Collapse of Baltija Bank sets off banking crisis in Latvia.
August 1998	Russian economic crisis temporarily interrupts economic recovery of Baltic states.
July 1999	Latvians elect first woman president of east central Europe, Vaira Vīķe-Freiberga.
2004	Baltic states join European Union and NATO alliance. Europa Tower in Vilnius becomes tallest building in the Baltics.
2005	The Baltic states record the fastest economic growth rates in the European Union.

1

The Land, People, and History

THE LAND

THE BALTIC STATES ARE three small countries nestled in northeastern Europe along the southern shore of the Baltic Sea. From north to south they are Estonia (*Eesti*), Latvia (*Latvija*), and Lithuania (*Lietuva*). The largest of them, Lithuania, encompasses 25,200 square miles and is only slightly larger than Latvia (24,900 sq. mi.). Each is comparable in size to West Virginia and is somewhat smaller than the Republic of Ireland. The smallest is Estonia. Including its lakes and islands, the country comprises 17,500 square miles, making it only slightly bigger than Denmark and comparable to New Hampshire and Vermont combined.

All three Baltic countries are low-lying and heavily forested. Located between 55 and 59.5 degrees latitude, the Baltic states occupy the same latitudinal space as the northern halves of the Canadian provinces British Columbia, Alberta, Saskatchewan, and Manitoba. Summertime visitors to northern Estonia enjoy up to 19 hours of sunlight; year-round residents, however, must endure the Baltic region's long, bleak winter nights. Whatever the season, the Baltic region is often damp, with wet, mostly cool summers and generally moderate but snowy winters. There are no mountains of any magnitude in the Baltic countries: the highest point in the entire region is Suur Munamägi (Great Egg Hill) in southeastern Estonia, which at 1,053 feet above sea level barely tops Gaiziņkalns in eastern Latvia at 1,030 feet. However, the region has thousands of lakes (many of which might more reasonably be classified as ponds), the largest being Lake Peipsi, which straddles Estonia and Russia.

Although forests and woodlands cover half of Estonia's territory, another fifth is covered by marshes. No European country has more living peat bogs than Estonia. Despite this distinction, Estonia's most significant geographical feature is its nearly 2,300 miles of coastline and its more than 1,500 islands and islets. The largest of these is Saaremaa (1,031 sq. mi.), known as Ösel when it was under Swedish control in the seventeenth century. Saaremaa is one of the most pristine parts of Estonia and is home to most of the country's 1,400 plant species as well as the scenic but sparsely populated Sõrve Peninsula. Tallinn (pop. 372,000), the capital, is not only the country's largest city, but with Toompea Castle and an extraordinarily well preserved medieval Old Town, it is also arguably its most beautiful. Although no other Estonian city rivals Tallinn in size or opulence, Tartu (pop. 100,000), whose university dates to 1632, can justly stake a claim to being the country's leading cultural center.

Latvia is divided into four regions. In the west is the Kurzeme, a largely rural region whose northernmost tip at the Kolka cape faces the Baltic Sea in the west and the Gulf of Riga in the east. Although Kurzeme's largest city is the port of Liepāja (pop. 80,000), some believe its most charming town is Kuldīga (pop. 12,400), whose castle is long gone but whose lovely waterfall, Europe's widest, seduces residents and visitors alike. Zemgale, Latvia's low-lying central region, is the seat of the country's capital, Riga (pop. 700,000). The indisputable center of Latvia's cultural, political, and economic life, Riga, like Tallinn, boasts a cozy and largely restored Old Town; but it is the city's stunning Art Nouveau architecture that sets it apart from the other Baltic capitals. Vidzeme, the hilly northern half of eastern Latvia, contains many of the country's historic castles (most notably those in Sigulda and Cēsis) as well as Gauja National Park. The southeastern part of Latvia is called Latgale. The location of Daugavpils (pop. 111,000), the country's second largest and most Russified city, Latgale is also the poorest and most rural region of Latvia.

Lithuania is both the biggest and the oldest of the Baltic countries, for its history as an independent state dates to the thirteenth century. Its four main regions are Aukštaitija (the Highlands, or Upper Lithuania) in the east, Samogitia or Žemaitija (the Lowlands, or Lower Lithuania) in the west, Suvalkija in the southwest, and Dzūkija in the south. Of the three Baltic states, Lithuania has by far the shortest coastline; however, it also possesses the northern half of the stunning Couronian Spit (Kaliningrad, which is part of Russia, controls the other half), a 61-mile sand bar that has several resort towns, pine forests, and spectacular sand dunes. While Kaunas in the south is the most "Lithuanian" of the country's larger cities, Vilnius (pop. 574,000),

The Baltic region before and after World War II. Courtesy of Cartographica.

the capital and the country's oldest city, is the most beautiful, baroque, and multicultural. At one time called the "Jerusalem of the North" for its once large Jewish population, Vilnius, known as Wilno to the Poles and Vilna to the Russians and Jews, is located in southeastern Lithuania near Poland, and in fact was governed by Poland in the 1920s and 1930s.

When compared with other countries that surround the Baltic Sea—Finland, Sweden, Germany, and Poland—Estonia, Latvia, and Lithuania are tiny and flat, no bigger than small, East Coast American states. There are no deserts or mountains, just lots of forests, woodlands, and lakes, more than a thousand rivers and streams, a few relatively sizeable cities, a thinly populated countryside, and a few thousand miles—if one includes Estonia's many islands—of mostly sandy coasts. A direct journey from the southern tip of Lithuania to the northernmost point of Estonia would carry a traveler only about 400 miles.

The small size of each of the Baltic countries is matched by their tiny populations. In 2004 Estonia's population dropped to about 1.35 million, down significantly from the 1.573 million people counted in the last Soviet census, which was taken in 1989 when the Baltic countries were still republics of the USSR. At 2.34 million (2003), Latvia's population has similarly declined since 1989, when the republic was home to 2.68 million people. Although Lithuania's population is also shrinking, the demographic situation is not quite as catastrophic there as in Estonia and Latvia. In 2004 Lithuania's population was estimated to be about 3.49 million, slightly up from 2001 but down about 200,000 from 1989.

Given their precarious geographical position and their history as a battleground on which larger powers such as Germany, Russia, Sweden, and Poland fought their many wars, it is amazing that the Baltic countries exist at all. Indeed, until fairly recently the Estonian and Latvian people did not even have their own states. Only as a result of World War I were Latvia and Estonia able to secure their independence from the Russian Empire, only to lose it again during World War II as the Soviet Red Army swept westward. Unlike Latvia and Estonia, Lithuania existed as an independent state during the later Middle Ages but was swallowed up first by Poland as the result of a dynastic union and later by an expansionist Russian Empire. However, Lithuania shared the fortunes of its northern neighbors during the twentieth century, securing its independence in 1920 only to be occupied by the Soviets during World War II. All three countries experienced physical devastation and catastrophic population losses during the two world wars. In 1991 all three Baltic states again gained their independence, and, in an effort to enhance their security and cement their ties to Western Europe, each joined the North Atlantic Treaty Organization (NATO) and the European Union in 2004.

THE PEOPLE

Because of their location and their shared history, observers tend to lump these three countries together as the "Baltic states" thereby overlooking the individual identities these nations have nurtured over the past 150 years or more. To be sure, Estonians, Latvians, and Lithuanians share some cultural similarities, but their survival has depended on the development of distinctive national identities. Estonians are closely related to the Finns and speak a Finno-Ugric language that is entirely unintelligible to the Latvian or Lithuanian ear. Latvians and Lithuanians, however, speak related Baltic languages of Indo-European origin. Although all three countries shared the experience of Russian and Soviet rule, Latvia and Estonia were heavily influenced by the Germans who conquered the region in the thirteenth century and who constituted the region's political, economic, and cultural elite right up until the early decades of the twentieth century. Lithuania, on the other hand, has closer cultural and historical ties to Poland, with which it was legally adjoined for more than two centuries. Indeed, like the Poles, Lithuanians overwhelmingly identify themselves as Catholics, whereas most Latvians and Estonians are Lutherans, when they are believers at all.

All three nations—and it should be noted that the word "nation" is not synonymous with "state" or "country"; it refers instead to a *people* sharing a common language, culture, and historical experience—locate the source of their identities in a folk culture that predates the arrival of Christianity. Indeed, folklore and folk traditions from pagan times continue to influence Estonian, Latvian, and Lithuanian music, literature, and art, and they remain integral to the cultural identities of the Baltic peoples. Summer solstice, for example, continues to be observed in all three countries and is accompanied by the performance of ancient rituals (such as jumping over a small fire) and the preparation of traditional foods. At Baltic song festivals and numerous other venues, one can still see on display the traditional costumes once worn by the Estonian, Latvian, and Lithuanian peoples.

Yet it can be misleading to talk about the Baltic states as countries belonging exclusively to the Estonian, Latvian, and Lithuanian peoples. As a result of foreign occupation, migration, and the myriad complexities of East European history, these are multiethnic societies. Although Russians are the largest national minority in each of the Baltic countries, their identity as a separate culture is murky, especially as so many of the people that are usually identified as "Russian" are in fact Ukrainian, Belarusian, or of mixed heritage. Therefore it is more useful to use the term "Russian speakers," which embraces not only Russians, but also Ukrainians and Belarusians. Of Latvia's total population, only about 60 percent are Latvians; most of the remaining

40 percent are Russian speakers. They form the majority in the capital, Riga, as well as in several other larger towns and are also concentrated in the Latgale region. Likewise, about two-thirds of Estonia's residents are ethnic Estonians; the remainder are mostly Russian speakers and reside largely in Tallinn and the area around Narva in the Estonian northeast. Although more than 80 percent of the Lithuanian population is ethnic Lithuanian, making it the most ethnically homogeneous of the Baltic states, the country also has substantial Russian-speaking and Polish minorities. The latter live mostly in Vilnius and the surrounding region.

While the Estonians, Latvians, and Lithuanians share their countries with significant Russian-speaking minorities, with whom they continue to work out the complicated issues of citizenship, education, and assimilation, the region also contains several smaller ethnic groups. In the Setumaa region of southeastern Estonia live several thousand Setus (Setus also live on the other side of the border in Russia), a linguistically distinct people who are culturally close to the Karelians of northwestern Russia. Estonia also has a small Swedish population as well as thousands of Ingrians, who are the Estonians' Finno-Ugric cousins. Livs, or Livonians, are also a Finno-Ugric people who once lived in settlements strung along the eastern and western coasts of Latvia's Kurzeme region. Despite recent efforts to preserve their unique culture, Livs have largely assimilated into the Latvian population, leaving no more than a dozen or so elderly native speakers of the Liv language today. Both Latvia and Lithuania today have substantial Roma communities, which live a completely separate existence on society's margins. Also living in Lithuania are several hundred Karaites (or Karaim); concentrated in Vilnius and nearby Trakai, the Karaites practice an ancient, pre-Talmudic form of Judaism. Of course, the Baltic countries were also once home to hundreds of thousands of Ashkenazi Jews called "Litvaks," most of whom lived in Lithuanian towns and villages and in larger cities such as Vilnius and Riga. More than 90 percent of the country's Jews were murdered during the Nazi occupation.

Although Estonia, Latvia, and Lithuania combined are home to about a million and a half Russian speakers (of a total population of little more than 7.2 million) and several other smaller ethnic minorities, the non-Baltic peoples, in particular the Russians, will be little discussed in this book. While Russians and peoples of other national origin share with the Baltic peoples their cities and resources, their cultures, customs, and traditions are fundamentally different. This may change in the future as the children of the Russian-speaking peoples become assimilated into the mainstream of Estonian, Latvian, and Lithuanian cultural life; but if that day comes they will no longer identify themselves as Russians or Ukrainians or Belarusians (it was perhaps easier when they could simply think of themselves as "Soviets") but as Estonians or Latvians or Lithuanians. There is some evidence that this process is already taking place. However, since space is limited and the book's main focus is not on one but *three* different nations, the large Russian-speaking community will by necessity be overlooked.

HISTORICAL BACKGROUND

Although 800 years have passed since the initial German conquests of the thirteenth century, the Latvians and Estonians have enjoyed an independent existence for only a few decades—that is, from the end of World War I to 1940, and then again from 1991 to the present. Unlike Latvia and Estonia, Lithuania existed as an independent medieval state, and then one closely tied to Poland, until it too fell under Russian and later Soviet rule. To understand how the cultures of the Baltic peoples developed in the nineteenth and twentieth centuries, it is important first to appreciate their position as peasants under the rule of foreign elites and as emerging nations that sought to define who they were in an age of nationalism and of Great Power domination. How did these tiny nations form? How did they survive Russification, Sovietization, and the great wars of the twentieth century? And how did they respond to the challenge of forming independent states not once, but twice in the twentieth century?

The Middle Ages

The first outside observer to take note of the peoples living along the southeastern Baltic coast was the first-century Roman historian Tacitus. In his book *The Germania*, Tacitus described a people called the Aestii: "They are the only people who collect amber—glaesum is their own word for it—in the shallows or even on the beach. Like true barbarians, they have never asked or discovered what it is or how it is made." Amber is a hard, yellowish fossil resin that was valued for its magnetic qualities, its alleged medicinal properties, and most of all for its ornamental uses. Traded by the ancient Balts, it was sought by the Romans and was distributed broadly throughout Europe. Throughout the ages the word *amber* has been almost synonymous with the coast that belongs to the Estonians and Latvians.

The Aestii to whom Tacitus referred were most likely the ancient Prussians—Indo-European peoples whose language, now dead, was closely related to that of the Lithuanians and of the proto-Latvian tribes such as the Cours, Zemgals, Latgals (or Latgalian), and Sels (or Selonians). Together these tribes are called the Balts, and they arrived in northeastern Europe from the Eurasian steppe at least 2,000 years before Tacitus took note of them. Estonians, who speak a Finno-Ugric language that is not related to the Indo-European languages spoken by the Latvians and Lithuanians, are not, at least in the linguistic sense, Balts. (However, here the Estonians are referred to as "Balts" in the geographical, cultural, and political senses.) Ancestors of the Estonians, like their Finno-Ugric cousins (Finns, Karelians, Hungarians, Ingrians), arrived from the Volga region of Russia even earlier than the Balts, somewhere between 3000 and 2500 B.C.E. Although both groups, the Finno-Ugric speakers and the Balts, were once broadly dispersed geographically, in later centuries they were consolidated in the region they now inhabit as a result of pressure from migrating German and Slavic tribes.

Before the German invasions and conquests of the thirteenth century, Balts and proto-Estonians were farmers who grew wheat, rye, and millet, while raising cattle, horses, goats, sheep, and chickens. They were also pagans, worshiping the spirits of the forests, mountains, fields, and water. Politically disorganized, they existed as a series of small, independent tribes that proved ineffective in protecting their independence during the era of German conquest. Only the Lithuanians managed to create a united kingdom by the thirteenth century, while Latvians and Estonians would have to wait until the twentieth to establish their own states. Surrounded by more populous and better organized neighbors such as Sweden, Poland, and Muscovy (the core of the emerging Russian state), during the Middle Ages the Baltic region became a battleground for their wars and the object of foreign conquest.

To the west of the Baltic tribes were German warriors, transformed during the Middle Ages into European knights and possessing the missionary zeal of new converts to the faith. While Orthodox Christianity had made an appearance in the region in the eleventh century with the arrival of Slavic missionaries, the German crusaders were bent on bringing Catholicism to Europe's last pagans. In 1198 Pope Innocent III (ca.1165–1216) authorized the launching of a holy war on the northeast with the same objectives as the recent crusades to the Near East: to defend Christian communities and to save souls, while at the same time creating new sources of papal revenue to meet the Church's growing commitments and ambitions. In Livonia the process of conquest and conversion began in 1201 with the creation of the Brothers of the Sword (*Schwertbrüder*). This knightly order was established by Albert von Buxhoevden of Bremen (ca.1165–1229), the Bishop of Livonia and the founder of the city of Riga, for the purpose of the subjugation and Christianization of the Baltic lands. The Livs and the Latgals, the weakest of the Baltic tribes, were quickly either conquered or won over as allies, while Albert and the Swordbrothers divided the spoils among themselves. The native populations were then baptized and subjected to an occupying elite of priests and landlords.

Medieval Livonia c.1500. Courtesy of Cartographica.

By 1227 the Estonian lands were conquered and fell under the rule of Denmark, while the Prussians held out for nearly six decades until they were finally defeated in 1283 by the Order of Teutonic Knights. The best organized of the Baltic peoples were the Lithuanians, who, in an alliance with the Zemgals, in 1236 defeated the Swordbrothers and killed most of their leaders. After this defeat the troubled Swordbrothers merged into the respected Teutonic Order, and their branch became known as the Livonian Order. Although never able to subjugate the Lithuanians, for several hundred years the Livonian Order ruled a state that comprised much of modern-day Latvia and the southern part of Estonia. Counterbalancing the Livonian Order's territories were those held by the Church, including the Riga Bishopric (later the Archbishopric), which comprised much of eastern Latvia; the Tartu (in German, Dorpat) Bishopric in eastern Estonia; the Bishopric of Courland (in Latvian, Kurzeme) in western Latvia; and the Bishopric of Saare-Lääne (in German, Ösel-Wik), which included western Estonia and most of its two large islands. The rest of Estonia belonged to Denmark until a peasant revolt, known as the St. George's Day Uprising (1343–45), resulted in the region's sale to the Livonian Order in 1346.

Thus from the thirteenth century onward most of the Baltic tribes were assimilated into a Christian world that was governed by the Holy Roman Empire (that is, medieval Germany), the pope, and the Livonian Order. While some surviving leaders and native elites were Germanized, the mass of subjugated peasants coexisted with a foreign upper crust of knights, clergymen, merchants, and noblemen in what was essentially a colonial relationship. This arrangement enabled the "Latvian" and "Estonian" peasants to preserve, with significant modifications, their languages and customs. Less fortunate were the ancient Prussians, who as West Baltic cousins of the Lithuanians were either assimilated by the Germans or destroyed by the seventeenth century.

Only the Lithuanians, for the time being at least, remained free of foreign rule and foreign gods. Around 1230 they united under the leadership of a ruthless tribal king named Mindaugas (?–1263), who agreed to accept Christianity as a condition for his assumption of the Lithuanian crown in 1253. However, Mindaugas's policy of coexistence with the Teutonic Knights so alienated his nobles that they killed him and his sons and reverted to paganism. It was not until the reign of Jogaila (1348–1434) in the late fourteenth century that the Christianization of Lithuania began in earnest. By that time Lithuania was on its way to becoming one of the largest states in Europe as it absorbed the lands of other Baltic tribes and of nearby eastern Slavs.

It was under the Lithuanian King Gediminas (ruled 1316–41) and his immediate successors that much of this expansion took place, as they took advantage of the destruction wrought by the Mongols in what is today Russia and Ukraine to augment Lithuania's territory. Gediminas's encouragement of western traders, artisans, and landowners to settle in his realm was also of lasting importance, for he provided them with protection of their person and their faith, thereby establishing the principle of religious tolerance in the Lithuanian lands. Among these settlers were Jews, who eventually formed a large community in Vilnius. By the time Gediminas's grandson Jogaila ascended the throne and converted to Christianity in 1386, the Grand Duchy of Lithuania, a mostly Slavic and Orthodox realm, stretched from the Baltic to the Black Seas. To the east lay a recovering Muscovy, whose leaders were bent on regaining the territories lost as a result of the fracturing of the Kievan Rus.

An important turning point in Lithuanian history was the Krevo Union of 1385, when Grand Duke Jogaila was offered Jadwiga, the 11-year-old queen of Poland, and with her the Polish crown. Six years later Jogaila, baptized as Władysław II Jagiełło, was forced to cede his title as Grand Duke of Lithuania to his cousin Vytautas (1350–1430). Together they defeated the Teutonic

Expansion of Lithuania to 1430. Courtesy of Cartographica.

Knights at Grünwald (Žalgiris to the Lithuanians) in 1410, thereby preventing the further eastward expansion of the Germans. Although the Lithuanian and Polish crowns were united, the Lithuanian administration functioned under a separate legal code known as the "Lithuanian Statute." Whatever the arrangement, it was always clear that Lithuania was the junior partner in this union, which ensured that tensions between them would persist. Over time the Lithuanian elites became Polonized, absorbing the language and culture of the Polish church and nobility, while the mass of Lithuanian peasants became enserfed, tied to the estates of the nobles.

Because of the threat posed by the growing might of their eastern neighbor, Muscovy, which openly interfered in the Grand Duchy's domestic affairs and launched a major war of conquest in the Baltic region in 1558, the Poles and Lithuanians strengthened their ties with the conclusion of the Treaty of Lublin in 1569. Henceforth the Polish Kingdom and the Grand Duchy of Lithuania would constitute a single indivisible state with a jointly elected leader and a parliament (*Sejm*) of nobles. While transferring parts of what is today Belarus and Ukraine to Polish administration (other areas in the south and east were lost to Muscovy), Lithuania also seized on the Livonian state's political and religious divisions to take possession of Courland, Zemgale, and southern Estonia (Sweden took northern Estonia) in 1561. Thus, just as Lithuania began its uncomfortable union with Poland, it also reoriented itself toward the Baltic coast.

For two centuries the noble-dominated Polish-Lithuanian Commonwealth (*Rzeczpospolita*) was one of the largest and most powerful states in Europe. However, it was a politically unstable and badly administered state that was unable to withstand the assaults of Sweden and Muscovy. Indeed, for nearly three-quarters of a century, from 1648 to 1721, the whole of Lithuania was either a site of warfare or a conduit for the foreign armies that moved across it. The Lithuanian population, reduced by half between 1648 and 1697, recovered during the eighteenth century, but the *Sejm*'s representatives, fearing the danger that a strong ruler might pose and seeking to protect their individual and corporate interests, rendered the country ungovernable and left it vulnerable to predators. While the Commonwealth was a de facto Russian protectorate during the first half of the eighteenth century, whatever remained of its independence disappeared during a series of partitions in 1772, 1793, and 1795 at the hands of the ambitious monarchs who ruled Austria, Prussia, and Russia. With the Commonwealth wiped off the map, Russia acquired most of Lithuania, as well as much of Poland, but the region called Lithuania Minor (*Mažoji Lietuva*) remained beyond Russian control and became part of Prussia (later Germany).

By this time Russia had already acquired most of the territories that would later be known as Latvia and Estonia. But before we turn to the place of the Baltic provinces within the Russian Empire, let us first consider the nature of German rule in Estonia, Livonia, and Courland because subservience to a German upper class was a constant feature of life in the Baltic region right up to World War I. The first century or so of German rule, beginning with the conquests of the early thirteenth century, was marked by clashes between the Church, which controlled about one-third of Livonia, and the Knights of the Order, who administered the rest. Over time, more territory fell under the control of the latter, whose territories were organized as the Livonian Confederation in 1418. Nevertheless, it was the Church that continued to control the most important institutions of Livonian life, including the parishes, congregations, clergy, and houses of worship. Merchants were another element of the Baltic elite, and they rushed into the region during the thirteenth century. Hansa ("flock") merchants had earlier formed the Hanseatic League, which by the middle of the fourteenth century included more than 100 towns and outposts throughout the North Sea and Baltic Sea regions, including Tallinn and Riga.

Just as the German nobles dominated the political and cultural life of Livonia, German traders dominated the economic life of the region. Nowhere was this truer than in Riga, the area's first and largest commercial center. However, Riga and other Baltic towns also became attractive destinations for fleeing peasants (*undeutsche,* as non-Germans were called). At the outset of German rule some Baltic peasants had small amounts of land, but most were landless. Their status slipped still further as the tax burden increased, forcing most peasants into serfdom. Some escaped this fate by moving to the cities to work as artisans or craftsmen.

The defining feature of Baltic life under German rule was the two separate worlds inhabited by Baltic Germans (*Deutschbalten*) and non-Germans: native Balts generally lived apart from the German-speaking elite, spoke their own languages, and maintained their own folk cultures. While Catholicism was common to both the German elites (as well as to the Poles who formed the elite in Lithuania) and the Baltic peasants, the latter retained many of their pagan practices for several centuries. Nevertheless, Baltic peasants were compelled to conform to the religious choices of the region's nobility: when the ideas of the Protestant Reformation entered the Livonian Confederation and much of the German elite converted to Lutheranism, the bulk of the peasantry had no choice but to follow suit. Because the impact of the Reformation in Poland was more limited and most of the nobles who had embraced Protestantism eventually returned to the Roman fold, Lithuanian peasants remained Catholic.

Russian Rule

While Livonia developed under the tutelage of its German elite, in the east the rulers of the growing Muscovite state were bent on "gathering" the Russian lands that had been lost as a result of the thirteenth-century Mongol invasions and the fracturing of Kievan Rus. By the sixteenth century Muscovy was a power that could no longer be ignored, and its Tsar Ivan the Terrible (Ivan IV, who ruled from 1547 to 1584), seeking a Russian outpost on the Baltic Sea, set his sight on the territory of the Livonian Confederation.

The Livonian War, launched in 1558 but continuing intermittently until 1582, was unsuccessful to say the least: it was devastating not only to the Livonian Confederation, which was partitioned in 1561, but also to Russia itself, which lacked the human and material resources to successfully prosecute this war and became impoverished under Ivan IV's mismanaged reign. With the dissolution of the Livonian Confederation, the former knights of the Order became the landed nobility of the Duchy of Courland and Zemgale, while Poland-Lithuania absorbed much of the eastern part of Livonia (called Inflanty under Polish-Lithuanian rule, but now known as Latgale). For decades after the partition, the Baltic region remained an object of contention for the region's great powers. The Swedes appeared to be the winners of the struggle, conquering much of the Baltic area by 1629; however, Poland-Lithuania retained Inflanty and the Duchy of Courland and Zemgale. The main losers, of course, were the Baltic natives, who suffered from the devastation wrought by war, hunger, and disease.

Estonians and Latvians of later eras tend to view the era of Swedish rule as a period of relative liberalism and enlightenment. This was partly because the Baltic German landlords were thought to be particularly harsh with their peasants, and also because the long era of tsarist rule that followed the Swedish period was likewise regarded as oppressive. Some historians believe that nostalgia for this "golden era" is somewhat misplaced: while Sweden's King Charles XI (ruled 1672–97) undertook initiatives that benefited the local peasantry, he also launched a policy of massive expropriation of land in an effort to expand his tax base. Not only did this hurt the German nobles who were forced to surrender much of their holdings, but aside from reducing the number of whippings meted out to the Livonian and Estonian peasants, Swedish rule seems to have done little to improve their conditions.

Swedish rule lasted for nearly a century. During this time Russia began to recover from the wars and domestic terror of Ivan the Terrible, the chaos of the Time of Troubles (1598–1613), and its consequent change of dynasties. Tsar Peter Alekseevich Romanov intended to succeed where Ivan had failed. The Great Northern War, which pitted Peter I (ruled 1689–1725) against his

The Baltic Provinces of the Russian Empire c.1850. Courtesy of Cartographica.

lifelong adversary, King Charles XII (ruled 1697–1718), once again devastated the Baltic region: as much as 40 percent of the population of the Latvian lands perished, and still more in Estonia. Under the provisions of the Peace of Nystad (1721), Russia acquired Livland (as northern Latvia and southern Estonia were known under Swedish rule), Estland (northern Estonia), and other territories in the region, along with a few hundred thousand new subjects. As a result of these and other conquests, Muscovy was transformed into an empire and Russia became the strongest state in the Baltic region.

Russia's incorporation of Livland and Estland preceded the absorption of Lithuania, Courland (Kurzeme), and Latgale by several decades; the latter territories were annexed during the Polish partitions of the late eighteenth century and were treated rather differently by the imperial authorities. While the Russian government was willing to confirm the privileges of the Baltic German elites in Estland and Livland, where centuries-old corporate bodies known as *Ritterschaften* and the provincial *Landtage* were allowed to function, it looked upon the elites of the Polish-Lithuanian provinces with considerable suspicion. Baltic Germans, who had the technical and political expertise that was in short supply in other areas of the empire, were allowed to administer local government in the Baltic provinces; they also served as diplomats and bureaucrats and were well represented in the officer corps of the Russian army. In exchange for their privileges, the Baltic Germans offered Russia their loyalty and service.

Yet as Russia's rulers sought to create a more rational and efficient state, the anomaly of serfdom held back substantive progress. The plight of the empire's serfs especially concerned Empress Catherine II (ruled 1762–96), who visited Estland and Livland in 1764 to familiarize herself with local conditions and ordered a commission to study the problem. However, the problem was not sincerely tackled until the reign of her grandson Alexander I (ruled 1801–25), who, having defeated Napoleon, acted resolutely on the serf issue by designating Livland and Estland as, in essence, experimental regions where the serfs would be liberated. Emancipation came first to Estland, in 1816, to Courland in 1817, and finally to Livland in 1819. Latgalian peasants (in the western part of what was known as Vitebsk province), like those of Lithuania, would have to wait until 1861 when the rest of the empire's serfs were liberated.

Although emancipation laid the necessary ground for the subsequent "awakenings" of the Estonian and Latvian (and later the Lithuanian) nations, the beginnings were not promising. The local nobility, who worked out the terms of the emancipation laws themselves, were willing to surrender their work forces but were not about to give away their lands. Thus, although the peasants gained their freedom, it came at the price of the protection they had traditionally enjoyed under their lords. While most of the former serfs remained agricultural laborers, in most cases working on the manors of German land-lords, others now took advantage of their freedom to join other occupations. Although in the post-Emancipation years many Latvian and Estonian peasants suffered from landlessness, this gradually changed during the second half of the nineteenth century as the Russian government pressured the German nobility to make more land available. Still, thousands drifted to Russia's interior to find land and work in factories. In the mid-1840s, at least 75,000 Estonian and Latvian peasants converted to Orthodoxy in the mistaken belief that they would be rewarded with land in the Russian south if they accepted the faith of the tsar. When this turned out not to be the case most quickly returned to the Lutheran fold.

It was during this period that Latvian and Estonian began to develop as literary languages. Indeed, one of the new fascinations of the German elite was the "discovery" of the Latvian and Estonian peasants, whose legends, fables, and songs began to be collected by Johann Gottfried Herder (1744–1803) in the 1760s. By the 1820s a weekly Latvian newspaper was being published, even if the native-language presses in the Baltic territories continued to be controlled by German intellectuals for several more decades. Equally significant was the fact that a native intelligentsia and a literate public were in the process of emerging—just as Estonians and Latvians were overtaking the German populations in the Baltic cities—thereby establishing the necessary preconditions for the "national awakenings" of the Baltic peoples in the second half of the century (this phenomenon is discussed in greater detail in subsequent chapters). Most significantly, the main impetus behind the national awakenings of the Estonians and Latvians was *not* the desire to free themselves from Russian rule—this was generally unquestioned and regarded as permanent—but rather to express their own national identities as well as their frustrations with the injustices of a system in which the Germans held all the cultural, political, and economic cards. Latvians and Estonians wanted to be recognized as more than just peasant people; they wished to assume a cultural and economic presence that reflected their preponderance in the provinces in which they lived.

But what of the Lithuanians? The Lithuanian provinces, principally Kovno (in Lithuanian, Kaunas) and Vilna (Vilnius), were never subject to the sort of experiments that were attempted in Estland, Livland, and Courland in the early nineteenth century. Nor, aside from the establishment of the constitutional Kingdom of Poland from 1815 to 1830 (in which the tsar was sovereign), were the elites of the incorporated Polish-Lithuanian areas granted the autonomy or rights and privileges enjoyed by the Baltic Germans. But like the Baltic Germans, however, the Polish-Lithuanian elites were far removed from the cultural life of the peasants who worked their lands. Indeed, until the latter half of the nineteenth century the Lithuanian language was spoken almost exclusively by Lithuanian peasants, while the Lithuanian upper classes lived in the cultural world of the Poles. There were so many Polish and Polish-Lithuanian nobles that to refer to them as an "upper class" can be misleading, as many were in fact poor and landless. Those who did have estates tended to have vastly larger estates than those possessed by the less numerous Baltic Germans in Estland, Livland, and Courland. Moreover, unlike the Baltic Germans, Polish and Lithuanian nobles were never reconciled to union with Russia.

Since the fate of the Lithuanians was in the nineteenth century inextricably linked to that of the Poles, the Poles' dissatisfaction with any limits on their sovereignty also affected the Lithuanians. A Polish uprising against the Russian authorities in late 1830 soon spread to the Lithuanian provinces but failed to achieve its objective. With the uprising crushed, the Polish constitution of 1815, which had awarded the Kingdom of Poland a special status in the empire, was revoked, and many of the estates belonging to the Catholic Church and the nobility were eventually transferred to mostly Russian landlords. Another Polish-Lithuanian rebellion took place in 1863, and it too was crushed. Exasperated with the rebellious Poles and seeking to lure the Lithuanians away from them and into the cultural orbit of Russia proper, "Russification" measures were undertaken that, for example, banned the use of the Latin alphabet in Lithuanian writing. From 1864 to 1904 Lithuanians who wished to write in their own language were required to use the Cyrillic alphabet used by the Russians.

By this time the Lithuanian peasantry had been liberated from serfdom as a result of the general emancipation of 1861. In terms of education and national development, Lithuanians were already far behind the Estonians and Latvians, who had become increasingly literate and self-aware. Thus, whereas the awakenings of the Estonian and Latvian peoples in Estland, Livland, and Courland were initiated by Germanized intellectuals, in Lithuania the leading role was played by priests such as Motiejus Valančius (1801–75) and Jonas Basanávičius (1851–1927). Following the press ban, Valančius struggled to keep the Lithuanian language and culture alive by encouraging the smuggling of books across the border from Lithuania Minor (in Prussia), where Basanávičius published the newspaper *Aušra* (The Dawn) in the mid-1880s. As a result of this national activity, many educated Lithuanians who had been raised in a Polish cultural milieu now made the conscious choice to identify themselves more closely with "the people"—that is, with the Lithuanian peasantry.

Meanwhile, thousands of Lithuanians left their native provinces to search for opportunities in other parts of the Russian Empire or in American

industrial centers such as Chicago. Likewise, Jews in the Lithuanian provinces, whose numbers had reached 755,000 by 1897 (they constituted the
largest ethnic group in Vilnius), were increasingly subject to local resentment and violence and began to leave during the last decades of the nineteenth century. Despite the cultural renaissance they were enjoying in the
Lithuanian provinces, thousands left for Prussia, Western Europe, and
southern Russia.

The Revolutionary Era

By the turn of the century, Livland and Estland were among the most indus-
trialized and urbanized provinces of the Russian Empire. Their leading cities,
Riga and Tallinn (or Reval, as the Germans called it), were increasingly multinational, home to significant numbers of Russians and Jews. By the 1890s,
however, and probably somewhat earlier, natives outnumbered the German
populations in the major urban centers. The situation was different in the
Lithuanian provinces. A small part of Lithuania (Lithuania Minor) was in
Germany, and the part that was in the Russian Empire was backward in comparison to the northern Baltic provinces. With Lithuanian peasants remaining
largely illiterate and industrialization arriving late, the Lithuanian provinces
retained their predominantly rural character until the middle of the twentieth
century. The few Lithuanian cities that existed in 1900 were hardly Lithuanian
at all: Vilnius, for example, was overwhelmingly Jewish and Polish.

It is paradoxical, then, given the absence of an urban proletariat in Lithuania,
that in 1896 Vilnius gave birth to the first political party in the region—and a
socialist one at that. Called the Lithuanian Social Democratic Party (LSDP),
it was the first party committed to achieving Lithuanian statehood. Its chance
arrived in 1905, when a revolution shook the Russian Empire. The context
of the revolution was a losing war with Japan, but the trigger was the massacre of 130 demonstrators by the St. Petersburg police in January. Although
sympathy strikes took place in the larger Baltic cities, most of the violence
took place in the Latvian and Estonian countryside and was directed less
at the Russian imperial authorities than at the Baltic barons: 184 of their
manor houses were burned down and hundreds of Germans (and Russians)
were killed. Tsar Nicholas II (ruled 1894–1917) managed to retain his throne
but was forced to grant political concessions that allowed for the creation
of a representative body, the State Duma, and the abolition of censorship.
Reversing its earlier Russification measures, the Russian government also
granted permission to use the Estonian, Latvian, and Lithuanian languages in
the schools. However, such compromises were coupled with the repression of
Baltic rebels, thousands of whom were imprisoned, sent to Siberian exile, or

executed. While Balts could voice their concerns in the Duma, they were not granted the political autonomy many had envisioned.

The period of relative normalcy and economic development that followed the repression of 1906–7 came to an end on August 1, 1914, with Kaiser Wilhelm II's declaration of war on the Russian Empire. While Latvians and Estonians initially supported the tsar and fought in his army, the Balts' attitudes about their place in the Russian Empire changed during the war as a result of German occupation and the two Russian revolutions. With war going badly for Russia and hunger threatening its cities, demonstrations broke out in Petrograd (as St. Petersburg was renamed) in early 1917, forcing Tsar Nicholas II to surrender his throne. For eight months Russia, under its Provisional Government, was the freest country in the world, and for the first time autonomy became a realistic goal for the peoples of Russia's western borderlands. While the government in Petrograd was reluctant to address the country's nationality problem, the Germans who occupied the western borderlands understood how "national self-determination," a phrase that was frequently invoked by U.S. President Woodrow Wilson (and by Vladimir Lenin), could be used to its advantage to detach the Baltic territories from Russia—most likely as a first step toward their annexation into the Reich. Indeed, in September 1917 Lithuanians in Vilnius, with German permission, formed a national council that voted for Lithuanian independence. Its chairman, Antanas Smetona (1874–1944) vaguely agreed that the country would enter into close relations with Germany.

Several months earlier, in March 1917, Latvians in the unoccupied territories (only Courland was at that time occupied by the Germans) formed a provincial council and discussed their competing visions of a unified and autonomous—or even independent—Latvia. At the end of the same month the Estonians formed their own representative assembly and, like the Latvians, abolished the old Baltic German-controlled institutions of local government. Meanwhile, sailors, soldiers, and workers formed their own councils called "soviets." Many among them, especially in Latvia, were sympathetic to the Bolsheviks' radical plans for a worldwide workers' revolution. Thus, by the time the Bolsheviks seized power in Petrograd in October 1917, the Estonians, Latvians, and Lithuanians had already taken decisive steps toward national independence.

Led by Lenin (1870–1924), the Bolsheviks were the radical wing of the Russian Social Democratic Workers' Party. An underground party—some historians prefer to call it a conspiracy rather than a party—that operated mostly from abroad, the Bolsheviks made their way back into Russia after the February Revolution. Taking advantage of the opportunity offered them by the ongoing war, general hunger, and the weakness of Russia's Provisional

Government, the Bolsheviks seized power in October 1917 with the declared intention of spreading the workers' revolution to the rest of Europe. Like the Germans and Wilson, Lenin too spoke of "national self-determination" for subject nations, but with the expectation that Russia's nationalities would choose socialism under the tutelage of the Bolsheviks. While the Bolsheviks contemplated how to end the war with Germany and took measures to create "socialism" in Russia, during the winter of 1917–18 the Latvian, Lithuanian, and Estonian peoples created impromptu assemblies that declared the existence of independent republics on their territories.

These declarations may have been inspiring, but they did not make independence a reality. In exchange for German recognition, Lithuania's authorities acknowledged the country's close ties with the Reich, which still occupied it. Just one day after the Estonian Committee of Elders declared the country's independence on February 24, 1918, German soldiers moved into Tallinn, where they stayed for several months. The struggling Bolshevik government, recognizing that it could not fight Germany *and* consolidate and spread the revolution at the same time, on March 3, 1918 finally concluded the Treaty of Brest-Litovsk with Germany, which ended the war and provided for Russia's surrender of vast stretches of border territory. Thus while the representatives of the Latvian, Estonian, and Lithuanian nations had declared their intentions to create independent states, such declarations bore little relationship to the actual facts, for the entire region was occupied by Germany.

Germany's successes on the eastern front were not duplicated in the west. Despite the modest gains from a spring offensive, an Allied blockade resulted in hunger in Germany's cities, and following a fresh infusion of American forces on the western front in April, by the autumn of 1918 Germany was forced to sue for peace. According to the terms of the November armistice, however, German forces were directed to remain in the east as a bulwark against a Bolshevik advance into Europe. Thus the Baltic region remained a scene of military activity for another year or so. While Russian anti-Bolshevik forces collectively known as "Whites" tried to save the empire under the slogan "Russia One and Indivisible," national forces in Estonia, Latvia, and Lithuania defended their independence from both the Whites and the Soviet Red Army. Indeed, on the arrival of the Red Army in late 1918, Latvian and Estonian Bolsheviks declared the existence of Soviet governments; these now competed for legitimacy with the provisional governments earlier created by the Baltic nationalists. The premature withdrawal of German forces (who soon reappeared in the form of the Baltic German *Landeswehr* and German *Freikorps* units) also gave the Bolsheviks the opportunity to declare the existence of a Lithuanian-Belarusian Republic. To add to the confusion, a newly reconstituted Poland attempted to take advantage of Russia's weakness by seizing parts of Belarus and Ukraine, as well as the Lithuanians' historic capital, Vilnius, which it held until 1939.

While the Bolsheviks were able to hold Russia's center (and eventually won the civil war), in the short term they realized that they had no choice but to enter into negotiations with the Baltic national governments. To save the revolution in Russia, Lenin ultimately concluded, it was necessary to amputate Estonia, Latvia, and Lithuania, with which the Soviet government concluded peace treaties in 1920. Only when the Allies lost hope for a democratic and united Russia, in 1921–22, did they also offer legal recognition to the new Baltic governments.

The First Era of Independence

The fighting that took place between 1914 and 1920 devastated the populations, landscapes, and economies of each of the Baltic countries. Worst affected was Latvia, most of whose industries were evacuated to the Russian interior, where they remained. More catastrophic still was the demographic impact of the war on Latvia, as its population fell from about 2.5 million before the war to fewer than 1.6 million in 1920. Hundreds of thousands of Latvian refugees fled to Russia, where many remained for some years.

In the meantime, the Baltic governments turned their attention to building democratic states and undertaking radical land reforms. As late as 1918 a relatively small number of Baltic Germans continued to hold most agricultural land in Latvia and Estonia, while many Latvian and Estonian peasants remained landless. Independence from Russia now offered the republics' new leaders an unprecedented opportunity not only to rectify this imbalance but also to break the Baltic barons' hold over the political and economic life of the region. Although the Baltic German landowners were permitted to make proposals, in the end Latvia and Estonia took radical measures and expropriated without compensation most of their property, which they then distributed to small farmers and veterans of the wars of independence. Land reform in Lithuania, a considerably more rural country with fewer landless peasants, was somewhat less radical.

For each of the Baltic countries, the era between the two world wars can be divided into a democratic period (until 1926 in Lithuania and until 1934 in Estonia and Latvia) and an authoritarian one. During the first period the Baltic states were among the most democratic in the world: parliaments held the upper hand in state politics, national institutions were built, and national minorities held civil rights and participated in public life. In each case, Baltic constitutions were based on the model of Weimar Germany, which provided for proportional representation in the national parliaments. In each the result was fragmentation, the proliferation of political parties, and frequent changes of government. For example, in the Republic of Estonia a *Riigikogu* was created (in Latvia it was the *Saeima* and in Lithuania it was the *Seimas*) with the power to dismiss the government at any time. However, the Estonian State Elder (effectively the prime minister), or *Riigivanem,* lacked even the basic power to veto parliamentary legislation. To a greater or lesser degree these conditions also existed in Latvia and Lithuania. Lacking strong executives to lead their countries and provide an effective counterbalance to their fractious parliaments, the new states were doomed to political paralysis. In Latvia, for example, no fewer than 27 parties were represented in the *Saeima* in 1925 and 1928; thus, 12 years of parliamentary democracy in Latvia produced 14 different cabinets.

Lithuania was the first of the Baltic states to succumb to authoritarian government. In December 1926 Antanas Smetona of the National Progress Party, who claimed to be saving the country from a communist putsch, launched his own coup. Installed as Lithuania's president with the support of the military, Smetona held this title until the Soviet takeover in 1940. It was not until 1934 that Latvia and Estonia succumbed to dictatorship, and by then Europe was in the grip of the Great Depression, which facilitated the emergence of extreme nationalist groups everywhere. In Estonia the main nationalist organization was the League of Independence War Veterans, which in 1932 proposed the creation of a strong chief executive to steer the country through difficult times. By January 1934 a new constitution was put into effect that reflected the League's preferences and Konstantin Päts (1874–1956) was made the acting president. However, sensing the imminent danger posed by the Veterans' League, which won a series of local elections and was preparing to compete in national elections, Päts declared martial law, arrested the leading members of the Veterans' League, and prohibited all political activity in Estonia, thereby inaugurating the "Era of Silence." In Latvia it was the executive's concerns about both the extreme Left *and* the extreme Right that were used to justify an authoritarian coup, but the result was still the same. In May 1934, two months after the coup in Estonia, Kārlis Ulmanis (1877–1942), the prime minister and one of the founders of the Latvian state, seized power in Riga.

While Soviet historians and propagandists liked to portray the Baltic governments as "fascist dictatorships," which was a justification for their incorporation into the Soviet Union in 1940, this is an exaggeration. Indeed, these *were* dictatorships—parliaments were shut down or ignored and political enemies perceived to be dangerous were arrested—but of the three only interwar Lithuania approaches the description "fascist." Supporting the activities of the Lithuanian Nationalist Union (*Tautininkai*) and the Iron Wolf paramilitary organization of Augustinas Voldemaras (who was dismissed from his post as prime minister in 1929), the Smetona government came closest to establishing a unifying nationalist ideology. As Jews were gradually deprived of rights, the Lithuanian government even took an openly anti-Semitic stance; nevertheless, many Jews clung to the belief that under these circumstances Smetona was their protector. The dictatorships of Estonia and Latvia, on the other hand, were based less on fascistic ideology than on a broad national consensus regarding the need for stability and national unity after more than a decade of what often appeared to be free-for-all politics.

These were authoritarian governments: they instituted press censorship and concentrated political power in the hands of a single individual who invariably portrayed himself as a national figure above the fray of ordinary politics. However, in none of the Baltic states was terror an instrument of the government; in none were the political police allowed to round up and murder the regime's political opponents. While the claims of Ulmanis and Smetona that they saved their countries from communist conspiracies are certainly subject to debate (as is the claim of Päts that he was saving the country from a right-wing coup), most will agree that their relatively mild authoritarian governments were far preferable to the monstrous totalitarian dictatorships that would run roughshod over this region after 1940.

Situated between two large and potentially powerful irredentist states, Germany and Soviet Russia, one might argue that the Baltic states never stood a chance. The Allies saw them as part of a *cordon sanitaire* designed to contain communism to the east and keep the Germans and Russians apart. While they were accepted as members of the League of Nations, the Allies provided the Baltic countries with few security guarantees; furthermore, by failing to cooperate among themselves in any systematic way on economic, political, and defense issues, the Baltic countries did little to help themselves. While they proceeded to industrialize, to build up their economic infrastructures, and to establish commercial ties with Western countries (mainly Britain and Germany), they made no serious provisions for a common defense beyond the creation of a narrow "Baltic Entente" in September 1934. Lithuania's main nemesis was Poland, which appropriated Vilnius, Lithuania's historic capital, for herself in 1920; this issue prevented the formation of any alliance between Poland and Lithuania. While the Soviet Union focused on its internal development ("socialism in one country") and signed a series of non-aggression treaties with its western neighbors, Germany appeared to be the most significant threat to the independence of the Baltic countries, especially after the Nazi seizure of power in 1933.

Soon after his assumption of the German chancellorship, Adolf Hitler began to dismantle the Versailles Treaty, which limited the German army and stripped Germany of some of its territory, but it was not until 1938 that he began his series of stunning and at first bloodless foreign conquests. First the Reich annexed Austria, whose citizens overwhelmingly favored it; then the Western powers acceded to Hitler's demand for the dismemberment of Czechoslovakia. Immediately after German troops marched into Prague in March 1939, Berlin demanded that Lithuania surrender the Klaipėda (known to the Germans who lived there as Memel) territory, which had once constituted part of Lithuania Minor under German rule but was detached from the Reich after World War I and placed under French administration. In 1923 Lithuania had seized the city and now Hitler wanted it back, leaving the Lithuanian government with no choice but to comply.

At the same time, Hitler posed as a friend of the Baltic states and offered Latvia and Estonia non-aggression pacts, which they signed under pressure in June 1939. In August Germany signed yet another non-aggression pact (the Molotov-Ribbentrop Pact), this time with the USSR. While it was to nearly clear everyone that Hitler was a threat to all of Europe, the Western powers were reluctant to make any deals with Soviet leader Josef Stalin to contain him. Meanwhile, Hitler realized that he could offer Stalin something they could not: a sphere of influence in Eastern Europe. On August 23, 1939, Germany and the USSR added a supplementary secret protocol to the earlier pact. This would divide northeastern Europe between them: each would receive part of Poland; in addition Finland, Estonia, and Latvia would fall under the Soviet sphere of influence, while Lithuania would go to Germany. (Lithuania was later transferred to the Soviet sphere in exchange for a larger hunk of Poland.) The pact went into effect when Germany attacked Poland on September 1.

Soviet Rule

Once the USSR occupied its half of Poland in mid-September, it pressured the three Baltic states and Finland to conclude "mutual assistance" treaties that would enable the Red Army to occupy strategic bases in these countries. In the treaty with Lithuania it was also agreed that the Vilnius territory would be transferred to Lithuania. During the following winter, more than 65,000 Baltic Germans were "repatriated" to the "homeland," which turned out to be mostly the areas of Poland that had been recently taken over by the Reich. These developments spelled the beginning of the end of the independence of the Baltic countries.

Accusing the Baltic governments of being unwilling or unable to carry out the terms of the mutual assistance pacts, Moscow issued each of them an ultimatum in the spring of 1940; these were quickly followed by the arrival of hundreds of thousands of Red Army soldiers. To send out the miniscule Baltic armies to defend their countries, the leaders of Estonia, Latvia, and Lithuania concluded, would have been useless. Thus there was no resistance to Soviet occupation in June 1940. Yet the official Soviet claim, based on the sham elections of July 14–15 and the subsequent resolutions of the Baltic parliaments, that the Baltic peoples "voluntarily" consented to their incorporation into the USSR was a lie—and this lie became the legal basis of nearly five decades of Soviet rule.

While Lithuania's President Smetona managed to escape to the United States (where he died in 1942), Ulmanis and Päts, along with dozens of other prominent Baltic leaders, were deported to the Soviet interior. The new leaders, chosen from either sympathetic or opportunistic natives, to which were added cadres imported from the USSR, quickly undertook the task of Sovietizing the Baltic countries. Large industries were nationalized, as well as private housing, banks, and commerce in general. Although large-scale collectivization would wait until after the war, the Soviet regime did its best to weaken the institution of private landholding. In an effort to eliminate as many potentially threatening individuals—that is, the Baltic cultural, intellectual, and political elite—as possible, on the night of June 13, 1941, the Soviet secret police (NKVD) began an operation that resulted in the deportation over the course of a few short days of 15,500 Latvians, 11,000 Estonians, and 21,000 Lithuanians to the Russian interior. Many died along the way.

While the packed boxcars made their way to Siberia or northern Russia, on June 22 Hitler broke his non-aggression pact and attacked the USSR. Revolts against Soviet rule immediately broke out in Lithuania, Latvia, and Estonia as the officials of the shattered Soviet regimes fled to the Russian hinterland. Hitler's plan was to eliminate the Soviet regime and create "living space" (*Lebensraum*) for Germans in the European parts of Russia. Because many Balts, and Estonians in particular, possessed the requisite racial qualities necessary for survival in Hitler's world, the Baltic republics were awarded a privileged position in the Reich's plans. While the Baltic region would in theory eventually be annexed to the Reich, for the moment native administrations wholly subordinated to German authority were set up under the supervision of the *Reichskommissariat Ostland* while thousands of Germans were invited to settle on some of the expropriated farms.

The Nazis' most important objective—even more pressing, it would appear, than winning the war—was the elimination of the Jewish population. By January 1942 most of Latvia's 80–85,000 Jews were killed; perhaps 180,000 Lithuanian Jews were killed. Most of Estonia's 4,500 Jews managed to survive because so many of them fled or were deported by the Soviets before the Germans arrived, but nearly all of the 950 who remained were killed. Many non-Jews were also killed during the German occupation, but they were not targeted for systematic extermination as were the Jews. The slaughter of the

Jewish population in Latvia and Lithuania has raised serious questions about the complicity of some Latvians and Lithuanians; it is only in the post-Soviet era that Baltic historians have begun seriously to address this uncomfortable but very important subject.

As the German war machine's momentum slowed in the second half of 1942, the Reich required more soldiers. Tens of thousands of Balts, at first voluntarily, and then by force, formed units under the Nazi flag to fight the Soviets. Since hundreds of thousands youths also managed to escape enlistment, this brings into question the notion, maintained by some historians of the Baltic countries, that many Estonian, Latvian, and Lithuanian men of military age had no choice but to serve the Nazis. While the pressure to do so was formidable (one could either fight for or labor under the Reich), many who joined these legions had unpleasant memories of the year of Soviet rule and believed that they were making the best of the available choices. Whatever the case, when the Red Army arrived in early 1944, this time it was met with fierce resistance by Baltic soldiers. However, just like the Nazis, the Soviet Union also formed national forces as its army overran the Baltic republics in the summer, recruiting, often by forcible mobilization, tens of thousands of Estonians, Latvians, and Lithuanians. Many resisters escaped to the forests to take up arms against the Soviet authorities. Despite being vastly outnumbered, undersupplied, and increasingly isolated, some of these "forest brothers" held out into the early 1950s.

Once again, the Baltic states were devastated by a war started by Germany, losing as much as 20 percent of their populations to death, deportations, and flight. At least a quarter of a million people fled ahead of the Red Army, thereby escaping the executions and deportations that would follow. Thus did the Baltic countries lose what remained of their intellectuals, property owners, and cultural and religious leaders. Damage to housing and infrastructure was extensive everywhere, but especially in Estonia. Still more damage was inflicted by the occupying Soviet regime, which picked up where it left off in June 1941. In 1947 the first postwar collective farms were set up in each of the Baltic countries, while prosperous peasants called "kulaks" were eliminated by the tried and true method of deportation. Rather than give up their animals to the collective farms, many farmers slaughtered their livestock, which resulted in a catastrophic drop in agricultural production in each of Baltic republics. In spring 1949, at the height of the collectivization drive, about 95,000 rural Estonians, Latvians, and Lithuanians—more than half of them women and children—were deported and dispersed to various locations throughout the USSR.

While the farms were being collectivized, the main economic focus in the Baltic republics, and especially in Latvia and Estonia, was industry. Latvian industry was concentrated in Riga, while in Estonia Soviet planners focused on the oil shale industry, for which a pipeline was built to supply the northern parts of the Russian republic (RSFSR). To meet Moscow's industrial requirements, waves of Russian, Ukrainian, and Belarusian laborers arrived in Estonia and Latvia, and to a lesser extent Lithuania, which until the 1960s remained predominantly agricultural. Latvia alone received more than 500,000 immigrants between 1945 and 1959. As a result, the Latvians' share of the republic's population fell from about 84 percent in 1945 to 60 percent in 1953. In Estonia these numbers were respectively 94 and 72 percent. By 1989 Latvians constituted less than 53 percent of the population of their republic and Estonians 61.5 percent of theirs. The percentage of Lithuanians in their republic held steady at 75 to 80—a figure that was heavily influenced by the ghostly but largely unacknowledged absence of Lithuania's once significant Jewish population and the repatriation of much of Vilnius's Polish population at the end of the war. Meanwhile, thousands of Latvians, Estonians, and Lithuanians migrated to the other Soviet republics in search of professional opportunities or education. Hundreds of thousands joined the Communist Party, often for the same reasons.

For the most part, the Estonians, Latvians, and Lithuanians were allowed to continue to develop their national cultures as long as this did not conflict with the political goals of the Soviet regime or suggest disloyalty to Soviet power. And it is true that Estonians and Latvians, and to a lesser extent Lithuanians, enjoyed a higher standard of living than the other peoples of the USSR. But is this a reasonable way of measuring their lives under the Soviet system? From another perspective; before World War II the standard of living in Estonia was comparable to that of nearby Finland, and although the Estonian standard of living remained high by Soviet standards into the 1980s, by then it was incomparably lower than that of Finland. Thus one may conclude that the economic development of the Baltic republics, although impressive on paper, was in fact held back by five decades of Soviet rule. Indeed, the purpose of economic development in the Baltic republic was not to raise the residents' living standards but to meet the Soviet need for energy, machinery, industrial equipment, oil shale, and processed food (among other things). This distorted economic development was perhaps the most significant obstacle that the Baltic republics faced when attempting to establish normalcy and international commercial relationships after the collapse of the USSR.

Many Latvians and Lithuanians (especially elderly ones), and to a lesser extent Estonians, remember the Soviet era as a time of stability and relative plenty. Others recall the "former times" with little nostalgia for what was: after all, the Soviet era was one of religious repression and of the suppression of entrepreneurship and private initiative; it was a time of massive Russian immigration and of obeisance to an ideology in which few actually believed. It was a period of foreign occupation. In protest against these conditions the Baltic states produced some of the USSR's boldest dissident movements. This was especially true of Lithuania, where Catholic religious activists emphasized the plight of believers. Some have gone so far as to argue that the Baltic republics were the pebbles that tripped the Soviet giant.

The End of the Soviet Era

In the 1970s the Soviet state appeared to be not only stable but perhaps stronger than ever. The place of the Baltic republics in the USSR seemed permanent. The long-term survival of the Balts themselves, and the Latvians and Estonians in particular, was less certain. Since Soviet policy had been to create a new "Soviet man"—one shorn of an overriding national and religious identity and dedicated to building a communist society—the future of the Baltic nations was in doubt. Immigration from the Soviet interior, particularly among Russians and other Slavs, continued into the 1980s (although it was much less intense than in the immediate postwar decades and took on the character of a revolving door), causing some scholars to suggest that in the long run the Estonians and Latvians were fated to disappear through assimilation.

While the first half of the 1980s was marked by renewed Cold War tensions, economic stagnation, and shortages of consumer goods, the era that began in 1985 with the appointment of Mikhail Gorbachev to head of the Communist Party saw the resurgence of national life in the Baltics and the other Soviet republics. A believer in socialist ideals who was determined to make the system work better, in 1986–87 Gorbachev launched the policies of glasnost (openness) and perestroika (restructuring). To improve the functioning of the Soviet system, Gorbachev reasoned, its people needed to be able to discuss their problems more openly. Intellectuals and politicians in the Baltic republics were quick to seize on this unprecedented opportunity, focusing first on environmental issues (the potential impact of a proposed hydroelectric complex in Latvia; intensive phosphate excavation in Estonia), then economic issues (Estonian economists and politicians drew up a plan for their republic's economic autonomy), and finally historical matters. By the summer of 1987 even the crowds had gotten involved, gathering in all three Baltic capitals on August 23 to mark the anniversary of the Molotov-Ribbentrop Pact of 1939. Although the Kremlin's response was uneasy, Gorbachev's approach was to permit such expressions. This more flexible policy had the effect of encouraging yet more demonstrations. On September 11, 1988, as many as 300,000 people gathered on the Song Festival Grounds in Tallinn, where slogans calling for democratization were displayed along with those calling for the restoration of Estonia's independence.

Latvian writers were particularly instrumental in exposing the Soviet lies about the putatively "voluntary" incorporation of the Baltic states into the USSR in 1940, as they demanded a public examination of the "secret protocols" of the Nazi-Soviet pact that divided northeastern Europe between them. In each of the republics "front" groups formed that were ostensibly in favor of Gorbachev's perestroika, but most of their activists were intent on steering their republics toward an exit from the USSR. Many local Communists, sensing the direction of the political winds, aligned themselves with the fronts; others remained completely loyal to the Kremlin. The most significant of the Baltic front groups was formed in Lithuania in May 1988. Under the leadership of musicologist Vytautas Landsbergis (b. 1932), Sąjūdis quickly emerged as the most popular (but by no means the most radical) force for Lithuanian nationalism. While such events made news in the USSR the world came to know of the Baltic peoples on August 23, 1989, when Sąjūdis and the other popular fronts organized the "Baltic Way" demonstration in which up to two million people held hands to form a human chain linking the three Baltic capitals. It was at this time that the satellite regimes of Eastern Europe were beginning to collapse, thereby emboldening the separatists in the Baltics and other Soviet republics to take still more decisive actions.

In early 1990 each of the Soviet republics held elections, but this time the ritual of voting for the official candidates was replaced with the possibility of choosing from among two or more competing candidates. In each of the Baltic republics the result was stunning victories for candidates who supported the popular fronts. The new chairman of the Lithuanian parliament was none other than Landsbergis, who immediately seized the opportunity to force a vote on Lithuania's independence. Gorbachev, understandably concerned that such defiance would be replicated by other Soviet republics, was infuriated, and a year-long stalemate between Moscow and Lithuania ensued. While the other Baltic parliaments also endorsed the goal of independence, they acted more cautiously than Lithuania.

After nearly two years of struggle, independence finally came in 1991. With the Soviet economy rapidly contracting as a result of Moscow's half-hearted economic reforms, and as national strife in the Soviet republics threatened to spin out of control, Gorbachev finally came to an agreement with most of the Soviet republics and in August planned to sign a new Union Treaty that promised its signatories significantly greater sovereignty. Although the Baltic republics, which by this time regarded their independence as an established fact that would eventually have to be recognized by Moscow, did not plan to sign this agreement, the Union Treaty galvanized Soviet hardliners into action. On August 19 a self-appointed Emergency Committee (GKChP) launched a coup that was intended to sideline Gorbachev and restore full Soviet power throughout the tattered USSR. However, the nerves of the plotters weakened and the coup fell apart. Although Gorbachev was immediately restored to the Soviet presidency, the country he once ruled in reality no longer existed. As the remaining Soviet republics declared their independence from Moscow one by one, on September 6 the USSR formally recognized the independence of Estonia, Latvia, and Lithuania. By the end of the year the Soviet Union was no more.

Independent Again

Having gained their independence the Baltic states now had to cope with myriad political, social, and economic problems. New constitutions would have to be created or old ones amended; the pressing matter of citizenship would have to be resolved (a special problem for the non-native populations); their economic systems would have to be reformed and their enterprises, many were convinced, would have to be privatized. In addition, the Baltic states would need to formulate foreign policies that would provide them with the protection they so sorely lacked during the first era of independence.

With the euphoria of triumph wearing off at the end of 1991, the Baltic peoples faced the problem of economic catastrophe, large-scale unemployment, and massive inflation. Worst affected were the elderly and infirm as pensions were slashed and government services were drastically reduced. While consumer goods soon became widely available, few could afford to buy them as most money was spent on food and other basic necessities. Indeed, the early to mid-1990s was a period of continual economic crisis; only in 1995 did Estonia, which benefited from considerable Scandinavian investment, appear to turn the corner and begin to register positive growth rates. Latvia was somewhat further behind and Lithuania, whose leaders were usually reluctant to leave the population vulnerable to the vagaries of the market, further still.

The politics of democracy have also posed a challenge to the Baltic states— one that they have met with considerable success. Despite the rapid proliferation of political parties and the general fragmentation of the political scene in each of the Baltic states in the early 1990s, in recent years the situation has stabilized. Estonia, with only two presidents since 1993 (first Lennart Meri, and Arnold Rüütel since 2001), has been a bulwark of stability and has been the driving force behind the efforts of the Baltic countries to forge closer ties with European institutions.

Lithuania's road has been a bit bumpier. In October 1992 voters dumped *Sąjūdis* and threw their support to the reform communists, now organized as the Lithuanian Democratic Labor Party (LDLP) under former Lithuanian Communist Party chief Algirdas Brazauskas. By 1996, however, the pendulum swung back to the right and then in 1998 to the left again. After a period of political stability from 1998 to 2003 under the popular Valdas Adamkus (an émigré who spent most of his life in the United States), Lithuanian politics have become more turbulent in recent years. The situation reached an especially low point in April 2004 when Rolandas Paksas was tossed out of office for a variety of improprieties, but the political situation seemed to have calmed following Adamkus's return to the presidency in July of that year.

Latvia too has traveled a difficult road since independence. In an effort to forge a more complete break with the communist past, in the mid-1990s Latvian politics veered in a nationalist direction. By 1998, however, a shift back toward the center could be seen with the formation of a broad-based parliamentary coalition. In June 1999 Latvia elected the first woman president of East Central Europe, Vaira Vīķe-Freiberga, a widely respected émigré and former academic whom some have likened to the thoughtful Vaclav Havel of the Czech Republic. As the president of the most multinational of the Baltic states, she has taken a moderate line on the nationality issue and in particular on the matter of citizenship for non-natives.

In general, a sense of optimism prevails in the Baltic countries. In 2004 each entered the European Union and NATO, and many Balts are convinced that their security is greater and their economic futures are brighter as a result. While they certainly are not lacking in specific complaints, the national minorities are reconciled to a life over which Moscow exercises little influence. Many Russian speakers—especially the young—are making attempts to learn the local language and meet the citizenship requirements of their countries. (Lithuania, unlike the others, offered automatic citizenship to all its residents, regardless of nationality.)

Life in the Baltic countries, most would agree, is getting better. The visitor to Tallinn, Vilnius, or Riga—especially those who managed to visit during Soviet times and have had the good fortune to return in the twenty-first century—will marvel at the largely restored "old towns" while taking notice of the many new high rises and modern hotels. Visitors to the countryside will, of course, see a different story: in most cases it is one of stagnation, poverty, and decay. However, it is in the countryside that one sees the forests, and it is in these forests where the cultures of the Estonian, Latvian, and Lithuanian peoples were born and developed.

SELECTED READINGS

Bilmanis, Alfred. *A History of Latvia.* Westport, Conn.: Greenwood Press, 1951.

Bojtár, Endre. *Foreword to the Past: A Cultural History of the Baltic People.* Budapest: Central European Press, 1999.

Dreifelds, Julia. *Latvia in Transition.* New York: Cambridge University Press, 1996.

Eglitis, Daina Stukuls. *Imagining the Nation: History, Modernity, and Revolution in Latvia.* University Park: Pennsylvania State University Press, 2002.

Gimbutas, Marija. *The Balts.* New York: Frederick A. Praeger, 1963.

Greenbaum, Masha. *The Jews of Lithuania: A History of a Remarkable Community 1316–1945.* Jerusalem: Gefen Books, 1995.

Hiden, John, and Patrick Salmon. *The Baltic Nations and Europe: Estonia, Latvia, and Lithuania in the Twentieth Century.* New York: Longman, 1991.

Kõll, Anu Mai, ed. *The Baltic Countries under Occupation: Nazi and Soviet Rule 1939–1991.* Stockholm: Almqvist & Wiksell, 2003.

Krickus, Richard J. *Showdown: The Lithuanian Rebellion and the Breakup of the Soviet Empire.* Washington, D.C.: Brassey's, 1997.

Lane, Thomas. *Lithuania: Stepping Westward.* New York: Routledge, 2002.

Levin, Dov. *The Litvaks: A Short History of the Jews in Lithuania.* Jerusalem: Vad Yashem, 2000.

Lieven, Anatol. *The Baltic Revolution: Estonia, Latvia, Lithuania and the Path to Independence.* New Haven, Conn.: Yale University Press, 1993.

Misiunas, Romuald, and Rein Taagepera. *The Baltic States: Years of Dependence.* Berkeley: University of California Press, 1993.

O'Connor, Kevin. *The History of the Baltic States.* Westport, Conn.: Greenwood Press, 2003.

Pabriks, Artis, and Aldis Purs. *Latvia: The Challenges of Change.* New York: Routledge, 2002.

Page, Stanley. *The Formation of the Baltic States.* Cambridge, Mass.: Harvard University Press, 1959.

Plakans, Andrejs. *The Latvians: A Short History.* Stanford, Calif.: Hoover Institution Press, 1995.

Raun, Toivo U. *Estonia and the Estonians,* 2nd ed. Stanford, Calif.: Hoover Institution Press, 1987.

Senn, Erich. *The Emergence of Modern Lithuania.* New York: Columbia University Press, 1959.

Smith, David J. *Estonia: Independence and European Integration.* New York: Routledge, 2002.

Snyder, Timothy. *The Reconstruction of Nations: Poland, Ukraine, Lithuania, Belarus, 1569–1999.* New Haven, Conn.: Yale University Press, 2003.

Thaden, Edward C., ed. *Russia's Western Borderlands, 1710–1870.* Princeton, N.J.: Princeton University Press, 1984.

Urban, William. *The Baltic Crusade.* DeKalb: Northern Illinois University Press, 1975.

Von Rauch, Georg. *The Baltic States: The Years of Independence: Estonia, Latvia, Lithuania, 1917–1940.* Berkeley: University of California Press, 1974.

2

Religion

SINCE THE LATE 1980s the Baltic countries have enjoyed a markedly freer spiritual atmosphere than was the case under Soviet rule. Amid great hope, traditional religious confessions have revived in this region and even non-traditional religions are tolerated. At the same time, there is also evidence of considerable indifference to spiritual affairs in Latvia and Estonia, countries in which relatively few people profess a religious affiliation. Although traditionally Lutheran countries, it is possible that most Estonians and Latvians are either atheists or nonreligious. The exception among the Baltic countries is Lithuania, where Catholicism and national identity have been closely tied for centuries—and where far fewer Russian-speaking people, who are usually Orthodox, reside.

To appreciate the complexity of religious life in the Baltic countries, the discussion must begin with the fact that the forested, remote region of north-eastern Europe that is now home to the Estonian, Latvian, and Lithuanian peoples was the last part of northern Europe to be Christianized. Until the late twelfth century the region's little-known Baltic and Finno-Ugric peoples seemed to lie well beyond the reach of Catholic Europe—although changing burial customs suggest that neighboring Danes and Swedes, as well as the Slavic missionaries representing the Orthodox variety of Christianity (inherited from Byzantium), did manage to make some inroads among the Estonian population as early as the eleventh century. However, this was the age of the Crusades, which was accompanied by a German drive to the east (*Drang nach Osten*). Thus for the Estonians, the ancient Prussians, and the tribes

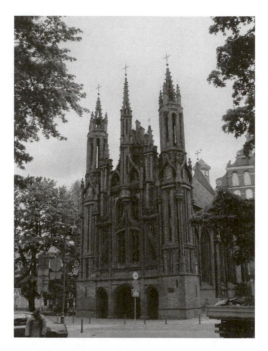

Church of St. Anne, Vilnius, Lithuania—a late
Gothic structure completed in 1581 and one of
Vilnius's great architectural gems.

that would eventually merge to become Latvians, Christianity in its Catholic, Western form was imposed from the outside, largely by force of arms.

Only Lithuania's leaders, after nearly two centuries of resistance, willingly embraced Christianity, and this was because they found themselves isolated and threatened in a world grown intensely hostile to pagans, Muslims, Jews, and other non-Christians. Yet deep in the forest the vestiges of pre-Christian beliefs survived, for if Christianity was the religion of the region's conquerors and rulers, paganism continued to influence the lives, customs, and outlooks of the Baltic peasantry into recent times.

PAGAN ORIGINS

Superficial accounts of the pre-Christian pagan beliefs of the Baltic peoples sometimes leave the reader with the impression that pagan mythology was static and unchanging. The reality is considerably more complex, for in the course of many hundreds of years the religious views of the Baltic and Finno-Ugric peoples underwent numerous changes, at least partly as a result of contacts with neighboring tribes and peoples. Various deities rose and fell in the pantheon of gods and goddesses, and regional peculiarities make generalizations more difficult still. Since written sources reflecting the beliefs and thought of the ancient Estonian, Latvian, and Lithuanian tribes are few (and were usually penned by hostile foreign observers), to reconstruct their religious worldviews, the folk tales and folk songs (*dainas*) that began to be systematically collected only in the late nineteenth century must be largely relied on. It is also important to distinguish between the pagan practices and beliefs of the Estonians, which largely resembled those of the neighboring Finns, and those of the Lithuanians and Latvians, which more closely resembled each other.

Natural phenomena were central to the belief systems of all the pre-Christian peoples of the Baltic region. Finno-Ugric peoples, including the Estonians (as well as the Livs and Setus), believed in a special force or power that was possessed by all living creatures. Since animals and human beings held most of their force in their heads, hearts, blood, hair, fur, nails, and teeth, it was an ancient Estonian custom to wear the teeth and tusks of the beasts of the forest, for it was believed that the bearer had taken possession of the animals' force. Thus the destruction of a slain enemy's force required his beheading and the removal of his heart, which in turn might be eaten in order to gain strength. To ensure their total submission to men, young women cut off their hair, the locus of their force, when they married.

Just as they believed that all living creatures possessed a force, the ancient Estonians believed in an eternal soul that existed apart from the physical body but at the same time was essential to keeping it alive. Depositing various objects in burial mounds that they thought the departed would require in the netherworld, the ancient Estonians believed that the dead continued their existence there in much the same way as they had lived on earth. Although regional beliefs varied, some Estonians believed that that upon a person's death the soul inhabited the forms of insects; most, however, seemed to believe that the soul continued in a new home such as a cemetery or sacred grove. Yet the souls of the dead were not completely cut off from the living. In late autumn, a traditionally quiet time called *hingedeaeg* or "spirit time," the souls of the dead were believed to roam about and Estonians traditionally left food out for them.

Not only humans, but animals, birds, insects, plants, and trees were also believed to possess souls; so did bodies of water, the sun, and the moon. Unlike the Western mindset that views nature as something apart from human existence—something to be mastered to serve humans' purposes—the ancient Estonians believed that they were a part of nature and that all aspects of nature ought to be respected and revered. To protect nature the Estonians looked to a variety of spirits and fairies. However, unlike the ancient religions of the neighboring Latvian and Lithuanian tribes, the Estonians had few greater deities to oversee the affairs of the world.

The Chronicle of Henry of Livonia, written in 1225 and 1226, identified Taara as the Estonians' high god. Sometimes connected with the Scandinavian thunder god Thor, Taara was thought to watch over everything and it was believed that he could manifest himself in everything. Although nineteenth-century scholars identified Taara as the god of war, modern devotees of Taara consider him to be undefined and undefinable. Other gods also played a significant role in the beliefs of the ancient Estonians: as the god of thunder and lightning, Uku provided rain and ensured a good harvest; as god of the dead, Vanetooni was a comforting companion who guided them to their final resting place; the gods of land and water were Maaema and Anti, who were also husband and wife; Vanejumi was a fertility god who made grain grow and flowers blossom and allowed women to have children.

As intermediaries between the physical world and the realm of gods, spirits, and fairies, shamans (*noed*) also played an important role in the lives of the ancient Estonians. Shamans, both men and women, were believed to have superior understanding of the forces of nature and passed this knowledge from one generation to the next. No less important were the sacred groves, stones, springs, and trees (oaks and lindens especially) where people went to sacrifice and pray. Since it was vital to keep on good terms with the various spirits, fairies, gods, and goddesses, it was to these special sacrificial sites that people brought offerings such as milk, meat, blood, wool, grain, and sometimes animals. According to Henry of Livonia, the will of the gods was revealed during animal sacrifice: if the animal fell on its right side, the coming endeavor (such as a raid) would be successful; however, the animal falling on its left side indicated the displeasure of the gods or spirits.

Whereas Estonian paganism shared many characteristics with the beliefs of other Finno-Ugric peoples, the ancient beliefs of the Balts—ancestors of the Latvians and Lithuanians—are quite distinct from those of the Estonians. While the Prussians, who were West Balts, and their customs disappeared by the seventeenth century, relics of the Lithuanians' and Latvians' pagan past have survived in the form of legends, fairytales, and mythological songs—some perhaps even older than the ancient Hindu Vedas to which they may be related. Indeed, as the elites and the cities converted to Christianity, the continuing devotion of Baltic villagers to their ancient religious customs—including animism, the cults of ancestors, and even the honoring of various deities—was a major source of consternation to their Christian leaders.

Since a common proto-Baltic language existed up to around 500 C.E., at which point the Lithuanian and Latvian (and Prussian) languages began to separate, it is unsurprising that the ancestors of today's Latvians and Lithuanians shared many of the same gods, goddesses, and religious customs. Yet a consensus about the hierarchy of the pre-Christian pantheon has not been reached. Whereas Marija Gimbutas (1921–1994), an expert on Lithuanian mythology, believed that the ancient Balts honored a variety of gods and goddesses, Endre Bojtár believes that there were in fact only two gods: Perkūnas (Pērkons in Latvian) and Dievas (Dievs in Latvian). The other "gods" he believes to be the inventions of mythologists who later transformed other idols and spirits into gods.[1] Whatever the status of the Baltic deities, the religion of the Baltic peoples and their pantheon of gods, goddesses, and spirits surely evolved over time in response to changing conditions and interaction with neighboring peoples.

An especially striking feature of Lithuanian mythology is the prevalence of goddesses, which underlines Gimbutas's belief that Lithuanian religion had a matriarchal structure.[2] Other experts have similarly suggested that the emphasis on feminine deities was the reflection of an earlier "matriarchal tribal system" that was later eclipsed by a "patriarchal tribal system" under which "most of the feminine deities lost their supremacy."[3] While some goddesses were associated with the fertility of the earth, others were able to transform themselves into birds, snakes, deer, or bears. However, all of them, Gimbutas wrote, "are associated with the mysterious forces of water, earth, and stone. It is from these sources that life is formed, and they represent this power."[4]

Some deities later identified with the Balts existed in Europe even before the Balts' arrival and eventually became part of the Baltic pantheon. For example, the Baltic goddesses Laima, Māra, and the Earth Mother (*Lith.* Žemyna, *Lat.* Zemes māte), may simply be different aspects of the one original Great Goddess. One expert on Lithuanian mythology has suggested that it would perhaps be most useful to view Lithuanian (and one might add, Latvian) religious beliefs in layers: at the base one finds the pre-Indo-European beliefs, onto which were grafted the ideas that arrived with the Indo-Europeans; Baltic and then more specifically Lithuanian beliefs and practices, having evolved most recently, occupy the upper strata.[5] Thus, for example, Laima, recognized by the ancient Latvian and Lithuanian tribes as the winged goddess of fate and happiness (as well as unhappiness), is believed to have been the chief goddess of Europe before Indo-Europeans reached the Baltic area. Dressed in white, Laima was most important to young women of marriageable age who desired a husband of good character; the good favor of Laima was no less important during childbirth.

Laima was closely associated with the supreme Baltic god Dievas/Dievs, the celestial father and god of the sky and the night. In the Latvian tradition she is his daughter. As the main god to which the ancient Balts appealed for help, Dievas's blessing and protection was the best shield against all evils. It is clear that Dievas, who was often represented as "an extremely handsome man, dress[ed] in a silver gown, a cap, his clothes adorned with pendants and with a belt and a sword attached," is related to the Dyaus of Sanskrit, the Greek Zeus, the Latin Deus, and the Germanic Tivas, as each of these words shares a common Indo-European root.[6] Although Dievas was not supreme in the sense that he could command other gods, together Laima and Dievas became a dominant pair akin to Hera and Zeus of Greek mythology. However, as each determined the fate of humans, they sometimes came into conflict with each other. Quick to note the analogies with the Christian God and Mary, Christianizers later assimilated Dievas, Laima, and the Earth Mother.

Another major Baltic god was Perkūnas/Pērkons, the god of thunder and of fire and storms; a fertility god as well, he is related to the Slavic god Perun (who in turn may be related to the Scandinavian god Thor). As the punisher, the reviver of life, and the protector of righteousness and order, Perkūnas/Pērkons may even have been the chief god of the Baltic rulers and nobility. Although numerous holidays are devoted to Perkūnas/Pērkons, it was believed that his special day was Thursday and that on that day fires should be lit in his honor. Writing in the year 1610, a Catholic priest named D. Fabricius observed that "during a drought, when there hasn't been rain, they worship Perkons in thick forests on hills and sacrifice to him a black calf, a black goat, and a black cock." When these were killed, Fabricius continued, the people would come together from the surrounding countryside to eat and drink. First paying homage to Pērkons by pouring beer into the fire, they then asked their thunder god for rain.[7]

Among the other popular gods of Lithuanian folklore is Gegutė, another goddess of fate, from which the word for the month of May (Gegužė) is derived. Manifested in the form of a cuckoo, Gegutė understands and is responsible for time. Her call announcing the spring, which marks the year's renewal, determines a person's fortune for that year. Of greater significance, however, were the Sun goddess Saulė (Saule in Latvian), to whom farmers prayed at sunrise and sunset, and the Moon god Mėnulis (Meness). Mėnulis was married to Saulė but fell in love with her daughter Aušrinė (Auseklis), the "morning star."[8] According to Lithuanian mythology, this so angered Perkūnas (not to mention Saulė), that he broke Mėnulis in two.

Velnias (Velns) is the god of the underworld and protector of the dead. A roguish spirit whose relationship with humans was ambiguous—sometimes he helped them, while at other times he misled them or tempted them into sin—Velnias was transformed into the Devil after the arrival of Christianity. Besides the pantheon of gods, goddesses, and spirits described, the Balts also had fairies called *laumės,* whom Gimbutas described as "peculiar naked women with long hair [who] dwelt in forests." Earlier legends, however, depicted the *laumės* as supernatural beings who lived in the water. Yearning for motherhood, they could be good, but they could also be mean spirited. According to Gimbutas, they "represented the irrational woman."[9]

The hierarchy of Baltic gods can be confusing, and it is probably best to avoid trying to understand Baltic mythology in terms of a universal hierarchy because each region had its own mythological orientation. Although a consensus on the matter has not been reached, one scholar has suggested that the mythology of the eastern Balts centered on the sky, that of the central Balts emphasized the earth, while the mythology of the western Balts focused on the underworld and water.[10] Thus, although Dievas/Dievs and Perkūnas/ Pērkons (who was unfamiliar to the ancient Prussians) were usually the highest gods, in some areas the supreme deity was the Earth goddess, who as the giver and sustainer of life is the mother of all.[11] Such regional variances contradict the notion, subscribed to by some later Christian chroniclers as well as by modern mythologists keen to make the ancient world fit their conception of order, that there was some sort of religious uniformity among the various Lithuanian and Latvian tribes.

Prior to the arrival of Christianity, religious activities such as harvest sacrifices appear to have been supervised by ordinary farmers. That the leading women of the community sometimes acted as priestesses is hardly surprising given that the pantheon of Baltic goddesses was even older than Perkūnas/ Pērkons, Dievas/Dievs, and their fellow male deities. Although in pre-Christian times there was no organized priesthood—the priests were simply wise old men who were chosen by the people—it seems likely that the arrival of Christian armies in the thirteenth and fourteenth centuries elevated and consolidated their position, at least in the Lithuanian lands. By this time the prince (*kunigas,* also the word for "clergyman") had emerged as the chief military and religious leader of Lithuania's small tribal units, and the grand duke was chief among these prince-priests. While the leading priests may have occupied a position in the community somewhat analogous to that of Christian bishops, Baltic pagans lacked anything like a pope or ruling chief priest.[12] During Gediminas's time, when Lithuania stood alone as the last pagan kingdom in Europe, the grand duke was surely the central figure of the pagan cult; but he was no "pope," and the sons of Gediminas made no claims of descent from any of the pagan gods.

Possessing no temples before Christianity began to penetrate the region (the first pagan temple—clearly the result of Christian influence—was built in Vilnius at the foot of Castle Hill during the era of Gediminas), the Latvians and Lithuanians, like the Estonians to the north, revered holy places such as sacred groves, forests, fields, and springs. This is hardly unique to the Baltic peoples, for the world of nature was also highly valued by their Scandinavian, Slavic, and Finnic neighbors. Yet the relationship of the Baltic peoples to their forests was special in its own way. Largely isolated from the outside world for many centuries before the arrival of Christian armies, it was in the Baltic forests that the people who would become known as Estonians, Latvians, and Lithuanians sang their sad songs of loss and lament and prayed to their gods.

CATHOLICISM

In 1237 the Livonian Order, a branch of the Teutonic Order of Knights, was established, and it held secular power in most of Latvia and Estonia for more than three centuries. Because Orthodox Slavdom was its neighbor, the order saw itself as an outpost of Catholic Europe charged with the mission to bring Catholicism to the east. And because the Crusaders tried to force the Balts to abandon their pagan beliefs and practices, Christianity's appearance in the region was marked by violence on a large scale. The Estonians and Latvians did not accept Christianity overnight, and in some places resistance to the knights was fierce; yet ultimately the pope's faith and authority prevailed in Livonia.

Lithuanian leaders, after a false start or two, waited nearly two centuries before making Catholicism the state religion of the Grand Duchy (even if most of its inhabitants were Orthodox). Unlike the insincere conversion of the Lithuanian chief Mindaugas in 1251, Jogaila's embrace of Christianity, although strategic to be sure—it was the price he paid for the Polish crown—was permanent. It was a final concession to the driving force of Western civilization. As one historian wrote: "In 1387 Władysław-Jagiełło went straight to Vilnius from his wedding in Cracow, and decreed the abolition of the pagan gods. The groves of sacred oaks were felled; the statue of Perkun overturned; the eternal fire extinguished." Vilnius now became the Polish Wilno, where a bishopric was installed.[13] Thirty years later the Diocese of Medininkai (later Samogitia) was created. As in Livonia 200 years earlier, Lithuanian peasants were baptized in droves, but the small number of churches and priests, the lack of schools of higher education, and the arrival of Polish priests who were unable to speak the local language meant that the process took centuries to complete.

Since local inhabitants throughout the eastern Baltic region tended to see Christianity as an alien phenomenon and most conversions were involuntary, many of their ancient traditions and beliefs survived for centuries. It has been observed that pagan beliefs "remained strong among the Estonians, and it would be difficult to assert that they actually accepted Christianity from the Catholic Church. Curious mixtures of pagan and Christian practices appeared, such as the worship of St. Anthony as a house god ... Christian marriage and baptism were slow to take root, and pagan burial customs continued more strongly among the Estonians than among any neighboring people in this period."[14]

The syncretistic impulse was even stronger among Lithuanians: as noted earlier, Dievas and Laima were assimilated by the Christian god and Mary, and pagan practices were Christianized. Summer solstice, known as *Kupoliu Švente*, became St. John's Day (*Jonines*); *Kučios* and *Kaledos* mark the winter solstice, and are celebrated today on December 24 and 25 (see Chapter 4). The Latvians, to the consternation of their Christian rulers, did much the same. Indeed, many scholars claim that with the arrival of Christianity, Baltic social traditions simply acquired an additional, Christian and Western, veneer, while underneath many of the old customs persisted, especially in the countryside.

Even if the villagers lived largely apart from their German masters for many hundreds of years, and even if Christianity remained primarily an urban phenomenon during that much of that period, the German colonization of Livonia introduced the Latvians and Estonians to European culture. Meanwhile, as Lithuania integrated into Christian Europe, the Grand Duchy's majority Orthodox and Slavic peoples were barely touched by the Catholic culture of the West. The regions they inhabited eventually became among the first to break away from the Grand Duchy. In Lithuania as elsewhere in Europe, the Christian clergy, drawn largely drawn from the Polish nobility and eventually from the Polonized part of the native population, became a privileged caste. They took part in state administration and were generally secluded from the rest of society. In Livonia the priesthood, like the nobility, was almost exclusively German.

Of the four bishoprics established in Livonia during the conquest the most important was the Riga Bishopric, which in the mid-thirteenth century became an Archbishopric. Monastic orders were also quickly established: the Cistercians, Franciscans, and Dominicans all arrived in Livonia in the thirteenth century. While the monasteries served to spread writing, several orders tried to work actively with the natives; many monks even attempted to familiarize themselves with the local languages. Yet it was the parish priest—when one could be found who was willing to serve outside urban centers such as Riga—who had the greatest contact with the lives of ordinary Latvians and Estonians: they were to conduct mass, share the seven sacraments, and teach the word of Christ. However, few were Estonian or Latvian, and the church rituals were offered in Latin rather than in the native tongues. The education provided by cathedral and monastic, intended for privileged Germans, was also in the Latin and German languages.

Catholicism faced no serious challenges in the region until the Protestant Reformation, the impact of which was felt most in Estonia and the central and western parts of Latvia, where the German upper classes embraced Lutheranism and the native peasantry had no choice but to follow. In Lithuania, however, where not a few magnates turned to Calvinism, the Catholic Church was eventually able to regain much of what it had lost.

Lithuania remained remarkably free of religious turmoil during this era. Indeed, from the fourteenth to the sixteenth century the Lithuanian state was inhabited by Orthodox, Catholics, Protestants, Muslims, and Jews, yet there were no domestic religious wars. Such relatively happy circumstances owed much to an earlier policy of tolerance practiced by Lithuania's earlier, pagan rulers when paganism was the officially recognized faith of the state but others, including Christians, were allowed to practice their religions freely. The situation after Lithuania's Christianization was analogous: Christians generally tolerated non-Christians, and Catholics tolerated other Christian confessions. Although Protestant communities briefly flourished in Lithuania, their success did not become an excuse for outbursts of murderous Catholic fanaticism. Indeed, at a time when Western Europe roasted its heretics in bonfires, when French Huguenots suffered the massacre of St. Bartholomew's Day (1572), and when thousands of religious exiles were forced to seek refuge far from their homelands, Lithuanian Catholicism (like Polish Catholicism) showed few signs of external militancy and largely refrained from sanctioning the use of such ferocious methods to deal with religious dissenters.

The Church's belated response to Martin Luther's Protestant challenge was the Council of Trent, a series of meetings that took place from 1545 to 1563, the purpose of which was to combat Protestantism and reaffirm and codify Church doctrine. This period of reflection and assertion was known as the Catholic Reformation (or Counter-Reformation). Faced with the threat of being overwhelmed by Protestantism, the Catholic Church focused on reforming itself from within while winning back areas that had been lost to its rival. Although it might seem that Catholicism's shallow roots among Lithuanians would have fated the region to follow the Livonian path, the Catholic Church was able quickly to make up its losses in Lithuania, and the Lithuanian peasantry was hardly affected at all.

It was in the spirit of the Catholic Reformation that the Society of Jesus was founded in 1540. While the controversial Jesuits were often criticized for their militancy and their devotion to worldly power, they helped to win back lost lands and peoples from the Protestants not only in parts of Western Europe, but in Poland-Lithuania as well. Devout and committed to learning, the Jesuits immediately began to build a higher educational system as a counterbalance to Protestant schools.

Wherever they went the Jesuits were especially concerned with strengthening popular religious devotion and attempted to learn the native languages. Religious books began to be printed in Vilnius by a Jesuit press; most of the texts, consisting principally of prayers and gospels, were translated from Latin into Polish or from Polish into Lithuanian. The Jesuits also delivered sermons in the native language while popularizing religious customs that remain popular in Lithuania today, such as the singing of the rosary and the chanting of the Little Office of the Immaculate Conception. Other monastic orders, such as the Franciscans, Benedictines, Dominicans, Basilians, Piarists, Vincentians, and Augustinians, similarly reinvigorated their apostolic work in Poland-Lithuania.

Another one of the more noteworthy effects of the Catholic Reformation in Poland-Lithuania was the renewed intensity of the Marian cult. This was most likely a response to the challenges posed not only by the Protestants but by Poland-Lithuania's Orthodox and Jews as well. According to one scholar, Poland-Lithuania was home to more than one thousand Marian shrines.[15] Among Lithuania's best-known Marian shrines today are those in the small towns of Pivašiūnai and Krekenava in the southern part of the country. This region had once converted to Protestantism, but in 1648 a Catholic church was built in Pivašiūnai and its central altar was decorated with the picture *Mother of God with the Baby*, an icon that was considered miraculous from its earliest days. Equally revered is *The Blessed Virgin Mary, Comfort of the Sorrowful*, which survived two major fires that consumed the churches that housed it. Perhaps the most famous example of the Marian Cult in Lithuania is located at the Gate of Dawn (*Aušros Gate*) in Vilnius, where the icon *Blessed Virgin Mary, Mother of Mercy* is reputed to have miraculous powers. The shrine continues to attract not only Lithuanian Catholic worshipers, but also Polish Catholics (whose services are conducted separately), as well as Orthodox Belarusians and Russians.

In none of the Baltic countries is religion more closely tied to national identity than in Lithuania. This is partly because of the country's historically close relationship with Poland. Poland received Christianity not from the invading Germans, but from the Czechs; likewise the Lithuanians received Christianity from the Poles, and the Lithuanian state and the Polish one were loosely tied from 1386. The Union of Lublin in 1569 formalized the arrangement and lasted until the last third of the eighteenth century, when the Russian Empire absorbed much of Poland and nearly all of Lithuania. Thus both Lithuania and Poland shared the experience of foreign rule—and since tsarist policies in this region were shaped by Russia's traditional mistrust of Catholicism, Catholic priests played leading roles in both the Polish and Lithuanian resistance movements of the nineteenth century.

The individual who best personified this symbiosis of Catholic and Lithuanian identity was Motiejus Valančius, a writer and from 1849 until his death in 1875 the Bishop of Samogitia. Ordained a priest in Vilnius, he worked in a poor parish for a time before being transferred to Samogitia, where he began writing the history of the Samogitian bishopric as well as other scholarly works on Lithuanian history. Father Valančius also promoted historical research and writing by his clergy and had their works illegally smuggled into Russian Lithuania (where writing in the Latin script was banned after 1864) from Lithuania Minor, or East Prussia. From 1866 onward Lithuanian books were printed in Königsberg (Karaliaučius in Lithuanian, but now Kaliningrad, an enclave of the Russian Federation) and smuggled across the border. Especially influential were Valančius's prayer books, intended for the Lithuanian peasantry. Caught in the middle of Russia's struggle with a rebellious Poland, from whose cultural grip nationally conscious Lithuanians hoped to extricate their people, Valančius had little choice but to support the existing authorities. At the same time, however, as Russian influence eclipsed Polish influence and as tsarist anti-Catholicism grew in Lithuania, Valančius used his moral authority to fuse popular passive resistance to St. Petersburg's Russification policies (most egregiously, the introduction of the Russian language into Church rituals) with the assertion of Lithuanian national consciousness.

Valančius's commitment to Lithuanian nationhood profoundly influenced the very public nature of the Church's involvement in later national activities, under tsarist rule and after the establishment of Lithuanian independence in 1918. (Given the very small size of the country's secular intelligentsia at the time it could hardly have been otherwise.) Priests participated in politics and administration, and the role of the Catholic Church loomed large in educational and cultural affairs. The secularization of the state—if that is the accurate term for the Soviet policy of excluding the Church from Lithuanian society and still harsher antireligious measures—was delayed until Lithuania's absorption by the officially atheistic USSR in 1940/1944.

PROTESTANTISM

Protestantism arrived in the eastern Baltic region not long after Martin Luther's revolt against Rome launched the Reformation. Germans, stirred by Luther's condemnation of Church abuses and tired of remitting taxes to Rome, were the first converts, and from Germany the revolution spread to the corners of Europe. While in Lithuania the effects of the Protestant Reformation were mostly temporary, Lutheranism, arriving first in cities such as Riga, Tallinn (Reval), and Tartu (Dorpat), quickly became the dominant religious confession in the urban areas of Livonia. Prussia, too, became a Lutheran state.

Since Luther's message, or its distorted reception, caused some disturbances in the countryside, the Baltic German gentry initially supported the Livonian Order's fight against the Lutheran reforms. However, resistance quickly gave way to adaptation, as most of the German gentry became Lutherans. Their conversion was followed by that of the Livonian peasants, who, in fact, had no choice of religious confession; they were obliged to conform to the religious choice of their German masters. Nevertheless, it is likely that many Estonian and Latvian villagers, who still resented the Germans' earlier attempts at forcible conversion to Catholicism, found solace in the Reformation's main message—that all men were equal before God. Despite three centuries of Christianity in first its Catholic and then Lutheran manifestations, pagan practices remained a part of everyday life for hundreds of thousands of Estonian and Latvian peasants.

The period of Swedish rule in the seventeenth century was in some ways a golden age for Lutheranism. While Poland sponsored the spread of Roman Catholicism in eastern Latvia and Russia attempted to bring Orthodoxy to neighboring Estonia, the Swedish administration was committed to upholding the Lutheran faith in its newly acquired territories of Livland (as northeastern Latvia and southern Estonia were now known) and Estland (northern Estonia). Lutheran pastors now faced the task of eradicating the old superstitions and destroying the places of sacrifice that had once again come into use. In seventeenth-century Estonia witchcraft trials were common.

While eradicating pagan practices, heresy, and witchcraft was no easy task for Lutheran pastors, in organizational matters the Swedish administration was remarkably successful: the new administration of the Evangelical Lutheran Church quickly ordained dozens of pastors while nearly half of the 50 Lutheran churches and chapels were restored.[16] Lutherans were also appointed to the theological faculty of Dorpat University, which opened its doors in 1632 and remained, despite interruptions, Estonia's leading institution of higher education (see Chapter 3). By the end of Swedish rule most Lutheran pastors had university educations and were able to deliver sermons in the local languages, which in turn strengthened the peasants' relationship with the church. Meanwhile, the Catholic Church, which had once held sway throughout the Baltic region, became nearly extinct in Estonia and northern Latvia.

Despite the official status of Lutheranism, even under the period of Russian rule, the most dynamic religious movement in much of what would become Latvia and Estonia in the eighteenth century was Pietism, which originated in Germany but arrived in the Baltic region in the 1730s. The Moravian Brethren (*Herrnhut,* from the German town where the movement originated) preached piety, morality, humility, equality, and self-education, and their ideas quickly made inroads among the Estonian and Latvian peasantry. Forming their own congregations and choosing their own preachers, the Moravians appeared in the eyes of the authorities to be organizing an opposition movement; however, their principal interest was not church reform but the moral improvement of the peasantry, and they did not break from the official Lutheran Church. Some among the old nobility (but not the Lutheran clergy) supported the movement, for the Moravians had quickly succeeded in raising the moral level of the peasantry: in the areas where they had congregations criminality and drunkenness declined substantially. The Moravians also fought against the old beliefs and, in an attempt to eliminate the vestiges of Estonian folk culture, destroyed the old places of sacrifice. As the movement's members began to exceed the bounds of religion and made social claims and moral demands, the authorities became alarmed, and in 1743 Empress Elizabeth forbade Moravianism. However, Catherine II later lifted the prohibition and the movement attained a new lease on life in the early nineteenth century.

ORTHODOXY

Among Christian faiths it is Orthodoxy that has the longest history in the region, for Orthodox congregations in eastern Estonia date as far back as 1030 when missionaries from the Russian principalities made their first appearance. Yet the Crusaders' arrival confined Orthodoxy to the Slavic peoples of the east; thus the Orthodoxy of Constantinople (and later Moscow) had little influence on the Estonians and none on the Latvians, Lithuanians, and Prussians during the Middle Ages. Indeed, until the nineteenth century the only significant Orthodox communities in Estonia were the Russians who lived in the towns, the Setus of eastern Estonia, and the Old Believers who, seeking to avoid the changes that were taking place in the Russian Orthodox Church, had fled from Russia in the seventeenth century. Their communities were concentrated on the western bank of Lake Peipsi and remain there to the present day.

During the first century of Russian rule Orthodoxy held little appeal to the native Baltic populations. In 1832, however, the regime passed a law that abolished the former privileged position of the Lutheran Church in the Latvian and Estonian provinces. Now Lutheranism was no longer the state religion of the Baltic region but just one of many religious sects permitted by the tsarist government, which upheld Orthodoxy as the official state religion. Although the tsar's faith never became predominant, tens of thousands of Estonian and Latvian peasants converted to Orthodoxy in the 1840s in the mistaken belief that they would be awarded grants of land. Understandably disappointed when they learned that the rumored land was in Siberia, many Baltic peasants later reconverted to Lutheranism, if not by formal registration (in the Russian Empire it was made illegal for Orthodox Christians to convert to another faith), then in practice. Meanwhile, hundreds of Lutheran pastors were prosecuted for the illegal act of performing rites for Latvians and Estonians who were still formally registered as Orthodox.

The tsarist regime's struggle with the cultural dominance of the Baltic Germans (who were in fact loyal to the regime) and the peasants' faithfulness to the Lutheran Church was accompanied by parallel efforts by both the Russian government and the German nobility to win the allegiance of the Baltic natives, now freed from serfdom and in the process of developing their own national identities. The regime's chief instrument of Russification during the reign of Tsar Alexander III (1881–94) was Orthodoxy, but only northern Estonians (those living in Estland) converted in significant numbers. It took the arrival of Russians to the region in the late nineteenth century for Orthodoxy to find a large following in the Latvian and Estonian regions, while in the Lithuanian provinces (as in Poland) Russification and Orthodox proselytization failed entirely. However, by the time Estonia was established as an independent republic, Orthodoxy had acquired a considerable following among Estonians: according to the official statistics (1935), of 212,000 members of the autocephalous Estonian Apostolic Orthodox Church (EAOC), 125,000 were ethnic Estonians.[17] In the Republic of Latvia, however, only a tiny minority of the titular population (4 percent) professed Orthodoxy; there, approximately two-thirds of all Orthodox Church members were Russians or Belarusians.

Lithuania's historical ties to Orthodoxy are of an entirely different nature, for throughout the life of the Grand Duchy, the Roman Catholic Lithuanians were a minority in a realm that contained large numbers of Orthodox Slavs (Belarusians and Ukrainians) and Jews. Yet Orthodoxy has historically held little attraction for ethnic Lithuanians, many of whom saw the colorful onion dome cathedrals erected in the nineteenth century as symbols of Russian imperial rule—which indeed they were. The imposing but beautiful Orthodox Cathedral, built in Riga between 1876 and 1884, was more than a house of worship: it was a symbol of Russia's attempt to promote the status of Russian Orthodoxy in the region during the era of Russification. Indeed, by the time Russia's last tsar abdicated the throne, just about every major city in every corner of the empire had its own Orthodox cathedral.

JUDAISM

Until nearly the entire Jewish community in Lithuania was murdered during World War II, Jews had a long and rich history in Lithuania, dating to

Gediminas's invitation to merchants and craftsmen to settle in the Grand Duchy in the fourteenth century. In the early fifteenth century Gediminas's grandson Vytautas granted Jews various privileges, including religious freedom and protection of both person and property. The number of Jews in Lithuania grew rapidly as the Grand Duchy attracted Jews who were expelled from Spain and other parts of Europe. (A decision to expel Jews from Lithuania in 1495 was reversed eight years later.) Iberian Jews were later joined by thousands of Jews who escaped persecution at the hands of marauding Cossacks in Ukraine. By the seventeenth century Poland-Lithuania had become the new cultural center of Jewish life in Europe. At first concentrated in the Zamut region (including Vilnius and areas north and west of it), Lithuania's Jews, called "Litvaks," eventually established communities throughout the western part of the Grand Duchy. By 1765 there were at least 120,000 Jews in ethnic Lithuania and nearly 750,000 Jews in the entire Polish-Lithuanian Commonwealth. Concentrated mostly in cities and towns, Jews lived separately from their Polish, Lithuanian, Belarusian, and Ukrainian neighbors.

The Commonwealth was home to the largest Jewish population in the world and conditions for Jews there were relatively good. For a long time Lithuanian Jewry was a religiously and culturally closed community, renowned for its religiosity, intellect, and dedication to the study of the Torah and the Talmud. Through their commercial contacts with the Jews the Belarusian and Lithuanian peasants became well aware of the Litvaks' different values and lifestyles. Townspeople regarded the Litvaks as noisy, dirty, sly, deceptive, and even diabolical but nevertheless tolerated this alien community in their midst. Despite tension between Jews and Gentiles, as well as pogroms in Vilnius in 1633 and Brest in 1637, accusations against Jews did not turn into bloodbaths, as was common elsewhere in Europe.

While most Jews were poor, some aspired to a noble lifestyle and a few even owned Lithuanian serfs. Most of the Grand Duchy's Jews, however, engaged in traditional activities such as moneylending, trading, and innkeeping while others established themselves as tailors, grocers, barbers, doctors (in short supply everywhere), goldsmiths, furriers, and tinsmiths. Jews were seen as especially useful by the Polish-Lithuanian nobility, who often allowed them to circumvent the regulations that governed economic life in the towns. However, under Russian rule, beginning in the late nineteenth century, the Jews' legal and socioeconomic status deteriorated as Russian-controlled parts of Lithuania and Poland were made part of the "Jewish Pale of Settlement" to which Jews were largely confined.

Latvia too once had a significant Jewish population, but its history is not as old as that of the Litvaks. Small numbers of Jews began to settle in Kurzeme (Courland) and Latgale as early as the sixteenth century; however, they began to arrive in Riga in significant numbers only in the nineteenth century, concentrating in the Maskavas district (behind the train station). In the small Latgalian town of Rēzekne, once a major trading hub (then known as Rezhitsa) but devastated during World War II, there once stood at least 8 (and possibly as many as 11) synagogues—a testament to the presence of Jews in this region a century ago.

SOVIET RULE

The Baltic countries were incorporated into the USSR in 1940 and for nearly half a century were subject to the Soviet regime's harsh antireligious policies. Although it claimed to uphold the rights of believers, the Soviet regime was officially atheistic and was deeply suspicious of religious institutions and of religion's appeal to ordinary people. While the Russian Orthodox Church, after two decades of ruthless persecution, was able to achieve a sort of concordat with the Soviet authorities that reflected its official favor (in turn the Orthodox Church was expected to support and promote the regime), Lutheran, Roman Catholic, Greek Catholic (called Uniates), and several other religious groups, viewed as "religious cults" that had supported the enemy during the war, were forbidden from establishing any kind of central administrative apparatus.[18] Some religious groups—most notably the Uniates (who were forced to merge with the Russian Orthodox Church under the control of the Moscow Patriarchate), Jehovah's Witnesses, Seventh Day Adventists, and Pentecostals—were simply barred from registering, but many sectarian groups nevertheless operated illegally. Clergymen of all faiths as well as ordinary believers were harassed, intimidated, threatened, and punished. To compete with and supplant religious holy days and rituals the Soviet regime created secular holidays and ceremonies, while marshalling its vast propaganda apparatus in an effort to change human consciousness and eradicate religious belief altogether.

At first the Lutheran Church was singled out for especially severe repression, as it was considered a "German" church, and Baltic Lutherans—clerics in particular—suffered in the arrests and deportations carried out by the Soviet authorities. Meanwhile, the Lutheran Church's educational functions were sharply curtailed and most of its theological institutions were closed. Although nearly two million Estonians and Latvians professed Lutheranism at the outset of the Soviet occupation, there is evidence that the prestige of the Church was already in decline even before the Soviet era, as rates of baptism dropped considerably during the 1920s and 1930s.[19] Some speculate that the harshness of Stalin's religious policies may have actually slowed down the existing trend toward secularization in the region. However, unlike the Catholic Church in

Lithuania, the Lutheran Church never developed a well-organized national-religious dissident movement in Latvia or Estonia.

The Soviet regime's attitude toward Orthodoxy, the religion of the Russian and other East Slavic people, was complex. The annexed western borderlands contained a sizeable Orthodox population—one that the Soviet regime was not eager to alienate further still by imposing excessively harsh religious policies. The main objective was to establish external control over the Orthodox churches, including those in the Baltic republics, where religious organizations were viewed as possible instruments of political separatism. Thus did Estonian autocephaly come to an end as each of the Baltic Orthodox Churches was placed under the control of the Moscow Patriarchate.[20] However, the autocephalous Estonian Apostolic Orthodox Church (EAOC) continued to exist for Estonian émigrés in the United States, Canada, and Sweden.

Many of those who came under Soviet rule in 1940–44 were Catholic, and these the Kremlin viewed with considerably greater suspicion. Associating the Catholic Church with nationalism, resistance, and foreign (i.e., Western) influence, the regime viewed this institution as inherently disloyal and as the one national body capable of defending Lithuanian culture, values, and traditions. Thus the Catholic Church was closely monitored, and priests thought to be disloyal to Soviet authorities were punished. By 1948 four of the five bishops who remained in Latvia after the occupation had been arrested, tried, and deported, while over the course of the first decade of Soviet rule Lithuania lost nearly half of its priests, especially during the great wave of deportations in 1946–49, when approximately 350 Lithuanian priests were exiled to the Soviet interior. Although the losses were not as great in Latvia, by 1959 there were almost twice as many parishes as there were priests.

After a brief thaw in religious life in the mid-1950s, during which Lithuania celebrated the consecration of two new bishops and 130 of the deported priests were allowed to return from internal exile, in 1959 Stalin's successor Nikita Khrushchev launched a new antireligious drive that resulted in the arrest of yet more clergymen and the closure of thousands of churches of all confessions throughout the USSR. The Vilnius Cathedral, taken over by the regime in 1953, was now turned into a gallery and concert hall, while Riga's famous Dome Cathedral (*Rigas Doms*) was restored and opened as a concert hall for organ music. Likewise, a more secular purpose was found for the city's huge Orthodox Cathedral, as it was transformed into a planetarium. Dozens of other churches and chapels were used as warehouses, stores, museums (of atheism, in some cases), movie theaters, and galleries, while enormous collections of pictures, sculptures, and other church articles were destroyed.

The harshness of the campaign lessened after Khrushchev was removed from the Soviet leadership in 1964. The Russian Orthodox Church, which had suffered most under Khrushchev, naturally stood to benefit the most from the more relaxed approach of his successors, but the greater breathing space benefited all religious confessions. The regime's somewhat greater flexibility on religious matters was demonstrated by the rebuilding of St. Peter's Church, long noted as one of Riga's great symbols because of the way its spire dominated the city's remarkable skyline. Bombarded during World War II, the church and its spire were rebuilt during 1968–73; however, nothing remains of its prewar collection of art and religious objects. Catholics also benefited from the regime's apparent softening on religious affairs: in 1964 Lithuanian priests were allowed, for the first time since the occupation began, to visit Rome. Jewish synagogues, however, were not rebuilt, and most evidence of Jewish life in the region before the war was eliminated.

Despite the more moderate line of Leonid Brezhnev's regime, few places of worship were reopened for services, and the regime continued to churn out atheistic propaganda as it monitored religious activities everywhere. The continued restraints on religious practice outraged the faithful and set the stage for the growth of a dissident movement in the 1970s, spearheaded by Lithuanian Catholics. When in 1968 the Soviet regime passed a law that allowed citizens to petition the government, Lithuanian Catholics immediately began petitioning for the return of exiled bishops, the publication of religious materials, and the lifting of rules that impeded their ability to practice their religion. Beginning in 1972 they published a small journal called *Chronicle of the Catholic Church of Lithuania,* which focused predominantly on the suppression of religious freedom in Soviet Lithuania. By the end of the decade a small group of priests had established a Catholic Committee for the Defense of the Rights of Believers, which documented the violations of the rights of believers.

Reprisals by the Soviet authorities seemed to have limited impact, as Catholic activism in Lithuania persisted. Despite the internal division between "loyalist" (who accepted the narrow confines the Soviet system imposed on Church activity) and "reactionary" (who insisted on the Church's independence) priests, the Lithuanian Catholic Church was far better able to preserve its influence than the Lutheran churches of Estonia and Latvia, which did comparatively little to resist Soviet antireligious policies. Indeed, atheistic ideology appeared to succeed especially well in Estonia and in Latvia, where by the 1960s most young people were estranged from religion.

RELIGIOUS LIFE TODAY

In the late 1980s, Soviet leader Mikhail Gorbachev launched a new policy of religious toleration as part of his overall reform program of "restructuring" (perestroika) the Soviet Union. With most religious restrictions lifted, spiritual life immediately began to flourish in the Baltic republics. The revival of religious life, there and elsewhere in the postcommunist world, is a testament to Marxist ideology's failure to penetrate the deepest layers of human consciousness in the captive nations. Although many people immediately hoped that their countries would reclaim the Christian values that had been largely lost during the Soviet era, over time religious idealism faded and religious values were eclipsed by secular values such as individualism, money, power, and social status. Spiritual life in the region, as in all times and places, has had to adjust accordingly.

Among the most notable features of contemporary religious life in the Baltic countries—and in Latvia and Estonia in particular—are its diversity and tolerance. Attaining their full independence in 1991, each of the Baltic governments has upheld the principle of full freedom of religion for its citizens. Thus not only have the region's traditional confessions—Lutheranism, Catholicism, and Orthodoxy—begun to revive, but other religious movements—Methodism, Baptism, Pentecostalism, and Seventh Day Adventism, for example—have made significant inroads as well. Although popular suspicion of nontraditional faiths lingers, Balts tend to be amused rather than offended by the sight of Hare Krishnas singing and dancing in their cities.

Just as the region is home to numerous confessions and sects, the nature of spiritual life differs in significant ways from one Baltic country to the next. Lithuanians tend to be staunchly Catholic, and as noted earlier have tethered their national identity as Lithuanians to their religious identity as Roman Catholics. Catholicism, therefore, is a very public matter in Lithuania, where one finds signs of outward religiosity—most notably wooden crosses—in even the most unexpected places. The contrast with Estonia could hardly be greater. Although the number of people who claim to be members of any particular church is rather low in Estonia, and although only 4 percent of Estonians say that they participate in weekly religious services, this does not necessarily mean that Estonians are nonreligious. Estonians, like their Finnish neighbors, are noted for their solitude and their private approach to religion. Religious convictions are considered extremely personal and Estonians are reluctant to engage in public discussions of religious questions. Latvia, the most ethnically and religiously diverse of the Baltic countries, is arguably the most tolerant when it comes to religious matters. Like Estonians, most Latvians tend to regard spiritual matters as private.

Estonia

Estonia is one of Europe's most secular countries. Since the scope of religious activity was allowed to widen in the late 1980s, spiritual life in Estonia was characterized first by a "church boom," during which the number of Lutheran baptisms temporarily skyrocketed, followed by a decline in the mid-1990s. Relatively few Estonians are affiliated with formal religious institutions, and even fewer are donating members.

The largest religious confession today among ethnic Estonians is the Estonian Evangelical Lutheran Church (EELC), which claims 175,000 members. While this represents a dramatic drop from the 874,000 Estonians who belonged to the church in 1934, Lutheranism still holds far greater attraction for ethnic Estonians than Orthodoxy, the faith of Estonia's Russian-speaking community. Constituting nearly three-quarters of the country's Orthodox Christians, Russian speakers belong to the Estonian Orthodox Church of the Moscow Patriarchate (EOCMP), which is now a separate organization from the Estonian Apostolic Orthodox Church (EAOC). The latter consists of 58 congregations with approximately 18,000 members, mostly ethnic Estonians. Congregations of Old Believers, who are Russians, are located along the coast of Lake Peipsi as well as in Tallinn and Tartu. They number about 2,500 people according to the 2000 census.

Despite its official status in the Middle Ages before the Lutheran revolt, Catholicism is the faith of only 5,700 or so Estonian residents today, only about 30 percent of whom are ethnic Estonians. The country's small community of Muslims, constituting fewer than 5,000 people, is a vestige of Soviet times when the Estonian republic was an attractive destination for emigrants from other parts of the USSR. Only 6 percent of the country's 1,387 Muslims (2000 census) are ethnic Estonians. Judaism has never made significant inroads in Estonia, and with the emigration or deaths of all but 10 Estonian Jews, Adolf Hitler was proudly able to pronounce the country *Judenrein* (cleansed of Jews). Thanks to the arrival of Russian-speaking Jews from the Soviet interior, the Jewish population in Estonia eventually recovered and peaked at around 5,500 in 1989; however, emigration, mostly to Israel, has taken a heavy toll. For 60 years Estonia did not have a single Jewish house of worship, but in early 2005 ground was broken in Tallinn for a new synagogue to serve the country's Jewish population of approximately 3,000.

Just as the country's traditional confessions have been able to revive their activities, relatively new charismatic movements such as Pentecostalism (which originated in the United States) have also made an appearance in Estonia. Established in 1991, the Estonian Christian Pentecostal Church (ECPC) today claims a membership of 3,500. Religious movements that had been banned by the Soviet authorities have also become active again, including Jehovah's Witnesses, the Moravian Congregation (a small group within the Lutheran Church), and the Salvation Army. A more recent arrival is "Word of

Life," which originated from Baptist and Methodist congregations in Estonia in the late 1980s and claims a membership of about 1,000.

Paganism, which the Christian faiths (not to mention the Soviet regime) tried for many centuries to eradicate, has also enjoyed a modest revival in Estonia. Its most visible manifestation in Estonia today is Taara belief, a religion that was created in 1928. Their organization (Tallinna Hiis, or the Sacred Grove of Tallinn), founded in 1933 and devoted to Estonian statehood, was repressed by the Soviet regime after less than a decade. Emerging openly once again in the late 1980s, Taara belief today claims a membership of more than 1,000. The reemergence of Taara belief has paralleled the appearance of "Earth Belief." Both are essentially modernized forms of paganism that emphasize nature worship. They are also skeptical of Christianity and regard it as an alien faith imposed by foreigners.

Perhaps the most significant religious question in Estonia today concerns the status of the Orthodox Church. In 1944 many leaders of the autocephalous Estonian Apostolic Orthodox Church (EAOC), which was canonically subordinate to the Patriarchate of Constantinople, fled Estonia and settled in Sweden, while Orthodoxy in occupied Estonia came under the control of the Moscow Patriarchate. With the restoration of Estonian independence in 1991, a struggle between the EAOC and the Diocese of the Moscow Patriarchate quickly ensued, each claiming to be the legal successor to the prewar EAOC. The main issue was property, including church buildings, lands, and housing for priests. Only in 2002 was an apparent solution found that required the Moscow-based church to surrender its claim to legal succession to the EAOC. Instead it was registered as the Estonian Orthodox Church of the Moscow Patriarchate and was awarded several buildings that had legally belonged to the EAOC. The nature of future relations between the two branches of the Orthodox Church can only be speculated, for the long history of troubles within Estonian Orthodoxy is unlikely to be buried entirely by the recent attempts at accommodation.

Latvia

Latvia today is truly a multiconfessional country. Since the fall of communism, the Christian population of Latvia, which includes a large number of Russian-speaking peoples, has been split fairly evenly between Protestantism, Orthodoxy, and Roman Catholicism. While most ethnic Latvians still belong to the Evangelical Lutheran Church, their relationship with this institution is rather tepid. As in Estonia, the status of the Lutheran Church in Latvia has clearly diminished since 1935, when it was the church of more than two-thirds of Latvians. The harsh antireligious policies of the Soviet period only partly explains this phenomenon; so does the general trend toward secularization and indifference to religion that one sees elsewhere in Europe. Another factor, and perhaps the most salient one, is the church's weakness as a Latvian institution, for it had been brought to Latvia by German barons and until the 1920s was dominated by German clerics. Latvians had only two decades to Latvianize this institution (e.g., train its own clergy, compose original Latvian hymns) before the Soviet occupation forced it into submission.

The Roman Catholic Church, by contrast, seems to have forged stronger links with its congregations and was better able to withstand the period of Soviet occupation. About half a million Latvian residents are Catholic, concentrated mainly in Latgale, a region with close historical ties to Poland. In recent decades it appears that Catholicism has become more evenly spread throughout the country, but this is due just as much to the failures of the Lutheran Church as it is to the successes of Roman Catholicism. During a period when all the traditional confessions were weakened, the Catholic Church, receiving guidance from Rome and better able than the Lutheran Church to tend to the spiritual needs of its flock, was able to preserve its status not only in Latgale but also in other parts of Latvia.

In Latvia the Catholic faithful continue to make regular pilgrimages to the Cathedral of Aglona (1699, rebuilt in 1780), located 40 kilometers east of Daugavpils on a site once considered sacred to the region's pagans. Aglona houses the painting *Our Lady in Aglona*, which many believers consider a holy icon. Upwards of 100,000 people converge on the tiny town during Whitsun, a Christian festival that takes place 50 days after Easter, and on the Feast of the Assumption of the Blessed Virgin Mary, held on August 15. In the summer of 1993 Aglona even received a visit from the Pope John Paul II.

As in Estonia, Latvian Orthodoxy was under the control of the Moscow Patriarchate during Soviet times, but in 1992 Latvia's Orthodox Church regained its independence. Most Orthodox Christians in Latvia are Russian speakers; likewise, the country's Old Believers, numbering as many as 70,000, are descendants of Russians who fled tsarist persecution more than three centuries ago. Riga's Old Believer parish, which worships in the golden-domed Grebenshchikova Church (*Grebenščikova baznīca*) in the city's heavily Russian Maskavas district, is probably the largest Old Believer parish in the world.

The Latvian government draws distinctions between the aforementioned "traditional" confessions (to which Baptism and Judaism must be added) and the "new" religions that compete for the souls of Latvia's believers. All religious groups must register with the government, but only Latvian citizens may do so. Because the Law on Religious Organizations prohibits the simultaneous registration of more than one church in a single confession, on occasion the government denies registration to one group or another. Thus the applications of the Confessional Lutheran Church and the Autonomous Orthodox Church to register have been refused, leading to charges of discrimination. Foreign evangelists and missionaries are allowed to hold meetings and to proselytize, but only if they are invited by domestic religious organizations. Once the restrictions on religious activities were lifted at the end of the 1980s, other Protestant groups began evangelizing, most notably Baptists (who are usually ethnic Latvians) and Pentecostals (the majority of whom are ethnic Russians).

Despite the murder of 80,000 or more Jews during World War II, a small Jewish community survives in Lithuania. Numbering 14,000 in 1995 but only 6,000 in 2002, this community continues to dwindle as Jews emigrate, mostly to Israel. A few remnants of Riga's old ghetto survive in the run-down Maskavas district, where the decrepit housing once occupied by Jews fell into the hands of the Russian-speaking immigrants (and their descendants) who arrived in the decades after World War II. Here stands a monument to the 300 Jews who were burned alive in the Great Choral Synagogue (1871) on July 4, 1941. Only 10 kilometers away is the infamous Rumbula killing field, a pine-forest enclave where around 25,000 ghetto Jews were murdered in just two days. Although there were once 40 synagogues in Riga, only one, built in 1905, has survived. Bombed three times in the 1990s (1995, 1998, and 1999), it is now under round-the-clock police surveillance.

While numerous religious confessions, both traditional and nontraditional, have revived in contemporary Latvia, the country's old pagan traditions are still far from dead. They continue to be preserved by the Dievturi ("those who hold God's laws"), whose beliefs are rooted in Dievturība—the "national Latvian religion"—of the interwar period. First established in 1926, Dievturība was based on ideas contained in the large body of *dainas* (folk songs), of which several thousand dealt with the subject of Dievs. Closely associated with some Latvian fascist-type groups, Dievturība was shut down by the Soviet authorities in 1940 and was not revived until nearly half a century later when interest in Latvian folklore began to revive. Like the Estonian Taara belief or the Lithuanian Romuva, Dievturība has a negative view of Christianity and is firmly rooted in respect for cycles of nature that governs all life. The Dievturi are also characterized by an optimistic view that focuses on the achievement of virtue rather than the avoidance of sin—a concept that appears to be alien to Latvian indigenous belief. It is hard to say how seriously the Dievturi take these beliefs, as in many cases the religion's practitioners are simply urban intellectuals who enjoy playing at being pagans.

Lithuania

Lithuania, whose patron saint is Casimir (1458–84), remains to this day a firmly Catholic country, with 649 parishes overseen by nearly 1,000 priests, who are aided by an equal number of nuns. Catholic archbishops reside in Vilnius and Kaunas, while five other bishops are responsible for other dioceses. Catholics constitute about three-quarters of the Lithuanian population, and as many as one of every three Lithuanians attends service at least once a month. The hundreds of wooden churches scattered throughout the country bear witness to Lithuania's Catholic heritage; the capital Vilnius has approximately 40 Catholic churches, mostly constructed in the Baroque style (see Chapter 8).

Of all the country's Catholic monuments, perhaps its eeriest is the Hill of Crosses (*Kryžių kalnas*). Located near Šiauliai in central Lithuania, the Hill of Crosses comprises tens of thousands of mostly wooden crosses both large and small.[21] While it began as a sacred pagan site where the symbol of the cross was used to provide protection against sickness or misfortune as well as to ensure a good harvest, today the Hill of Crosses is a symbol not only of Christianity but of Lithuanian nationalism as well. The site was bulldozed by the Soviet regime on several occasions, but devout and national-minded Lithuanians did not hesitate to plant new crosses in defiance of the authorities. Although Catholic shrines in Šiluva and Žemaičių Kalvarija continue to attract crowds, Soviet authorities managed to destroy several other important shrines, including the seventeenth-century Stations of the Cross in Vilnius, which once drew influxes of more than 100,000 pilgrims. Its 36 chapels were dynamited in 1962.

While Russian Orthodoxy has the support of around 5 percent of the population (mostly Russians), less than 1 percent of Lithuanians are Protestant. Most of these belong to the Lutheran Church, which is especially strong in the Klaeipėda area and has 45 congregations throughout the country. Evangelical Protestants and fundamentalists have also made an appearance in the country, but they pose no challenge whatsoever to the primacy of the Catholic Church.

Jewish life in Lithuania has nearly disappeared altogether. Visitors to Vilnius may still visit the city's old Jewish quarter, which lay in the streets west of *Didžioji gatvė,* but like the tiny Jewish ghetto in Kaunas it fails to do justice to the history of Jewish life in a country that was once home to hundreds of thousands of Jews. Twentieth-century efforts to make the historically multinational Vilnius more recognizably "Lithuanian" have obscured the fact that Jews constituted 36.2 percent of the city's population as late as 1920 (when the city was under Polish administration). Of course, the "Lithuanization"

A Hill of Crosses (Kryžių kalnas), near Šiauliai, Lithuania. A sacred spot where a church once stood, the Hill of Crosses became a symbol of anti-Soviet resistance.

of Vilnius was simply the result of government policy, for the war and the accompanying Holocaust played the most important role in the destruction not only of the Jewish community, but also of the Jewish ghetto and the city's synagogues, including the Great Synagogue (1572) that could once accommodate more than 3,000 believers. Soviet authorities destroyed much of the rest. Only street names such as *Žydų* (Jews) and *Gaono* (Gaon, or genius or sage) serve as living reminders of the Jewish past in Lithuania.[22] The number of Jews living in Vilnius today is fewer than 5,000 —fewer than half of what it was at the end of the 1980s (12,400) and a mere 5 percent of the prewar Jewish population—and they have but one synagogue (there were once more than 100) and one Jewish newspaper.

The Ashkenazi Jews were destroyed, but a small but endangered Jewish community has survived in Lithuania called the Karaites (or Karaim), a sect whose origins were in eighth-century Mesopotamia. In some ways the Karaites' theological position, which is distinct from the Rabbinical Jewish tradition, is analogous to that of the Protestants during the Reformation, for it emphasizes a return to the written word of the Old Testament and a rejection of the Talmud. The Karaites' language is Turkish and, arriving from present-day Ukraine and Crimea during the Middle Ages, they retain a Tatar-like appearance and way of life, which sharpened the distinctions between Karaites and the country's other Jews. About half of Lithuania's remaining 300 Karaites live in Trakai, where there is a museum devoted to

Another view of the Hill of Crosses.

them; most of the remainder live in Vilnius. In Lithuania as elsewhere their numbers are dwindling rapidly, leaving perhaps only 5,000 Karaites in the entire world today.

Despite the small number of Jews in Lithuania, a miniature Jewish cultural revival has been taking place since the late 1980s. To its credit the post-Soviet Lithuanian government has condemned the crimes against the Jews of Lithuania (which were largely ignored by the Soviet regime) and has officially recognized the Jewish State Museum of Lithuania. Synagogues, closed during the Soviet era, are open in Vilnius and Kaunas. Thirty or so Jewish social organizations are registered in Lithuania, and the tiny Jewish community coexists peacefully alongside Lithuanians, Russians, and Poles without official discrimination. However, anti-Semitism has by no means completely disappeared in Lithuania, whose neo-Nazi organizations regularly publish anti-Semitic articles as hooligans desecrate Jewish graves and decorate buildings and monuments with Nazi symbols.[23]

As in Estonia and Latvia, paganism has enjoyed a significant revival in Lithuania since 1991, when Romuva ("Sanctuary" or "Temple") congregations were once again established in Vilnius, Kaunas, and elsewhere. A nature-centered religion that observes a pantheon of many gods and goddesses, Romuva was first established in 1929 but was disbanded and persecuted during the period of Soviet occupation. According to Lithuania's "Law on Religious Communities and Association," Romuva has the status of a nontraditional religion, which means that it does not receive the state support given traditional religions such as Catholicism and Orthodoxy.

NOTES

1. Endre Bojtár, *Forward to the Past: A Cultural History of the Baltic People* (Budapest: Central European Press, 1999), 307–17.

2. Marija Gimbutas, "Religion and Mythology of the Balts," in *Of Gods and Holidays: The Baltic Heritage,* ed. Jonas Trinkūnas (Vilnius: Tvermė, 1999), 21.

3. Prane Dunduliene, "Ancient Lithuanian Mythology and Religion," www.litnet.lt/litinfo/religion.html.

4. Gimbutas, 20.

5. Norbertas Vėlius notes that Lithuanian religious beliefs are further divisible into those of the Aukštaičiai (Highlanders) and of the Samogitians (Lowlanders). Norbertas Vėlius, "Mythology and the Religion of the Early Lithuanians," in Trinkūnas, 49.

6. Gimbutas, 41.

7. "Pagan Lithuanian Folk Beliefs," www.geocities.com/Athens/Delphi/3503/lecture.html.

8. The relations between Mėnulis and Aušrinė, while controversial, are also confused. Is she his girlfriend, his wife, or his daughter?

9. Gimbutas, 38.

10. Norbertas Vėlius, *The World Outlook of the Ancient Balts* (Vilnius: Mintis Publishers, 1989), 61.

11. Scholars continue to debate the syncretistic links between Māra and Mary. Was Mary created from *Māra* and her Indo-European variants? How did the concept of Māra change as a result of Christianization?

12. Some early scholars were convinced that a pope-like figure by the name of Krivė lived in Lithuania in the 1320s, but this appears to be more legend than fact. See S. C. Rowell, *Lithuania Ascending: A Pagan Empire within East-Central Europe, 1295–1345* (New York: Cambridge University Press, 1994), 125–28.

13. Norman Davies, *God's Playground: A History of Poland, Volume I: The Origins to 1795* (New York: Columbia University Press, 1984), 124.

14. Toivo U. Raun, *Estonia and the Estonians* (Stanford, Calif.: Hoover Institution Press, 1987), 23–24.

15. Davies, 171.

16. Alfred Bilmanis, *A History of Latvia* (Westport, Conn.: Greenwood Press, 1951), 171.

17. Founded in 1923, the autocephalous EAOC sought to distinguish itself from the Russian Orthodox Church, which was controlled by the Moscow Patriarchate. The Estonian Orthodox tried to Westernize their church by reducing the number of icons in their churches and reducing ceremonies as much as possible while placing greater emphasis on sermons. Estonian Orthodox were also considerably less hostile to Catholicism than the Russian Orthodox. Walter Kolarz, *Religion in the Soviet Union* (New York: St. Martin's Press, 1961), 118–20.

18. Riho Altnurme, "'Religious Cults,' Particularly Lutheranism, in the Soviet Union in 1944–1949," *Trames*, 6, no. 56/51 (2002): 3–16.

19. Romuald Misiunas and Rein Taagepera, *The Baltic States: Years of Dependence 1940–1990* (Berkeley: University of California Press, 1993), 125.

20. From 1961 to 1990 the Bishop of Tallinn was Aleksei Ridiger (b. 1929), a bilingual descendant of a Baltic German baron, who then became Aleksii II, Patriarch of Moscow and All-Russia. Accusations that Aleksii II cooperated with the KGB while heading the Estonian Orthodox Church has bred only further mistrust of the Moscow Patriarchate among many Estonians.

21. This is not to be confused with the considerably more modest Hill of Crosses on the Tahkuna Peninsula of Estonia's Hiiumaa island. This dune marks the spot where the island's 1,200 Swedes performed their final act of worship before being forced to leave in 1781.

22. The street name *Gaono* refers to Vilna Gaon Elijah ben Solomon Zalman, reputedly the greatest sage of the eighteenth century.

23. The swastika, today inextricably linked with Nazi barbarity, is one of the special life symbols of the ancient Lithuanian religion, along with the spiral, the cross, the wheel, as well as sun and moon symbols.

SELECTED READINGS

Bourdeaux, Michael. *Land of Crosses: The Struggle for Religious Freedom in Lithuania, 1939–78.* Chulmleigh, UK: Augustine Publishing, 1979.

Greimas, Algirdas J. *Of Gods and Men: Studies in Lithuanian Mythology.* Bloomington: Indiana University Press, 1992.

Hoppenbrouwers, Frans. "Romancing Freedom: Church and Society in the Baltic States since the End of Communism," *Religion, State & Society,* 27, no. 2 (June 1999): 161–73.

Vardys, V. Stanley. *The Catholic Church, Dissent and Nationality in Soviet Lithuania.* Boulder, Colo.: East European Quarterly, 1978.

Velius, Norbertas. *The World Outlook of the Ancient Balts.* Vilnius: Mintis Publishers, 1989.

Other Sources and Websites

There are many articles in *Journal of Baltic Studies* concerning religion in the Baltic countries. Also see the surveys by Toivo Raun and Andrejs Plakans, listed at the end of Chapter 1. For up-to-date statistics on religious demography in the Baltic states, see the U.S. State Department's International Religious Freedom Reports, www.state.gov/g/drl/rls/irf/. On religion in Estonia today, see The Estonia Page's overview at www.esis.ee/ist2000/einst/society/SOreligion.htm. For more on paganism in Estonia, see "The Heathens in Tartu in 1987–1994. Heritage Protection Club Tžlety," vinland.org/heathen/pagancee/taara.html. On Lithuanian paganism see www.lithuanian.net/resource/myths.htm. On Latvian paganism, see Jānis Tupešis's article in *Lituanus,* www.lituanus. org/1987/87_3_06.htm.

3

Marriage, Family, Gender, and Education

In MANY WAYS the Baltic countries are societies in transition. In recent decades they have experienced stagnation, liberation, depression, and recovery. Stability has returned in most places, but the transition left its mark on every aspect of society. Many families adapted to the changing conditions with some success; others were destroyed as parents succumbed to despair and many younger people sought opportunities elsewhere—in the shadow economy, in the larger cities, or even abroad. While most of this book highlights the cultural accomplishments of the Baltic peoples, this chapter focuses less on what the Balts have achieved than on the way they live. Its principal concerns are marriage and the family, the challenges faced by women in Baltic societies, and the educational systems of Estonia, Latvia, and Lithuania. As the Baltic peoples become more modern and European in their habits and ways of thinking, so have their institutions adapted to the changing times: although marriage is commonly viewed less as a necessity than as an option, the one-child (and frequently single-parent) family has become the norm. Higher education, now adapted to the European model, is more essential now than ever for one to get ahead—or just to keep up. Meanwhile, as everywhere in the Western world, women face the challenge of balancing work and family in a climate that is at best indifferent to women's concerns.

MARRIAGE AND THE FAMILY

Traditional Weddings

As Latvian, Lithuanian, and Estonian societies become increasingly modern and urban, many of the traditional wedding customs of the Baltic countryside have disappeared or have taken new forms. In the peasant societies of northeastern Europe it was customary for marriages to be arranged by the parents of the bride and groom, often utilizing the services of a matchmaker; yet it was also possible for young suitors to choose mates with whom they were already acquainted. Since most people in these peasant societies were quite poor the most important factor in choosing a bride was not her looks or her financial status but her diligence, for a wife must be able to labor outdoors while maintaining the household, attending to her husband, and raising their children. (As shall be seen the obligations of ordinary women in the Baltic countries have changed little over the centuries.)

Before the modern era marriages typically took place in late autumn or winter, with ceremonies and celebrations taking place at the homes of both sets of parents. While an old-fashioned wedding might last one week or even longer, over time these were shortened to just two or three days. Church weddings did not become common until the middle of the nineteenth century, but these were largely replaced by secular ceremonies during the Soviet era.

Contemporary Balts, much like Westerners, typically think of a wedding as a joyous affair that celebrates a serious commitment witnessed by family, friends, and God. Yet it was not long ago that marriage was viewed with much more gravity. Songs that were sung at weddings, especially in Lithuania and parts of Latvia, often had a mournful tone, for now the young woman was leaving her parents' home and her carefree life to enter the household of her husband. One might go so far as to say that the wedding was considered a sort of death for the bride. Unlike the marriages of today, those of the Baltic peasants were indissoluble, whether the husband was kind or mean, drunk or sober, handsome or unattractive.

Wedding customs and traditions varied from Lithuania to Latvia to Estonia (even though they have existed as countries for less than a century), and they also varied by region. Some customs common to northern Estonia were unfamiliar in the south and vice versa; likewise, the traditions of Samogitia differed noticeably from those of Dzūkija or eastern Lithuania. Many widespread customs had regional variants. For example, an old Latvian custom was that of the groomsmen "kidnapping" the bride; to get her back the groom had to sing a song or pay some other ransom. Variations of this custom were practiced in Estonia, in Bohemia, and elsewhere. In some places, like the

Central Asian republic of Kirgizia, the prewedding kidnappings continue to this day–but these are often not games. A Lithuanian wedding eve tradition was the braiding ceremony, during which the bridesmaids sang their sad farewell songs as the bride prepared to leave her home.[1] In Estonia a coifing ceremony took place at the home of the groom, whose mother traditionally placed a cap or kerchief on the head of the bride to signify her passage from maidenhood into womanhood.[2]

Throughout the Baltics the leading roles in the wedding ceremonies were played not by the groom and the bride, who were essentially passive participants in a celebration that took place around and for them, but by the best man (and groomsmen) and the matron of honor (and her bridesmaids). Weddings have traditionally been—and remain—participatory events, at which the singing, dancing, and feasting is all done for the central purpose of honoring a man and a woman who are embarking together on life's journey. Many of the older traditions have disappeared in the cities, but some are maintained in the countryside where old rural customs are better preserved. Just as traces of the traditional wedding customs have survived in modern nuptials, new traditions have been added over the centuries and especially in recent times. The contemporary custom of demanding that the groom kiss the bride by shouting "bitter" became customary in the Baltic countries only in the twentieth century, thanks to Russian influence. Likewise, in the Latvian capital it is fairly common to see newlyweds standing at the bank of the Daugava River to be photographed before a panoramic view of Old Riga (just as Muscovite wedding parties often end up in Red Square).

The Shrinking Family

While marriage has traditionally been viewed as a lifelong commitment that is necessary for the fulfillment of one's social and biological functions, in the Western world this timeless arrangement is now widely understood as optional and revocable. Family patterns in the Baltic states today parallel general European and American tendencies toward high divorce rates, small nuclear families, and households headed by single parents. Indeed, the attitude toward marriage has changed dramatically in the Baltic countries in the past two decades, and in the twenty-first century marriages are increasingly delayed, broken, or avoided altogether. Attitudes toward marriage and family remain most conservative in Lithuania, where families are traditionally large and divorce is less common, but even there the trends of recent decades have followed the patterns of the country's northern neighbors.

Among the explanations commonly given for the general decline in the marriage rate is the dramatic ageing of the Baltic populations, which itself is a consequence of the shrinking nuclear family. There are simply fewer people in the Baltics today in their twenties and thirties—the age when most people marry—than there were in previous decades. Moreover, men and women of the younger generations are choosing to remain single longer. Whether this is because of the universal social effects of urbanization, or the priority that many young people place on higher education and getting established in their professional careers, or the practical obstacle of finding affordable housing, or the simple and increasingly common desire to prolong one's carefree adolescence into middle age, the age of first marriage steadily climbed during the Soviet era and is now at its highest level in many decades.[3] Lithuanian women, for example, typically marry at 24.3 years of age today (2002), while the average man marries at 26.4. These figures still put Lithuanians at the low end of the European spectrum, but they represent a steady upward trend in the past decade. For Latvians and Estonians those figures are 24.9 and 25.5 years for women and 27.0 and 28.2 years for men.[4]

Paralleling the marriage slump of recent years has been a similar decline in the absolute number of divorces. Yet the divorce rate in the Baltic states is quite high by world standards and is comparable to that in the United States, where about half of all marriages end in divorce. Divorce was quite rare in Catholic Lithuania up to the 1950s, but as in the rest of the USSR the divorce rate increased dramatically in the 1970s and 1980s and peaked in the early 1990s, when the country and the entire region endured a profound economic crisis. Although divorce rates have leveled off in recent years, in Lithuania today it is still the case that more than 40 percent of all marriages end in divorce.[5] In Latvia, where there are 61 divorces per 100 marriages (2002), the trend is even more pronounced, but ethnic Latvians are less likely to divorce than are Russians and members of most other ethnic groups living in Latvia. The Estonian figure of 70 divorces per 100 marriages in 2002 actually represented an improvement over the 2001 figure.[6]

The western republics of the USSR experienced high rates of immigration from the 1940s to the 1980s (Latvia and Estonia far more than Lithuania), so it is not surprising to find that a high proportion of marriages in the Baltic countries are between partners of different ethnic groups. Although the trend of Baltic-Russian marriages, which was especially pronounced among city dwellers, began to reverse itself somewhat in the 1980s, about one out of every five marriages that takes place in Latvia today is between partners of different ethnicity, typically Latvians and Russians (or Ukrainians and Russians, etc.).[7] Lithuanians, whose country is much more ethnically homogenous, and Estonians, who tend to live separately from Russians, are much less likely to marry outside their ethnic group than are Latvians; yet even in these countries interethnic marriages are fairly common.

While Latvians, Estonians, and Lithuanians have different patterns of inter-ethnic marriage, all three Baltic states, like the rest of the former European USSR (Ukraine, Belarus, Russia), are experiencing a family crisis that began in the 1960s and continues to worsen. Sixty years after World War II decimated the Baltic republics, the ethnic Estonian and Latvian populations have still not reached their prewar levels. The total populations of all three Baltic countries, including the immigrants who arrived after the war (and their descendants), have been declining since the end of the Soviet era. Despite the pronatalist policies of today's Baltic governments, Estonia, Latvia, and Lithuania have among the world's lowest birthrates, well below the population replacement level (2.1) that each had been able to maintain into the late 1980s.[8] Families having three children are regarded as large and are the exception today, whereas families with only one child have become the norm.[9]

The decline in fertility during the Soviet era was largely because of the effects of modernization and urbanization, including the growth in the number of families having two parents working outside the home. Although the Soviet regime encouraged motherhood and provided day-care facilities for parents of young children, there were numerous practical issues that discouraged people from having large families, chief among them being low wages (which meant that both parents had to work), the lack of child-care options, and small living quarters—typically only two rooms in an apartment.[10] The economic uncertainties of the 1990s only exacerbated the trend toward smaller families. Likewise, the widespread availability of contraception has likely played an important role in suppressing the birthrate. Thanks to the unavailability of reliable contraceptives in the USSR, as well as the nonexistence of sex education, the main method of birth control in the Soviet era was abortion. In all three Baltic republics there were typically more abortions than live births in any given year—sometimes nearly twice as many. Although the abortion rate remains quite high, today the Balts rely on other means of birth control such as condoms and intrauterine devices (IUDs).

Although Baltic families continue to grow smaller, they are also increasingly being created outside of wedlock. In the United States, single motherhood is commonly thought to be an adolescent phenomenon, but in the Baltic states the overwhelming majority of unmarried mothers give birth to their first child while in their twenties. Parenthood outside of marriage is not the exception but the rule in Estonia, where couples are increasingly choosing to cohabit rather than marry. Thus, while more than half of all births in Estonia take place outside of marriage, two-parent households are still very much the norm. In Latvia, where more than 40 percent of births are outside of traditional marriage, the number of unmarried mothers is rapidly catching up to Estonian levels. In Lithuania the proportion of children born outside marriage doubled in the 1990s and by 2002 constituted nearly 28 percent of all births.

WOMEN

The Soviet Era and Today

It is sometimes remarked that *feminism* is a dirty word in Eastern Europe, where gender issues were for the most part ignored under the dictatorships of the proletariat. Some East European feminists—a tiny minority of women in this part of the world, to be sure—believe that the elimination of Marxist regimes did little to solve the problem, and that public discourse in the region today is dominated by an antifeminist agenda. It often seems that in the Baltic states, as in the former Soviet bloc as a whole, discussions of feminism and gender issues are largely confined to universities, academic journals, and conference halls—places where there is little hope of influencing public attitudes.

This rejection of feminism is partly a legacy of five decades of communist rule, during which the Soviet regime and its satellites, despite an official ideology that was favorable to equality between the sexes, did little to discourage the prevailing conservative attitudes toward women and the family. As feminists are, as a rule, members of the middle class, the limited appeal of feminism in the Baltic countries may also be explained by the relatively small (but nevertheless growing) size of the class that is most receptive to its ideas. To this must be added the rise of nationalism and the accompanying nostalgia for tradition in the Baltic countries. In Lithuania in particular there has been a renewed emphasis on women's roles as the producers of future citizens (hence there is a movement, absent in Latvia and Estonia, underway to outlaw abortions in Catholic Lithuania); in Latvia, too, the perception that Latvians are dying out has given added weight to traditionalist claims regarding the centrality of procreation and motherhood.[11] Such an atmosphere, feminists lament, inhibits the broad dissemination of feminist ideas and perpetuates the relegation of women to a secondary role in civic life.

Despite these concerns, the traditional cultures of the Baltic peoples have in many ways been favorably disposed toward women. As noted in Chapter 2, many of the Balts' most important deities were goddesses, and as priestesses, women were accorded a great deal of respect. As mothers and grandmothers, and as singers of the traditional *dainas* (see Chapters 5 and 7), women were the transmitters of Baltic cultures and were the repositories of its accumulated wisdom. And when educational opportunities became more widely available for Estonian and Latvian peasants (the Lithuanian peasantry was well behind) in the nineteenth century, women in several provinces were able to achieve literacy levels nearly equal to those of men.

However, before independence Baltic women had little experience in organizing to defend their rights and advance their interests. Although middle-class women in Latvia had participated in temperance movements, charity organizations, and women's leagues, these were not by their nature political. In a part of the world where gender issues were always subordinate to national and class concerns, no women's movements of any consequence existed to advance the cause of gender equality.[12] Because the governments of the inter-war Baltic states immediately granted women full political rights, including the right to vote, Baltic women never struggled for the franchise as their counterparts did in Britain or the United States. While women organized in various associations and exercised their right to vote, they did not share political power with men: a woman was not elected, for example, to the Latvian parliament for the first time until 1931. Although most women worked in the interwar Baltic republics, this did not further the economic independence of Baltic women, for most of that work was on the family farms that dotted the Baltic landscape.[13] Moreover, as the work of women was usually seen as being less valuable than that of men, women were paid considerably less even when doing the same job.

The arrival of the Soviet era marked a major change for women: in addition to the socialist duty of motherhood, there was an obligation to contribute to the rapidly industrializing Soviet economy as workers. After the war women entered the workforce in unprecedented numbers—indeed, many had little choice but to fend for themselves, as a large proportion of Baltic men had been deported or killed during the war. However, the positions they typically occupied—as teachers, doctors, nurses, secretaries, clerks, shop workers—were defined as "women's work" and thus were typically of low status and poor remuneration.[14] Meanwhile, Soviet women were expected to meet their obligations as workers while also fulfilling their traditional roles as wives and mothers; thus one had to work while finding the time to shop under conditions of chronic queues and shortages. While state child-care facilities were available to alleviate some of the burdens of child rearing (which to some extent liberated women from dependency on men), women were also expected to do most of the housework.

On the positive side, in Soviet times women enjoyed unprecedented opportunities to pursue higher education, and by the end of the Soviet era women in the Baltic countries outnumbered men in institutions of higher education. However, most women found that their salaries and opportunities for advancement lagged behind those of men. While women enjoyed the right to vote, the votes of women and men alike were meaningless in the Soviet system. Women occupied far more positions in national bodies under Soviet rule than they ever had during the first era of independence, but they rarely had positions at the highest echelons of power (i.e., the Central Committees of the USSR and of the Estonian, Latvian, and Lithuanian republics).

Although autonomous political organizations were prohibited during the Soviet era, the new freedoms of the perestroika era made it possible for women to organize and create organizations to advance their causes. During the 1990s hundreds of women's and family organizations emerged in the Baltic countries, yet few political parties today give a great deal of attention to women's issues, gender equality, or the family. While each of the Baltic constitutions guarantees equal rights, women have seen only marginal improvement in their situation; in some respects their condition has actually worsened since the Soviet collapse. Women in all three Baltic countries continue to demonstrate higher percentages of higher education and academic excellence than men, yet a significant salary gap remains. Moreover, because persistently retrograde attitudes about proper male and female roles at home and in the workplace continue to force women into secondary positions, women have little chance of competing with men for the most lucrative positions. Although women remain over-represented in the poorly remunerated medical, educational, and service sectors, relatively few have found success as entrepreneurs or in upper management.

To make matters worse, the transition to a market economy in the 1990s resulted in proportionally greater unemployment for women. Although the Baltic economies have stabilized in recent years, employment discrimination remains common and is worst for older women. Indeed, job advertisements sometimes explicitly call for the applications of younger (under age 35), attractive women. Moreover, with the closing of numerous child-care centers in the 1990s, many women experienced the double blow of losing their income while trying to raise children at home, which in turn complicated their efforts to find work.

The women who suffered worst during the economic crises of the 1990s were the elderly, who constitute a growing portion of the total populations of the Baltic countries. With a life expectancy of about 77 years in each of the Baltic countries (on average about 11 years longer than men), women make up more than two-thirds of all pensioners, who subsist on meager government payments. Despite these conditions, it is men—especially men in their sixties—who are far more likely to take their own lives in the Baltic countries, which have some of the world's highest suicide rates.[15]

Sexual Commodification

One of the saddest developments for women since the end of the Soviet era has been their commodification in the sexual marketplace. The free flow of information that began in the early 1990s begat an avalanche of pornography in the Baltic states, from videos viewed privately at home to "adult" magazines sold openly in kiosks. While the public display of revealing magazine covers has abated in recent years, the makers of television commercials and of street and magazine advertisements know that sex sells, and that the images of attractive teenage girls sell best. While feeling attractive has been important to young people at all times and in practically all places, the value placed on physical attractiveness has never been higher in the Baltic countries than it is today, as fashion models and film stars set the standard for physical beauty in a way that was inconceivable in Soviet times. Dieting is far more common today than it was during the Soviet era. In 1996 the typical 18-year-old Estonian girl reportedly weighed nearly 12 pounds less than her counterpart did only seven years earlier.[16]

Of still greater concern is the growth of prostitution and trafficking in women and children. Although their trade is illegal in the Baltic states, prostitutes are more numerous than they were in the Soviet era and have more venues in which to operate, including the new hotels, brothels, and strip clubs that have sprung up in each of the Baltic capitals. While Riga, with its hundreds of establishments offering a range of sexual services, is the sex capital of the Baltics, prostitution is hardly confined to the largest cities.[17] Moreover, sex is an export industry in the Baltic states, as naive young women are frequently lured to Western countries with promises of well-paid jobs as waitresses, dancers, models, or nannies. On arrival their identification is stolen, making it impossible to return home, and they are forced to have sex with clients. Children are also at risk of sexual exploitation as prostitutes or pornography "models." Although sex trafficking has been given a great deal of press attention and is illegal, its profitability makes its demise in the near future rather unlikely.

Political Participation

In politics the record for Baltic women has been somewhat mixed since 1990. Women were relatively well represented in the Soviet parliaments (called Supreme Soviets), but these institutions did not really govern, exercising real power for only a brief period in the Gorbachev era. With the creation of new democratically elected parliaments in the early 1990s, representation for women contracted substantially; however, the trend began to reverse itself in the latter half of the decade as more women took up seats in the Baltic parliaments. Although conditions remain far from ideal—women, for example, are underrepresented at the top of party lists—women in the Baltic countries have never had greater opportunities to participate in public life. Of the 101 deputies elected to the Estonian *Riigikogu* in 2003, 19 were women (18 percent). Latvia's parliamentary election of October 2002 awarded 18 of the *Saeima*'s 100 seats to women. While the 2000 elections in Lithuania brought only 15 women into the 141-member *Seimas* (10.6 percent), the elections of October 2004 gave seats to 31 women (21.9 percent). Although these figures are a far cry from Scandinavian levels (following Sweden's 2002 parliamentary elections, 45 percent of the deputies were women), they still represent a considerable advancement toward gender equality.

In general women in the Baltic countries are better represented in local government councils than in national bodies. Nevertheless, several women have achieved national recognition for public service. Lithuania's prime minister from March 1990 to January 1991 was Kazimiera Prunskienė (b. 1943), who in 1995 became the leader of the Lithuanian Women's Party. Narrowly defeated by Valdas Adamkus in the presidential run-off election of June 2004, Prunskienė remains one of Lithuania's most prominent politicians. Although no woman has been seriously considered for the largely ceremonial position of Estonian president since 1992, when Lagle Parek was a candidate, and although Estonia has never had a female prime minister or county governor, there have been several women cabinet ministers (five in 2002, but only two in 2004). While few women exercise real political power in Estonia today, it is worthwhile to note that a woman, the poet Lydia Koidula, helped define Estonian national identity in the nineteenth century (see Chapter 5).

Among the most prominent women in Estonian politics in recent years are Marju Lauristin (b. 1940) and Kristiina Ojuland (b. 1966). Lauristin is a journalist and academician who was one of the most widely respected leaders of the Estonian independence movement; a leader of several parties that formed in the early 1990s, Lauristin served as Minister of Social Affairs (1992–94) and afterward took a seat in the *Riigikogu* (1995–2003). The younger Ojuland is a relative newcomer to Estonian politics. In 2005 she returned to the *Riigikogu* after serving for two years as the Estonian Minister of Foreign Affairs. In an interview with one of Estonia's leading newspapers Ojuland discussed the continued relevance of femininity in political life: "Women's great chance lies in whether or not they can use their appearance in [sic] their advantage. Of course a woman attracts more attention, especially if she is blonde. Blondes make people talk. If such a woman also proves herself to be a serious worker, she will have got her chance."[18] Similar views of the role of women in the political sphere are not unusual in the Baltic countries.

The first two post-independence governments in Latvia had no women, but after 1994 women began to occupy several important posts. Most significantly, in July 1999 Vaira Vīķe-Freiberga (b. 1937), the daughter of refugees who fled Latvia in 1944, was elected as Latvia's first woman president after spending more than three decades as a professor in Canada. Popular and articulate, Vīķe-Freiberga was reelected to a second four-year term in 2003, making Latvia the only post-communist country that has a woman as head of state.

EDUCATION

Historical Background

Until the arrival of Christianity in the High Middle Ages, there was no formal education in the regions that now comprise Estonia, Latvia, and Lithuania. As elsewhere in Europe, the first schools in the Baltic region were Latin-language church schools whose main purpose was to prepare students for theological study. Dome churches were first established in Riga, Tartu, and Tallinn in the thirteenth century and in Vilnius at the end of the fourteenth, but it was only in the fifteenth and sixteenth centuries that secular town schools for the sons of the nobility were founded in the northern Baltic provinces. By the end of the seventeenth century, under Swedish rule, the Livland Diet decided that the noble landowners were obligated to build a school in each parish. Whether under the authority of Sweden or Russia, the educational system in Estonia and most of Latvia was almost purely German: the language of instruction was German, and German teachers provided instruction to the children of affluent Germans and to only a small number of Estonians and Latvians. These conditions did not change substantially until the mid-nineteenth century, when some Russian officials belatedly began to recognize that the existing educational system threatened to lure Latvians and Estonians toward German rather than Russian culture.

It was only during the late eighteenth century, after the region had recovered from the calamitous Great Northern War, that literacy levels among Latvian and Estonian peasants began to rise significantly, quickly exceeding the literacy rate of the empire as a whole. Generally speaking, literacy and education were more advanced in the Protestant Baltic regions than in Orthodox Russia or Catholic Lithuania. More than one-third of Latvian youth could read by the first decades of the nineteenth century, and more than three-quarters of all Latvians were literate by 1897.[19] Although the literacy rate for all Estonians over the age of 10 approached 90 percent by mid-century—by far the best performance in the empire—the harsh Russification measures that were introduced in Estonian and Latvian schools in the early 1890s may have actually had a negative effect on literacy rates in Estonia.[20] As will be seen, the struggle over languages in Latvian and Estonian classrooms has hardly abated, although today it is Latvian and Estonian that have the upper hand.

Since Christianity arrived later in Lithuania, schools were not established in the Grand Duchy until the end of the fourteenth century. The first was located near the Vilnius cathedral, and others were soon established elsewhere. Literacy was obligatory for Lithuanian magnates and nobles who wished to participate in public life, so it was for their children that these schools were originally established. By the sixteenth and seventeenth centuries schools for primary and secondary education were being established throughout the Grand Duchy, thanks in large measure to the competition between Protestants and Catholics seeking to consolidate their influence among the population. While Catholics, led by the Jesuit Order, ultimately came to dominate the educational system of the Grand Duchy, Protestants, Uniates, and Orthodox also maintained schools in their respective communities. A testament to the Jesuits' success was the fact that there were perhaps 300 elementary schools in Vilnius alone by the time the pope dissolved the order in 1773. Still, only a small proportion of the Lithuanian population attended these schools.[21]

When compared with the educational successes of the Estonian and Latvian provinces during the second half of the nineteenth century, Lithuanian education appears to have stagnated: a large proportion of the country's large urban-dwelling Jewish population achieved literacy at the dawn of the twentieth century (Vilnius was an important center of learning for European Jewry), but most Lithuanian peasants had not. As late as 1923 nearly one-third of the country remained illiterate; the corresponding figures for Latvia and Estonia were 14.3 and 5.6 percent, respectively.[22] Moreover, it was not until 1936 that Lithuania instituted the system of free, compulsory six-year education that had been in place in Latvia and Estonia from the beginning of their independence. However, by the end of the 1930s the system of primary education was nearly universal in the Baltic countries. Voluntary secondary education gymnasia, whose main focus were vocational education, were also established to meet the need for a skilled workforce.

Schools for linguistic minorities had legal status in the independent Baltic republics, but schools were considered national institutions whose purpose was not only to educate children but to foster national identity and to inculcate patriotic attitudes, regardless of ethnic background. The government, proclaimed Latvia's president Kārlis Ulmanis in 1936, would "take care that the school in Latvia [would] really be a sanctuary of culture that calls, stimulates, prepares and strengthens our sons and daughters of the nation in their honorable work for the good of the fatherland."[23] With only the slightest amendment, this declaration might just as well have been uttered by the presidents of Lithuania and Estonia in the second half of the 1930s. Since the patriotic images of the interwar republics continue to inspire today's politicians (and those who vote for them), to fully appreciate the meaning and purpose of the contentious educational reforms presently being undertaken in Latvia and Estonia one must consider the earlier efforts by Baltic governments to carry out their own national aspirations in education.

Education Reform

The educational system that the Baltic states inherited from the Soviet era was well developed and far more extensive than the educational systems that had existed in the independent Baltic republics of the 1920s and 1930s. Being heavily centralized and standardized, however, the educational system (like the economic infrastructure) that was in place from the Stalin era to 1991 was tailored to meet the needs of the USSR rather than those of the Baltic republics themselves. The only major allowance for difference was the length of the curriculum, which after 1965 was 11 years (8 years of basic education followed by 3 years of secondary education, which was made compulsory only in the 1970s) in Estonia, Latvia, and Lithuania but only 10 years in the other Soviet republics.

Modeled largely on the German educational system, the Soviet educational emphasis was vocational, with students tracked into either general (academic) or vocational programs after completing basic education. While not at all unusual in Europe, the system is unfamiliar to Americans, whose educational paths remain open until the completion of high school. While some might object to the system's inequality—students who are tracked into vocational training have a considerably smaller chance of attaining university education—the purpose of vocational education is to prevent the marginalization of the most vulnerable young people (i.e., those who have not completed basic education, which now lasts for nine years, by age 15) by providing them with training to become skilled workers. Unsurprisingly, most students today prefer to continue their studies in general, academically oriented secondary schools (gymnasia).

As was the case during the Soviet era, teaching is a female-dominated profession in the Baltic countries. In Lithuania, for example, 98 percent of all teachers in primary schools and 82 percent of all secondary school teachers are women. Only in the universities is the situation different: there more than half of the lecturers are men.[24] The ratios vary somewhat in Latvia and Estonia, but the story is still basically the same. Although diminishing birthrates in each of the Baltic countries has resulted in declining enrollments, the student–teacher ratio has not really changed except in higher education, where the hiring of teaching staff has not been able to keep pace with the rapid increase in students. In recent years the Baltic governments have also made efforts to improve teacher remuneration, which was meager in the 1990s.

One of the major successes of the education system in the Baltic countries today is the increased attention that is being paid to students with special needs. In the Soviet era a common approach to the physically and mentally handicapped was to institutionalize them rather than provide them with educational and professional opportunities. In contrast, in Latvia today there are 63 state-funded special education institutions (2002–3) to serve the needs of the approximately 10,000 students who attend them. An even greater contrast between Soviet attitudes and Baltic attitudes in the educational sphere concerns religious education. Forbidden during the Soviet occupation, the question of religious education reemerged in the early 1990s when communist restrictions on "religious propaganda" were loosened. Now legal, private religious schools have been established in the Baltic counties, but they often struggle to find funds for salaries and textbooks.

Religious education in public schools is a somewhat more controversial matter. Latvia and Estonia especially are highly secular societies in which, thanks in part to 50 years of communism, most people have lost their connection with their traditional churches and are wary of the introduction of another ideology into public life. Thus the passage of a law in 1996 that would allow religious classes in Latvian public high schools caused uneasiness in some quarters. However, the religion courses that are now offered in Latvian high schools are simply voluntary electives; no student is obliged to study religion.[25] Likewise, in Lithuania, where religious education was compulsory in public schools during the interwar period (despite the fact that the country had no official state religion), religious instruction is now provided only on the wishes of the students' parents.

Far more contentious than religious education is the matter of language. In the interwar era instruction in the Baltic countries at the primary, secondary, and tertiary levels was given mainly in the mother tongue; at the same time ethnic minorities were allowed to set up their own schools using their own languages. Under the Soviet system people could be educated in their own languages, but this had to be supplemented with the study of Russian. A drive in the late Brezhnev era to develop the Russian-language skills of the USSR's non-Russian population resulted in the introduction of Russian in native-language schools as early as the preschool level. This was not accompanied by a parallel campaign to encourage Russian speakers to learn the languages of the republics in which they lived. For example, although the study of Estonian in Russian-language schools in the Estonian republic began in third grade, only a small number of hours were devoted to it and few Russian-speaking students took it seriously. The principle of encouraging the universal mastery of Russian was also applied at the university level, for doctoral dissertations were now required to be written in Russian.

Since regaining their independence, one of the educational priorities in both Latvia and Estonia has been the development of policies toward ethnic minorities that will encourage their integration into national life. The policies that they have pursued toward that end have not always sat well with the more vocal elements of their Russian-speaking communities. This is less of a concern in Lithuania, where more than 80 percent of the country's residents are ethnic Lithuanians and Lithuanian is the language of 90 percent of all students enrolled in general schools. Latvia and Estonia have schools where ethnic minorities can be taught in their own languages, but in recent years each has taken concrete steps to encourage linguistic minorities to learn the national tongue. In Latvia a bilingual program that obliges minority-language high schools to teach 60 percent of their classes in Latvian began in September 2004. It immediately prompted accusations of discrimination and nationalist extremism by some Russian speakers (and by their spokespeople in Russia).

Estonia is undertaking a similar reform intended to ensure that all students in Estonia become proficient in the Estonian language. When it is fully implemented in 2007, Estonian-language instruction will make up 60 percent of the curriculum in Russian-language schools. While entirely Russian communities like those in Narva are unhappy about the change, many Russian-speaking families are preparing their children for full Estonian citizenship. The fact that only 23 percent of all students in Estonia study in Russian-language schools in a country where Russian-speakers make up nearly one-third of the population suggests that non-Estonian parents have become more willing to place their children in Estonian-language schools.[26] Likewise, in Latvia, where Russian speakers are about 40 percent of the population, about three-quarters of all first-graders began studying Latvian in the 2004–5 school year.[27]

Foundations of Higher Education: Vilnius and Tartu Universities

The basic infrastructure of higher education in the Baltic states was created during the first era of independence as the Baltic governments set up a series of institutions that ranged from academies and technical schools to conservatories and universities. While some were destroyed during the war or closed by Soviet authorities, several of these institutions are still functioning today. In interwar Lithuania there was Vytautas Magnus University, the

Agricultural Academy, the Veterinary Academy, the Art Institute, and the Conservatory in addition to the various teachers' and commercial institutes. The Pallas Art School (see Chapter 9) and the Higher Music School were located in Tartu, Estonia's leading cultural center, while the Technical University, the State School of Industrial Arts, and the Conservatory (reorganized in 1923 as the Higher Music School) were established in the Estonian capital. Among Latvia's institutions of higher education were the University of Latvia, the Conservatory in Riga, the Art Academy, and the Agricultural Academy in Jelgava. Yet the Baltic region can boast of only two classical humanistic European universities that predate the era of independence. These are Vilnius University and Tartu University, which during their respective golden ages were among the leading centers of higher education in all of Eastern Europe.

Older than Harvard (1636), Yale (1701), and Moscow University (1755), Vilnius University was established in 1579 and quickly became the spiritual and cultural center of Lithuania. Before there was a university in Vilnius, Lithuanians from the noble class studied abroad: in the late fourteenth century some went to Prague, but by the fifteenth century the university in Cracow had become attractive to students who intended to make careers in the Church. Students who attended institutions of higher education in German cities such as Leipzig, Wittenberg, and Heidelberg in the sixteenth century often returned as defiant Protestants. While Lithuanian Protestants played a leading role in the development of nearby Königsberg University (1544), the arrival of the Jesuit Order several decades later transformed education throughout the Grand Duchy.

Tartu University, Estonia. Built in the Classical style in 1803–1809, the main building is one of the national symbols of Estonia.

Of the 10 or so new colleges the Jesuits established in the Lithuanian and Belarusian lands, the most important was the one they founded in Vilnius in 1570, which within nine years was promoted to the status of an academy and then a university. Although its students were drawn overwhelmingly from the Lithuanian and Belarusian regions of the Grand Duchy, the language of instruction at the Vilnius University was, as elsewhere in Europe, Latin. During its golden age, from the late sixteenth to the eighteenth centuries, Lithuanian scholarship was developed principally by the university's own graduates, who produced works both in the humanities (logic, rhetoric, literary theory) and the sciences (mathematics, physics, astronomy, optics). By the 1720s, however, this golden age was coming to an end as enrollments flattened and the curriculum became fossilized.

With the abolition of the Jesuit Order in 1773, all Jesuit schools were closed, and eight years later the university was reorganized as a secular institution, now called the Principal School of Lithuania. Under Russian administration after 1795, the university became the biggest in the Russian Empire and in 1803 was appropriately renamed the Imperial University of Vilnius, where most of the lectures were given in Polish. With Russian added to the curriculum as well, the number of students more than quadrupled to 1,321 in 1830, but the university was shut down as a punishment for the rebellion of 1830–31, leaving Lithuania without a single institution of higher education for nearly a century. When the university was finally reopened by Polish authorities in 1919 it was renamed Stephen Bathory University and was given a distinctly Polish orientation. Meanwhile, the traditions of Vilnius University were continued in the temporary capital, where in 1922 the University of Lithuania in Kaunas (renamed Vytautas Magnus University in 1930) was established.[28]

After the war, with Vilnius incorporated into what had become the Lithuanian Soviet Socialist Republic, Vilnius University was reorganized according the principles of the country's new rulers. Lithuanian replaced Polish as the language of instruction, but some classes were taught in Russian to meet the needs of its Russian-speaking students. While numerous other academies and colleges were established in Lithuania during and after the Soviet era, Vilnius University remains the country's flagship institution of higher education. Located in the heart of the Lithuanian capital, its distinctively handsome campus is also of some architectural interest (see Chapter 8).

The Estonian counterpart to Vilnius University is Tartu University, which was opened in 1632 as Academia Gustaviana in honor of Sweden's King Gustavus II Adolphus, who signed its charter. With origins similar to that of Vilnius University, the academy's precursor was a grammar school founded by the Jesuits in 1583 when Tartu (Dorpat) was under Polish rule. The university struggled for much of its early history, falling victim to the almost constant fighting between Sweden, which took Tartu in 1625, and Russia, which occupied the city in 1656 and again in 1704, when it was permanently absorbed into the empire. Closed in 1710, the university was reopened in 1802 as the University of Dorpat and given a series of new buildings. With Latin replaced by German as the language instruction, for most of the century the university maintained a dual identity as a German-language institution under Russian administration.

Although few ethnic Estonians studied there in the first decades of the nineteenth century, Dorpat University was nevertheless an important center for research on the Estonian language. It was only during the "national awakening" between 1860 and the 1880s that the enrollment of Estonians increased significantly; however, the number of Estonians at Dorpat University declined in the 1890s thanks to the Russification measures imposed by the authorities in St. Petersburg and the appearance of educational opportunities elsewhere. Just as Russian replaced German as the principal language of instruction, so in 1889 did the Russian name Iur'ev replace the German name Dorpat.

In the decades that followed Iur'ev University was a battleground between the Russian government, which controlled academic appointments, and the Baltic German faculty, most of whom departed and were replaced by Russians; meanwhile the relatively few Estonians who enrolled at the university were simply expected to assimilate and speak Russian. Only in 1919, following the establishment of Estonian independence, was the name Tartu restored to the university.[29] Although at first perhaps half of the lectures at the now indisputably Estonian institution were delivered in Russian, Estonian gradually became the predominant language of instruction. By the 1930s enrollments had climbed to more than 3,000, making Tartu University one of the largest and most influential institutions of higher education in the Baltic states.

Like Vilnius University, Tartu University was Sovietized and reorganized after World War II; resources devoted to Russian studies expanded while Estonian ethnic disciplines contracted. Unlike Vilnius, however, Tartu, which was located near a Soviet airbase, was a closed city during much of the Soviet era; thus it remained isolated from contact with Western languages and research. Since the collapse of the USSR Tartu University has become one of the Baltic region's most Westernized and English-friendly institutions of higher education; it presently enrolls large numbers of Finnish students attracted to its high standards and relatively low fees.

Higher Education Today

Like many other countries in East Central Europe, the Baltic countries have been experiencing a period of spectacular growth and dynamism in their systems of higher (or tertiary) education over the past decade or more. With a wide range of educational choices that includes universities and professional higher schools, both public and private, record numbers of students are now working toward degrees. In Latvia alone, where there are now 20 public and 15 private educational institutions (compared with 10 public and 2 private educational institutions at the end of the Soviet era), enrollments have nearly tripled since 1990–91, reaching 130,000 in 2004–5. As has been the case for several decades, over half of all students enrolled in universities are women, who constitute the majority in programs such as health, social service, teaching, and the humanities. Men outnumber women in areas such as engineering, computer technology, the physical sciences, and agriculture.

The system of higher education presently in place in the Baltic countries is binary, divisible into academic universities and professionally oriented higher schools or colleges. Although universities are more prestigious and competition for a place in them can be fierce, the non-university sector provides vocational training that is no less valuable for finding employment. The system is also divided into public and private institutions. Most students attend public higher educational institutions, where tuition is free for a limited number of students. However, many public institutions have a dual-tracking system whereby some students are admitted but do not receive funding from the state. All private institutions charge tuition, and while the private educational sector is growing much faster than the public one, it is also more unstable. To help students cope with the financial challenges posed by the decrease in state funding for public institutions and the relatively high cost of attending private ones, each of the Baltic governments has instituted financial aid programs consisting of grants (for students exhibiting high academic performance) and subsidized student loans.

There are only three classical universities in the Baltic states. The oldest are Vilnius University and Tartu University, which were discussed earlier. The third, the University of Latvia, is the largest university in the Baltics today and is attended by 25,000 students. Formed on the basis of the Riga Polytechnicum, which was founded by Russian imperial authorities in 1862, it was taken over by the Latvians in 1919 and became the country's national university. Called Latvian State University during the Soviet era, it remains the country's most prestigious institution of higher education. While Latvians seeking higher education have plenty of other options, most of these are located in Riga, where four out of five of the country's university students are enrolled. Founded on the basis of the small educational institutions that were created during the first era of independence, institutions such as Riga Technical University (which grew out of the Riga Polytechnical Institute established by the Soviets in 1958), the Latvian University of Agriculture (in Jelgava), Riga Stradiņš University (formerly known as the Medical Academy of Latvia), and Daugavpils University (formerly called Daugavpils Pedagogical University) are well established, but they face competition from newer institutions like Vidzeme University College (1996). Small, flexible, and in some ways on the cutting edge of educational reform, this little university in northeastern Latvia emphasizes English-language education and transnational programs.

Of all the systems of higher education in the Baltic states, Estonian universities are the most English-friendly. Whereas in Soviet times it was necessary to write one's doctoral dissertation in Russian, today Estonian dissertations, like scientific papers, are often written in English. Indeed, an increasing proportion of lectures are delivered in foreign languages—mostly English—in Estonian universities, several of which offer degree programs in English. All together Estonia has six public universities, six private ones, and around two dozen other accredited applied higher educational institutions, both public and private. However, the system remains dominated by Tartu University (17,500 students) and Tallinn University of Technology (more than 9,000 students), which was the first and leading center of cybernetics research in the USSR. More than half of the nearly 50,000 students attending institutions of higher education study at one of these universities. Many Estonians choose to study abroad: more than one-quarter of Estonian students abroad attend institutions in Russia, but Finland, Germany, and Latvia are also popular places to study.

Like the other Baltic countries, Lithuania too has experienced a significant increase in the number of tertiary educational institutions since the end of the Soviet era: today there are 15 universities (the main ones are Vilnius University, Vytautas Magnus University, Kaunas Technological University, Klaipėda University, and Vilnius Technical University) and nearly twice as many higher educational institutions without university status. However, private education has developed more slowly in Lithuania than in Latvia or Estonia: it was not until 1999 that the first two private institutions of higher education were established in Lithuania, and even today only a tiny proportion of students attend such institutions.

The reform of higher education began in the Baltic states just as the USSR was about to collapse. As higher education began to be decentralized the most important decisions about curriculum and organization were devolved to the educational institutions themselves. With the elimination of compulsory courses in Marxism-Leninism, higher education was immediately de-ideologized. Meanwhile, a variety of reforms were undertaken in an effort to align the Baltic systems of higher education with European practices and standards.

Some of the more recent reforms have come about because of the commitment made by the Baltic states to the Bologna Process in 1999. While in a way this phrase nicely captures the feelings that many educators share about the initiatives undertaken by the bureaucracies that rule them, the process is actually a serious and complex undertaking that involves 40 European countries, thousands of institutions of higher education, and millions of students. With a larger goal of creating a European Higher Education Area (EHEA) by 2010, the Bologna Process's main objective is to have members adopt a set of comparable degrees and systems of credit while promoting educational quality and mobility.

Even before the Bologna Process got under way the Baltic countries had already begun to reform the old Soviet-style degree system. Soviet universities, like Russian universities today, offered three degrees: diploma, candidate of science, and doctor of science. A diploma (analogous to a bachelor's degree) could be earned after five years of study, although this varied with the area of specialization. The candidate of science degree typically took three or four additional years and was roughly comparable to an American Ph.D. The doctor of science degree is held by a relatively small group of doctors and scientists who had already made significant research contributions in their areas of specialization. This system was in place in the Baltic countries into the 1990s, but recent reforms have reduced undergraduate programs from five years to four, making the diploma equivalent to the bachelor's degree. After earning a bachelor's degree a student who is interested in pursuing a specialized advanced degree may earn a master's degree (which takes two years) and then a doctorate (typically three or four years).

In many respects, educational reform is simply another aspect of the Westernization of the Baltic states. With the implementation of these and other reforms, many Baltic universities are working to promote transnational ties that will not only further their integration into Europe but will also attract students from abroad.

NOTES

1. Danutė Brzytė Bindokienė, *Lithuanian Customs and Traditions* (Chicago: Lithuanian World Community, 1989), 264–304.

2. Ülo Tedre, *Estonian Customs and Traditions* (Tallinn: Perioodika, 1985), 50–75.

3. While the age of first marriage in the Baltic region is higher today than it was in the Soviet era, the age of marriage among Baltic peasants in the late nineteenth century was higher than in other parts of Eastern Europe and was more comparable to that of Western Europe. Rural men in western Latvia, for example, usually married at 27 to 29 years if age, while the average woman married between the ages of 24 to 26. Vita Zelče, *Nezināmā: Latvijas sievietes 19. gadsimta otraja puse* (Riga: Latvijas Arhivistu biedriba, 2002), 263–64.

4. See the country pages for Estonia, Latvia, and Lithuania on the Council of Europe website, www.coe.int.

5. Ethnic Poles living are least likely to divorce, while Lithuania's Russians are most likely to divorce.

6. For Soviet era statistics on marriage and divorce, see Romuald Misiunas and Rein Taagepera, *The Baltic States: Years of Dependence* (Berkeley: University of California Press, 1993), 366. For more recent figures, see the chapters on the Baltic countries in Lynn Walter, ed., *The Greenwood Encyclopedia of Women's Issues Worldwide: Europe* (Westport, Conn.: Greenwood Press, 2003), 174; Women's Issues Information Centre Web site www.lygus.lt/mic2/women_in_lithuania/angl-gyventojai.html; Council of Europe Web site www.coe.int.

7. As a whole for the period 1970–2003, about one in three marriages in Latvia was between partners of different ethnicities; at the same time, ethnic Latvians are significantly less likely to marry outside their ethnic group than are Russian speakers. Children of mixed Latvian-Russian marriages almost always opt for Latvian nationality. Christiaan W. S. Monden and Jeroen Smits, "Ethnic Intermarriage in Times of Social Change: The Case of Latvia," *Demography*, 42, no. 2 (May 2005): 323–45.

8. Women in the Baltic countries are eligible for maternity leave and state subsidies for child care, but the value of these benefits is thought to be meager. Some women may choose not to have a child for fear that their positions will be eliminated once they return from leave. Men, too, are eligible for paternity leave, but since the compensation is so meager very few are willing to take time off work.

9. Despite the emphasis placed on childbearing in Lithuanian culture, the average woman in Lithuania today is expected to have only 1.3 births in her lifetime; for Estonia this figure is 1.2 and for Latvia it is only 1.1. UNICEF Web site, www.unicef.org/infobycountry/.

10. The high cost of apartments forces many young couples to live with their parents and is another disincentive that inhibits marriage and the creation of new families.

11. Daina Stukuls Eglitis, *Imagining the Nation: History, Modernity, and Revolution in Latvia* (University Park: Pennsylvania State University Press, 2002), 205.

12. While women were dominant in the social structure of the Riga Latvian Charity Society, an organization that was active during the last third of the nineteenth century, their activities were basically apolitical. The principal women's organization in early twentieth-century Latvia, the German Women's League in Riga (1905–39), was concerned less with women's issues per se than it was with the needs of ethnic Germans in Latvia. See Robert G. Waite, "The German Women's League in Riga, 1905–1939: An Ethnic Women's Organization in the Baltic States," *Journal of Baltic Studies,* 28. no. 4 (Winter 1997): 339–56.

13. Eglitis notes that in 1934 about 56 percent of Latvian women worked for wages, which was the second-highest rate in Europe at the time. Eglitis, 195.

14. Although the medical profession was dominated by women, most surgeons and leading specialists were men. This is still the case today.

15. While high suicide rates are common to many former Soviet republics, Lithuania is the world leader. There suicides are committed at a rate of 43.1 per 100,000

residents (2002). Estonia (37.4) and Latvia (36.5) are not far behind. (This compares with 13.9 in the United States.) Men are typically three to five times more likely than women to take their own lives.

16. Ain Hans, Edgar Kaskla, and Anu Laas, "Estonia," Walter, 176.

17. For a variety of reasons, not least of which is the Russian dominance of the shadow economy, Russian speakers constitute the overwhelming majority of prostitutes in Riga. Eglitis, 222.

18. As appears in Raili Põldsaar, "Women in Estonian Politics: Baltic and Global Perspective," in *Women in Baltic Societies: Past and Present,* ed. M. Goloubeva and D. Hanovs (Riga: N.I.M.S., 2002), 73.

19. Andrejs Plakans, *The Latvians: A Short History* (Stanford, Calif.: Hoover Institution Press, 1995), 68, 95.

20. Toivou U. Raun, *Estonia and the Estonians,* 2nd ed. (Stanford, Calif.: Hoover Institution Press, 1987), 55; Mati Laur, Tõnis Lukas, Ain Mäesalu, Ago Pajur, and Tõnu Tannberg, *History of Estonia,* 2nd ed. (Tallinn: Avita, 2002), 180–81.

21. Zigmantas Kiaupa, Jūratė Kiaupienė, and Albinas Kuncevičius, *The History of Lithuania before 1795* (Vilnius: Arlila, 2000), 347.

22. Zigmantas Kiaupa, Ain Mäesalu, Ago Pajur, and Gvido Straube, *The History of the Baltic Countries,* 3rd ed. (Tallinn: Avita, 2002), 153.

23. Gaston Lacombe, "Nationalism and Education in Latvia, 1918–1940," *Journal of Baltic Studies,* 28, no. 4 (Winter 1997): 309–39.

24. Ministry of Education and Science of the Republic of Lithuania, "Education in Lithuania 2003: Figures and Trends," www.mtp.smm.lt/dokumentai/english/Education_LT2003.pdf.

25. Anta Filipsone, "Time of Uncertain Conversations: Religious Education in Public Schools of the Post-Soviet Latvia," *Religious Education,* 100, no. 1 (Winter 2005): 57–60.

26. Estonian Ministry of Education and Research, www.hm.ee/.

27. Ministry of Foreign Affairs of the Republic of Latvia Web site, www.am.gov.lv/en/policy/4641/.

28. In 1950 Vytautas Magnus University was reorganized as the Kaunas Polytechnic Institute and the Kaunas Medical Institute. Only in 1989, in a moment of patriotic fervor in the Lithuanian Supreme Soviet, was Vytautas Magnus University reestablished.

29. Property belonging to Tartu University was moved to Vorenezh during the war. Most of it was returned after 1922, but the university's art collection remained in Voronezh.

SELECTED READINGS

Family

Domsch, Michel E., and Désirée H. Ladwig, eds. *Reconciliation of Family and Work in Eastern European Countries.* Frankfurt: Peter Lang, 2000.

Juozeliuniene, Irena. "Political Systems and Responsibility for Family Issues: The Case of Change in Lithuania." *Marriage and Family Review,* 28, nos. 3–4 (1999): 67–77.

Zvinkliene, Alina. "The State of Family Studies in Lithuania." *Marriage and Family Review,* 22, nos. 3–4 (1996): 203–32.

Gender Issues

Eglitis, Daina Stukuls. "(Re)Constructing Gender in Post-Communism." In *Imagining the Nation: History, Modernity, and Revolution in Latvia,* ed. Daina Stukuls Eglitis, 186–224. University Park: Pennsylvania State University Press, 2002.

Goloubeva, Maria, and Deniss Hanovs, eds. *Women in Baltic Societies: Past and Present.* Riga: N.I.M.S., 2002.

Kaskla, Edgar. "The National Woman: Constructing Gender Roles in Estonia," *Journal of Baltic Studies,* 34, no. 3 (Fall 2003): 298–312.

Walter, Lynn, ed. *The Greenwood Encyclopedia of Women's Issues Worldwide: Europe.* Westport, Conn.: Greenwood Press, 2003.

Zelče, Vita. *Nezināmā: Latvijas sievietes 19. gadsimta otrajā pusē* (The Unknown: Latvia's Women in the Second Half of the Nineteenth Century). Riga: Latvijas Arhivistu biedriba, 2002. This book contains a useful English-language summary on pages 261–79.

Other Sources and Websites

For women's issues, see the United Nations Development Project Web site, which has links to the Baltic countries as well as other former Soviet states: gender.undp. sk/index.cfm. Estonian Women's Studies and Resource Center (ENUT), www.enut.ee/.

The most up-to-date information about education in the Baltic states may be found on various Web sites. Especially helpful are the ministries of education. For Estonia, see www.hm.ee/. For the report by the Lithuanian Ministry of Education and Science, www.mtp.smm.lt/dokumentai/english/Education_LT2003.pdf. Latvia: www.ibe.unesco.org/International/ICE47/English/Natreps/reports/ latvia.pdf. A useful source for the financial aspects of information on higher education in the Baltic countries and elsewhere is The State University of New York at Buffalo's *The International Comparative Higher Education Finance and Accessibility Project,* www.gse.buffalo.edu/org/inthigheredfinance/.

4

Holidays, Cuisine, and Leisure Activities

MEMBERS OF ALL extended kinship groups, whether these are nations, villages, or tribes, share a common set of customs and traditions that are passed down from one generation to the next. Many of these traditions are—or are commonly believed to be—deeply rooted in a rural past, in which holidays, feasts, and traditions developed over the centuries in a relationship with the seasons, the soil, and the spirits. Others are not quite as ancient and eternal as they might seem: these "invented" traditions are often the conscious creations of modern nation-builders—whether they are poets, politicians, or historians—who shape the nation's past to suit the political needs of the present. Still other customs that are commonly regarded as native are in fact the result of foreign influences.

All of these conditions are true of the Baltic nations. Although the ancestors of the Estonians, Latvians, and Lithuanians arrived in the Baltic region earlier than the Germans and Slavs and although many attributes of their indigenous cultures developed more or less independently, they have nonetheless been extremely vulnerable to foreign conquest and alien cultural influences. German, Polish, Scandinavian, and Russian influences may still be seen in the impressive architectural monuments that have survived in the region's larger cities (see Chapter 8); and while the Germans and the Poles who dominated the region for centuries tended to live apart from the Baltic peasantry, their cultures and traditions clearly affected the Latvians, Estonians, and Lithuanians living in the countryside. Most significant was the arrival of Christianity, which spread throughout the region slowly but thoroughly by the seventeenth century. However, rather than changing the customs and world-views of the Baltic peoples, Christianity simply added another dimension or layer. As shall be seen, while the names and even the content of the Balts' festivals and holidays changed in accordance with the spiritual requirements of their adopted faith, in many ways their essence was undisturbed.

The greatest assault on the cultures and traditions of the Baltic peoples took place during the Soviet era, when forced ideological conformity combined with demographic Russification to make many Estonians, Latvians, and Lithuanians feel almost like strangers in their own countries. Yet the allowances the post-Stalin regime made for the development of national culture at least partly mitigated the Soviet system's overall insidiousness. Moreover, thanks to the Soviet Union's attempt to isolate its people from Western influences, the cultures and customs of the Baltic nations were in effect preserved (to use the appropriate metaphor) like insects in amber. Latvia, for example, may have become one of 15 Soviet Socialist Republics, but in many essential respects it remained Latvia.

It was only a quarter-century ago that some observers lamented the eventual disappearance of the Estonian and Latvian nations (the Lithuanian population was always larger and more insular), and with them their ancient customs and cultures. Yet 15 years after the Baltic states regained their independence it may be said with confidence that more has been preserved than has been lost. Larger cities such as Riga and Vilnius may be multinational, but the

The largest of its kind, the Latvian Open-Air Ethnographic Museum, Lake Jugla, features replicas of ancient Latvian villages, traditional Latvian food, handmade furniture, and folk art.

villages of rural Latvia are quite Latvian and those of Lithuania are unquestionably Lithuanian (except when they are Polish or Belarusian). Estonians, usually regarded as the most aloof of the Baltic peoples, remain the most enigmatic: frequently insisting that their country is "European" rather than "Baltic," Estonians are nevertheless the most culturally distinct of the Baltic peoples. Preferring family farms rather than communal village life, the Estonians too speak the language of their ancestors, eat many of the same foods, and celebrate the same holidays as they did more than a century ago, but with new additions. While current demographic trends are not working in favor of the Baltic nations, their cultural memories remain intact and their national traditions—both their timeless rural traditions and the invented traditions of the nineteenth and early twentieth centuries—promise to endure for the foreseeable future.

HOLIDAYS

A nation's annual calendar cycle reveals much about its history, its self-consciousness, and its traditional worldview. Although today most Balts do not don traditional peasant costumes to celebrate St. John's Day and only elderly women participate in the religious processions that take place on feast days, it may be argued that on the whole Estonians, Latvians, and Lithuanians are more faithful to the essence of their holiday traditions than are most Americans or Western Europeans. Having awakened to their own national identities only in the nineteenth century and threatened with cultural and even physical extinction during the wars and Soviet occupation of the twentieth century, the Baltic peoples are profoundly attached to many of their old customs and traditions. Likewise, as nations that have struggled to achieve and maintain their independence, they observe numerous holidays devoted to celebrating their nationhood and to remembrance of past suffering.

Folk Calendar Holidays

Baltic cultures have their origins in the countryside and its traditions. Since the Baltic peasants of earlier times believed that their survival and prosperity depended on the gods and spirits who inhabited their world, their celebrations of today's calendar holidays such as Christmas and Easter are in fact deeply rooted in the traditions of pagan worship. Over time these older practices were reworked to reflect the Christian beliefs and traditions that were acquired after the thirteenth century. In the peasantry's conception, time was separated into blocks according to the agricultural year, whose division points were the traditional saints' days and other holidays.[1] Thus the calendar holidays observed by the Latvians, Estonians, and Lithuanians today must be understood in light of the agricultural cycle, which begins with the spring planting and ends with the autumn harvest. In between, from November until March, there was much time for celebration.

The late autumn celebrations that follow the harvest festivities begin on November 2 with All Souls' Day, a day devoted to remembrance of the dead. A Catholic holiday that is observed throughout Europe, All Souls' Day is of particular significance in Lithuania (there it is called *Velinės;* in Latvia it is *Veli*), where a pagan autumn festival in honor of the dead known as *Ilges* was celebrated before Catholicism was firmly established in the country. The holiday retained its special meaning in the twentieth century, when thousands of Lithuanians lost their lives in defense of their faith and their country.

The next important day in the autumn celebratory cycle is St. Martin's Day on November 10, which marks the end of the agrarian year in northern Europe and the beginning of winter. Unlike the solemn All Souls' Day, St. Martin's Day (or Martinmas) is celebrated in a manner reminiscent of Halloween. It is of particular significance in the Estonian folk calendar, which two weeks later observes a similar holiday known as St. Catherine's Day (*Kadripäev*). Still popular in rural Estonia, the customs of St. Catherine's Day (November 25), although more associated with herding than with farming, are similar to those of St. Martin's Day: both holidays traditionally involve feasting and entertainment at home, while costumed children go door to door singing songs and collecting gifts and treats. However, instead of the menacing threat "Trick or treat!" shouted by American children on Halloween, on St. Martin's Day (*Mardipäev*) Estonian children have traditionally greeted their elders with the refrain "Please let us in because Mardi's fingers and toes are cold." If the children are not welcomed into the house, the house dweller risked being assaulted not by eggs, shaving cream, and toilet paper but by rude songs; more likely the children are admitted inside and given apples, nuts, cookies, and other treats.

In the short days and long nights of December the late autumn celebrations give way to the winter celebrations that peak during the Christmas holidays. Indeed, Christmas in the Baltics, as elsewhere in Europe, is less a single holiday than it is the high point of a winter festival season whose celebration begins with the winter solstice on December 21 (also known as St. Thomas's Day) and ends on January 6, when the Feast of the Epiphany is observed. In Latvia the year-ending season is known as *Ziemas svetki* (winter fest); in Estonia it is called *talvistepühad* or *jõulud,* from the ancient Scandinavian word *Jul,* from which the English word Yuletide is derived. In the Christian tradition the holiday celebrates the birth of Christ, but in the Baltic region's folk traditions the Christmas holiday is tied to the winter solstice, which signified the rebirth of the Sun maiden. Everywhere the holidays are celebrated with a variety of traditional dishes that provide the festivities with a distinctive local flavor.

Thanks to centuries of German rule, many of the Christmas traditions of the Baltic countries have their origins in Germany, including the custom of the Christmas tree. Despite this unassailable fact, a series of myths about the Latvian or Estonian origins of the Christmas tree persist. Since the pagans of the region regarded trees of all kinds with spiritual reverence, and since fir trees are quite common in northeastern Europe, this is not at all surprising. However, the notion that in 1510 Martin Luther, struck by the moonlight shining on the fir trees, brought one into his house in Latvia (an interesting proposition because Martin Luther never lived in Latvia) and decorated it with candles for his children, is unsupported by evidence. Estonia, too, has a claim on the first Christmas tree: according to legend the Fraternity of Blackheads—a group of unmarried, wealthy German merchants—first put up a Christmas tree on Tallinn's Town Hall Square in 1441. When the celebration ended they allegedly burned the tree.

In reality the Christmas tree is actually a rather recent Christmas symbol in the Baltics. In Estonia and Latvia it was adopted from the local German populations in the nineteenth century; the custom began in Lithuania only during the 1920s. The tradition of a red-robed Santa Claus bringing Christmas presents to good little girls and boys is also relatively recent but has become customary in each of the Baltic countries. However, the custom of bringing home Christmas straw, which was connected with the biblical legend of Christ's birth, was widespread in Baltic peasant tradition long before any Christmas trees could be found in their homes.

Under Soviet rule the Balts were discouraged from celebrating the Christmas holidays. To enforce the policy, school was in session on both Christmas Eve and Day, which were regarded as regular work days. Thus, the emphasis during those years, at least until the 1970s, was on New Year celebrations, when Father Frost—a slimmed-down Soviet imitation of Santa Claus, dressed in a silver caftan—arrives to reward all deserving boys and girls with gifts. Since the end of the Soviet era Christmas has reclaimed its former place in the Baltic countries, where the holiday is once again celebrated with simply decorated trees, exchanges of gifts, and the familiar seasonal gluttony. In fact, the frenzied shopping atmosphere that has almost come to define the Christmas holidays in the West is now becoming more familiar in the Baltics and other parts of East Central Europe.

In the Baltics the focal point of the holiday celebrations is not Christmas Day but rather Christmas Eve, a quiet time that is reserved exclusively for the family. While the old Christmas Eve traditions are best preserved in heavily Catholic Lithuania, many customs are disappearing. In Estonia, as elsewhere, the traditional edible home-made Christmas tree decorations have been largely replaced with store-bought ornaments. Likewise, the Christmas tradition of mumming, once common in the rural parts of the Baltic countries, is gradually fading into memory. In this tradition, merrymakers (mummers) disguised in various masks—animals such as bears, horses, wolves and goats, as well as fortune-tellers, dwarves, and living corpses—would travel from house to house or village to village, bringing blessings to a home, encouraging fertility, and frightening away evil spirits. As in the rest of Europe, however, rural life gave way to modern urban living in the twentieth century and such masquerading customs, like the tradition of dragging the Yule log—signifying last year's misfortunes—through the village and burning it, began to disappear in the Baltic countries.

Despite this loss, the tradition of having one's fill at the dinner table is as secure as ever. In Lithuania the Christmas Eve celebration is known as *Kūčios,* the focal point of which is an elaborate dinner. A sober occasion, household members are expected to refrain from eating meat or drinking alcoholic beverages; carp typically takes the place of meat, while water, cider, or fruit juice is served instead of wine, beer, or some other strong drink. While today this may be more a matter of principle than actual practice in many households, the spread at every Lithuanian table is nevertheless impressive. Consisting of 12 different dishes (formerly 13, representing the months of the pagan calendar) to represent the Apostles, the *Kūčios* feast typically includes foods prepared the previous summer and fall—for example, fruits and vegetables that were dried or otherwise preserved for the winter. It also includes fish, boiled or baked potatoes, a meatless sauerkraut, salads, mushrooms, biscuits (*slizikai*) with poppy seed milk, cranberry pudding (*kisielius*), compote or a dried fruit soup, and bread. As a token of peace, thin wafers called *plotkeles* are traditionally broken and eaten by each member of the household, who later gather around the Christmas tree to sing songs. The holiday custom of visiting neighbors occurs on Christmas Day (or the day after), when the family exchanges gifts, attends mass, and at last eats a meat-filled dinner.

In Latvia and Estonia, which are traditionally Protestant countries where the old Catholic restrictions on meat consumption did not apply, the celebration of Christmas differs mainly in the details and in the sorts of foods that are prepared. Observant Latvians and Estonians typically attend religious services on Christmas Eve (sometimes called *Ķūķi* in Latvia) rather than on Christmas Day, but as in Lithuania food is essential to the celebrations. According to Estonian and Latvian traditions one should eat nine (or seven) meals on Christmas Day to assure wealth during the coming year, but the custom is rarely observed today. Indeed, it would be difficult to imagine digesting more than one or maybe two meals consisting of pork dishes (snouts and feet are particular favorites), blood sausage, fried meat, liver pâté, bacon, sauerkraut, many varieties of small pies, pepper biscuits, knotted bread or coffee cake with nuts and raisins (Estonian or Latvian *kringel,* which has German origins), and gingerbread—which are typically washed down with beer, mead, mulled wine, or cultured milk.

The Christmas season in the Baltic countries lasts through the Feast of the Epiphany, or Three Kings Day, which is observed on January 6. On the islands and coastal regions of Estonia the holiday continues through January 7, which is known as St. Canute's Day in honor of the medieval Danish king. Before the demands of the modern workplace intervened, the winter holidays were traditionally a time when hard work was avoided and replaced with visiting and popular amusements. But the 12 days of rest and games ended on Epiphany, which in earlier times was a day of religious processions in honor of the Three Wise Men of Biblical lore. As a commemoration of Christ's baptism, the Epiphany is of special significance to the Orthodox churches, and thus Russians and other Orthodox believers living in the Baltic countries place more emphasis on this holiday than on Christmas.

The next important holiday in the calendar cycle is Shrove Tuesday, a movable feast day that falls somewhere between February 3 and March 9. Called *Mardi gras* in French-speaking countries and *fetter Dienstag* (Fat Tuesday) in Germany, Shrove Tuesday is celebrated in all three Baltic countries, where it marks the end of the long Baltic winter. As the culmination of the four-day meat-eating period known as Shrovetide, Shrove Tuesday is the last day before Lent, a period of fasting that begins on Ash Wednesday and lasts for 40 days until Easter.

Although today these holidays are celebrated in the Baltic countries in the Christian tradition, the season also has numerous associations with older pre-Christian traditions. In Lithuania the week of mirth and feasting before Lent is called *Užgavėnės,* which blended with an older festival marking the end of winter and the ushering in of spring. In Latvia Shrove Tuesday's early analog was the ancient *Meteni* feast, which was celebrated on the seventh Tuesday before Easter. A Latvian spirit associated with the growing of flax, Metenis was believed to arrive on a sleigh; thus Latvians, like Estonians and Lithuanians, celebrated by sledding, which they believed would make the flax grow longer.[2] The holiday is also believed to have had special meaning for Livonian fishermen, since the arrival of Shrovetide indicated that the fishing season was drawing near and thus winter preparations must soon be completed. Suppressed under Soviet rule, Shrove Tuesday is once again celebrated as a day of gorging, principally on pancakes and meat.

St. Casimir's Day, celebrated by the Lithuanians, usually follows Shrovetide. The grandson of the Lithuanian king Jogaila, St. Casimir is celebrated by Lithuanians for his piety, virtue, good works, and royal lineage.[3] Among the miracles St. Casimir is thought to have performed was his intercession— 35 years after his premature death from tuberculosis—to aid Lithuanian soldiers in their defense of the city of Polotsk against Russian forces in 1518. Today his casket lies in the Church of St. Peter and St. Paul in Vilnius, where it is visited by pilgrims arriving from all over Lithuania on March 4, the day that marks his death. These gatherings gave birth to the St. Casimir's Fair (*Kaziuko mugė*) in Vilnius, which attracts musicians, folk artists, and people of all ages from all over. Vendors brave the chilly weather as they sell food, handicrafts, trinkets, and Vilnius *verbos,* the country's traditional Palm Sunday flowers.

While St. Casimir's Day is a uniquely Lithuanian religious holiday, the most important holiday in the Catholic Church calendar is Easter. Observed on the first Sunday of the full moon after the spring equinox (March 21), Easter arrives at the end of the Lenten period of fasting and signifies the resurrection of Jesus Christ. However, like many other religious holidays it has merged with older traditions related to the agricultural cycle. Called "Great Days" in Lithuania (*Velykos*) and Latvia (*Lieldienas*) and "meat-taking holidays" (*lihavõttepühad*) in Estonia, the Easter rituals begin on Palm Sunday, which commemorates Christ's entry into Jerusalem. The main days of observance are Good Friday and Easter Sunday, a family holiday that, arriving after the solemnity of Lent, is celebrated by feasting and attending religious services.

As a holiday that has always been associated with fertility, Easter is also celebrated by swinging. For centuries this has been a favorite spring pastime in the Baltics, as it was believed that swinging on village swings tied to tall trees would make the livestock healthier and make the flax crop grow faster. Likewise the tradition of the decorated Easter egg, a symbol of life, has long been celebrated in the Baltics. Hidden by adults on Easter Saturday and hunted by children—who attribute the eggs to an imaginary Easter Granny (*Velykė* in Lithuania)—the following morning, Easter eggs are central to games such as egg-breaking and egg-rolling contests. They also appear in the Easter meals that are prepared in every home.

The seventh Sunday after Easter is known as the Pentecost, from the Greek word for "fiftieth," for on the fiftieth day after Easter the Apostles received from the Holy Spirit the ability to speak in other languages; this provided them with the ability to spread the word of Christ. While the Pentecost in the Baltic countries is mainly associated with Christian religious observances, its traditions also include older practices related to nature and the start of summer agricultural labors. In Lithuania, for example, where it merged with a cattle holiday known as *Sėkminės,* the celebration of the Pentecost incorporates elements of nature worship. This is best represented by the newly sprouted birch tree—whose branches were inserted under the roof to provide the Holy Spirit (believed to take the form of a white dove) with a resting place—and the wreaths that were typically fashioned from field flowers.

Another important spring holiday is St. George's Day, which is celebrated on April 23. While the historical St. George was a Christian warrior who died a martyr in 303 C.E., he later became associated with the legend of a mythical dragon slayer who symbolized the victory of Christianity over paganism.[4] Since contracts between farm owners and farmhands were written to end on April 23, this was also the day when renters, land lessors, and farmhands—like the landless peasants of earlier times—would move from one place to another.

In Estonia, where it was once believed that the earth remained poisonous until vegetation appears, St. George's Day was associated with the anticipated emergence of greenery. "With his key," says one Estonian proverb, "George makes the grass grow." St. George's Day was also associated with snakes, as the image of St. George the dragon slayer merged with the belief that after this day the poison of the earth enters snakes and toads. In recent centuries St. George's Day became one of the most important days in the Estonian folk calendar for yet another reason: it was on this day in 1343 that thousands of Estonians rebelled against the Danish king. Although the rebellion failed and Estonia was soon sold to the Livonian order, the revolt has left a strong psychological impact on the Estonians, who revere this holiday as symbolic of Estonia's fight for freedom. To this day bonfires marking the uprising of 1343 are lit all over Estonia on St. George's Eve.

Bonfires can be seen all over the Baltics during the summer solstice celebrations that make a late June visit to the Baltic countries a unique delight. In Estonia this mid-summer holiday is called *Jaanipäev*. For the Lithuanians it is *Joninės* or *Rasos,* its old pagan name. The Latvians call it *Jānu Vakars* or simply *Jāņi*. In all three countries St. John's Day falls on June 23–24, when the sun barely sets in northern Estonia. Like many other folk holidays, the solstice celebrations are deeply rooted in ancient pagan traditions but eventually acquired something of a Christian veneer as the Balts gradually adopted their new faith.

The biggest St. John's Day (named for the Apostle John) celebrations are in Latvia, where the holiday is stretched out over three days. In ancient times, the celebrations began on St. John's Eve (also called Līgo Eve or Herb Day), when boys and girls would meet on village squares and go off to gather flowers, herbs, and grasses to make wreaths to be used in the next days' ceremonies. In Latvia they also sang the traditional *līgo* songs and performed traditional Latvian folk dances (see Chapter 7), while drinking beer and eating pies and cheese. To this day St. John's Eve is an evening of eating, drinking, and singing; many revelers stay up all night to watch the sun sink and rise again.

Everywhere the focal point of St. John's Day is the lighting of a bonfire, over which the revelers jump with considerable courage (some of it liquid) and contagious enthusiasm. When asked why they do this, most young people are hard-pressed to come up with a suitable answer; they just know that jumping over a bonfire is great fun. For the ancient ancestors of the Estonians, Latvian, and Lithuanians, however, bonfires were lit to guarantee prosperity and to avoid bad luck, to ensure a good harvest, and to drive away mischievous spirits. For hardworking agricultural peoples, the summer solstice marked the transition from spring sowing to summer reaping and haymaking; for contemporary Balts, however, St. John's Day is a celebration that marks the real beginning of summer, as many will soon begin their extended summer holidays. Of all the holidays celebrated in the Baltics, it is simply the most fun.

The end of the summer brings annual celebrations associated with the harvest. St. Jacob's Day (July 25) traditionally marked the end of haymaking and the beginning of harvesting, while St. Batholomew's Day (August 24) is associated with reaping. The main harvest holiday has always been St. Michael's Day (or Michaelmas), which is celebrated on September 29. Nearly coinciding with the autumn equinox (September 23), St. Michael's Day marks the formal end of the short Baltic summer. Historically this was significant because with the completion of the harvest, the seasonal peasant contracts that covered the interval between St. George's Day and St. Michael's Day ended and Baltic peasants were free to move elsewhere.

Many harvest festivities from pagan times were transferred to St. Michael's Day. Other harvest customs have survived to the present day without being syncretized. Some rural regions of Estonia, for example, still celebrate the Festival of Killing the Pigs every September. Likewise, on October 5 Lithuanian farmers still observe the Festival of the Old Woman (*Nubaigai*), during which an old woman, or *Boba* (*Baba* in Slavic languages), symbolically binds the last sheaf of grain and is carried with it in procession to the farm while the procession sings. It is probably from similar harvest traditions in other European countries that the American custom of placing a wreath on the door is derived.

In addition to these traditional religious holidays, whether they are of pagan or Christian origin, the Baltic peoples also celebrate two important personal holidays: birthdays and name days. While birthdays are celebrated by the immediate family, name days, which are rooted in saints' days (i.e., a person was named for the saint on whose day he or she was born) are even more important and are celebrated by the extended family as well as by friends and coworkers. Each day in the Estonian, Latvian, or Lithuanian calendar usually has two or more names attached to it: for example, all Latvian men named Ainars celebrate their name day on July 17; likewise, May 7 is the name day for all Estonian women named Helma.[5] For many people it is a day to stay home and enjoy the company of friends and family, who drop by to offer gifts, chocolate, and flowers. A generous meal and numerous toasts are usually in order.

National Holidays and Commemoration Days

In addition to celebrating Christmas, New Year's Day, and Easter, people in the Baltic countries also observe several other international holidays. Since the 1920s the Baltic states, like other European countries, have observed Labor Day, a May 1 holiday that is celebrated mainly by not laboring. Earth Day, which falls on March 20, entails no such reward and therefore is barely noticed in the Baltic states. Mother's Day, an international holiday that falls on the second Sunday in May, is also observed in the Baltic states in much the same way it is observed elsewhere—with presents of flowers and candy. However, the May 9 holiday, which the countries of the former Soviet bloc celebrate to commemorate the victory over Germany in World War II, is more controversial in the Baltic states. After all, many Balts view it less as a day of victory than a reminder that the USSR's defeat of Germany was followed by half a century of Soviet occupation. The issue was addressed openly in 2005, when world leaders gathered in Moscow to celebrate the sixtieth anniversary of the defeat of Nazism. While Latvia's president Vaira Vīķe-Freiberga reluctantly agreed to attend the May 9 celebration, Estonia's Arnold Rüütel and Lithuania's Valdas Adamkus sent Russia an unambiguous message by opting to stay home.

In addition to celebrating the international, religious, and folk holidays discussed, each of the Baltic states also has its own distinctive national holidays and remembrance days that commemorate the triumphs and tribulations of the nation's past. The most important state holiday in each of the Baltic states is Independence Day. Since each of the Baltic states declared its independence from Russia on a different day in 1918, each country has its own official holiday, which naturally is accompanied by official ceremonies. In Lithuania the holiday falls on February 16, on February 24 in Estonia, and on November 18 in Latvia. There are also other holidays—not all of which are official state holidays—that celebrate the state's very existence. On November 11 Latvians celebrate Lāčplēsis Day, which celebrates the victory of Latvian Freedom Fighters over German and Russian Forces during the Latvian War of Independence (1918–20). A similar holiday, known as Victory Day (*Võidupüha*), is observed in Estonia on June 23 to mark a decisive battle over German forces in 1919. Lithuania, the only Baltic state to have enjoyed a period of independence before 1918, has its own unique Statehood Day (July 6), which commemorates the coronation of Grand Duke Mindaugas around 1230.

Indeed, none of the Baltic countries devotes more days to celebrating the nation than Lithuania. On March 11, Lithuania celebrates its Restoration of Independence Day, which commemorates the Lithuanians' declaration of independence from the USSR in 1990. (Similar occasions are observed in Estonia on August 20 and on the following day in Latvia.) On the fourth Sunday in May Lithuanians celebrate Partisans' Day, which commemorates the thousands of Lithuanians who continued to fight for their country's freedom during the early years of the Soviet occupation. September 8 is the Day of the Nation, and October 25 is Constitution Day. As on Independence Day, these commemorative holidays usually involve official ceremonies and the displaying of national flags outside buildings and homes.

The Baltic countries also observe numerous remembrance days devoted to commemorating the trauma of Soviet oppression. A pause from the otherwise light June atmosphere occurs on June 14, the day that marks the deportations of tens of thousands of Estonians, Latvians, and Lithuanians to Siberia in 1941. In Lithuania it is called the Day of Mourning and Hope, but in each of the Baltic countries it is a somber day of commemoration and reflection. On January 13 Lithuanians commemorate the Defenders of Freedom Day, dedicated to the memories of the 13 Lithuanians who died while defending the country's move toward restoring independence in early 1991. The Latvian version is called Commemoration Day of the Defenders of the Barricades, which remembers the Latvians who were killed by Soviet forces in Riga the same month. Another important Latvian national holiday is Commemoration Day of the Victims of Communist Terror, a day devoted to remembering the 43,000 Latvians who were deported in the spring of 1949. Lithuanians commemorate the unhappiness of Soviet occupation by observing Black Ribbon Day on August 23, the day on which the Molotov-Ribbentrop Pact (see Chapter 1) was signed in 1939.

Both Latvia and Lithuania also observe commemorative holidays in remembrance of Jewish suffering during World War II. On July 4 Latvia observes the Commemoration Day of the Jewish Genocide, as it was on this day in 1941 that Nazi forces burned down Riga's main synagogue, while Lithuania observes Genocide Day of the Lithuanian Jews on September 23, which commemorates the liquidation of the Vilnius ghetto on that day in 1943.

FOOD AND DRINK

Baltic Cuisine

Although not nearly as generously proportioned as Americans or even Western Europeans, the Estonians, Latvians, and Lithuanians are certainly hearty eaters. Most of the food eaten in the Baltic countries today is simple, everyday fare that has been prepared and consumed by generations of countryside dwellers. Other dishes require time and imagination and are usually prepared only during the holidays. One way to imagine Baltic cuisine is to recall a dining experience at a favorite Indian, Japanese, Chinese, or Thai restaurant—and then to think of the opposite. Japanese cuisine, for example, is known for being light, delicate, and expensive. Food in the Baltic countries, however, tends to be heavy, simple, and relatively cheap. A sturdy wok for quick stir-frying is the most important culinary tool in the Szechuan region of China, whose food is famed for its spiciness. In the Baltic region, however, where the food is fairly bland and sometimes bitter, the most important cooking instruments are a large pot for boiling and a pan for frying. While typical Indian recipes feature rice, peppers, and rich sauces, meals in each of the Baltic countries are heavy on dairy products and dill, breads and various kinds of meat, and potato dishes in their many forms.

Although many of the gastronomic traditions discussed here originated in the Baltic countryside, the culinary traditions of the Baltic peoples have also been shaped by the customs of their neighbors. Many Lithuanian dishes have Polish origins, while Estonian food tends toward Scandinavian culinary sensibilities. At the same time, both the Estonians and the Latvians inherited many of their traditions from the Germans who once ruled the region. In each of the Baltic countries there are obvious Russian (or Soviet) influences as well. Indeed, one of the most popular quick bites among Latvians is *belashi:* originating from the Crimean Tatars, *belashi* are a deep-fried dough filled with ground beef and onions (and who knows what else) that one can easily find today at marketplaces, where they are sold by Russian babushkas. With the appearance of pizzerias, Chinese restaurants, and American fast food restaurants in the larger cities, the culinary scene in the Baltic countries is becoming truly international. This discussion, however, will focus less on the wide array of dining options in Tallinn or Riga than on the traditional foods and drinks that have been enjoyed by the Baltic peoples for generations.

The main influences on any nation's culinary traditions are its location, its geography, and its weather. The long Estonian and Latvian shorelines mean a heavy emphasis on fish in those countries; this is also true of Lithuania, whose dozens of rivers make up for its relatively short coast. Since Baltic weather is cool and the region has a short growing season, fruits and vegetables are less common than grains such as wheat, rye, barley, and oats.[6] Potatoes, which were introduced in the eighteenth century (but were initially resisted by the Baltic peasants), can be grown almost anywhere and accompany each and every meal. Picking mushrooms is a national form of entertainment throughout Eastern Europe; once they have been "hunted" in the forests the mushrooms may be boiled, fried, made into a sauce, or pickled for the winter. Pork is the most important meat throughout the Baltics, but beef and chicken are also quite common. Dairy products are absolutely central to the national cuisines of Estonia, Latvia, and Lithuania. Sour cream is as ubiquitous as potatoes and is typically lopped onto salads, soups, meats, sauces, and vegetables alike. To add flavor to their simple food the Balts tend to rely on locally grown enhancers such as onions, garlic, caraway seeds, and dill; honey is the main sweetener.[7] Mustard and horseradish have traditionally been among the most important condiments, but most Balts keep a bottle of ketchup in the cupboard as well.

Fish

There are about 40 fish species in the Baltic Sea and in the 250 rivers that flow through Lithuania, Latvia, and Estonia. The most commonly eaten fish are herring, trout, pike, eel, and salmon, which are typically smoked, fried, eaten as salted appetizers, or incorporated into a fish soup. A distinctive Latvian dish is fried salmon with plum compote, while the tiny Baltic sprat (*kilu*) is the principal Estonian fish. Preserved with spices and packaged in bright blue tins, sprat pâté (*kiluvol*) was one of Estonia's best-known exports during the Soviet era.[8] Sturgeon is available in many restaurants but is comparatively expensive. Black caviar is also quite expensive, while red caviar is more moderately priced and is sometimes used as a pancake filling.

Located in former zeppelin hangars near the railway station, Riga Market was once the largest in Europe. It is still the preeminent market in Riga, where thousands of shoppers buy meat, dairy products, baked goods, and other products daily.

Meat

Vegetarians may find life in the Baltic countries difficult, especially those who are horrified at the common sight of pig and cow carcasses hanging in the shops. Roast pork is a holiday favorite. While boiled pork (or veal) in jelly is a common Estonian recipe (it is called *sült*), pork most commonly appears in the forms of bacon—liable to be incorporated into almost any dish—and sausage. Salamis and frankfurters are the most common sausages, while blood sausages wrapped in a pig's intestine are an Estonian Christmas favorite. Estonians seem to enjoy a number of blood-based foods, such as fried blood bread (*verileib*) and *verikäkk,* which consists of blood and bits of pig fat rolled into balls with flour and eggs. A typical Latvian meal might include *pīrāgi* (bacon rolls), which are related to Russian *pirozhki.* Among the most popular meat dishes in Lithuania are local versions of the Polish *zrazy,* which are rolled fillets of ground beef, typically stuffed with mushrooms. While the standard *kotlett* (Lithuania) or *kotlete* (Latvia), consisting of pork or beef that is flattened, breaded, and fried, is a universal dish, it is fairly common for rural inhabitants to enrich their dining tables with game such as goose, pheasants, hares, wild boar, deer, and elk (in Estonia).

Soups and porridges

The variety of soups and porridges in the Baltic countries is limitless. However, each country or region has its own specialties. If Latvia has something that might be called a national dish, it is *putra,* a porridge with pork fat to which may be added meat or smoked fish. Fish soups are common in each of the Baltic countries. Among the numerous Russian connections in Baltic cuisine is beet soup (*borshch*), which in the summer is often eaten cold.

Cold dishes

Salted cabbage (sauerkraut), salted herrings, cucumbers, boiled eggs, vegetable salads, potato salads, and various meats and cheeses are among the most common cold dishes, and they are usually accompanied by dark (rye) bread.

Dairy products

Dairy products are central to the diets of Estonians, Latvians, and Lithuanians. These include milk, cultured milk, curdled milk, milk soups, milky sauces, hard cheeses, and cottage cheese. Generous heapings of sour cream, which is also the base of many sauces, are served alongside or on top of almost any meal, and butter—truly a wonderful Baltic treat—is on every table.

Bread

Although there are dozens of different kinds of breads in the Baltic countries of all shapes and sizes, the most common bread is dark rye bread. The more exotic breads may contain sunflower seeds, carrots, nuts, and raisins, while sweet breads are frequently topped with berries, apples, or sweetened cottage cheese. A popular Lithuanian appetizer is crunchy fried bread with garlic (*kepta duona*).

Potatoes

Although there is hardly a method of potato preparation that has not been attempted and perfected in the Baltic countries, boiled potatoes accompany most meals and are a common pancake ingredient. Lithuania deserves special mention for its potato dishes. *Cepelinai* are a national favorite and constitute an entire meal in themselves. Made from grated potato dough in the cylindrical shape of a zeppelin, *cepelinai* are often stuffed with meat, cheese, or mushrooms and topped with a sour cream sauce with onions, butter, and bacon bits. Another Lithuanian potato dish is *kugelis,* a grated potato pudding with bacon that is baked and served with sour cream.

Desserts and sweets

While often quite tasty, desserts in the Baltic countries tend to be less sweet than American desserts or those of Western Europe. Cakes, biscuits, cookies, sweet breads, and spiced gingerbread are popular holiday desserts throughout the region. Kringel (*klingeris*), a pretzel-shaped coffee cake stuffed with raisins and almonds, is a common Latvian birthday treat. Fruits prepared in various ways—fruit pies, fruit loaves, fruit puddings, and various stewed fruit dishes—are also essential to the dessert menu. Wild berries (strawberries, raspberries, loganberries) and cranberries are seasonal favorites and are often canned, preserved, or turned into compote or puddings.

Like people everywhere, the Balts are chocolate lovers. The Laima brand is Latvia's largest confectionary maker, with numerous shops in Riga and elsewhere providing a limitless variety of chocolates and other candies. Its Estonian counterpart is the Kalev chocolate factory in Tallinn, which actually has its own museum. In the late 1960s Kalev became the first company in the USSR to attempt to make chewing gum (a thoroughly Soviet concoction, as it was made of synthetic rubber), which the authorities viewed as propaganda for the capitalist lifestyle and thus banned immediately. When the ban was rescinded a decade later Estonia quickly became the main source of chewing gum in the USSR.

Beverages

American soft drinks such as Pepsi and Coca-Cola are available in restaurants, grocery stores, and kiosks everywhere. These products, now produced locally, join the existing array of traditional drinks long enjoyed by Latvians, Lithuanians, and Estonians. Milk, both hot and cold, is consumed throughout the region, and in various forms. Balts like their milk plain, curdled (a Latvian favorite, called *rūgušpiens*), cultured, and fermented. While skim milk is a less popular drink, skim milk powder is one of the region's major dairy exports. Tea remains the most common hot beverage, but the number of coffee drinkers in the Baltics is rapidly growing. While in restaurants and cafes coffee is usually prepared in espresso machines, at home it is frequently of the instant variety.

Juices and mineral water are two of the most popular soft drinks in the Baltic countries. A typical Latvian drink is birch juice (*bērzu sula*), made from the birch tree sap that is gathered every March. Since birch forests also cover parts of Belarus and Russia, it is also drunk in those countries and is believed to possess medicinal qualities. Lithuanians like the sweeter sap of maple trees, from which a fermented tree beverage called *rauginta sula* is made.

The most popular summertime beverage in Latvia is *kvass,* a mildly sweet fermented drink that, despite its virtual disappearance in the 1990s, has regained the popularity it enjoyed during the Soviet era. Typically made from rye bread, water, yeast, and honey or sugar, *kvass* is a nonalcoholic beverage that is served cold or at room temperature. The Lithuanian version of rye bread *kvass* is called *gira,* but Lithuanians also drink caraway seed *gira,* barley *gira,* cranberry *gira,* and honey *gira.* The Estonian version of *kvass* is known as *kali,* the most popular brand of which, Linnuse Kali, is now owned by Coca-Cola. Coca-Cola's acquisition of a number of *kvass* brands in Russia and the Baltics has prompted complaints that its corn syrup-based *kvass/gira/kali* bears little resemblance to the traditional beverage.

As for alcoholic beverages, the choices are many and the price is cheap. While the Baltic countries are too far north to produce wine, there is a tradition of making sparkling beverages from imported grapes and locally produced fruits and berries.[9] Honey-based mead has a long and distinctive history in the Baltic region and is presently enjoying a revival in Lithuania.

Hard spirits have been drunk in the Baltic region for centuries, but the taste for vodka did not develop among the Baltic peasantry until the eighteenth and nineteenth centuries, when Baltic landowners began to grow potatoes and establish distilleries on their estates in an effort to boost their incomes. Vodka remains the most popular strong alcohol in the Baltics and is produced under dozens of labels.[10] However, legal producers of vodka face stiff competition from the trade in illegal vodka, which is unsafe and has contributed to hundreds of poisoning deaths in recent years.[11] As the Baltic governments began to crack down on the illicit trade, at the end of 2004 Lithuanian border guards discovered a plastic hose that ran three kilometers from Belarus, a producer of some of Europe's cheapest vodka.

While coastal Estonian cities such as Tallinn and Pärnu are favorite destinations for Finnish vodka tourists, increasingly the alcoholic beverage of choice for many Estonians and Lithuanians is beer. Latvia's per capita beer consumption lags well behind that of its neighbors and is one-quarter that of the Czechs, but it is beginning to catch up as strong alcohol loses its attraction for young people. Today most of the Baltic breweries are owned by European companies. Unfortunately for beer lovers, Baltic brews are often difficult to find in other European countries or the United States. Those who wish to sample the wide array of Lithuanian lagers will probably have to journey to Lithuania. But beware, Lithuanian beer, long reputed to be the best beer in the Baltics, is stronger than the beer brewed in Western Europe and is often nearly twice as strong as American beer. The high alcohol content of Lithuanian beer does little to deter beer lovers from celebrating the national beverage each September at the annual Three Days, Three Nights beer festival at Vilnius's Vingis Park.

Throughout the region, particular breweries are usually associated with certain cities or regions. Of Lithuania's 12 brewers the most popular are Utenos Alus (located in Utena) and Kalnapilis (Panevėžys). Perhaps the most distinctive beer in Lithuania is the Švyturys (Klaipėda) brand *Baltijos,* an award-winning German-style Märzen/Oktoberfest. The leading brewery in Latvia is Aldaris (located in Riga), but the oldest is Cēsu Alus (in Cēsis), which has been in operation since 1590 but is now owned by Finland's Olvi brewery. Most Latvians prefer light lagers, but several breweries also offer darker stouts (*tumšais;* in Lithuania dark beer is called *porteris*). Originally made in imitation of the English Imperial Stouts that were produced for the tsar's court, the reddish-copper Baltic porters that are produced today are quite strong (usually upwards of 6.5 percent alcohol) and are often of excellent quality. Estonia's leading brewer is Saku (in Harjumaa), which is one of the few Estonian breweries that exports its products to the United States. Saku produces 13 different lagers, ranging from its premium lager *Originaal* to a dark Christmas porter (*Jõuluporter*) that is regarded as one of the brewery's finest.[12] At the other end of the brewing spectrum is *Viru Õlu*, a pale lager made by the Viru Brewery that comes in plastic bottles.[13]

The Baltic countries also produce a variety of liqueurs, some of which are specifically aimed at tourists. Lithuanian mead (*midus*) has a long tradition and is fairly mild. *Krupnikas,* a honey-based liqueur, and *Daivana* and *Palanga,* which are made from mixed berries, are considerably stronger and make nice after-dinner drinks. Estonia's most famous liqueur is the dark, syrupy *Vana Tallinn* (Old Tallinn), which has a mild rum taste and is produced in four different strengths, ranging from 16 to 50 percent alcohol. Especially noteworthy is *Rigas Melnais Balzāms* (Black Balsam), a bitter black drink that has been around for 250 years.[14] Like *Vana Tallinn,* it is often mixed with coffee or vodka or served over ice cream, but unlike the Estonian liqueur it was originally marketed for its medicinal qualities. A newspaper advertisement in 1762 claimed that the balsam "is advisable for different conditions: fever, stomach ache, toothache, headache, burns, chilblain, dislocations of limbs, white and red erysipelas, tumor, poisonous stings, fractured bones, and especially in cases of closed, stabbed, and chopped wounds. The most dangerous wound will be healed in five or, at most, six days."[15]

LEISURE AND SPORTS

The Baltic peoples take pleasure in many other leisure activities, most of which do not differ fundamentally from activities enjoyed by Americans or other Europeans. In the Latvian and Lithuanian countryside many women still enjoy weaving homemade fabrics and clothing, while men occupy themselves with woodcrafts, fashioning furniture and various smaller items from the firs and oaks of the Baltic forests. Likewise, many rural people continue to collect their own honey, ferment their own *kvass,* and bake their own bread. Indeed, while Baltic cities become ever more modern and Western, many villages retain some of their timeless traditions. Among the more enduring traditions of the people living along the Latvian coast is the collecting of amber, which has been prized since ancient times for its ornamental qualities.

Despite the relative slimness of many Balts, few are physical fitness fanatics: walking to and from the bus stop, shopping, and tending to one's business is more than enough exercise for most adults, who remain aloof from the sedentary automobile and fast-food culture that has come to define the United States. However, although Balts have not embraced the cult of physical fitness (or plastic surgery) on the level of southern California, it is more common now to see joggers and rather courageous bicyclists in the busy Baltic streets. Likewise, the appearance of a small number of 24-hour gyms, which cater mostly to the affluent, in the larger cities attests to the increasing popularity of physical fitness. Judo has become quite popular in Estonia, as has cross-country skiing—an activity in which the whole family may participate. Luge and bobsledding are popular winter sports in each of the Baltic countries.

Popular American sports such as baseball and football have had no impact in the Baltic region, but other team sports such as baseball, soccer, and hockey are wildly popular. Lithuanian basketball teams have been internationally competitive since the interwar era, winning the European Championship in 1937 and 1939 (when it defeated Latvia in Kaunas) and again in 2003. Lithuanian players dominated the Soviet basketball teams that won so many Olympic medals and European championships; since the Soviet collapse many of Lithuania's best players—including Arvydas Sabonis, Šarūnas Marčiulionis, Žydrūnas Ilgauskas, and Darius Songaila—have enjoyed successful careers in the United States' National Basketball Association. Other Lithuanian players star in European leagues or for the Lithuanian Basketball League, whose top teams include Vilnius's Lietuvos Rytas and Kaunas's Žalgiris. The former won its first Union of European Basketball Leagues (ULEB) championship in 2005, while the latter won the ULEB cup in 1998 and Euroleague Basketball championship in 1999.

Soccer (called football) is Latvia's most popular team sport. Latvia fielded competitive soccer teams during its 20-year period of independence in the 1920s and 1930s, when it first formed its own national association, and. The eight-team Latvian Football Federation League was reconstituted after Latvia regained its independence, and since that time it has been dominated by Skonto Riga, which has won every league title since 1991. Latvian soccer gained international attention in 2004—the same year the Baltic countries joined NATO and the European Union—when the national team, consisting primarily of semi-professional and amateur players, qualified for the European Football Championship. Although the Latvian team did not win Euro 2004 (Greece defeated Portugal for the championship), the achievement of qualifying was widely hailed as nearly miraculous in Latvia.

Although Estonian sports teams have not achieved the level of success enjoyed by Lithuanian basketball teams or Latvian soccer clubs, individual athletes from Estonia have earned international acclaim ever since the heavyweight wrestlers Georg Hackenschmidt, Georg Lurich (who also set world weightlifting records), and Aleksander Aberg became world champions a century ago. While Estonians were among the best wrestlers and weightlifters in the Russian Empire, during the interwar era Estonia ranked behind only Sweden, Finland, and Germany in Greco-Roman wrestling. Among the best Estonian athletes of recent years are Erik Nool (b. 1970), who was the decathlon gold medalist at the 2000 Summer Olympics in Sydney, Australia, and the cyclist and two-time Olympic gold medalist Erika Salumäe (b. 1962). Estonian skiers such as Andrus Veerpalu (b. 1971) and Kristina Šmigun (b. 1977) have also earned international acclaim, while the cyclist Jaan Kirsipuu (b. 1969) has won four stages of the Tour de France since 1999.

Indeed, numerous Baltic athletes have won Olympic medals in various individual sports both as Soviet athletes and as representatives of their individual countries. Since 1989 Estonians, Latvians, and Lithuanians have also competed on a smaller scale in the Baltic Sea Games, which are held every four years. Participation is limited to the 10 countries surrounding the Baltic Sea, each of which fields athletes who compete in sports such as basketball, boxing, canoeing, cycling, fencing, Greco-Roman wrestling, gymnastics, handball, judo, rowing, rugby, shooting, sport dance, swimming, track, weightlifting, and volleyball.

The Baltic states have also produced some of the world's top-ranked chess players, including Latvia's Mikhail Tal (1936–92) and the young Aleksei Shirov (b. 1972), who was born in Riga but has represented Poland and Spain in recent years. Chess is so revered in Estonia that its greatest player, Paul Keres (1916–75), is featured on the five-kroon note. In 2000 Keres was named Estonia's Sportsman of the Century.

NOTES

1. Toivo U. Raun, *Estonia and the Estonians,* 2nd. ed. (Stanford, Calif.: Hoover Institution Press, 1982), 55.

2. In Latvia the *Meteni* holiday was traditionally followed by Ash Day (*Pelnu Diena*), during which farmers took the ashes from the previous day's fire and spread them on their fields.

3. There are 12 churches in Lithuania named for St. Casimir.

4. The Greek form *Georgius* means ploughman, or cultivator of the land; thus, St. George's Day traditions are often connected with the arrival of spring and the season's first outdoor herding.

5. With the appearance of new names that are not distinctly Estonian, Latvian, or Lithuanian, there is a continuing debate in the Baltic countries about which names to include on these calendars. For a link to European name-day calendars, see www.mynameday.com/namedaylinks.html.

6. It appears that vegetable consumption in the Baltic countries is directly related to latitude. According to surveys taken in the summer of 1997, 78 percent of respondents in Lithuania claimed to eat vegetables (excluding potatoes) daily, but only 60 percent of Latvians and 48 percent of Estonians did so. J. Pomerleau, Martin McKee, Aileen Robertson, Kamelija Kadziauskenie, Algis Abaravicius, Sirje Vaask, Iveta Pudule, and Daiga Grinberga, "Macronutrient and Food Intake in the Baltic Republics," *European Journal of Clinical Nutrition,* 55 (2001): 202.

7. In Lithuania, bees and honey are symbols for friendship and hospitality. One word for friend is *biciulis,* which is derived from the word for "bee" and literally means "dear fellow beekeeper."

8. Estonian sprats were a favorite throughout the USSR. To punish Estonia for its attitude toward Russia and Russians, in 1994 the Russian government slapped prohibitively high tariffs on Estonian sprats.

9. The world's northernmost vineyard is located in Sabile, a Latvian town near Kuldīga. Sabile is the home of Latvia's largest Roma community.

10. The Baltic countries, like Russia, Ukraine, and Belarus, are plagued by staggeringly high rates of alcoholism, which rose substantially during the troubled 1990s. One report notes that "between 1990 and 1995, age standardized death rates from chronic liver disease and cirrhosis doubled in Estonia and Latvia, and increased by 50% in Lithuania." Estonia has the highest rate of alcohol consumption, followed by Lithuania and then Latvia. Beer is the most commonly consumed beverage, followed by spirits for men and wine for women. Martin McKee, Joceline Pomerleau, Aileen Robertson, Iveta Pudule, Daiga Grinberga, Kamelija Kadziauskenie, Algis Abaravicius, and Sirje Vaask, "Alcohol Consumption in the Baltic Republics," *Journal of Epidemiology and Community Health,* 54, no. 5 (2000): 361–66.

11. Although the number of reported alcohol poisonings has declined since its peak in the mid-1990s, the dangers associated with illicit alcohol production have remained. The region's worst case of mass alcohol poisoning took place in August 2001 in Pärnu. It resulted in 68 deaths.

12. Most of these breweries have been acquired by Baltic Beverages Holding, a Finnish-Swedish joint venture that was formed in the early 1990s. It has majority ownership of Saku, Aldaris, and Švyturys-Utenos, as well as various breweries in Russia (such as Baltika) and Ukraine.

13. Some beer lovers are horrified by the trend of selling beer in polyethylene terephthalate (PET) bottles in Estonia and Latvia. Because the use of two-liter plastic bottles allows producers to cut prices, about 70 percent of all beer in Latvia is sold in plastic bottles.

14. Its manufacturer, Latvijas Balzāms, is the largest alcohol producer in the Baltics, claiming nearly half the Latvian market.

15. Andris Kolbergs, *The Story of Riga* (Riga: Jāņa sēta Publishers and Printers, Ltd., 1998), 118.

SELECTED READINGS

Holidays and Traditions

Bindokienė, Danutė Brazytė. *Lithuanian Customs and Traditions.* Chicago: Lithuanian World Community, 1989.

Tedre, Ülo. *Estonian Customs and Traditions.* Tallinn: Perioodika Publishers, 1985.

Cuisine

Davidson, Alan. *The Oxford Companion to Food.* New York: Oxford University Press, 1999.

de Gorgey, Maria Gieysztor. *Art of Lithuanian Cooking.* New York: Hippocrene Books, 2001.

Doub, Sire Lisa. *A Taste of Latvia.* New York: Hippocrene Books, 2000.

Imbrasienė, Birutė. *Lithuanian Traditional Foods.* Vilnius: Baltos lankos, 1998.

Kalvik, Silvia. *Estonian Cuisine.* Tallinn: Perioodika Publishers, 1993.

Other Sources and Websites

General

"Baltic Cuisine," www.russia-in-us.com/Cuisine/Dadiani/balticindex.htm.

Cookery Art, www.cookbook.rin.ru/cookbook_e/national.html.

Cooks.com. www.cooks.com.

Estonian Food

The Estonia Page, "Estonian Cuisine," www.esis.ee/ist2000/einst/culture/cuisine.htm.

Estonian Institute, "Estonian Cuisine," www.einst.ee/publications/cuisine/.

"Estonian National Dishes," www.kokaraamat.ee/rahvustoidud.php?cat=2.

Inyourpocket Essential City Guides, "Estonian Cuisine," www.inyourpocket.com/estonia/tallinn/en/feature?id=55202.

Latvian Food

Evangelical Lutheran Church of America, "Recipes from Latvia," www.elca.org/countrypackets/latvia/recipe.html.

The Latvian Institute, "Latvian Cooking Traditions and Eating Customs," www.li.lv/en/?id=30.

Steinbergs, A., "Latvian Cuisine," www.angelfire.com/al2/LatvianStuff/Cuisine.html.

Lithuanian Food

Anthology of Lithuanian Ethnoculture, "Lithuanian Traditional Foods," http://ausis.gf.vu.lt/eka/EWG/default.htm.

Baltic Roads, "Lithuanian Dishes," www.balticroads.lt/en/learn/dishes.asp.

House of Lithuania, "Lithuanian Recipes," www.houseoflithuania.org/recipes.html.

5

Language, Folklore, and Literature

AMONG THE MOST cherished beliefs shared by Estonians, Latvians, and Lithuanians is the centrality of language in their conceptions of national identity. Over the centuries the pressures of cultural and linguistic assimilation have resulted in the disappearance of languages on every continent, yet the Baltic peoples, who have been subject to foreign conquest and occupation during much of their history, have nevertheless managed to maintain, develop, and standardize their own languages while developing their own distinctive literary traditions.

The survival of the Estonian, Latvian, and Lithuanian vernaculars and their transformation into literary and official state languages was by no means a foregone conclusion. When German was the tongue of Estonia's and Latvia's elites the upwardly mobile natives naturally, though their numbers were small, gravitated toward it and became, in effect, Germanized. The situation in Lithuania was somewhat different: from the sixteenth century onward its elite was either Polish or Polonized, and with the delay in modernization and urbanization the Lithuanian peasantry faced little pressure to learn Polish or Russian. Yet when the winds of Romantic nationalism swept from Western Europe into the borderlands of the Russian Empire during the nineteenth century, educated (and usually Germanized or Polonized) Baltic natives embraced their traditional languages, now convinced that these were central to their national identities. With the rise in the nineteenth century of an intellectual class fluent in the native tongue, the transformation of Estonian, Latvian, and Lithuanian into literary languages began, and by the first decades of the twentieth century a classical literary canon was created.

Yet the survival of these languages—and consequently of Estonian, Latvian, and Lithuanian national identities—was by no means assured even after the establishment of independent Baltic states in the early twentieth century. Lasting only 20 years, the era of independence was followed by another 50 years of Russian occupation. Under it the Baltic peoples were subjected to the forces of Sovietization: the creation of new factories was accompanied by the arrival of waves of Russian-speaking workers from the Soviet interior; Russian became one of two official languages in the newest Soviet Socialist Republics. While the Soviet regime required Baltic children to learn Russian in school, it made much smaller demands of Russian-speaking immigrants. This double blow of demographic and linguistic Russification caused many foreign observers to conclude that it might not be long before the Estonians and Latvians suffered the fate of the many other small peoples who have vanished into history.

Despite such pressures, the intellectual elites of the Baltic republics dug in their heels during the 1960s and 1970s: while Russian speakers assumed command of much of the region's industry, native intellectuals took refuge in the academies, educational institutions, and creative unions where they investigated folklore and history and wrote thousands of novels and poems. Many played conspicuous roles in the nationalist movements of the late 1980s. They urged the passage of laws in each of the Baltic republics that would protected the legal status of the native languages. Not only was this a major step toward the establishment of political independence, it was, from the Balts' perspective, essential for national survival.

LANGUAGES AND LITERARY BEGINNINGS

The Baltic languages are among Europe's oldest living languages. Like Finnish and Hungarian, the Estonian language is part of the Finno-Ugric linguistic group; thus it is not, strictly speaking, a Baltic language. Lithuanian and Latvian are the only surviving East Baltic languages of the Indo-European linguistic family. Old Prussian, a West Baltic language, died when its surviving speakers were Germanized in the eighteenth century. Although a common proto-Baltic language probably once existed, it had begun separating by 500 C.E., and over the following centuries the people that we now call Latvians and Lithuanians absorbed neighboring tribes such as the Cours (Couronians), Zemgals (Zemgalians), and Sels (Selonians), and developed distinct languages that eventually became Latvian and Lithuanian.

Estonian is the most homogenized of the Baltic region's three principal native languages, but even among the country's fewer than one million native

Estonians there are significant differences between the northern and southern dialects. In the end it was the northern Estonian dialect that emerged as the nation's literary language.[1] There also remain strong regional dialects in Latvia. Indeed, the Latgalian dialect of eastern Latvia is so distinctive that some linguists regard it as a separate language altogether, and it was accorded such status under the first Latvian republic. Spoken Lithuanian also varies somewhat from one region to the next, but its standardized form is based on the dialect of the Suvalkija region.

The survival of these languages is due in part to the social division between natives and Germans that began with the latter's conquest of the region. For hundreds of years the German-speaking lords regarded the peasant tongues spoken by the Estonian and Latvian villagers with disdain; the toilers of the countryside were simply non-Germans (*undeutsche*) from whom the Germans maintained a separate existence in what was essentially a colonial relationship. Aside from a few words and phrases, the Latvian and Estonian languages were not even written down for the first time until 300 years after the German conquest. Indeed, there was little need to do so, for the languages of administration, commerce, science, and theology were Latin and German; church services, too, were conducted in Latin.

Over the centuries, hundreds of older loanwords entered into the Estonian and Latvian languages from German (or Old German); hundreds more have been borrowed from Russian. Estonian, while exceptionally difficult for foreigners to master, is well suited to the adoption of foreign words because of its phonetic spelling. In recent decades many English words have entered the Estonian language and have become Estonianized by phonetizing their spelling and then declining or conjugating them according to the rules of Estonian grammar.

The absence of a written Lithuanian language before the sixteenth century made it necessary to borrow from Lithuania's Slavic and German neighbors. In the fourteenth and fifteenth centuries the Grand Duchy used no fewer than three languages for official business: foreign relations were usually conducted in Latin; German was used for correspondence with the Livonian Order; and Chancery Slavonic was used for relations with the Russians and for the writing of chronicles, laws, state documents, and other internal matters.[2] Lithuanian existed only as a spoken language, even at court, and its use was gradually abandoned by much of the Lithuanian elite, which began adopting the Polish language, faith, and customs. Finally in 1697 the Lithuanian state, which for more than a century formed the eastern half of the Polish-Lithuanian Commonwealth, replaced Slavonic with Polish, which was made the official language in the Grand Duchy's chancelleries.

The main impetus for the creation of written Baltic languages was the arrival of Lutheranism in the region in the third decade of the sixteenth century. As elsewhere in Europe, for the first time the Bible, or portions of it, was translated into indigenous languages. In 1525 a prayer book was published in Lübeck that apparently contained texts in Estonian, Livonian (a Finno-Ugric language once spoken in parts of northern Latvia), and Latvian; but, wary of the fanaticism of Martin Luther's followers, members of the Lübeck council destroyed them without a trace. A decade later a Lutheran catechism was printed in Wittenberg: its left-hand pages were in Low German, while on the opposite side the text appeared in Estonian. However, it was quickly deemed a forbidden book "due to the many mistakes in it," and no copies have survived.[3] Fifty years later, in 1586 or 1587, a Latvian-language Lutheran handbook was printed. Commissioned by churchmen in Courland, it contained a catechism, part of the New Testament, and a hymnal. This appeared shortly after another Latvian-language Catholic catechism, translated by Peter Canisius (1520–97), was printed in Vilnius. Still more Latvian-language materials appeared in the seventeenth century: Georg Mancelius (1593–1654), a Lutheran clergyman and later a professor at Dorpat (Tartu) University, published sermons as well as nonreligious books in Latvian, while Ernst Glück (1651–1705) contributed to the development of the written language with his translation of the New and Old Testaments (1688–94). However, another century would pass before Latvians themselves would begin to write.

It is hardly surprising that most of the first writings in the Estonian, Livonian, and Latvian languages were religious in nature. Knowledge of multiple languages was common among Lutheran pastors and Catholic priests (Jesuits in particular) alike; having learned the local language of the people to whom they wished to bring the word of God, they then wrote in it. In Tartu, south Estonia's predominant Catholic center before the era of Swedish rule, Jesuit priests such as Thomas Busaeus, Johannes Ambrosius Weltherus, and Wilhelm Buccius wrote in Estonian, but their works did not survive the struggles of the era. Toward the middle of the seventeenth century Lutheran pastors began contemplating the production of a complete translation of the Bible, but it was not until 1739 that the first Estonian Bible was printed— about 50 years after the appearance of Glück's Latvian translation. The fact that the first Estonian Bible was published in the northern dialect facilitated its emergence as the dominant form of the written language.

The New Testament did not appear in Lithuanian in its entirety until 1701, a century and a half after the first Lithuanian book, Martynas Mažvydas's (1520–63) *Catechismusa Prasty Szadei* (*Catechism*, 1547), was printed by Lutherans in Königsberg. Among the first Lithuanian books printed in Vilnius were a catechism (1595) and a collection of homilies titled *Postilla Catholica* (1599), both of which were translated into Lithuanian by Canon

Mikalojus Daukša (1527–1613) and published by a Jesuit press. Written in a polished literary style, the latter retains its significance for linguists because it is accented and contains a large number of archaic forms. In *Postilla*'s "Prefatory Word to the Gentle Reader" (written in Polish), Daukša explained the importance of the native tongue, imploring his readers not to abandon it:

> Through all ages people have spoken in their native tongue, and striven to preserve it, to enrich it, to perfect it and to make it more beautiful.... Nations live not by the richness of their soil, not by the diversity of their dress or the beauty of their countryside, not by the strength of their cities and castles, but mostly by preserving and using their native language.[4]

While books of a religious nature continued to be published in seventeenth-century Lithuania, some secular books also began to appear, including a translation of Aesop's fables, published in Königsberg in 1706. It was here in Lithuania Minor, rather than in the Grand Duchy, that most Lithuanian book publishing took place until the beginning of the twentieth century. Although during the eighteenth century Lithuanian folksongs began to be written down and Lithuanian grammars and dictionaries written in Latin and in German appeared, Lithuanian book publishing generally became impoverished during this period. Only late in the nineteenth century, with the rise of a Lithuanian intelligentsia and the belated appearance of Lithuanian national consciousness, did the written Lithuanian language begin to recover and to develop into a true literary language.[5]

FOLKLORE

Every national group has its own collection of folklore, legends, and folk music. In the case of the Baltic peoples, however, it would be difficult to overestimate the significance of the oral tradition. Since the Baltic peasants—the only native speakers of their languages—were overwhelmingly illiterate until the nineteenth century, folklore was passed from one generation to the next through a well-established oral tradition. One may think of Baltic folksongs (discussed in Chapter 7) as a sort of lyrical poetry for a pre-literate age—they were the repository of ancient wisdom, embodying the values and beliefs of peoples who had yet to be transformed by the demands of modernity.

Folksongs and folklore have had a lasting impact on the way the Baltic peoples understand themselves and their world. In the absence of ancient chronicles or native religious literature, scholars turn to native folklore to provide important clues about the Balts' pre-Christian religious beliefs. It was on the basis of well-established oral traditions that nineteenth-century intellectuals created national epics for peoples who lacked their own Homer; even today many fiction writers turn to these ancient sources for inspiration.

Lithuanian folksongs began to be written down as early as the seventeenth century; likewise, the first Latvian folksong was published as early as 1632 in Fredericus Menius's *De origine Livonorum*. However, the systematic collection of Lithuanian folk songs and folklore had to wait until the Lithuanian national awakening of the late nineteenth century. In the Latvian and Estonian lands the collection and analysis of folklore was first taken up by Baltic Germans and then by Germanized native intellectuals. Such activity was closely linked to the national Romantic movement that swept through Europe after the French Revolution. Reacting to the Enlightenment's focus on rationality and universality, the National Romantics emphasized feeling and national uniqueness. Many believed that the traditions, songs, and folklore of the peasantry were the truest expressions of the national spirit.

In German lands, intellectuals emphasized the *Volk* (people), with its oral traditions of legends, fables, and songs, as the key to understanding the essence of Germanness. The peoples of the Baltic region played an important role in this development, for in the last decades of the eighteenth century Germans in the eastern Baltic region began to "discover" the local peasantry, identifying them too as *Völker* possessing their own characteristics and traditions. This scientific approach to the Estonian and Latvian peasantry was taken most famously by Johann Gottfried Herder, a minister who taught in Riga in the late 1760s. Taking an interest in the languages and cultures of the Estonian and Latvian peasants, Herder realized that beneath the "high culture" of the German overlords there existed a variety of local cultures with their own rich oral traditions, and that folksongs and folklore gave voice to the distinctive national spirits of the people who created them. Herder included several Estonian and Lithuanian folksongs in his *Stimmen der Völker in Liedern* (Voices of the Peoples in Song), published in 1787.[6]

Scholarly publications dealing with the Estonian and Latvian languages and their folklore, prepared mainly by Baltic German intellectuals, began to appear in the first decades of the nineteenth century. Consciously following the lead of Herder, in 1824 a group of German pastors established the Society of Friends of Latvians, whose members studied the Latvian languages (necessary for delivering sermons), collected Latvian folksongs, and published their findings. Likewise, in 1839 the Estonian Learned Society was founded at the initiative of Friedrich Robert Faehlmann (1798–1850), a Germanized Estonian intellectual; it became the central organization for the collection and study of Estonian folklore. Only after the middle of the nineteenth century, as the national "awakenings" of the Estonian and Latvian peoples gathered momentum, did natives assume full proprietorship of their history and folklore.

Convinced that their cultural development had been inhibited by centuries of servitude to foreign masters, Germanized Estonians and Latvians sought to bring their peoples up to the cultural level of the Germans and themselves began the systematic collection and analysis of native folklore.

A landmark event in the development of Estonian literature—and of Estonian national consciousness—was the publication in 1857–61 of the epic poem *Kalevipoeg* (Son of Kalev) by the doctor Friedrich Reinhard Kreutzwald (1803–82), who completed a work that had been outlined earlier by F. R. Faehlmann. The inspiration for this Estonian epic came partly from the Finnish epic *Kalevala* (first published in 1835–36), to which *Kalevipoeg* bears considerable resemblance. Each of these epics was written in trochaic verse consisting of four disyllabic feet per line (common in old Estonian poetry), and in both the main hero possesses superpowers that allow him to speak the language of birds and other animals.[7] Despite this resemblance, the heroes and themes of *Kalevipoeg* were derived from the Estonian folk tradition, in which supernatural forces and the struggle of good against evil were prevalent motifs. Heroic deeds, honesty, and peaceful labor are depicted as supreme virtues, while the German conquerors are portrayed as devils bringing ruin to a once free and prosperous people. Although the hero and king, Kalevipoeg, retires to the forest following a journey to Hell (where he defeats Savrik, the Devil) and defeat by invading forces, the people believe that Kalevipoeg will return some-day "To bring his children happiness / and build Estonia's life anew." Although its importance has diminished over time, *Kalevipoeg* was the first truly Estonian book—one that profoundly influenced a generation of Estonian intellectuals and became a symbol of the Estonian national awakening.[8]

Of more enduring value has been the Latvian national epic, *Lačplēsis* (The Bear Slayer), published by Andrējs Pumpurs (1841–1902) in 1888. Set in pagan Latvia in the thirteenth century, *Lačplēsis* recounts the exploits of a bear-eared giant—the son of a man and a female bear—who defends his homeland from invaders. In the end the Bear Slayer is defeated and the Latvians are sub-jected to 700 years of misery. Like the Estonian epic *Kalevipoeg,* the Latvian epic is based on traditional folk tales and, through its rough portrayal of the Teutonic Knights who invaded the region in the thirteenth century, gave vent to the Balts' increasing resentment of the Germans' continuing cultural and economic dominance in the region. Also like *Kalevipoeg,* the Latvian epic was meant to show that the oppressed Latvians had a history and culture no less grand than those of their German masters.

Such epics served the national need to create, in the words of the writer Anatol Lieven, an "imagined pagan past" in lands that had been sadly deprived of their own histories, as well as to showcase the potential of the Baltic lan-guages to produce great modern writers.[9] Since Latvia had no epics, Pumpurs had to make one up from fragments of Latvian folklore. Yet *Lačplēsis,* at least in terms of its influence and political significance, was far more than a folk epic: in 1919 the government of the first Latvian republic designated the Lačplēsis Military Order as the country's highest official award. Indeed, the epic's lasting cultural resonance even for younger generations of Latvians has not been lost on the producers and marketers of local beer and vodka products that cannily bear the Lačplēsis label.[10]

Pumpurs's Latvian epic, certainly the grandest of all of Latvia's early literary works, must be viewed in the context of the efforts by fellow Latvian intellectuals to promote a Latvian national identity. Some recognized that one of the most important tasks that the Latvian "awakeners" must undertake was that of collecting and organizing the Latvian people's vast repository of folksongs and folktales, which at the moment lived mostly in the collective consciousness of a peasantry that was fated eventually to disappear due to Germanization and the forces unleashed by modernization. In the 1860s the *jaunlatviesi* (Young Latvians) movement, led by Krišjānis Valdemārs (1825–91), began to promote the Latvian press, literature, and science in an effort to raise Latvian national consciousness. While Valdemārs, a folk writer, provided the inspiration for the movement to collect Latvian folklore, Krišjānis Barons (1835–1923), a fellow staff member of the short-lived but hugely influential newspaper *Pēterburgas avīzes* (Saint Petersburg Newspaper), was entrusted with this enormous project and took over the materials previously collected by Fricis Brīvzemnieks (1846–1907), another Young Latvian. Trained as a mathematician and an astronomer, Barons took a systematic, scientific approach to the task that took up the rest of his life. Writing down the *dainas* that were sent to him over the years on tiny pieces of paper, he enumerated and classified the verses by subject (wedding songs, mythological songs, songs of death and burial, and so on) in his famous 70-drawer oak cabinet. Of the 217,996 folksongs he published in his six-volume *Latvju dainas* (1894–1915), most were quatrains (consisting of four lines), but some were longer songs. Since then the total number of *dainas* collected has reached 1.3 million, or about one for every Latvian. The fact that many are regional variants of similar songs hardly diminishes the magnitude of this achievement.

In Estonia the leading folklore collector was Jakob Hurt (1839–1906), the son of a rural schoolteacher and, like his predecessors F. R. Faehlmann and F. R. Kreutzwald, a Germanized Estonian. Acquiring doctorates in theology and philology, Hurt was surely one of the most learned Estonians of his time and was also one of the strongest proponents of the cultural development, rather than the political emancipation, of the Estonian people. With the help of his friends and relatives, in 1860 Hurt began to collect Estonian folklore, but like the Latvian folklore collectors Brīvzemnieks and Barons he realized that folklore collection would have to be a nationwide undertaking. As president of the Society of Estonian Literati, in the 1870s he recruited 1,400 volunteers to visit nearly every dwelling in Estonia. Hurt's resulting 162-volume collection remains the most valuable contribution to the Estonian Folklore Archive (1927).

The investigation of Lithuanian folklore began somewhat earlier than similar undertakings in the Latvian and Estonian lands but was at first less systematic. One reason for this early interest was the establishment of the Kingdom of Prussia in 1701 by the Hohenzollern dynasty. Having defeated and, over the course of several hundred years, exterminated the native Prussians (whose name they ironically appropriated for their own state), the German conquerors turned their attention to the Prussians' closest living relatives, the Lithuanians of multinational East Prussia (Lithuanic Minor). Buoyed by a heightened interest in the Prussian past, early German ethnologists became aware of Lithuanian folklore and folksongs. Most notably, in 1745 Philipp Ruhig (1675–1749) published three Lithuanian songs, along with a number of Lithuanian proverbs and idiomatic expressions, in a book about the Lithuanian language. This apparently made an impression on Herder, who, as noted, later began to collect Estonian folksongs.

As Prussia's most important intellectual center before Berlin assumed this distinction, Königsberg was the leading center for the study of the Lithuanian language and Lithuanian religious literature in the eighteenth century. Convinced that the Lithuanian language was losing its purity as a result of an influx of German colonists into Prussian Lithuania, in 1825 Ludwig Rhesa (1776–1840) published the first collection of Lithuanian folk songs. During the second half of the nineteenth century, however, the Lithuanians living under Russian rule faced greater obstacles to publishing native literature, for in 1864 the government imposed a ban on publishing in the Lithuanian language. Until the ban was rescinded in 1904 most books on Lithuanian folklore were published in Lithuania Minor (in Germany) and the United States. However, folkloric studies in Lithuania soon reached the level of scholarship that was earlier achieved in Latvia and Estonia. The University of Kaunas became the country's main center for folkloric studies after 1918, and the Lithuanian Folklore Archive, established in 1935 by the writer Jonas Balys, was placed in charge of the collection. By 1940 it included about half a million items of diverse kinds of folklore.

Songs were more popular in the eastern area of Baltic culture (Latvia and the eastern parts of Lithuania), while central Lithuania is known for its folktales and legends. As far as it is possible to tell, Baltic narrative folklore used to be told—or rather performed—indoors in the evenings or at night, usually by elderly people. Its main motifs included nature, anthropomorphism, and human interaction with gods and goddesses, and its central characters were the sun and birds (associated with the sky), snakes and toads (associated with the earth), goblins (associated with the underworld), and venerated plants and trees (e.g., the image of the world tree in Lithuanian lore). The same motifs often appear in the modern literatures of Lithuania, Latvia, and Estonia as well.

LITERARY DEVELOPMENTS TO 1940

Lithuania

Before the nineteenth-century national awakening the most significant work of Lithuanian secular literature was *The Seasons,* by Kristijonas Donelaitis (1714–80) of East Prussia. A pastor, an accomplished musician, and a maker of precision instruments (such as barometers, thermometers, and optical glasses), Donelaitis was also a polyglot who spoke Greek, Latin, Hebrew, German, French, and Lithuanian and composed verse in several of these languages. Although he wrote his poem in Lithuanian between 1765 and 1775, it was not until 1818 that it was published and then only in German. Composed in classical hexameter, *The Seasons* may be read as a sermon in verse: portraying everyday life of the Lithuanian peasants during the four seasons of the year, it aimed to teach them the virtues of piety, hard work, and satisfaction with life's precious gifts. Written after the German colonization of East Prussia had come to an end, *The Seasons* also showed how the region's Lithuanian peasantry had unconsciously managed to resist the influence of the newcomers as they maintained their own unique way of life. If the lyric tradition of Lithuanian poetry is represented by the folk songs of the peasantry, then Donelaitis is the first representative of Lithuania's epic tradition.

One of the central features of Lithuanian literature from its earliest days is its close relationship with religion. While many of the early poets and prose writers of Lithuania were priests, there developed even among lay writers a tradition of simultaneously addressing both God and nature. The result was a vision of their beloved Lithuania that was tinged with spirituality. Indeed, for some writers the articulation of their belief in Lithuania was nothing less than an act of religious faith. This blend of Catholicism and Romanticism was responsible for an explosion of creativity not only in the literature of Lithuania, but in its art and music as well.

After Donelaitis's *The Seasons,* the next important landmark of Lithuanian literature was the narrative poem *The Pine Grove of Anykščiai* (1859) written nearly a century later by Antanas Baranauskas (1835–1902). Composed in Polish-influenced syllabic meter, it is considered the first Romantic poem in Lithuanian literature. Its subject is the forest of Anykščiai, which was destroyed during the era of Christianization in an attempt to chase away the pagan gods. Baranauskas laments the ruin of this paradise as a tragedy for Lithuania's folk culture and national traditions.

Like Donelaitis's *The Seasons,* Baranauskas's great poem was not read widely until after the Romantic nationalism of Central and Eastern Europe had swept into Lithuania. This trend was helped along by Adam Mickiewicz (1798–1855), a Polish poet who is also acclaimed by the Lithuanians, who know him as Adomas Mickevičius. Although Mickiewicz lived and taught in Kaunas, he wrote solely in Polish and spent much of his life separated from his homeland. His most famous work, the epic poem *Pan Tadeusz* (Lord Thaddeus, 1834), was set in provincial Lithuania during the Napoleonic era, not long after most of it was absorbed by the Russian Empire. Sentimentalizing the author's homeland and glorifying the heroism of the Polish-Lithuanian medieval past, *Pan Tadeusz* (subtitled *The Last Foray in Lithuania*), although written in Polish, became one of the foundation stones of Lithuanian national literature. To this very day every Lithuanian and Polish schoolchild knows its beginning: "Lithuania! My fatherland! You are like health! Only he who has lost you may know your true worth."[11] Decades later the Lithuanian poet Vincas Kudirka (1858–99) incorporated this line (which he modified to read "Lithuania! Our fatherland!") into a poem that eventually became Lithuania's national anthem.

While Mickiewicz could not imagine a Lithuania separate from Poland, there were others who could. Simonas Daukantas (1793–1864), who was once Mickiewicz's classmate at Vilnius University, wrote scholarly works in which he chronicled a great Lithuanian state before its union with Poland and the resulting destruction of Lithuania's superior culture. Daukantas was the first to write Lithuanian history in Lithuanian, and by emphasizing the glory of medieval Lithuania, Daukantas was working within a Romantic literary-historical tradition that located the origins of a nation's glory in a mythologized medieval past. While later Lithuanian writers appropriated Mickiewicz's colorful images, it was Daukantas's view of Lithuanian history from which many drew their inspiration.

If the priest Jonas Basanávičius, who founded a Lithuanian-language newspaper and had it smuggled across the border from Germany, is the father of the Lithuanian national revival, then the movement's great Romantic poet was another cleric named Jonas Mačiulis (1862–1932), better known as Maironis. Although he worked in multiple genres, ranging from drama to history, Maironis's reputation rests on the poems in his collection *The Voices of Spring* (1895), which glorified the Lithuanian countryside. His other great literary achievement was the publication of *Young Lithuania* (1907), a semiautobiographical account of young Lithuanian patriots' struggle for political and cultural freedom.[12]

Another prominent Lithuanian nationalist writer of that era was Julija Žymantienė (1845–1921), a self-taught peasant better known as Žemaitė. Beginning her literary career at the late age of 49, her stories and novellas addressed the most significant problems of the era, such as the effects of the emancipation of the Lithuanian peasantry as well as the struggle against Russification. With a focus on the everyday life and family relations of ordinary Lithuanian peasants, Žemaitė's stories reflect the emergence of realistic prose in Lithuania at the end of the nineteenth century.

By the turn of the century Lithuanian writers had begun to embrace Symbolism, a popular literary and artistic movement that was characteristic of Russia's Silver Age. Arising out of the earlier Romantic tradition, Symbolism's main premise was that all is not as it seems: the reality around us is merely one of appearances. Thus Symbolist writers and poets presented a symbolic rather than a literal reality. The first true Lithuanian Symbolist was Jurgis Baltrušaitis (1873–1944), who began publishing his heavily abstract and philosophical verse in the 1890s and early 1900s. Most of his works, however, were in Russian. Only in 1927 did he begin to publish in Lithuanian, and in fact most of his Lithuanian poetry was written during his final years in Paris. By this time, however, his poetry can no longer be characterized as Symbolist; in its attempt to convey the richness of Lithuanian rural life it had grown more earthy and concrete.

The canon of modern Lithuanian literature began to take shape during Lithuania's brief era of independence from 1918 to 1940. Among the most outstanding writers of this period were Vincas Krėvė-Mickevičius (1882–1954) and Vincas Mykolaitis-Putinas (1893–1967). A playwright and a poet, Krėvė first rose to fame in 1912 for his prose poem *Legends of the Old Folks of Dainava,* which, like his later short story collection, *Under a Thatched Roof* (1922), was based on Lithuanian mythology and legends. Infused with folkloristic elements, these works were intended to encourage Lithuanian self-awareness. The matter of Lithuanian national identity was also present in Krėvė's first play, *Šarūnas* (1911), which depicts the predecessor of Lithuania's first great king, Mindaugas. Like the later *Skirgaila* (1922), its main issue is the dilemmas of political power, of the tensions between the desires of ordinary people and the needs of state.

Vincas Mykolaitis-Putinas's major landmark work was the semiautobiographical trilogy *In the Shadow of the Altars* (1933), whose main subject was the dilemma with which Putinas himself long struggled: whether to give himself to his calling as a poet or devote himself to his work as a priest. Like his protagonist, Putinas eventually left (or was expelled from) the priesthood. Folkloristic influences could be seen in his poem *Rūpintojėlis* ("pensive Christ"), a word that refers to the wooden statues carved by village artisans and placed at roadsides that depict a seated peasant in a sad, contemplative pose. Published in 1926, *Rūpintojėlis* portrays a young man standing before such a sculpture, reflecting on its fate and that of humankind.

Folkloristic influences can also be found in the poetry of Liudas Gira (1884–1946), who, like Krėvė, adopted the stylistic devices of traditional Lithuanian folksongs. Indeed, with the Lithuanian government actively encouraging interest in folklore and folk art, many artists tried to find ways to infuse folklore into their work. Among them were the poets Antanas Miškinis (1905–83), Jonas Aistis (1904–73), and Salomėja Nėris (1904–45), and the prose writer Petras Cvirka (1909–47). Numerous other authors made significant contributions to the corpus of interwar Lithuanian literature, but only a few can be mentioned here. Balys Sruoga (1886–1947) was a poet, dramatist, and literary critic whose early work was influenced by Russian Symbolism. Antanas Vienuolis-Žukauskas (1882–1957) began his literary career as a war correspondent, covering Lithuania's war of independence, and afterward settled down to write Chekhov-influenced stories.

An especially distinguished place in Lithuanian literature is occupied by Kazys Binkis (1893–1942). Considered by some to be the creator of Lithuanian Futurism, others regard him as an Expressionist. Whatever he is labeled, at the height of his career in the mid-1920s Binkis was the editor of the influential journal *Four Winds,* which was also the name of the group of avant-garde poets who briefly thrived under his leadership.

Estonia

While Russian and Polish influences are evident in the modern literature of Latvia and Lithuania, Estonian literature has always been characterized by a distinctly north European orientation. A handful of surviving Estonian-language poems, written mostly by wealthy German amateurs, date back to the seventeenth century. However, Estonian poetry really begins with the appearance of Käsu Hans's *Lamentation for the Destruction of Tartu* (1708). Written in the south Estonian dialect—which had not yet lost the battle with the northern dialect for literary supremacy in Estonia—the poem expresses the author's grief over the devastation his homeland suffered during the Great Northern War, whose end result was the incorporation of Estonia into the Russian Empire.

Also appearing in the first half of the eighteenth century was Estonian narrative literature, consisting principally of storybooks translated from the German language by clergymen. Products of the Pietistic movement (see Chapter 2), these stories were intended for the moral edification of the Estonian peasantry.

Most notably, in 1782 Friedrich Wilhelm von Willmann (1746–1819), a pastor from the Estonian island of Saaremaa, published a collection of stories under the title *Tales and Deeds*. Receptive to these stories, the Estonian peasants assimilated some into their own rich body of folklore. It was also around this time that Johann Gottfried Herder published translations of a handful of Estonian folksongs in his *Volkslieder* (1779). Otto Wilhelm Masing (1763–1832) also influenced Estonia's literary development with the books, Bible stories, and school texts he published for Estonian peasants. Masing also published the first newspaper in the Estonian language (see Chapter 6).

Kristjan Jaak Peterson (1801–22), whose literary career was cut short by the tuberculosis that killed him at the age of 21, is commonly regarded as a herald of Estonian national literature. Although gifted in many languages, it was his poetry in the Estonian vernacular that causes present-day Estonians to celebrate Mother Tongue Day on March 14, the day of Peterson's birth. His verse, influenced by European classical and Romantic literature as well as by Estonian folksongs, was probably the first Estonian literature to achieve a high level of artistry. While Peterson now occupies an iconic position in the pantheon of Estonian authors, his unpublished poetry lay completely forgotten until the first quarter of the twentieth century.

The accomplishments of F. R. Faehlmann and F. R. Kreutzwald in the area of Estonian folklore, discussed previously, laid the foundations for the emergence of a genuinely national literature. Faehlmann, Estonia's central literary figure of the second quarter of the nineteenth century, published German versions of a series of Estonian myths as well as some poems in Estonian. Likewise, Kreutzwald not only recorded Estonian folksongs and completed the epic *Kalevipoeg*, but also published various moral and instructive items (such as *The Plague of Vodka*, 1840). He also authored a collection of folk stories and legends based on both genuine Estonian folktales and German fables, under the title *Old Estonian Fairy Tales* (1866).

By the 1860s Estonia was fully in the throes of its national awakening. Its literature was characterized by patriotism and concern for the future of the Estonian people. The most important publicist of the Estonian national awakening was Johann Voldemar Jannsen (1819–90), a teacher, poet, story writer, and journalist who founded the newspaper *Perno Postimees* (Pärnu Courier) in 1857. Adopting a colloquial tone that was accessible and appealing to ordinary Estonians, Jannsen did more than anyone to bring newspaper reading to the Estonian peasantry. Writing under the pseudonym Koidula, Jannsen's daughter Lydia Koidula (1843–86) first achieved recognition for her work in the literary section of *Eesti Postimees* (located in Tartu after 1863). Also a writer of numerous short stories and plays, Koidula is best remembered for her Romantic poetry, which is characterized by its alliterated trochaic style and its intense patriotism. Every Estonian has read her poems; some have been set to music. Indeed, during the Soviet era, when national symbols were prohibited, Koidula's poem, *My Fatherland Is My Love,* earlier set to a melody by Gustav Ernesaks, became regarded as the country's unofficial anthem.

Koidula's romanticism and patriotism were common to her generation of poets, which includes Mikhel Veske (1843–90), Ado Reinvald (1847–1922), and Friedrich Kuhlbars (1841–1924). Each found inspiration not only in the examples of Kreutzwald and Koidula, but were also influenced by Carl Robert Jakobson (1841–82), a polemicist, poet, and, in the years before his untimely death, editor of the intensely nationalist newspaper *Sakala*—Estonia's most popular in the 1880s. The works of Mikhel Veske, who was Jakobson's closest collaborator, focused on social issues and displayed a highly idealized vision of the Estonian fatherland. Reinvald's poetry—simple, naturalistic, and frankly anti-German—reflected the outlook of the Estonian peasant. Kuhlbars, who borrowed heavily from Kreutzwald's *Kalevipoeg,* is best remembered for his romantic poems, many of which were published in his collection *Vanemuine* (1870).

While Juhan Liiv (1864–1913), a tragic figure who suffered from mental illness, is renowned as one of the outstanding Estonian poets of the late nineteenth century, the country's first truly great prose writer was Eduard Vilde (1865–1933), whose classic novels reflect the gradual transition to realism that took place in Estonian literature in the 1890s. Many of his works depict the hardships experienced by the Estonian peasantry under their German landlords. Among Vilde's greatest achievements were *To the Cold Land* (1896), regarded as a seminal work in Estonian critical realism, and his epic historical trilogy *The War at Mahtra* (1902), *When the Peasants of Anija Visited Tallinn* (1903), and *The Prophet Maltsvet* (1906).

During the era between the revolutions of 1905 and 1917—a period that Vilde spent in self-imposed exile—Estonia's most significant literary movement was *Noor-Eesti* (Young Estonia). Founded by the poet and literary scholar Gustav Suits (1883–1956), the *Noor-Eesti* group was oriented toward the literature and culture of Western Europe (France and Scandinavia in particular) and was especially concerned with elevating the level of Estonian culture. Suits's call captures well the mood of the Young Estonians: "More culture! More European culture! Let us remain Estonians, but let us also become Europeans!" Although their greatest innovations were in poetry, short prose, and literary criticism, the *Noor-Eesti* journal also introduced the hitherto unknown works of Juhan Liiv and the forgotten poetry of Kristjan Peterson.[13]

It is hard to overstate the impact that World War I had on art and culture throughout Europe; some scholars believe that it was the cataclysm of the Great War that gave birth to modern art, music, and dance.[14] In Estonia the rationality of the *Noor-Eesti* writers was eclipsed by the abstractness of the group who wrote for the journal *Siuru* (1917–19), which was founded by Friedebert Tuglas (1886–1971), a former contributor to *Noor-Eesti*. *Siuru*'s greatest poets were Henrik Visnapuu (1890–1951) and Marie Under (1883–1980), whose early works were characterized by their sensuality and emotionalism. As the founder of several other literary periodicals, most notably *Looming* (Creation), Tuglas himself was at the center of Estonia's cultural and literary life, writing scores of short stories and novels while participating in numerous cultural organizations. Unfortunately, few of his works have been translated into English, a barrier that has prevented most Baltic authors from gaining an Anglophone audience.

Despite the limited international impact of Estonian-language literature, its new vitality within Estonia became evident in the founding of periodicals such as *Eesti Kirjandus* (Estonian Literature) and *Looming* and the creation of writers' groups of various orientations. The development of Estonian literary culture was directly encouraged by the fledgling new state, which sponsored the creation of the Estonian Writers' Union in 1922. Its purpose was to provide members with the material means to pursue their professional literary work; likewise, the Cultural Endowment was established three years later for the purpose of awarding grants in the arts, and it remains the main source of funding in the arts in Estonia today.

The Estonian literary canon is filled with writers who made their mark during the era of independence. Estonia's most acclaimed author is Anton Hansen Tammsaare (1878–1940), whose books are considered national treasures. Tammsaare's literary career began in the early 1900s with the publication of a string of naturalistic rural stories. His first novel, *The Farmer of Kõrboja* (1922), was also among his most successful, but *Truth and Justice* (1926–33), a five-volume tour de force that depicts the development of Estonian rural life from the last decades of the nineteenth century through the 1920s, was his most ambitious and became an instant classic. While Tammsaare is sometimes said to be the Estonian Shakespeare, his works have found only a small audience outside his homeland.

Another outstanding critical realist of the independence era was Mait Metsanurk (1879–1957), whose short stories and novels such as *The White Cloud* (1925) and *The Red Wind* (1928) describe the lives and problems of ordinary working people or small farmers. During the 1930s Metsanurk turned to the genre of the historical novel—a popular genre then and today in Estonia. *On the River Ümera* (1934) realistically depicts the Estonian resistance to the thirteenth-century German conquest, while *Fire Under the Ashes* (1936) is set during the great famine of the seventeenth century.

The works of August Gailit (1891–1960) occupy a distinctive place in the literature of interwar Estonia. In contrast to the realism of Tammsaare and

Metsanurk, Gailit's writing continued to be romantic and fantastical. Shaped by his experience as a member of the *Siuru* literary group, Gailit found an international audience with the publication of the novel *Toomas Nipernaadi* (1928), which has as its hero a vagabond who wanders the roads of Estonia from spring to autumn.[15] However, the most popular Estonian writer of the period, and perhaps of the entire twentieth century, is Oskar Luts (1887–1953). The author of scores of novels and short stories, Luts is best known for a series of books about the farmboy Toots, whose adventures have made him a folk hero to generations of Estonians.

By the second half of the 1930s, following the establishment of an authoritarian regime in Estonia, poetry began to supplant the epic realist narratives that had characterized the best of Estonian literature in the late 1920s. Among the innovative young Estonian poets of the 1930s were Betty Alver (1906–89) and Uku Masing (1909–85) of the *Arbujad* (Soothsayers) group and August Sang (1914–69), but each lost several decades during the Stalinist terror before reemerging with new collections during the more relaxed atmosphere of the 1960s.

Latvia

The national literature of the Latvian people began only in the nineteenth century. The first writer of Latvian origin to have his work published was Indrikis the Blind (1783–1828), whose first collection, which consisted of 14 poems on nature, love, and religion, was published in 1806. The first widely published Latvian poet, however, was Juris Alunāns (1832–64), whose *Little Songs* (1856) laid the foundations for Latvian written poetry. Juris Neikens (1826–63), whose short stories dealt with familial themes such as prodigal sons, was the pioneer of Latvian prose.

By the last quarter of the nineteenth century Latvia had become an awakened nation and Latvian writers had begun to produce genuinely artistic works of prose and verse. Rural themes were prevalent in many works from this period, such as the short stories of Apsīšu Jēkabs (1858–1929). *Surveyors' Times* (1879), a novel by the brothers Matīss Kaudzīte (1848–1926) and Reinis Kaudzīte (1839–1920) was appreciated for its humorous portrayal of village life. Yet the classical Latvian literary canon is filled with writers who rose to national prominence in the 1890s and early 1900s. It includes the realist poet Vilis Plūdonis (1874–1940), the Romantic poet Jānis Poruks (1871–1911), the dramatist and short story writer Rūdolfs Blaumanis (1863–1908), Augusts Deglavs (1862–1922), who wrote the trilogy *Riga* (1909–22), and the revolutionary poet and dramatist Aspāzija (1865–1953).

Towering above all these figures is Aspāzija's husband, Jānis Rainis (*nee* Pliekšans, 1865–1929). A lawyer, poet, and dramatist who was able to reconcile his nationalist proclivities with his social democratic (Marxist) convictions, Rainis was arrested in 1897 for his political radicalism. Freed from prison in 1903, Rainis returned to his activism and became a central figure in the 1905 revolution. It was at this time that he completed one of his most forceful plays, *Fire and Night* (1905), an allegorical epic based on the *Lāčplēsis* tale about the Latvians' struggle for freedom. Forced to flee abroad, Rainis, like many activists from the Russian Empire, emigrated with his wife to Switzerland, where he published collections of his poetry and wrote many of his greatest plays. In 1920 this poet who had proclaimed "Wherever I am, Latvia's soul is with me" returned to the independent Republic of Latvia, where he became involved in state politics while directing the Latvian National Theater from 1921 to 1925. Three years after his death in 1929 the state commissioned a statue of Rainis, which occupies a prominent place in Riga's pretty Esplanade Park.

Some scholars believe that Rainis's wife, Aspāzija (Elza Rozenberga), might be better known today had she not sacrificed years of her career to nurturing the talents of her famous husband.[16] Although she first came to public attention for her penetrating dramas, in particular the intensely political play *The Silver Veil* (1905), Aspāzija also worked as a journalist and began publishing poetry in the late 1890s. Not limited by any one form, her poetry was a mirror that reflected the state of her mind at any given moment; this was particularly evident in the poetry she parsimoniously published during her years in exile. Increasingly estranged from her husband, Aspāzija's most prolific period came after she returned to Latvia. As Latvia succumbed to dictatorship under President Ulmanis, in 1936 Aspāzija wrote her *Hymn to Latvia,* which concluded with the words "Latvia will live forever and dying will never die!" Four years later the USSR established its claim to Latvian territory, and when Aspāzija died in 1943 the country was occupied by the Germans.

Joining Rainis and Aspāzija in the Latvian literary elite during the era of independence was Jānis Jaunsudrabiņš (1877–1962), a remarkably prolific writer who is also known for his paintings. His best-known work is a self-illustrated book of short stories called *The White Book* (1914, 1920), about a little boy's childhood in the Latvian countryside. Originally published in various periodicals before being compiled into a single volume (since published in more than 25 editions), these realistic stories are still read by Latvian schoolchildren today. In the editions published during the German and Soviet occupations, however, many of the stories (which originally numbered 100) were censored: stories that favorably depicted Jews were omitted during Nazi rule, while stories that departed from the established Socialist Realist norms were eliminated by the Soviets.[17]

Among the great Latvian poets of the interwar era was Edvards Virza (1883–1940), whose verses frequently exhibited national themes. Although first and foremost a poet, his most noteworthy work is the novel *Straumēni* (1933), whose subject is the seasonal rhythms of Latvian rural life. The national theme is also taken up in Jēkabs Janševskis's (1865–1931) six-volume masterpiece, *The Native Land* (1924–25). Meanwhile, the poet Kārlis Skalbe (1879–1945) continued his work as Latvia's foremost writer of fairy tales, in which he recreated a world of fairies, nymphs, giants, and elves. Other leading Latvian poets and prose writers of the independence era included Jānis Ezeriņš (1891–1924), Mārtiņš Zīverts (1903–90), Zenta Mauriņa (1897–1978), Aleksandars Čaks (1901–50), and Kārlis Ābele (1896–1961). Many would flee Latvia during World War II and the Soviet occupation; some would lend their services to the new regime; still others suffered internal exile or simply disappeared from public view.

BALTIC LITERATURES SINCE 1940

The Stalin Era

During the Soviet era the literature of the Baltic peoples was split: at least half of the recognized literary figures of the prewar era chose exile from their Soviet-occupied countries; those who remained at home were subject to rigid ideological controls or simply chose to remain silent altogether. Numerous writers found work as translators of Russian books, and when they did write original works they did so with little expectation of having them published anytime soon. Some, including a number of Baltic writers who had spent the interwar era in Soviet Russia, offered their talents to the regime out of ideological commitment, while others were coerced or lured into collaboration with the promise of significant print-runs and material rewards. And there was much to be done: as one scholar later recalled, "The history of the Balts had to be rewritten, their poetry had to be revised, and even their memories had to be reshaped."[18]

Consider, for example, the Latvian experience: most poets and writers who had been active during the era of independence were discredited and classified as "reactionary" or "bourgeois" and their works were banned. To monitor those writers who remained a Latvian Writers' Union, consisting at first of only nine members, was immediately set up under the realist writer Andrējs Upīts (1877–1970), who had earlier earned a reputation as a polemicist and a prolific novelist, comparable to Russia's Maxim Gorky. The first Latvian to win a Stalin Prize (1946), Upīts was joined by another established writer, Vilis Lācis (1903–66), who was rewarded for his loyalty and service with the post of Commissar of Internal Affairs and two Stalin Prizes (1947 and 1952). Latvia's remaining writers were expected to celebrate their liberation from capitalism, and poets were instructed to write tributes to Stalin. Few original prose works were published during the early years of the occupation, and although the earlier works of the classic Latvian writers Rainis and Blaumanis were briefly deemed useful for gaining the allegiance of the Latvian people, much of the literature of the past was condemned to oblivion.

Similar stories could be told about literary life in Estonia and Lithuania in the first occupation in 1940–41 and again in the years after World War II, when the campaign to bring cultural affairs completely under the control of the Communist Party was at its most ferocious. Literature was valued less for its aesthetic qualities than for its usefulness—and no writer could expect to get published unless he demonstrated the ideological usefulness of his work. A prerequisite for getting one's work published was membership in the Soviet Writers' Union, whose branches were quickly established in each of the Soviet republics. However, before a work of literature could be published it had first to go through Glavlit, the Soviet censorship organ. As the "engineers of human souls," all Soviet writers were expected to make positive contributions to the construction of socialism and to embrace Socialist Realism, the dominant literary mode in the USSR. Symbolism, fantasy, and allegory were now superseded by the unambiguously "positive hero" committed to the building of socialism. The safest bets for any author were war stories that depicted the heroism of the Soviet people or those that portrayed the maturing of the people in the course of Soviet construction.

Exile Literature

During the first decade or more of the Soviet occupation the most significant works of Baltic literature were published by exiles who fled to the United States, Canada, Germany, Australia, and elsewhere. Sweden was the primary destination for exiled Estonian writers. While writers such as Gustav Suits, Marie Under, Henrik Visnapuu, August Gailit, August Mälk, and Albert Kivikas were free to publish their works in Stockholm, their books were mostly unavailable in their native Estonia. It was in Sweden that the poet, novelist, literary scholar, and publisher Bernard Kangro (1910–94) published the cultural magazine *Tulimud* (The Fire Soil), beginning in 1950. Few writers anywhere could match Kangro's productivity: between 1945 and 1969 he published 10 collections of his own poetry in addition to 10 novels and several other collections of plays and poems. Karl Ristikivi (1912–77), a poet and the author of numerous historical novels, including the "Tallinn trilogy" (1938–42), also occupies a distinctive place in the community of Estonian writers in exile. Perhaps his most innovative prose work in exile was the surrealist novel *All Souls' Night* (1953), in which the protagonist, wandering the streets of Stockholm on New Year's Eve, finds himself in the labyrinthine Dead Man's House—a place where one arrives at the top floor by going down the stairs. Frequently compared with Herman Hesse's *Steppenwolf* and Lewis Carroll's *Alice in Wonderland,* Ristikivi's *All Souls' Night* is a story of alienation: the narrator, who has spent seven years in exile, is trapped inside himself; there is no exit.

For more than four decades the Estonian literary community was split in half. While Estonian writers in exile were cut off from developments in their homeland, those living in occupied Estonia could obtain banned émigré writings only by smuggling them into the country. To the end of the Soviet era misunderstandings persisted on both sides: some Estonians who remained at home were not entirely convinced that the official Soviet myths about those who fled—i.e., that they were traitors seeking material riches abroad—was without foundation; many diaspora Estonians, on the other hand, dismissed their homeland culture as collaborationist. The split that divided the Estonian literary world for half a century came to an end in the years that followed the collapse of the USSR. Symbolizing this reconciliation was the merger in 2000 of the Estonian branch of the Soviet Writers' Union and the Stockholm-based Estonian Writers' Union in Exile.

The main destinations of Latvia's exiled writers were the United States, Canada, and Australia. The works they composed in exile frequently bore witness to the sufferings of the Latvian people: the experience of flight from the homeland, the challenges of life in displaced persons camps, and the feelings of disorientation in their new environments. Latvia's leading playwright, Mārtiņš Zīverts, produced some of his best plays while abroad, while the bard Anšlavs Eglītis (1906–93) wrote passionate poems and stories about the loss of his homeland. The prolific novelist Zenta Mauriņa emerged as one of the country's best-known writers in exile; although especially popular in Germany, her works were translated into many languages. Jānis Jaunsudrabiņš, Kārlis Skalbe, Aivars Ruņģis also continued to write while in exile, as did the poets Zinaīda Lazda (1902–57), Kārlis Ābele, and Dzintars Freimanis.

Most Lithuanian exile writers ended up in the United States. Like their Estonian and Latvian counterparts, exiled Lithuanian writers continued to write about their native land and life in the countryside and provincial towns as if they had never left them. Among them were the poet Henrikas Radauskas (1910–70) and the novelist Vincas Ramonas (1905–85). Radauskas is regarded by some as the greatest Lithuanian poet of the twentieth century or indeed of any time. Born in Cracow and fleeing to Germany at the end of World War II, Radauskas ultimately immigrated to the United States in 1949, where he managed to publish four short volumes of poetry and translated numerous German literary works into Lithuanian. Like Radauskas, Vincas Ramonas fled to Germany and ultimately ended up in Chicago. His most significant work, *The Crosses* (1947), depicted the tragedy of the first Soviet occupation in 1940–41.

Although not strictly speaking an "exile" writer, Czesław Miłosz (1911–2004), an internationally renowned poet and essayist born in Lithuania, deserves mention nevertheless. Born in Seteiniai, he completed his studies in Polish-occupied Vilnius and left Poland in 1951, eventually emigrating to the United States, where he won the 1980 Nobel Prize for Literature. His most famous work, a collection of essays titled *The Captive Mind* (1953), condemns Eastern European intellectuals' accommodation to communism after 1944. If for no other reason, this masterpiece of twentieth-century literature warrants mention because of its success in drawing the world's attention to the tragedy of the Baltic countries.

Estonian Literature

While exiled authors, soon joined by a younger generation of Baltic authors who grew up in foreign lands, continued to write novels, novellas, and poems, little of their work was read at home until the end of the Soviet era. Meanwhile, literary life in the Baltic republics, as in the rest of the USSR, began its long road to recovery during Nikita Khrushchev's "thaw" in the second half of the 1950s. Only then were some of the punished and banned Baltic writers rehabilitated. Although several deported writers returned from Siberia and the works of some so-called bourgeois nationalists soon came to light, it was clear that the Soviet regime preferred the classics, which in effect left Baltic literary life stuck in the world of the previous century. Whatever the thaw's limits, at least the Socialist Realist monopoly was broken and writers were allowed to explore other literary avenues.

Among the most important thaw-era works in Estonia was *The Land and the People* (1956) by Rudolf Sirge (1904–70), the author of a number of successful books during the prewar era. Set in the Estonian countryside in 1940–41, the novel presents a realistic description of the Sovietization of Estonia, including the mass deportations of June 1941. Its publication was soon followed by the literary debut of Jaan Kross (b. 1920), who published his first collection of poems under the title *The Coal Concentrator* (1958). Although this collection, based on Kross's experience in the mines of Vorkuta (a Soviet forced-labor camp in far northern Russia), was controversial when it first appeared, it came to be regarded as a true landmark of Estonian verse that influenced the renaissance of Estonian poetry in the 1960s.

While it was his poetry that first earned Kross his reputation as one of Estonia's premier writers, he is also renowned as the country's greatest contemporary historical novelist. His most ambitious work is *Between Three Plagues* (1970–80), a four-volume biographical novel about the sixteenth-century Tallinn city elder Balthasar Russow. However, Kross's best-known work internationally is the widely translated novel *The Tsar's Madman* (1978). Set in Russia in the late 1820s, its protagonist is Timotheus (Timo) Eberhard von Bock, a Baltic German nobleman from Estonia who once served as Tsar Alexander I's aide-de-camp. A maverick who defied aristocratic convention by marrying an Estonian peasant girl, von Bock is imprisoned for nine years and declared insane for telling his emperor unpleasant truths about the Russian autocracy. Successfully outwitting Soviet censorship, Kross published his novel at a time when the Soviet KGB under Yuri Andropov routinely confined dissidents to psychiatric hospitals. In recent years Kross's novels have been of a more autobiographical nature: *Mesmer's Circle* (1995) chronicles student life in Tartu during the final days of the first Estonian republic and the first Soviet occupation, and *Treading Air* (1998) describes the end of Estonian independence during his youth.

Kross's generation also includes Artur Alliksaar (1923–66), a poet who, like Kross and so many others, was imprisoned by the Soviets. After his release in 1957, Alliksaar abandoned classical forms and became known for his unrhymed free-verse poetry. A complete collection of his poems, *Lavishing Sunlight,* appeared in 1997. The poetry of Kross, Alliksaar, Kersti Merilaas (1913–86), and Ellen Niit (b. 1928) that began to appear (or reappear) in the late 1950s provided a backdrop before which emerged an extraordinary group of young writers in the 1960s. Named for the small cardboard boxes, called *kassets* in Estonian, in which poetry collections were packaged at the time, many of the "cassette generation" writers worked successfully in multiple genres, including poetry, drama, and prose. Rejecting the reigning literary orthodoxy of Socialist Realism, these writers introduced modernism into Estonian letters.

The most widely translated and internationally famous writer of this generation is Jaan Kaplinski (b. 1941), whose first poetry collection, *Tracks at the Spring* (1965), launched a writing career that has now spanned four decades. A disciple of the theologian-poet Uku Masing, Kaplinski composed his early nature poems in unpunctuated free verse. A hallmark of his poetry over the decades has been its growing concision; to the present day his simple descriptions allow readers of his poems to grasp deeper truths. In addition to being a poet, essayist, journalist, and translator, Kaplinski is also well known for his social activism and his interest in Eastern philosophies. After serving in the Estonian parliament from 1992 to 1995, Kaplinski returned to writing

and translating full-time; both he and Jaan Kross (who also took a seat in the
Riigikogu) have been candidates for the Nobel Prize.

About a dozen or so writers are said to belong to the "cassette generation."
Among the better known are the novelist Enn Vetemaa (b. 1936), the poet, dramatist, and translator Paul-Eerik Rummo (b. 1942), the absurdist urban writer
Arvo Valton (b. 1935), and the multitalented Mati Unt (b. 1944). Mati Unt,
the youngest of this group, was a published writer before he was even out of his
teens. Beginning in the mid-1960s, a time when prose forms began to revive
in Estonia, Mati Unt composed a series of stories set in the university town of
Tartu; the focus of these stories was his own generation coming to terms with
the world. Despite his early success as a prose writer, today Unt is better known
as a dramatist who has staged more than 100 plays (see Chapter 7).

Arvo Valton, like Unt one of Estonia's leading modernist authors, began his
career in the 1960s as a writer of realistic stories; his mature works, however,
grew more abstract. For example, Valton's first novel, *The Path to the Other End
of Infinity* (1978), has as its subject the Genghis Khan's relationship with a Taoist
scholar. A later work titled *Despondency and Hope* (1989), on the other hand, is
an autobiographical novel about the deportations of 1949 and the ruined lives
of those who were sent to Siberia. Although the most prolific Estonian author
of the 1960s and 1970s was Aimée Beekman (b. 1933), her works have not
earned a prestigious place in the pantheon of Estonian literary classics.

Among the Estonian classics the most prevalent are historical novels. This
genre has a tradition that dates to the turn of the century, when Eduard Vilde
produced his great trilogy. *Ahasuerus's Dream,* one of the country's most widely
discussed novels of recent years, falls in this esteemed category. Published by
the novelist and poet Ene Mihkelson (b. 1944) in 2001, its subject is the
"forest brothers" who resisted the Soviet takeover in the years after World
War II. Many of Mihkelson's works grapple with the way her own generation
was affected by Estonia's twentieth-century tragedies; thus *Ahasuerus's Dream*
contemplates the Estonian resistance from the perspective of the daughter of
a partisan who was killed in the early 1950s. Although this topic was taboo
in Estonia during the Soviet era, the exiled writer Arved Viirlaid (b. 1922)
wrote about it in his novel *Graves Without Crosses* (1952), which many critics
consider the classic treatment of this cruel episode in Estonian history.

Few people in any country can hope to make a living solely as a writer; given
the size of Estonia's literary marketplace it is almost impossible. Moreover, after
the collapse of the USSR the works of Estonia's struggling young novelists and
poets faced competition from various formerly "forbidden fruits," including
émigré literature, the works of previously suppressed authors, so-called manu-
scripts from the drawer, and foreign literature. (This might also be said of
the Latvian and Lithuanian literary markets.) Despite these obstacles, younger

writers have managed to find an audience in Estonia today.[19] Some, such as Andrus Kivirähk (b. 1971), have found success by leaning heavily on Estonia's ancient literary heritage. Kivirähk's third novel, *The Old Barny* (2001), a comedy set during the era of serfdom, draws heavily on Estonian folklore. It portrays archetypal characters that would be familiar to any Estonian reader, including the witty and wise old farmer (the protagonist) and the greedy and cruel manor overseer.

Two of the most successful post-Soviet writers in Estonia are Ervin Õunapuu (b. 1956) and Tõnu Õnnepalu (b. 1962). Ervin Õunapuu's reputation as a novelist and storywriter was established only after he had become known as a painter, playwright, scriptwriter, and film director. Instantly turning its author into a favorite cult writer, Õunapuu's *Olivia's Master Class* (1996) has been made into an opera and a play. Although younger, Tõnu Õnnepalu first won recognition in the 1980s for his poetry. Sometimes publishing under the pseudonym Emil Tode (*tõde* is Estonian for "truth"), Õnnepalu later earned critical acclaim for a series of postmodernist novels, including *The Border State* (1993), *The Price* (1995), and *Princess* (1997).

A little-noticed development in Estonian letters in recent years is the use of the Võru dialect of southern Estonia, which now has its own standardized spelling. Until recently the only literary forms in Võru were poems, but now it is not uncommon for plays and novels to be written in the southern dialect. Likewise, Latvia today is witnessing the revival of the Latgalian dialect as a literary form. In recent years poetry collections by Anna Rancane and Antons Kūkojs (b. 1940) have included verses in Latgalian.

Latvian Literature

Like writers in Estonia, Latvian writers who survived the era of war, terror, and silence also began to explore life in the Soviet homeland somewhat more realistically in the first years of the post-Stalin era. Among Latvian writers associated with the thaw-era, three in particular—Ēvalds Vilks (1923–76), Jēzups Laganovskis (b. 1920), and Visvaldis Eglons-Lāms (b. 1923)—stand out for their courage in confronting the deformities of Soviet reality. While the short stories of Ēvalds Vilks never went so far as to reject the party line, they implicitly criticized the abuses and incompetence of provincial party bosses and collective farm chairmen. The stories in Jēzups Laganovskis's collection *When the Winds Rustle* (1956) mounted a somewhat bolder attack on the absurdities of the Soviet bureaucracy.

Another thaw-era writer who managed to surpass the boundaries of Socialist Realism was Visvaldis Eglons-Lāms. In 1959 his controversial story about the Latvian Legion (created by German forces to fight the Soviets during the last years of World War II) began to appear in serial, but the authorities had it discontinued. Censured by the Writers' Union for his "wobbly ideological position," Lāms encountered difficulties in getting this work (or any other) published, and for much of the 1960s he remained silent.[20] Lāms had to wait until 1989 before the novel was published in full under the title *The Glimmer of Northern Lights.*

Alberts Bels (b. 1938) was similarly willing to test Moscow's limits. A writer who once defined the essence of Socialist Realism as praise of the bosses in a manner that the bosses can comprehend, Bels debuted in 1967 with the short novel *The Investigator,* about a sculptor's coming to terms with his family's experiences during the first decades of Soviet power. His next novel, *The Cage* (1972), is an allegorical story about contemporary life in Soviet Latvia: its protagonist is trapped in a cage from which there is no escape. *Insomnia* (1987), which concerns the taboo subject of the Latvian Legion, encountered official resistance when it was first written in the late 1960s. Like Lāms's earlier novel *The Glimmer of Northern Lights,* Bels's story had to wait until the more liberal glasnost era to be published in full. As the greatest Latvian prose writer during the "era of stagnation," no Latvian novelist has been more widely translated than Bels.[21]

While generalizations about any literary genre in any part of the world are always risky, it is not a stretch to say that Soviet-era literature, whether written by Baltic authors or by Russians, was frequently characterized by a certain sense of mission. Poets in particular often believed that their words were an expression of the collective consciousness, whether that of a triumphant class or of a threatened people. Poetry in the Soviet era was more difficult to police than prose; thus poets, because of the very nature of their art, had more freedom to explore national and personal themes. This sense of mission— a calling to express the collective yearning of the nation—was especially pronounced among Latvian poets, both at home and abroad.

As in Estonia, the 1960s was the era of the poet in Soviet Latvia. Among the most widely read of the young poets who rose to prominence during this period were Voldemars Avens (b. 1924), Imants Aužiņš (b. 1937), Jānis Peters (b. 1939), and Māris Čaklais (b. 1940). One of Latvia's most beloved "woman's poets" was the physician Arija Elksne (1928–84), whose verse has been read and admired by many Latvian women. But the best-known Latvian woman poet of the second half of the twentieth century is Vizma Belševica (1931–2005), whose nature poems and short stories have been translated into more than 40 languages. Frequently subjected to the criticism of party zealots, whose censors ensured that many of her works were altered before publication, Belševica survived periods of forced silence through her work as a translator.

Another favorite Latvian poet of the 1960s and 1970s was Ojārs Vācietis (1933–83), who was known as the "Latvian Yevtushenko" both for his mercurial lyrics and his status, like that of the Russian bard Yevgeny Yevtushenko, as an acceptable dissident. However, if any poet can be considered Latvia's "national bard" it is Vācietis's contemporary Imants Ziedonis (b. 1933). To many Latvians Ziedonis is more than a great literary authority; he is a spiritual leader. Also known for his prose "miniatures" and short stories, Ziedonis has published fairy tales and children's stories in addition to his innumerable poems. While he was never a dissident like Vācietis, Ziedonis is, like so many cultural figures in Eastern Europe, a social and political activist. In the 1970s he became involved in the campaigns to protect the Latvian environment from the excesses of Soviet industrialization, and at the end of the Soviet era he helped establish the Latvian Culture Fund to promote the development of Latvian arts and letters.

Of the writers who rose to prominence in the 1980s and 1990s, one of the most distinctive is the poet and dramatist Māra Zālīte (b. 1952). Folkloric imagery is embedded in many of Zālīte's poems, which are famed for their lyrical quality. In recent years she has turned her attention to writing librettos for rock operas such as *Lāčplēsis* (1988) and *The Birds' Opera* (2000). Zālīte's musical poem *The Wild Swans,* which was heavily influenced by the tales of Hans Christian Anderson and was set to music by the beloved composer Raimonds Pauls (see Chapter 7), premiered in 1995 and has remained a popular favorite on the Latvian stage ever since. The recipient of nearly every major Latvian literary award, Zālīte is presently the president of the Union of Latvian Authors.

While the list of promising young Latvian authors is long, it is worthwhile briefly to mention a few. Andra Neiburga (b. 1957) is the author of several short-story collections and a children's book, while the novels of Gundega Repše (b. 1960) center on the lives of famous Latvian painters. One of the most popular young authors in Latvia today is the dramatist, poet, and story writer Inga Ābele (b. 1972), who made her literary debut in 1998 with a collection of poems. Three years later Ābele published her first novel, *Fire Will Not Wake You.*

Lithuanian Literature

While it has often been noted that Lithuania enjoyed greater autonomy under its wily First Secretary Antanas Sniečkus (1903–74) than did Estonia or Latvia, its literary life was no less devastated by the imposition of strict ideological controls and the exile of some of its greatest talents. Since the simple but elegant *dainas* and *raudos* (songs of lament) represent the heart of premodern Lithuanian culture, it should come as little surprise that Lithuania's poets responded vigorously to the thaw that began in the mid-1950s. While new writers of a younger generation arose to take the place of the dead, deported, or exiled authors, some of the older writers who survived began to speak in a different voice.

Among the great innovators of the 1950s and 1960s was Eduards Mieželaitis (1919–97). A communist idealist in his youth and a Romantic and Symbolist in his maturity, Mieželaitis was awarded a Lenin Prize for his poem *Man* (1962), which showed that it was possible to use unorthodox forms as long as the ideological content was acceptable. Following his lead, poets such as the former prisoner of war Paulius Širvys (1920–79), the nature poet Janina Degutytė (1928–90), as well as Algimantas Baltakis (b. 1930) and Alfonsas Maldonis (b. 1929), were able to widen the boundaries of the permissible. Many poets of this generation were concerned with the issue of ethnic identity, and nature and what civilization has done to it. Indeed, the lyrics of Justinas Marcinkevičius (b. 1930), the "national bard" of postwar Lithuanian poetry, frequently express his love for his native land, his deep attachment to Lithuania's rural culture, and his indignation at the harm done to its people. Over the decades Marcinkevičius also established a reputation as a fine historical dramatist whose works—most notably *Mindaugas* (1968)—have been translated into more than 20 languages.[22]

Among the strongest representatives of Lithuania's "village verse" tradition is Sigitas Geda (b. 1943), who is regarded as one of the most innovative poets writing in the Lithuanian language today. The poems collected in his *26 Songs of Autumn and Summer* (1972) express Geda's deep reverence for the living things in nature; indeed, "magical" and "mystical" are the words that literary scholars most frequently use to describe the aesthetic qualities of Geda's nature poems. In more recent collections such as *The Jotvingian Mass* (1997), Geda has taken up historical themes. As always, however, the religion of nature remains central to his art.

While it often seems that communion with nature—a literary tradition that dates to Donelaitis's *The Seasons*—is a condition for full membership in the community of Lithuanian national bards, the poet Judita Vaičiānaitė (1937–2001) was more interested in the ambience of urban landscapes. Her poems spoke not of skyscrapers and the night life of Vilnius, but of dilapidated streets, shops, and parks and of nostalgia for the past. Tomas Venclova (b. 1937), who began publishing his poems in the early 1970s, is more difficult to categorize. The son of the influential Soviet-Lithuanian poet Antanas Venclova (1906–71), Tomas Venclova has always been more than a poet: he is also an essayist, a translator, a literary critic, and the author of an outstanding guidebook to his beloved Vilnius. One of Venclova's admirers recently described him as "the most influential social and cultural critic in twentieth-century Lithuania."[23] Having run afoul of Soviet authorities for his dissident activities, he emigrated to the West in 1977 and later became a professor of Slavic literature at Yale University. But Venclova has always remained close to his homeland: in 2000 he received Lithuania's National Prize for Culture and Art for poems and essays that he published in the late 1990s.

As in Lithuanian poetry, some of the most common themes in Lithuanian prose are nature, and the nation's unique identity and tragic history; usually these motifs are inseparably intertwined. For example, one of the major thaw-era landmarks of Lithuanian prose is the novel *Steps to the Sky* (1963) by Mykolas Sluckis (b. 1928). Its themes were the Lithuanian peasantry's attachment to the land and the tragedy of collectivization. Sluckis is also well known for his literary innovations: while his earlier short stories were realistic, his novels of the 1960s, such as *Adam's Apple* (1966), introduced the stream of consciousness narrative (or the "inner monologue") and other Impressionist techniques into modern Lithuanian literature.

One of the most widely translated Lithuanian prose writers of the era of "developed socialism" was Jonas Avyžius (1922–99), whose trilogy *Village at the Crossroads* (1964), *The Time of the Emptying of Homesteads* (1970), and *Scorched Land* (1982) dealt with the forced transformation of Lithuanian villages into collective farms in the early years of the Soviet occupation. A series of novels by Romualdas Granauskas (b. 1939), including *The Bread Eaters* (1975) and *Homestead under the Maple Tree* (1988), also bore witness to the loss of hope in the countryside. Icchokas Meras (b. 1934), a Jew from Kaunas, was one of the few writers of Lithuania to mention the Holocaust. Several of his novels dealt with Jewish-Lithuanian relations during the Nazi occupation and were well received by Soviet critics. Nevertheless, Meras emigrated to Israel in 1972 and consequently became a nonperson in the eyes of Soviet authorities.

During the 1980s a number of younger Lithuanian writers emerged who were less concerned with nature and the tragedy of collectivization than with the darker side of life under (and after) Soviet rule. Among the most notorious was the novelist, playwright, and journalist Ričardas Gavelis (1950–2002), whose works since the late 1980s focused on the many problems facing Lithuanian society. Although his most popular novel is the controversial *Vilnius Poker* (1989), a dark mockup of Soviet society set in Vilnius in the 1970s, some believe that his best work is *The Memoirs of a Young Man* (1991), whose young hero aspires to become a great physicist but is held back by the tyranny of Soviet officialdom. The last novel in the Vilnius trilogy, The *Last Generation of People on Earth* (1995), is also the most grotesque and fantastical, as it focuses on the sometimes shocking consequences of freedom in contemporary society.

The seedier side of Lithuanian life is explored in the social satires of Jurgis Kunčinas (b. 1947), who began publishing his novels only in the early 1990s. Kunčinas's unique blend of humor, fantasy, and sorrow is on display in the novel *Tūla* (1993), which is widely regarded as his best. Set in the late Soviet era in a neglected section of downtown Vilnius called Užupis, it depicts an urban landscape and its inhabitants who exist at the margins of the Soviet utopia.

One of the most widely read Lithuanian writers today is Jurga Ivanauskaitė (b. 1961). Her novel *The Witch and the Rain* (1993), a story about a priest's love affair with a woman, was immediately condemned as pornography and banned. Naturally, this act of censorship only boosted its sales. A subsequent series of nonfiction works on Tibet introduced her compatriots to another country with its own peculiar spiritual practices that has endured decades of occupation by a more powerful neighbor. While Ivanauskaitė continues to write novels with religious themes, her recent series of exhibitions have revealed her additional talent as a painter.

NOTES

1. In the early years of the twentieth century, the linguist Johannes Aavik (1880–1973) and others introduced a series of reforms to the Estonian language in an attempt to transform it from a peasant tongue into a European cultural language. Among these innovations were the introduction of hundreds of new words and the alteration of Estonian word order, which previously had been identical to the word order of German sentences.

2. Similar to Belarusian, Chancery Slavonic was based on the Church Slavonic that was introduced by Orthodox clergy from the south.

3. Mati Laur, Tõnis Lukas, Ain Mäesalu, Ago Pajur, and Tõnu Tannberg, *History of Estonia,* 2nd ed. (Tallinn: Avita, 2002), 93.

4. "Book, in the Lithuanian Language," www.spaudos.lt/LietKalba/Books.en.htm.

5. As written Lithuanian began to revive in the late nineteenth century, it acquired a new orthography to distinguish it from Polish. Borrowing from Czech orthography, Lithuanian began to use "č" instead of the "cz" (pronounced "ch" in English) and "š" rather than "sz" (pronounced "sh"). Timothy Snyder, *The Reconstruction of Nations: Poland, Ukraine, Lithuania, Belarus, 1569–1999* (New Haven, Conn.: Yale University Press, 2003), 35–37.

6. Gotthard Stender (1714–96), a professor of geography and a publisher of Latvian grammar books, warrants mention for his fairy tales for Latvian peasants. In 1774 he also published a "peasants' encyclopedia" titled *Augstas gudrības grāmatā no pasaules un dabas* (A Book of High Wisdom on the World and Nature), Latvia's first popular scientific book.

7. Troachic verse is alliterated, rather than using end rhymes in the German tradition.

8. On Saaremaa, Estonia's largest island, the natives have their own legend of Suur Tõll (Big Tõll), who fought a series of battles against evildoers.

9. Anatol Lieven, *The Baltic Countries: Estonia, Latvia, Lithuania, and the Path to Independence* (New Haven, Conn.: Yale University Press, 1993), 116, 121.

10. Although *Lāčplēsis* has been translated into several languages, English was not among them until 2005, when the retired Australian Professor Arthur Cropley completed a poetic translation of the Latvian epic in rhymed iambic pentameter. As of this writing it has not found a publisher.

11. With Lithuania and Poland in a virtual state of war during the 1920s and 1930s over the latter's seizure of Vilnius, Lithuanian schoolchildren read an abridged translation of *Pan Tadeusz* that removed all references to Poland and to Poles. Snyder, 78.

12. Maironis later wrote the historical dramas *Kęstutis* (1921), *Vytautas with the Crusaders* (1930), and *King Vytautas the Great* (1930), which are still performed today.

13. Other leading writers associated with the Young Estonia movement include the poet Ernst Enno (1875–1934), the nature poet Villem Grünthal-Ridala (1885–1942), and the prose writers Jaan Oks (1884–1918) and Aino Kallas (1878–1956).

14. See Modris Eksteins, *Rites of Spring: The Great War and the Birth of the Modern Age* (Boston: Houghton Mifflin, 1989).

15. Other noteworthy Estonian prose writers of the independence era include the humorous storyteller Oskar Luts (1887–1953), the realistic short story writer Peet Vallak (1893–1959), and August Mälk (1900–87), the author of a series of historical novels.

16. See Astrida B. Stahnke, *Aspazija: Her Life and Her Drama* (Lanham, Md.: University Press of America, 1984).

17. Anette Reinsch, "Adaptation of a Latvian Classis: *Baltā grāmatā* during the Nazi and Soviet Occupations," in *The Baltic Countries under Occupation: Nazi and Soviet Rule 1939–1991,* ed. Anu Mai Kõll (Stockholm: Almqvist & Wiksell, 2003), 269–77.

18. Rolfs Ekmanis, *Latvian Literature under the Soviets, 1940–75* (Belmont, Mass.: Nordland Publishing Co., 1978), 44.

19. These include Jaan Undusk (b. 1958), Peeter Sauter (b. 1962), Mart Kivastik (b. 1963), Jüri Ehlvest (b. 1967), Aarne Ruben (b. 1971), and Mehis Heinsaar (b. 1973). Estonia's leading poets include Juhan Viiding (1948–95), Doris Kareva (b. 1958), and Triin Soomets (b. 1969).

20. Juris Sileniks, "World Literature in Review: Latvian," *World Literature Today,* 64, no. 3 (Summer 1990): 501.

21. Other leading Latvian prose writers of the late Soviet era included Regīna Ezera (b. 1930), Aivars Kalve (b.1937), Egīls Lukjanskis (b. 1937), Andris Jakubāns (b. 1941), and Skaidrīte Kaldupe (b. 1922).

22. Lithuania's most important postwar playwright was Juozas Grušas (1901–86). Following in the tradition of Vincas Krėvė-Mickevičius and Balys Sruoga, his plays such as *Barbora Radvilaitė* (1971), set in sixteenth-century Poland-Lithuania, dealt mostly with historical themes. However, his tragicomedy *Love, Jazz and the Devil*

(1967) deals with the moral conflict between the teen generation of the 1960s, whose only values appear to be themselves and their excesses, and their parents.

23. Leonid Donskis, *Identity and Freedom: Mapping Nationalism and Social Criticism in Twentieth-Century Lithuania* (New York: Routledge, 2002), 121.

SELECTED READINGS

Cedrins, Inara, ed. *Contemporary Latvian Poetry.* Iowa City: University of Iowa Press, 1984.

Ekmanis, Rudolfs. *Latvian Literature under the Soviets, 1940–1975.* Belmont, Mass.: Nordland Publishing Company, 1978.

Kareva, Doris, ed. *Windship with Oars of Light: Modern Estonian Poetry.* Tallinn: Huma, 2001.

Kurman, George. "Estonian Literature." In *A Case Study of a Soviet Republic: The Estonian SSR,* ed. Tõnu Parming and Elmar Järvesoo. Boulder, Colo.: Westview Press, 1978.

Nirk, Endel. *Estonian Literature,* 2nd edition. Tallinn: Perioodika, 1987.

Rubulis, Aleksis. *Baltic Literature: A Survey of Finnish, Estonian, Latvian, and Lithuanian Literatures.* Notre Dame, Ind.: University of Notre Dame Press, 1970.

Silbajoris, Rimvydas. "Post-Soviet Literature in Lithuania: An Overview." *World Literature Today,* 72, no. 2 (Spring 1998).

Sruoginis, Laima, ed. *Lithuania: In Her Own Words.* Vilnius: Tyto alba, 1997.

———. *The Earth Remains: An Anthology of Contemporary Lithuanian Prose.* Vilnius: Tyto alba, 2002.

Other Sources and Websites

Lituanus has a wonderful archive of articles on Baltic culture in general and Lithuanian literature in particular: www.ltuanus.org. *Estonian Literary Magazine* (ELM) addresses recent developments in Estonian literature: www.einst.ee/historic/literary/index.html. The literary journal *Soviet Literature,* no. 1 (1989) is dedicated to the literature and art of Estonia and features a selection of Estonian short stories, poems, and essays from the 1980s. The Spring 2004 issue of *Descant* focused on recent Latvian literature. Also see the academic journals *World Literature in Review, World Literature Today,* and *Journal of Baltic Studies.*

6

Media and Cinema

WITH POPULATIONS OF only 3.6 million, 2.3 million, and 1.35 million people, the media markets of Lithuania, Latvia, and Estonia are among the smallest in Europe. During the transition in the 1990s from a system in which the state owned and operated nearly all media to one that is privatized and pluralistic, many of the region's newspapers, television stations, and film studios struggled. While continuing to cope with the financial challenges arising from the collapse of state subsidies, the increasing reliance on advertising in tiny commercial markets, and the competitive pressures of the global marketplace, the Baltic media landscape appears to have stabilized. The Baltic countries now enjoy an impressive variety of newspapers, magazines, television channels, radio stations, and Internet portals that are able to meet most of their citizens' needs for information and entertainment. Even the film industry, which appeared to be idle in the late 1990s, is making a modest comeback. While the contemplative cinema of Estonia, Latvia, and Lithuania will never commercially outperform Hong Kong action films, Hollywood blockbusters, or Bollywood musicals, the appearance in recent years of several high-quality films with broad international appeal augurs well for the future of Baltic cinema, where the release of any film is truly a national event.

THE MEDIA

Historical Foundations

The foundations for the emergence after 1918 (and again after 1991) of a regular national press in the Baltic countries began to be laid more than three centuries ago, when most Estonians, Latvians, and Lithuanians were illiterate and much of the region was dominated by elites who spoke foreign tongues. Until the emergence of a native intelligentsia in the second half of the nineteenth century, journalism in Estonia and Latvia was the preserve of the Baltic Germans, who had their own press in Riga since 1588 and in Tallinn since 1631. Their first newspaper was titled *Ordinari Freitags* (later *Donnerstags*) *Post-Zeitung,* which appeared from 1675 to 1678 and was probably published in Tallinn. By the early 1680s Riga's German-speaking community had begun to publish the newspapers *Rigische Novellen* and *Rigische Montags* (later *Donnerstags*); this was followed by the appearance of *Revalsche Post-Zeitung* in Tallinn in 1689.

Because of the devastation wrought by the Great Northern War, no newspapers or magazines were published at all in either Estonia or Latvia between 1710 and 1761; in the last third of the century, however, periodical publishing began to recover. While German-language newspapers such as *Rigasche Zeitung* (1778–1889) and *Dörptsche Zeitung* (1789–1875) enjoyed a dependable market of educated readers, the absence of literate Estonians and Latvians rendered impractical the creation of a native-language press. Nevertheless, 41 issues of an Estonian-language magazine called *Lühhike öppetus* (Short Instruction) were published in Põltsamaa in 1766–67, around the same time as the appearance of the Latvian-language magazine *Latviešu Ārste* (Latvian Doctor). It was not until 1806, however, that the first Estonian-language newspaper, *Tarto maa-rahwa Näddali-Leht* (Tartu Countryman's Weekly), began to be published by German intellectuals for simple rural readers.[1] The first Latvian-language newspaper, *Latviešu Avīzes* (Latvian Newspaper), was first published in 1822 and remained active until World War I.

Due to Lithuania's different historical conditions, journalism developed differently there. In Vilnius a Polish-language newspaper, *Kurier Litewski* (Lithuanian Courier) was published from 1760 to 1763, and other newspapers were published in French, German, Russian, and Yiddish during the first half of the nineteenth century. Although Protestant missionary periodicals had been in circulation in Prussian-ruled Lithuanian Minor since the 1820s, the first Lithuanian-language weekly newspapers did not appear until 1849, when *Keleivis* (The Traveler) began to be published in Königsberg (Kaliningrad), followed by *Lietuviškas Prietelis* (The Friend of Lithuanians), which was published in Russian-ruled Lithuania proper. With the imposition of the press ban following the Polish-Lithuanian rebellion of 1863–64, all Lithuanian-language publishing in the Russian-ruled areas of Lithuania was prohibited for the next 40 years.

During a period when Lithuanians were smuggling printed materials, including the nationalist periodicals *Aušra* (Dawn) and *Varpas* (Bell), over the border from Lithuania Minor, journalism in Latvia and Estonia was maturing and becoming politicized. In Estonia newspapers such as *Perno Postimees* (Pärnu Courier) and *Eesti Postimees* (Estonian Courier), both founded by Johann Voldemar Jannsen, played pivotal roles in the Estonian national awakening of the 1860s and 1870s. While these newspapers were at first conservative and religious, advocating cooperation with the Baltic Germans, Carl Robert Jakobson's newspaper *Sakala,* founded in 1878, was more radical in its advocacy of social and political reform.

The Latvian awakeners inspired—and drew their inspiration from—the influential *Pēterburgas Avīzes* (St. Petersburg Newspaper), which was published in the Russian capital. Because of the controversies provoked by its editors Krišjānis Valdemārs and Krišjānis Barons, *Pēterburgas Avīzes* was published for only three years (1862 to 1865) before it was shut down. While these and other newspapers discussed a variety of cultural, economic, and political (often anti-German) themes, all materials published in the Russian Empire were subject to censorship and Russian press laws. Meanwhile the Lithuanian-language press, which was banned in Russia until 1904, thrived in American cities such as New York and Chicago, where from 1884 onward Lithuanian immigrant communities founded their own periodicals. These were, unsurprisingly, usually supportive of the Lithuanian nationalist movement and uncompromisingly critical of tsarist rule.

Newspaper publishing developed rapidly during the first decade of the twentieth century, and especially during the years that followed the first Russian revolution of 1905. Estonia, for example, had just one daily newspaper in 1900, but by 1907 there were 12. With the appearance of a wide variety of dailies, weeklies, and specialized magazines—many of which, especially in Lithuania, were associated with the new political parties and movements that emerged after the first revolution—the basic structure of the national presses of Estonia, Latvia, and Lithuania was created.

During the independence era from 1918 to 1940, hundreds of newspapers and other periodicals appeared in the Baltic countries in numerous languages—including Russian, German, Yiddish, Hebrew, and Polish—under relatively free conditions.[2] Because of the small Baltic markets and the unstable economic conditions of that era, many failed to last more than a year or two. Freedom of the press, although curtailed during the 1930s, was entirely obliterated during the Soviet era, when Baltic media served the propaganda needs of the Soviet state and thus were subject to stringent censorship. Most prewar journalists were killed or deported, or defected to the West, and even the professionally educated journalists who emerged during and after the thaw of the Khrushchev era remained inadequately trained.

While the media were by no means free and its content—at least until the 1980s—was often boring and predictable, there was, on the other hand, a lot of it, as newspapers and print periodicals, book publishing, broadcast media, and film studios were heavily subsidized by the Soviet state. What was not allowed to be published officially was sometimes published underground. Lithuanian dissidents were the most active publishers of these *samizdat* materials and were responsible for the *Chronicle of the Lithuanian Catholic Church*, which appeared from 1972 to 1988. Thus, when the Baltic states attained their independence in 1991 the media structure they inherited was relatively well developed, even if Western journalistic standards were at first lacking.

The Contemporary Press

The perestroika and glasnost years represented the peak of press circulation in each of the Baltic states. Newspapers and journals proliferated along with cultural networks and, after 1988, New political organizations. Indeed, the role played by the media in mobilizing the Estonian, Latvian, and Lithuanian populations during the national "reawakenings" is inestimable. Freed from the censorship that had for more than 40 years rendered impossible any honest discussions of the past, present, and future, Baltic newspapers such as *Atmoda* (the weekly newspaper of the Latvian Popular Front) began to publish the appeals and resolutions of the newly emerging political movements, while television and radio stations broadcast sessions of the Baltic parliaments and reported on the protests and mass meetings.

After the Baltic countries attained their independence in 1991, however, the main role of the media shifted from culture and politics to entertainment and economic news. During the 1990s newspapers proliferated and became more diverse; state television and radio channels were privatized as ties with Moscow were cut; state subsidies shriveled, and the media became driven by advertising and commercial concerns. While inflation ate away at the standard of living and the prices of newspapers and magazines skyrocketed, periodical circulations plummeted as television viewing and radio listening increased.

The price that Baltic media paid for their political independence was a new dependence on their unusually small and unreliable markets. As a result, many media outlets drastically downsized or closed down entirely; others merged or came under the control of foreign, typically Scandinavian, media corporations such as Schibsted (Norway), Orkla Media (Norway), the Bonnier Group (Sweden), the Modern Times Group (Sweden), and Polsat Media (Polish-Dutch). Yet it can be argued that the outcome has been a more professional, politically independent, and diverse media environment that better meets the needs of Estonian, Latvian, and Lithuanian media consumers. The situation for Russian speakers is somewhat different: while they are able to maintain their own press, broadcast laws in the Baltic countries favor the native languages. Although it is likely that these conditions have encouraged some Russian speakers to learn the local languages and become more attuned to local developments, others continue to get most of their information from foreign (Russian) sources, which in turn may reinforce their sense of alienation.

With nearly three million speakers of the native language spread out over its four regions, Lithuania has by far the largest and most diffuse media market in the Baltics. While the Latvian market is dominated by Riga, and Estonia's is concentrated in Tallinn and the northwest, Lithuanian media have a more local character. In addition to its more than 60 local newspapers, in 2005 Lithuania had three national daily newspapers—*Lietuvos rytas, Respublika,* and *Lietuvos aidas*—and two tabloids: *Lietuvos žinios* and *Vakaro žinios.* The largest of the dailies is *Lietuvos rytas,* a former communist youth organization newspaper (then called *Komjaunimo tiesa*) that is now left-leaning but pro-market. As the first daily to be privatized, *Lietuvos rytas* now claims more than 50 percent of the audience share and controls several regional newspapers. Its main competitors are *Respublika,* an investigative tabloid that was originally associated with the *Sąjūdis* movement but that now claims to be nonpartisan, and *Lietuvos aidas,* a right-wing newspaper that was first published in 1988 by the Lithuanian parliament. The leading Russian-language newspapers in Lithuania are the daily *Ekspres–Nedelia* and the weeklies *Obzor* and *Litovskii Kur'er',* while the best-selling Polish daily is *Kurier Wilenski.*

Lithuania's regional newspapers were mostly founded during the Soviet era and generally fare much better than regional and local newspapers in Latvia and Estonia. Lithuania's most significant regional newspaper is *Kauno diena,* a high-quality newspaper that is published in Kaunas but that has steadily penetrated the national market. In 1998 it was acquired by Orkla Media, a Norwegian enterprise, while *Verslo žinios,* Lithuania's leading business newspaper, was acquired by the Bonnier Media Group of Sweden.

Latvian newspapers were completely privatized by 1992 but remain divisible into two groups, Latvian-language and Russian. A striking characteristic of the Latvian press is its concentration in Riga, where more than one-third of the country lives. Regional newspapers such as *Kurzemes Vārds* and *Zemgales Ziņas* combined garner only about 30 percent of the daily newspaper audience. Most of these are owned by larger media groups.[3] About one-third of the local and regional newspapers are owned by the joint stock company (JSC) Diena, most of which is in turn owned by the Bonnier Group. JSC Diena's most important products are the national daily *Diena,* a high-quality centrist newspaper with considerable editorial independence, and the evening paper *Spogulis.* While *Diena* presently enjoys the widest circulation in Latvia, its main competition is *Latvijas Avīze* (formerly *Lauku Avīze*), a nationalist, conservative, and anti-Russian paper that focuses mostly on rural concerns. Latvia's third-largest national daily is *Neatkarīgā Rīta Avīze,* a Latvian-language broadsheet that is owned by Mediju Nams and the printing facility Preses Nams, both of which are in turn owned by the Latvian oil transshipment company, Ventspils Nafta—which in turn is believed to be controlled by Ventspils mayor Aivars Lembergs.[4] While the evening tabloid *Vakara Ziņas,* which was the country's first "yellow" newspaper, enjoys a wide readership, the more sober *Latvijas Vestnesis,* published by the Latvian state, has relatively few readers. Latvia's leading weeklies are *Ieva,* which is marketed to women, and *Privātā Dzīve,* a celebrity tabloid.

Latvia has the largest Russian-speaking media market in the Baltics, consisting of nearly one million people. While the Latvian-language press has consolidated in recent years, the Russian press has remained fragmented and unstable, as daily and weekly newspapers appear and then seem suddenly to disappear. Another area of contrast between the Latvian- and Russian-language press is the pattern of ownership: whereas the Bonnier Group of Sweden has interests in a number of Latvian newspapers through its majority ownership of JSC Diena, the privately owned Russian-language press in Latvia has enjoyed only limited—if increasing—cooperation with foreign (Russian) media concerns.

The Russian-language dailies with the widest circulation in Latvia are the scandal tabloids *Vesti segodnia* (published by Fenster) and *Chas* (published by Petits), and the privately owned newspaper *Telegraf,* which was called *Respublika* back in the Soviet era. The leading Russian-language business newspapers are the pink broadsheet *Bizness & Baltija,* which owns an FM radio station of the same name, and the weekly *Kommersant Baltic* (published by Fenster). These Russian-language newspapers—like several others that have already come and gone—have attempted to fill in the space left by the disappearance of *Sovetskaia molodezh,* which for many years was circulated throughout the USSR.

During the past decade or so the Estonian press has been transformed in much the same way as the Latvian press: it is bifurcated into two market segments, one Estonian and the other Russian-language; newspaper circulations have dramatically decreased; after a period of privatization and proliferation the press consolidated, much of it coming under the control of large, usually foreign-owned, media enterprises. Of the country's six daily newspapers, four are in Estonian and two are in Russian. The leading Estonian-language daily is *Postimees,* a newspaper with a history that echoes that of the Estonian nation. Founded in Pärnu in 1857, the weekly newspaper *Perno Postimees* was published until 1885, while a sister version called *Eesti Postimees* was created in Tartu in 1863. During the Soviet era the latter was transformed into a Communist Party newspaper (*Edasi*), reverting to its traditional name only in 1989. Privatized in the early 1990s and relocated to the capital in 1997, *Postimees* is now owned by Schibsted.

The other Estonian-language dailies are the popular *SL Õhtuleht,* an evening tabloid that has been in existence since the year 2000, *Eesti Päevaleht,* a financially troubled paper that resulted from a 1995 merger of three Estonian dailies, and the pink-paged *Äripäev,* which was founded in 1989 and is Estonia's leading business newspaper. The tabloid *Eesti Ekspress,* which was also founded in 1989, is one of two popular Estonian-language weeklies. The other is *Maaleht,* which has been discussing rural issues and events since 1987 but is nearly invisible in the cities. Among the nearly 20 Russian-language newspapers in Estonia are the dailies *Estoniia* and *Molodezh Estoniia* and the weekly newspapers *Den za dnom* and *Vesti nedelia plius.*

Since the late 1990s Scandinavian media enterprises have taken over numerous Estonian media outlets. Norway's Schibsted controls *Postimees,* whose publishing group, known as Eesti Meedia, controls about one-third of the nationwide press market, including 50 percent of the profitable *SL Õhtuleht.* Sweden's Bonnier Group is part-owner of *Eesti Päevaleht;* it also indirectly owns the business newspaper *Äripäev* as well as its Lithuanian and Latvian counterparts, *Verslo žinios* and *Dienas Bizness.* Many television and radio stations are controlled by foreign media concerns as well.

Although state control of the media and its concomitant dangers disappeared with the demise of the USSR, the growing concentration of media ownership remains a source of concern. The mergers described may have saved some struggling newspapers (while pushing local those like Lithuania's *Kauno žinios* out of the market), but there are concerns that this trend is a threat to pluralism and that the resulting commercialization of the print media encourages trivialization and sensationalism. Indeed, market pressures have forced Baltic newspapers increasingly to emphasize crime, scandals, and human interest stories at the expense of hard news. Moreover, the tightening job market for journalists leaves them vulnerable to pressure from their employers. Thus, while state censorship is absent in the Baltics today, self-censorship has not disappeared.

On the other hand, it may be argued that the foreign acquisition of Baltic media outlets has helped ensure stability and greater financial transparency, which in turn probably creates more favorable conditions for balanced reporting. Thanks in part to the journalistic traditions of Scandinavia, Baltic newspapers are largely editorially independent and the media in all three countries have consistently been rated "free" by Freedom House. Despite the trend toward consolidation, Lithuanians, Latvians, Estonians, and Russian speakers still have access to a wide variety of daily and weekly newspapers, many of which have achieved financial stability as their circulations begin to recover. In addition, the weekly newspaper *Baltische Rundschau* keeps Germans up to date on current Baltic events, while English-speaking tourists and expatriates have the weekly newspapers *The Baltic Times* and the magazines *The Baltic Review* and the free *City Paper,* which are available in kiosks and some of the more expensive hotels in Tallinn, Riga, and Vilnius.

Just as the choice of newspapers has improved since Soviet times, the selection of magazines on display at newspaper stands has vastly improved since the Soviet era, when cheaply made magazines were targeted to broad audiences (children of various ages, women) rather than to specific interests. Each of the Baltic countries has several weekly and monthly magazines devoted to news, business, television, and entertainment. The largest share of the magazine market in the Baltic states, however, now belongs to women's magazines. In Latvia, for example, the Soviet women's magazine *Sieviete* (Woman) has been eclipsed by magazines such as *Zeltene,* based on a journal of the same title published in the 1920s and 1930s, and *Santa,* a Western-style magazine that is targeted to an urban female audience. Russian-speaking women in Latvia have *Lilit,* which resembles the American magazine *Cosmopolitan,* and *Lubliu* (I Love). The leading women's magazines in Estonia are *Eesti Naine* (Estonian Woman) and *Kodukiri* (Home Magazine), while Lithuania's top women's magazines are *Moteris* (Woman) and *Panelė* (Miss). *Cosmopolitan* now appears in all three Baltic languages in addition to Russian.

The Baltic countries' magazine markets are even more concentrated than the region's newspaper markets. Titles published by Zurnals Santa, such as *Santa, Ieva,* and *Privātā Dzīve,* dominate the Latvian magazine market. Likewise, Ajakirjade Kirjastus, a joint venture that brings together the Ekspress Group (owned by Hans H. Luik) and Eesti Media (owned mostly by Schibsted), captured two-thirds of the Estonian magazine market in 2004 with its 20 titles—mostly women's, youth, and home and garden magazines. In each of the Baltic countries the best-selling weekly periodicals of all tend to be TV guides.

News Agencies and Electronic Media

Many of the stories carried by Baltic newspapers originate with the *Baltic News Service* (*BNS*), a news agency produces 500–700 news items daily in the Baltic languages as well as in Russian and English. Founded in Moscow in 1990 by a group of Baltic students, *BNS* is now owned by a variety of Finnish and Swedish media concerns. Today it is headquartered in Tallinn and also has regional offices in Riga and Vilnius. Until recently, each of the Baltic states had its own individual news agency—*LETA* (Latvia), *ELTA* (Lithuania), and

ETA (Estonia)—but the financially troubled *ETA* was shut down in 2003, leaving Estonia with only *BNS*. One of the most popular information portals on the Internet is *Delfi,* a trans-Baltic news service that is accessible in all three Baltic languages plus Russian.[5] Some of the other popular information portals are Google, takas.lt, Sala.lt, tvnet.lv, and elinks.lv.

Young people in the Baltic countries, and especially in Estonia, have embraced the new developments in communications technology that have taken place since the 1990s. With Internet cafes dotting the Estonian urban landscape, Estonia (or E-stonia) is one of the most Internet-connected countries in Eastern Europe. In an effort to expand computer use to the countryside, a project was launched in 2002 to provide free basic computer and Internet education to 100,000 Estonian adults. By early 2003 more than one-third of the Estonian population had a home computer, and more than two-thirds of these were connected to the Internet. According to a 2004 study by the Estonian marketing research company EMOR, 52 percent of the Estonian population between ages 6 and 74 used the Internet. This figure compared with 27 percent for Latvia and 29 percent for Lithuania, where the fastest gains are being made.[6] Many Baltic radio stations are accessible through the Internet and nearly all the major daily newspapers have Internet sites.

Radio

The initial launching of radio broadcasts in Estonia, Latvia, and Lithuania in the mid-1920s coincided with that of most other countries, but the medium was not really developed until the Soviet era, when radio, like television, became not only an informational, educational, and cultural medium but was primarily an instrument of propaganda.[7] Until nearly the end of the Soviet era all telecommunications were under strict state control, as all radio and television frequencies belonged to the state. However, the privatization of broadcast media in the early 1990s resulted in the rapid proliferation of radio and television stations before a period of consolidation at the end of the 1990s, when much of the broadcast media, like the Baltic press, came under foreign control. Estonia's *TV1,* Latvia's *LNT,* and Lithuania's *Baltijos TV* are presently owned by Polsat, a Polish-Dutch media concern, while the *TV3* television network and the radio networks *Power Hit Radio* and *Star FM,* which broadcast throughout the region, are all owned by Sweden's Modern Times media group. Indeed, with every turn of the Baltic media kaleidoscope another newspaper, radio station, or television channel comes under the control of an international conglomerate or a local media baron like Latvia's Aivars Lembergs or Estonia's Hans H. Luik.

One thing is clear, however, and that is that the Balts love radio just as they love the music it magically transmits. Perhaps this mania for having the radio on at all times and in all places is partly because of the relative newness of the notion of radio as a source of music. Today music makes up the bulk of the programming on commercial stations, whose broadcasts can be heard in boutiques, sidewalk cafes, and in coffee shops in Vilnius, Tallinn, and Riga, as well as in smaller cities. A long bus trip can be maddening to the weary traveler, as many bus and taxi drivers appear to be indifferent to whether or not their passengers want to hear the bouncy beats of Russian pop or Euro dance music delivered by the tinny, crackling speakers that are invariably located directly overhead.

In Estonia three radio networks control the major portion of the market: state-owned Estonian Radio, the Trio Group (owned by Eesti Meedia, which is mostly owned by Schibsted), and Sky Media. Estonian Radio (*Eesti Raadio*) has been broadcasting since 1926 and remains, like Estonian Television, a public broadcasting organization that now has four stations. Its flagship channel is *Vikerraadio,* a public service station that is targeted to the general public. The oldest and still the most popular station in Estonia, *Vikerraadio* focuses on news, information, education, and entertainment. Its Russian-language counterpart is *Raadio 4. Raadio 2* serves the youth market with its format of popular music, while *Klassikaraadio* is oriented toward high culture.

Of Estonia's more than 30 private radio stations, the first to be established was *Raadio Kuku,* which began broadcasting in Tartu in 1992 and now broadcasts in Tallinn as well. Owned by the Trio Group, *Raadio Kuku* is oriented toward an educated audience and remains the main competitor with Estonia's public stations. The Trio Group also owns *Raadio Elmar,* whose programming consists mainly of popular music for a middle-aged audience. Other popular Estonian-language radio stations include *Pereraadio* (Christian programming), *Raadio Uuno* (Top 40), *Radio Mania* (rock), and the adult contemporary stations *Sky Plus, Power Hit Radio, Star FM,* and *Raadio Eeva.* While all of them broadcast in Tallinn, most have networks that reach other parts of Estonia as well. Estonia's four commercial Russian-language radio channels are *Radio 100 FM, Sky Radio, Russkoe Radio,* and *Radio Katiusha.*

Latvian radio broadcasting is similarly divided between public radio, whose focus is informational, and the commercial stations, whose content is overwhelmingly musical. Latvia's public station is Latvian Radio (*Latvijas Radio*), which, like its Estonian counterpart, broadcasts on several frequencies and therefore is the easiest to receive throughout the country. Although its main market is older listeners, Latvian Radio offers a variety of programs on its four channels: *Radio 1* is mostly a news station, but it also plays Latvian music; *Radio 2* seeks to compete with the commercial stations and features mixed programming; *Radio 3* is a classical station; and *Radio 4,* also known as *Doma laukums,* features programming in Russian and other minority languages.

In early 2005 there were seven commercial radio stations with national coverage in Latvia. With three stations based in Riga, the leading commercial network is *Radio SWH,* whose stations, like Latvia's second most-popular station, *Star FM,* have an adult contemporary format. *Capital FM* plays European hits, *SWH Rock* prefers English-language rock music, and Christian music is broadcast on *Latvijas Kristīgais Radio* (Christian Radio). Several stations aim at the Russian-speaking audience, including *Mix 102.7* (Euro hits), *Radio SWH+* (mixed programming), *Top Radio* (European dance music), and *Radio PIK* (pop). For those who quickly tire of the soul-deadening repetitiveness of European dance music and bouncy Russian pop, there is *Radio NABA,* an alternative Latvian-language station run by students at the University of Latvia.

As in the other Baltic countries, Lithuania's public radio broadcasting network, which is operated by Lithuanian Radio and Television (LRT), commands a large proportion of the audience share. Lithuanian Radio broadcasts on numerous frequencies throughout the country on its two national radio stations. *LR1* is a general public service station that broadcasts information and music, and *LR2* ("*Klasika*") is oriented toward high culture. While Lithuanian Radio is state-owned and about 80 percent state-financed, the country's commercial broadcast stations are owned mostly by individuals or small groups of shareholders rather than by the large media conglomerates that now control many of the region's newspapers and television stations.

Nevertheless, two entities dominate the Lithuanian commercial radio market: the Achema Group, which owns more than 30 enterprises in various fields as well as the *Radiocentras* and *RC2* radio stations, and Hubertas Grušnys, who owns the national radio stations *M-1, M-1 Plus,* and *Lietus.* These commercial radio stations mostly play Lithuanian, European, and English-language pop music and adult contemporary. The national radio network *Pūkas,* which is owned by Kęstutis Pūkas, plays Lithuanian pop, while *Pūkas-2* and *Relax FM* offer a jazz/blues format. *Žiniu Radias,* which is owned by the American Equitable Finance Corporation, has a news/talk format, and *Marijos Radios* offers Christian programming. Lithuania's Russian speakers can listen to contemporary hits on *Russkoje Radio Baltija* (another Achema concern), which leads the Vilnius market, while *Znad Wilii* broadcasts a variety of programs in Polish. Given the small size of the Lithuanian advertising market, it is difficult to imagine that the country will be able to sustain 46 (as of 2004) commercial radio stations indefinitely.

Television

Television began broadcasting in the Baltic countries in the mid-1950s and remained one of the Soviet government's most important instruments of propaganda into the mid-1980s. During the Soviet era each of the Baltic republics had only one state television station located in the capital, but that changed with the reestablishment of independent Baltic states and the enthusiasm for privatization that accompanied it. With too many television channels struggling to compete in the tiny Baltic markets, the industry began to consolidate in the late 1990s and appears now to have achieved a certain degree of stability.

Television in the Baltic countries today, like radio, is divided between public, state-supported networks and private, advertising-driven stations. In addition to the public Lithuanian Television network (*LTV*), Lithuania also has three private commercial networks (*LNK, TV3*, and *Baltijos TV*) and a number of regional stations (*TV1, TV5, Tango TV, Pūkas TV*, and *KRT*). While *Tango TV* targets the youth market with music-oriented programming, the most-watched stations are *TV3* and *LNK*, each of which commands more than one-quarter of the television audience. *TV3* was founded in 1993 as Lithuania's first independent station, but it is now owned by the Modern Times Group, a Swedish concern that has also acquired television stations in Estonia and Latvia. However, it is the history of *LNK* over the past decade that best illustrates the recent history of the Baltic broadcast media: founded in 1995 and acquired by the Lithuanian media mogul Hubertas Grušnys in 1998, *LNK* was quickly sold to Marieberg Media, a subdivision of Bonnier, before being acquired by MG Baltic Investment (which also holds a majority stake in *ELTA*) in 2003.

Latvian television is similarly divided into public networks (*LTV1* and *LTV7*), national commercial television stations (*LNT, TV3*), and a series of regional channels whose broadcasts are usually limited to a few hours a day. With the exception of the financially troubled *LTV1*, whose programming is entirely in Latvian, all of Latvia's television stations have programs in both Latvian and Russian. *LTV7* provides programming in Latvia's minority languages, principally Russian. While *LNT* (*Latvijas Neatkarīgā Televizija*), the result of a 1996 merger between *NTV-5* and *PICCA-TV*, is by far the country's largest national broadcasting station, the strongest regional television station in Latvia is *TV5*, which broadcasts for the Riga region. The ownership structure of each of these stations is unclear: while 60 percent of *LNT* is owned by Polsat, another 40 percent belongs to something called Baltic Media Holdings, which is registered in the Netherlands but is believed to be a division of Rupert Murdoch's sprawling media empire.

Estonian television has only one public channel (*ETV*) and two national commercial channels (*TV3* and *Kanal 2*). Public television is primarily cultural and informative, and it is the country's main outlet for Estonian animation films and documentaries. Of the commercial stations, *TV3* (Modern Times Group) is the more economically successful, but *Kanal 2* (Schibsted) is steadily edging toward profitability as it increases its audience share. While the public station is now entirely commercial-free (in Latvia and Estonia advertising is allowed on public television) and reaches nearly the entire population, there is no regional television in Estonia, as the local media market is incapable of supporting it. Broadcasts from Finland can reach about 40 percent of the Estonian population; as sources of Western culture and information, these were very popular during the Soviet era but are considerably less popular today.

Broadcasting in the Baltic countries faces certain language restrictions. For example, Latvian law used to require that a minimum 75 percent of all commercial radio and television broadcasting be done in Latvian, but this law was repealed by the Constitutional Court in 2003. While Estonia's public television provides some Russian-language programming, the Broadcasting Act of 1994, which contain provisions aimed at the protection and development of the Estonian language and culture, mandates that broadcasts in non-Estonian languages be translated into the state language. However, it makes no reciprocal provisions for the benefit of the large Russian-speaking community. Since there are no Russian-language television stations in Estonia and since few Russians speak Estonian or tune into Estonian-language broadcasts, Russian speakers living in the larger cities (and in Latvia) turn to cable television, through which they can receive broadcasts from Moscow and St. Petersburg. Since 2004, however, Russian speakers throughout the Baltic region have been able to watch *First Baltic Channel* (*PBK*), a Russian-language station that is broadcast via satellite from Latvia. In February 2005 it launched a 24-hour music channel targeted to younger viewers.

Like people throughout the developed world, Balts are becoming increasingly addicted to television, as it is cheap and the programming is reasonably diverse and informative, as well as at least somewhat entertaining. According to a survey taken in February 2003, Estonians spend 4.5 hours per day watching television (a figure that only slightly trails the number of hours Americans spend watching television), while Latvians watch just under 4 hours per day of TV and Lithuanians less than 3.5 hours.[8] The region's most avid TV watchers, however, are Russian speakers, most of whom have cable TV in order to watch broadcasts from Russia.

But just what are these people watching? In Estonia, the most popular television programs are news programs, but most television in the Baltic countries—like television everywhere—consists of light entertainment. While public television provides viewers with news, documentaries, and educational and cultural programming, commercial TV in each of the Baltic countries is saturated with imported programming and locally produced imitations of popular American and European shows. The entertainment value of imported programming, however, is severely diminished by the tendency in Lithuania and Latvia to use voice-overs rather than subtitles. Although cheaper than subtitles, dubbed shows often feature a single voice for all characters, male or female, and there is usually little attempt to synchronize the dubbed words with lip movement. Estonia, on the other hand, emulates Scandinavia, where foreign shows are usually subtitled.

One of the biggest players in the Baltic television market is Sweden's Strix Television, which has produced popular reality shows such as *Expedition Robinson* (a Swedish version of the American show *Survivor*) and *The Farm* (reminiscent of *Big Brother*) for *TV3*. While European game shows (*Panorama Europe*) and Mexican soap operas (*Simply Maria*) are quite familiar to many television viewers in the Baltics, entertainment shows made in the United States continue to dominate. It is cheaper to broadcast foreign programs than to produce new ones, so TV stations in the Baltic countries broadcast an endless stream of American sitcoms (*The Golden Girls*), cop shows (*CSI: Crime Scene Investigation*), and soap operas (*Santa Barbara*).

Television is the most important medium for the advertisement of foreign commodities, ranging from chewing gum and toothpaste to cigarettes and alcohol. This flood of foreign images and products has contributed to concerns, exacerbated by the Baltic states' entry into the European Union, that that the Estonians, Latvians, and Lithuanians are undergoing a creeping process of denationalization.

BALTIC CINEMA

While television in the Baltic countries, like everywhere else, is viewed primarily as a medium for entertainment, news, and information, cinema has traditionally been revered as a medium for artistic expression. The Baltic countries have produced many fine filmmakers and actors, but the local cinema market is quite small, and thus Baltic films are rarely profitable. Thanks to generous state funding under the Soviet regime, for several decades Baltic filmmakers were spared from commercial concerns but were constrained by the political and ideological requirements of Soviet officialdom. Today the situation is the reverse: Baltic filmmakers no longer need to worry about interference by officials from the Film Section of the CPSU Central Committee's Department of Culture, but state funding evaporated after the collapse of the USSR. Competing with imported—overwhelmingly American—films for a limited audience, Baltic cinema struggled during the 1990s. In the early twenty-first century, however, it appears to be staging a modest comeback as the local economies recover and audiences, increasingly tired of Hollywood productions, yearn for something they can call their own.

Early History

The history of cinema in the Baltics is nearly as old as cinema in the rest of Europe: short films were created in Estonia in 1908, in Lithuania in 1909, and in Latvia in 1910, and by 1914 all the major Baltic cities had their own cinemas. While Baltic audiences were able to watch newsreels, documentaries, and short films (mostly foreign-made), the first locally produced feature films were not screened until the mid-1920s and were produced on a regular basis only starting in the 1960s. The origins of Baltic cinema are indeed rather modest. Johannes Pääsuke (1892–1918), who created the first Estonian documentary in 1912 and two years later created a primitive, short satire called *A Bear Hunt in Pärnumaa,* is sometimes regarded as the father of Estonian film; however, that appellation might equally be applied to Konstantin Märska (1896–1951), who in 1924 directed Estonia's first full-length feature film, called *Shadows of the Past* (it has not survived), as well as a number of documentaries for the state-subsidized Estonian Culture Film studio (1931). Despite the work of these pioneers, it is Theodor Luts's *Young Eagles* (1927), a stylish patriotic film set during Estonia's War of Independence, that is generally regarded as the cornerstone of Estonian cinema.

Lithuania's first important filmmaker was Jurgis Linartas, the director of films such as *The Soldier, Lithuania's Defender* (1928), and *Onytė and Jonelis* (1931). The latter was Lithuania's first full-length feature film, in which the main roles were played by actors from the State Theater. The first Latvian feature film, on the other hand, was a largely amateur production directed by the Latvia-born Lithuanian Aleksandrs Rusteiķis (1892–1958). Influenced by Sergei Eisenstein's *October,* Rusteiķis's film *Lāčplēsis* (1930), whose title is derived from the Latvian national epic, is a love story that glorifies the birth of the Latvian state. While Baltic cinema developed quickly during the first decade of independence, the modest markets and the onset of the global depression of the 1930s brought the production of feature films to a standstill. The only important production during this period was the Latvian classic *The Fisherman's Son* (1939, dir. Vilis Lapenieks), which was completed just before the Baltic states were incorporated into the USSR.

Soviet Film

The Soviet authorities were well aware of cinema's propaganda potential— the artistic works of the Riga-born filmmaker Sergei Eisenstein are among the most prominent examples—and wasted little time in setting up filmmaking institutions in the USSR's newest republics. While the Lithuanian Film Studio (originally founded as the Documentary Film Studio in Kaunas, it later moved to Vilnius), the Riga Documentary Film Studio, and Tallinnfilm were immediately created during the first year of the occupation, the Balts themselves were hardly involved in the creative process during the first two decades of Soviet rule, for the filmmakers were mostly Russians from the Soviet interior whose job was to produce propaganda pieces that depicted the victory of socialism. Thus, during the 1940s and most of the 1950s nearly all the films shown on Baltic screens—with the exception of imported Russian feature films—were newsreels and documentaries. While "Lithuanian" films such as *Dawn Over the Nemunas River* (1953, dir. Aleksandr Faintsimmer) and *Ignotas Has Returned Home* (1956, dir. Aleksandr Razumnyi) were produced in collaboration with the major Moscow and Leningrad film studios, it was only in 1957 that Soviet Lithuania was able independently to produce its first full-length feature film, *Blue Horizon,* directed by Vytautas Mikalauskas.

Despite the fact that local filmmakers now enjoyed greater artistic control, the State Committee for Cinematography (Goskino) in Moscow provided the money and, along with Glavlit (the state censorship body) and the CPSU Department of Culture, had the final say about whether or not the resulting product would be released. Indeed, many films made in the USSR were shelved or enjoyed only limited circulation. Since films had to meet the ideological requirements of the Soviet regime, typical Latvian fare included movies such as *The Story of a Latvian Rifleman* (1957, dir. Pavels Armands), which was about the fight for social justice at the time of Latvia's birth, and *"Tobago" Changes Its Course* (1965, dir. Aleksandrs Leimanis), a film set in the summer of 1940 as Latvian sailors returned home to what had become Soviet Latvia.

While Lithuanian films of the 1950s also focused on politically correct social themes, by the 1960s and 1970s historical concerns had moved to the forefront of Lithuanian cinema. A classic of this period that highlights the Lithuanians' concern about their past—and future—was Marijonas Giedrys's (b. 1933) *Herkus Mantas* (1972), a historical drama about an uprising by the ancient Prussians, whose sad fate was to be assimilated or exterminated by their German conquerors. The country's most popular and influential filmmaker during the Soviet era was Vytautas Žalakevičius (1930–96), the director of movies such as *The Chronicle of One Day* (1963) and *Nobody Wanted to Die* (1966). By the early 1980s Žalakevičius had even achieved international recognition—no small feat for Baltic filmmakers in a country where the bulk of the resources went to the major Russian studios, Mosfilm and Lenfilm—for films such as *The Story of a Stranger* (1980), an adaptation of a Chekhov story. While his films launched the careers of actors such as Regimantas Adomaitis, Bronius Babkauskas, Donatas Banionis, Vaclovas Blėdis, Juozas Budraitis, Algimantas Masiulis, and Laimonas Noreika, as director of the Lithuanian Film School Žalakevičius also influenced a younger generation of directors.

Among the many directors who appropriated the techniques of Žalakevičius were his contemporary Almantas Grikevičius (b. 1935) and Algimantas Puipa (b. 1951), a filmmaker of the younger generation. Grikevičius first earned acclaim for his documentaries of the mid-1960s but by the end of the decade had begun making feature films. The most notable of these are *Feelings* (1968), a film set at the end of World War II that Grikevičius codirected with Algirdas Dausa, and *Fact* (1980), another historical film about a Nazi atrocity in a Lithuanian village. Both of these films came from screenplays by Žalakevičius. Algimantas Puipa's best Soviet-era works include *The Devil's Seed* (1979)—also from a Žalakevičius screenplay—and the epic psychological drama *The Woman and Her Four Men* (1983).

In Soviet Latvia two of the most popular makers of feature films were Aleksandrs Leimanis, who in the 1970s directed a series of entertaining historical adventure films, and Gunārs Piesis (1931–96), who was best known for adaptations of fairy tales and dramas based on Latvian classics. In *Blow, Wind!* (1973), Piesis brought to the screen a love story by Latvia's most beloved author, Jānis Rainis, while *In the Shadow of Death* (1971), adapted from a story by Rūdolfs Blaumanis, explored the theme of Latvians' attachment to the sea. Jānis Streics's (b. 1936) most popular film is the comedy *Limousine the Color of St. John's Night* (1981). A light parody of the Soviet system, it has the qualities of a folk tale and is usually shown on Latvian television during the summer solstice celebrations.

Among the other celebrated Latvian directors of the Soviet era were Aivars Freimanis (b. 1936) and Rolands Kalnins (b. 1922), while the country's top actors included Eduard Pāvuls (who appeared in many of the most popular films of the 1970s), Lilita Berzina, Gunārs Cilinskis, and Kārlis Sebris. Although not as broadly popular as Leimanis, Piesis, and Freimanis, Latvia's hippie filmmakers of the early 1970s such as Andris Grīnbergs (b. 1946) are noteworthy for the unusual films they produced outside the confines of Soviet institutional cinema (see Chapter 9).[9]

While Riga Film Studio became known within the USSR for its police and detective films, it also produced some of the country's best documentaries. Indeed, documentaries and newsreels comprised the majority of films produced in the Soviet Baltic republics. While each of the Baltic republics might produce from two to five feature films in a typical year during the 1970s and 1980s, Baltic film studios created dozens of documentaries. The artistic trend in Latvian documentary films was reflected in the works of filmmakers associated with the Riga School of Documentary Cinema. It emerged in the early 1960s when filmmakers such as Uldis Brauns (b. 1932) and Herz Frank (b. 1926) began to revive the approach taken by the nearly-forgotten Russian filmmaker Dziga Vertov in the 1920s, that is, that the documentary film can be a work of art with its own unique visual language.

While the films of Brauns and Frank were rarely seen outside of Soviet Latvia, they were important in stimulating Latvian social consciousness in the decades before perestroika. Uldis Brauns launched his career with a series of artistic documentaries about labor, while Frank took a more philosophical approach to film, focusing on individuals at crucial points in their lives. Among Frank's boldest works were: *The Trace of the Soul* (1972), about a collective farm chairman; *Forbidden Zone* (1975), about a teenager who is descending into criminal activities; and *The Last Judgment* (1987), a film about a confessed murderer condemned to death, which in turn raised questions about the death penalty.

During the perestroika era, Latvia's most celebrated filmmaker internationally was Juris Podnieks (1950–92). Working first as a cameraman on some of Frank's films in the 1970s, Podnieks struck out on his own in the 1980s with a series of highly regarded documentaries before his premature death in 1992 from an automobile accident. While later films such as *Soviets* (1990) and *Homeland* (1991) explored the rising tide of Baltic nationalism, his most famous film was *Is It Easy to Be Young?* (1986), which was one of the first films candidly to explore youth culture in the USSR. It broke box office records throughout the USSR and was also viewed in the West. Another achievement was his documentary series *Hello, Do You Hear Us?* (1990), in which Podnieks examined the Soviet government's responses to crises such as the Chernobyl disaster and the earthquake in Armenia.

It was not until well into the 1960s that feature films of any artistic (or entertainment) value were made in Soviet Estonia. *Madness* (1968), a Kaljo Kiisk (b. 1925) film about a German officer who hides in a lunatic asylum while searching for a spy, has become an Estonian cult classic, while Grigori Kromanov's (1926–84) *The Last Relic* (1969), an allegorical adventure set in the sixteenth century, earned worldwide distribution and remains one of Estonia's most popular films. As Estonian cinema was becoming established it displayed a close relationship with the country's classic literature. One of the most noteworthy cinematic adaptations of the period was Leida Laius's (b. 1923) *The Milkman from Mäeküla* (1965), based on a story by Eduard Vilde.

Following a lull in the early 1970s, the latter part of the decade is regarded as the golden age of Soviet Estonian film. Kaljo Kiisk's *Ask the Dead What*

Death Costs appeared in 1977, followed two years later by Olav Neuland's *Nest of Winds* and Leida Laius's *Landlord of Kõrboja,* another historical film set in an Estonian village. The Estonian countryside is also the setting for Peeter Simm's (b. 1953) best-known Soviet-era film, *The Ideal Landscape* (1980), which portrayed a young man who became a commissar on a collective farm in the 1950s.

In the 1980s more Estonian films were set in Tallinn's urban environment, which features prominently in the frankly anti-Soviet feature film *I'm Not a Tourist, I Live Here* (1988, dir. Peeter Urbla) and the television film *Flamingo—Bird of Fortune* (1986, dir. Tõnis Kask), based on a novel by Raimond Kaugver. By the close of the Soviet era, Jaan Kolberg (b. 1958) had emerged as a promising young director for films such as *The Lost Way* (1989) and *Creditors* (1991). Among the leading actors in the cinema of Soviet Estonia were Rein Aren (1927–90), who acted in more than and 100 stage productions in addition to his 30 films, Jüri Järvet (1919–95), and Leonhard Merzin (1934–90).

The quality of Estonian feature films was uneven during the Soviet era, but Estonian animation has maintained an international reputation for many decades. The tradition dates to 1931, when a short, silent, Disney-style animated film was created called *Adventures of Juku the Dog.* However, Estonian animation did not really get off the ground for another 26 years, when Tallinnfilm created a division for puppet animation under Elbert Tuganov (b. 1920). (This tradition is now carried on by the independent Nukufilm Studio.) From his first film in 1958, titled *Little Peter's Dream,* Tuganov went on to direct more than three dozen animated films. The father of Estonian drawn animation is Rein Raamat (b. 1931), who in 1971 founded another Tallinnfilm division called Joonisfilm, which is now independent. Animated features such as *Suur Tõll* (1980), based on a character from Estonian mythology, and *Hell* (1983), which brought to life the characters inhabiting Eduard Wiiralt's etching of the 1930s (see Chapter 9), made Reimat Estonia's first internationally acclaimed animator.

Although most animated films in the USSR were made for children, there is little question that Reimat's intended audience was more mature. Indeed, Estonian animators exhibit a wide variety of visual styles and are known for their willingness to experiment. Estonia's best-known animator today is Pritt Pärn (b. 1946), who has been making animated films since *Is the Earth Round?* was released in 1977. Among his classics are *Breakfast on the Grass* (1987), which is known for its unvarnished depiction of Soviet life, *1895* (1995), a tribute to the Lumière brothers and the birth of cinema, which Pärn codirected with Janno Põldma (who directs the children's serial *Tom & Fluffy*), and *The Night of the Carrots* (1998). Other highly regarded Estonian animators include Kalju Kivi (b. 1947), Mati Kütt (b. 1947) and Rao Heidmets (b. 1956). Rijo Unt (b. 1956), the director of *Cabbagehead* (1993) and *Back to Europe* (1997), is among the country's leading puppet animators.

Contemporary Film

Now operating as independent film studios, Nukufilm and Joonisfilm are among the great success stories of post-Soviet cinema in the Baltics. More broadly, however, the 1990s was a decade of crisis for Baltic film as incomes dropped, the numbers of moviegoers plummeted dramatically, the cost of making films skyrocketed, and state funding for the cinematic arts disappeared. The nadir of Baltic filmmaking was reached in 1996, when not a single fiction film was produced in any of the Baltic states. One of the problems is the lack of permanently working cinemas: in Estonia alone the number of screens declined from 611 in 1991 to only 12 in 2003. (Latvia had 33 cinemas in 2003, while Lithuania had 65.) While the film industry shows signs of revival in the first decade of the twenty-first century, even today so few feature films are produced in the Baltic countries that the release of any movie is a major event.

With the growth of private-sector funding and the establishment in 1997 of the Estonian Film Foundation by the Ministry of Culture, Estonian film appears to have turned the corner. Although state financing of the Estonian film industry is considerably more generous than in Latvia or Lithuania, some of the recent success of Estonian cinema may be attributed to innovative financing, such as the trend toward joint film productions. For example, Peeter Simm's *Good Hands* (2002), about a Latvian woman thief and her romance with a local policeman in a small Estonian town, was a joint Latvian-Estonian production, while *Korini!* (2005), Simm's next film, was an Estonian-German coproduction. Funding for *Heart of the Bear* (2002, dir. Arvo Iho), about a European in Siberia who meets a woman untouched by civilization, came from Germany, Russia, and the Czech Republic. Finland provided much of the funding for Estonia's most expensive and most commercially successful film, *Names Engraved in Marble* (2002). Directed by one of the country's top theater directors, Elmo Nüganen (b. 1962), the film is about the schoolboy volunteers who fought in Estonia's War of Independence in 1918. The comedy *Made in Estonia* (2003, dir. Rando Pettai) also achieved commercial success, topping even the international blockbuster *The Lord of the Rings: The Two Towers* on its way to selling more tickets than any other film in Estonia in 2003.

While other Estonian films such as *Firewater* (1994, dir. Hardi Volmer), *Too Tired to Hate* (1995, dirs. Renita and Hannes Lintrop), and *All My Lenins*

(1997, dir. Hardi Volmer) failed to achieve this level of commercial success, they were shown in film festivals throughout Europe to some critical acclaim. One of the most visually beautiful and philosophically ambitious Estonian films of the 1990s was Sulev Keedus's *Georgics* (1998), about a mute boy sent to a remote Estonian island for rehabilitation. No less aesthetically appealing was Keedus's next film, *Somnambula* (2004), which was set during the Soviet reoccupation of Estonia in 1944 and depicts the plight of Estonians who fled to Sweden.

Despite the artistic successes of films by filmmakers like Hardi Volmer and Sulev Keedus, commercial success often remains elusive as the number of screens in Estonia are few and ticket prices are rising to European levels. And although Estonian films have begun to reclaim part of the domestic market, cinema in Estonia remains largely a Hollywood enterprise: thanks in part to the practices of the monopolistic film distribution company Finnkino, four out of every five new films shown on Estonian screens (accounting for nine out of ten admissions) each year are American productions or coproductions.

Latvian cinema has struggled to match even the modest successes of recent Estonian film making. Ivars Seleckis (b. 1934), Dzintra Geka (b. 1950), and Laila Pakalnina (b. 1962) have carried on the tradition of the Latvian documentary, but feature film production came to a standstill in the mid-1990s—the only exception being Aivars Freimanis's black-and-white *The Nest* (1995), a documentary-like film about a forester's family living in a nature reserve. Although conditions have improved since 1996, only a handful of Latvian feature filmmakers have been able to work consistently. Jānis Streics, who has been making films since the early 1960s, has returned in recent years with *The Mills of Fate* (1997) and *The Mystery of the Old Parish* (2000), while Una Celma (b. 1960) directed the romantic comedy *Follow Me!* (1999) and *Handful of Bullets* (2002). Laila Pakalnina, meanwhile, has ventured into feature films, directing *The Shoe* (1997), a black-and-white picture set on Latvia's sandy beaches at the height of the Cold War in the 1950s, and *The Python* (2003), a color drama that depicts the totalitarian qualities of school. Innovatively responding to the crisis in state funding for films, Latvian producers have formed several international partnerships that have yielded promising results. Una Celma's *Follow Me!* was a joint Swedish-Latvian production, while Peeter Simm's *Good Hands* (2002), which featured both Latvian and Estonian actors, was the first ever Estonian-Latvian coproduction.

Post-Soviet filmmaking in Lithuania can be said to have begun in 1987, when the 23-year-old Šarūnas Bartas (b. 1964) ended the monopoly of the Lithuanian Film Studio by founding Kinema, the first independent Lithuanian film studio. Since then Kinema has produced Bartas films such as *In Memory of a Day Gone By* (1990), *Three Days* (1991), *The Corridor* (1995), and the internationally acclaimed *Few of Us,* a French, Portuguese, and Lithuanian coproduction that was screened at the Cannes Film Festival in 1996. Kinema has also produced or coproduced films by documentary and feature film directors such as Valdas Navasaitis (b. 1960), who frequently collaborated with Bartas, and Audrius Stonys (b. 1966), whose documentary *The Land of the Blind* won the Felix Award from the European Film Academy for the best documentary film of 1992.

Established directors such as Andrius Šiuša (b. 1952) and Algimantas Puipa also continued to make films under the new circumstances. Šiuša, who is best known for documentaries such as *A Musical Marathon* (1979) and *The Picture* (1981), continued the metaphorical tradition in Lithuanian cinema with a highly acclaimed feature film titled *And He Bid You Farewell* (1993), about a man who awakens after a four-year coma to find that he is an inmate in a sanatorium on an island. Šiuša's contemporary Algimantas Puipa managed to make six feature films during the 1990s, including *The Necklace of the Wolf's Teeth* (1997) and the commercially successful *Elze's Life* (1999), Puipa's fifteenth film. Theater director Jonas Vaitkus's major film contribution thus far has been *Utterly Alone* (2003), a hugely popular film that dramatizes the life of a Lithuanian partisan who fought against the Soviets.

Although *Courtyard* (1999), Valdas Navasaitis's first fiction film, was less of a commercial hit, it highlighted the high artistic quality of contemporary Lithuanian film. Set in the late Brezhnev era, *Courtyard* examines the lives and hopes (or hopelessness) of different people living in the same house during what was called the "era of stagnation." Instability rather than stagnation was the theme of the dramatic comedy *The Lease* (2002), the feature film debut by Kristijonas Vildžiūnas (b. 1970). Depicting a recently divorced woman struggling to adapt to her lonely new life, it appealed to its small audience of Lithuanians who also found themselves adapting to trying circumstances in post-Soviet Lithuania.

Of the three Baltic countries, it is Lithuania, the region's leading film producer during the Soviet era, that has struggled the most to adapt to post-Soviet filmmaking conditions. Although Lithuania's Cinema Law declared that film is a cultural priority of the Lithuanian state, the government's grants for the film industry are considerably smaller than the subsidies enjoyed by filmmakers in Estonia and Latvia. As in these countries, movie screens in Lithuania have been overwhelmed by foreign productions against which the poorly financed Lithuanian films cannot hope to compete. Moreover, the price of movie tickets today is beyond the reach of many Lithuanians. Thus Vilnius, the country's largest city, has only a handful of theaters—the largest of which is owned by the monopolistic Finnkino, which favors foreign commercial productions.[10] Despite these bleak conditions, the feature films produced by Lithuanian directors tend to be of unusually high quality and are often shown at the leading film festivals at Cannes, Venice, and Berlin.

NOTES

1. Otto Wilhelm Masing (also see Chapter 5), a man of mixed heritage, was the newspaper's first publisher. His work was carried on by Heinrich Rosenplänter (1782–1846).

2. After an attempted communist coup in Estonia in 1924, the periodicals associated with the Estonian Communist Party, which itself was banned, were shut down. Censorship was introduced in each of the Baltic countries after 1933.

3. "The Latvian Media Landscape," www.ejc.nl/jr/emland/latvia.html.

4. Lembergs appears to be the country's biggest "invisible" press baron. Through concerns such as Ventspils Nams he is believed to control *Neatkarīgā Rīta Avīze, Vakara Ziņas, Rigas Balss, Sporta Avīze,* and the Russian-language newspaper *Vechernaya Riga.*

5. In 2003 *Delfi* was bought by Findexa, a Norwegian company.

6. Halliki Harro-Loit, "The Baltic and Norwegian Journalism Market," in *The Baltic Media World,* ed. Richard Baerug, www.politika.lv/polit_real/files/lv/Baltic_Media_World_novaks.pdf.

7. Despite Soviet attempts to jam their broadcasts, *Radio Free Europe* and *Voice of America* also reached Baltic audiences.

8. TNS Emor Web site www.emor.ee/eng/arhiiv.html?id=65&page=2&keyword=30.

9. Mark Allen Svede, "Lights, Camera, Subversive Action! Latvia's Hippie Auteurs," in Anu Mai Kõll, ed. *The Baltic Countries under Occupation: Nazi and Soviet Rule 1939–1991* (Stockholm: Almqvist & Wiksell, 2003), 341–46.

10. In 2003 Finnkino opened a 14-screen multiplex in Riga's giant Coca-Cola Plaza that reportedly has the largest screen in northern Europe. In 2003 about 88 percent of all cinema tickets in Latvia were sold in Riga.

SELECTED READINGS

Media

Baerug, Richard, ed. *The Baltic Media World.* Riga: Flēra, 2005. www.politika.lv/polit_real/files/lv/Baltic_Media_World_novaks.pdf.

Høyer, Svennik, Epp Lauk, and Peeter Vihalemn, eds. *Towards a Civic Society: The Baltic Media's Long Road to Freedom.* Tartu: Nota Baltic, 1993.

Petković, Brankica, ed. *Media Ownership and Its Impact on Media Independence and Pluralism.* Ljubljana: Peace Institute, 2004. www.mirovni-institut.si/media_ownership/.

Radio and Television in Lithuania: Comprehensive Guide to Broadcasting Sector. Vilnius: Petro Ofsetas, 2004. www.rtk.lt/.

Vihalemn, Peeter, ed. *Baltic Media in Transition.* Tartu: Tartu University Press, 2002.

Cinema

Sokmann, Reet. *Estonian Film,* 1991–1999. Tallinn: F-Seitse OÜ, 2000.
Tapinas, Laimonas. *Lithuanian Film Makers.* Vilnius: Mintis, 1988.

Other Sources and Websites

Much of the most up-to-date information about media in the Baltic countries is
available on the World Wide Web. See, for example: "The Estonian Media
Landscape," www.ejc.nl/jr/emland/estonia.html; "The Latvian Media
Landscape," www.ejc.nl/jr/emland/latvia.html; The Lithuanian Media Landscape," www.ejc.nl/jr/emland/lithuania.html.
A useful resource for international cinema is the annual edition of *Variety International
Film Guide.* Lithuanian Film Center, www.lfc.lt/en>. Overviews of Estonian
film: www.estonica.org/ and www.efsa.ee/eng/estonianfilm.html. On-line
journal *Kinoeye* www.kinoeye.org.

Newspapers

In English

The Baltic Review: www.tbr.ee/
The Baltic Times: www.baltictimes.com/
Baltic Business News: www.balticbusinessnews.com/

In Estonian

Äripäev: www.aripaev.ee/
Eesti Ekspress: www.ekspress.ee/
Eesti Päevaleht: www.epl.ee/
Postimees: www.postimees.ee/

In Latvian

Diena: www.diena.lv/
Dienas Bizness: www.db.lv/online/
Latvijas Vēstnesis: www.vestnesis.lv/
Neatkarīgā Rīta Avīze: www.nra.lv/

In Lithuanian

Kauno diena: www.kaunodiena.lt/lt/
Lietuvos aidas: www.aidas.lt/
Lietuvos rytas: www.lrytas.lt/
Lietuvos žinios: www.lzinios.lt/

In Other Languages

Baltische Rundschau (German): www.baltische-rundschau.de/
Bizness i Baltiia (Russian, Latvia): www.bb.lv/
Chas (Russian, Latvia): www.chas-daily.com/
Kommersant Baltic (Russian, Latvia): www.kba.lv/
Litovskii kur'er' (Russian, Lithuania): www.kurier.lt/
Molodezh Estonii (Russian, Estonia): www.moles.ee/
Nasz Czas (Polish, Lithuania): nasz-czas.tripod.com/

7

Performing Arts

NEARLY TWO DECADES have passed since the world's attention was focused on the breathtaking changes then taking place inside Mikhail Gorbachev's Soviet Union, a country that for half a century appeared to be the permanent prison of the Estonian, Latvian, and Lithuanian peoples. Of all the unforgettable images of the perestroika era, few are as striking as that of the hundreds of thousands of Estonians who gathered at the Tallinn Song Festival Grounds on September 11, 1988. Viewed through the prism of American pop culture, the scene in Tallinn was reminiscent of Dr. Seuss's famous Christmas story in which the serene chorus of the innocuous "Whos" of "Whoville" melts (or, to be more accurate, enlarges by three sizes) the stony heart of the scowling, unloved Grinch, now suddenly unable to summon the will to prevent the Whos from celebrating their beloved holiday. "The Song of Estonia" was the largest mass gathering in the history of any of the Baltic countries. To both participants and observers it was an unforgettable day in which the Estonians' century-old national tradition of song festivals converged with the swelling desire for independence shared by their Latvian and Lithuanian neighbors. It was the pinnacle of the Balts' "Singing Revolution."

While the song festival, a Baltic tradition that merges centuries-old folk culture with mass popular entertainment, is more familiar to outsiders than most other aspects of Baltic culture, the reality is that apart from those who claim an Estonian, Latvian, or Lithuanian heritage, few people living outside the region possess any knowledge at all about the music, art, and literature produced by the Baltic peoples. For decades western Europeans, North

Americans, and others have typically viewed Estonia, Latvia, and Lithuania simply as the "Baltic countries"—as three tiny and rather obscure Soviet (and then ex-Soviet) republics—rather than as three individual countries possessing unique cultures and customs. Indeed, the reality that each of the Baltic countries has its own distinctive theatrical, dance, and musical traditions is often obscured by their shared political past. This chapter highlights some of these traditions, focusing not only on the forms of folk singing and dancing that have survived into the twenty-first century, but also on those modern forms of theater, dance, and music that have been greatly influenced by European, Russian, and folk sources.

MUSIC

Folk Music

In recent decades Baltic folk music and dance have undergone a remarkable revival. The folk festivals held in each of the Baltic countries always feature groups of women—young, middle-aged, and elderly—clad in romanticized versions of traditional, colorful peasant garb. Often smiling as they perform the songs once sung by their ancestors hundreds of years ago, it is through such women that the national ethos is passed on from one generation to the next. Open-air museums near Riga, Tallinn, and Kaunas attempt to preserve the heritage of these tiny peoples by maintaining reconstructed peasant homes, tools, and musical instruments.

Other small, threatened peoples of Europe such as the Welsh, Bretons, and even the little-known Sorbians of eastern Germany have also made concerted attempts to maintain their once-threatened indigenous cultures and languages, but few have done so with the commitment and verve of the Estonians, Latvians, and Lithuanians. In the third quarter of the nineteenth century, a time when tsarist rule appeared to be permanent, Baltic nationalist intellectuals, sensing that the forces of urbanization and modernization, as well as the twin threats of Russification and Germanization (or Polonization), would sweep away the local peasant cultures, began the systematic collection of folk music in an attempt to preserve for posterity this essential expression of the national soul. The result is some of the largest folklore and folksong collections in the world, entirely out of proportion to the relatively small numbers of Estonian, Latvian, and Lithuanian people.

At the heart of Lithuanian and Latvian folk cultures is the *daina,* a short song of only one or two stanzas, or quatrains, each consisting of two non-rhyming couplets. Although the quatrains themselves are short, the singing can go on for quite some time. Lithuanian and Latvian folksongs can be sung solo or, during traditional festivities, in groups. Usually it is women who are doing the singing. References to nature are abundant; especially common is the symbolism of the oaktree.

While *dainas* were traditionally sung throughout the territories that are today inhabited by Latvians and Lithuanians, the form, content, and performance of the song varies by region: Lithuania's northeastern region (Aukštaitija) is distinguished by its tradition of the polyphonic *sutartinė* (to agree), whose melody may be duophonic, consisting of two voices or groups of voices (*dvejinės*) singing in harmony; in the case of the *trejinė* there are three overlapping parts in which two are sung at a time. Similar forms may be heard in nearby western Latvia (Kurzeme), while in Latvia's eastern Latgale region singing in thirds, in which the upper voice sings the melody, is usual.

Of particular interest is the vocal drone—a polyphonic song with one or more parts sung only in one tone. The vocal drone is sometimes compared with the drone of honeybees in their combs, which should not be surprising since beekeeping, as well as the collecting and exporting of honey and wax, has long been one of the region's traditions. Inherited from the East Baltic tribes who settled in the region millennia ago, drone singing is characteristic of some Latvian group songs but is likely to be heard mostly in the country's central and western regions and parts of Latgale, as well as in northeastern Lithuania. Some vocal drones appear to share affinities not only with Estonian drone songs—which is striking since the Estonians do not share common ethnolinguistic roots with their Estonian neighbors—but also with the vocal drones of the Balkans and far-away Georgia.[1]

Yet it is the *daina* that is most associated with the Lithuanian and Latvian folk music tradition. How far back these songs go is a matter of speculation: some musical ethnographers claim that the *dainas* were created in the seventeenth century; others say that elements of the genre may date from before the tenth century. Whatever their origins, the earliest folk music of Lithuania and Latvia was mainly functional, consisting of work and ritual songs, as well as songs connected with the events of everyday life. The dramatic stories and heroic epics typical of other countries' folksongs are absent in Lithuania and Latvia, for in the Baltic area there are few songs about battles, kings, nobles, or princes. Lyrical rather than narrative, the *dainas* are concerned with subjects ranging from the mythological to the mundane: they sing of youth, love, fate, and sorrows.

The following is a classic *daina*, known to nearly every Latvian:

> Liku bēdu zem akmeņa
> Pâri gâju dziedâdama.

I placed my sorrow under a stone
Then I jumped over it singing.[2]

Many *dainas* had ritualistic functions and were sung at weddings, christenings, feasts, and funerals. Wedding songs are particularly varied and are important to the Baltic folk tradition, as are the laments (*raudos*) sung at funerals and on other occasions. Sung for the departed, *raudos* were performed at weddings, too, for it is a sorrowful event indeed when the bride is separated from her parents and driven off to the home of her husband. The tradition of singing *raudos* over the corpse of the departed continues in Lithuania and Latgale to the present day. Created and sung by women, traditional *raudos* often speak "of parting, of anxious waiting at home and a soldier's homesick dreams far away, of a joyous return or the arrival of a messenger of doom."[3]

Oh earth, my earth
Earth ashen-gray!
You took my father,
Mother away.
You took my father,
Mother away.
So take me also,
Take maiden gay.

The hardships of life near the sea were reflected in the *dainas* of Lithuania Minor, which under Prussian rule was separated from the rest of Lithuania. Although these songs disappeared more than a century ago, they reflected the perspective of women who pined for a loved one—a husband or a son—whose return they awaited.

The work song is also typical of the Baltic folk tradition. Lithuanians and Latvians had songs, sung in groups, for almost every kind of work, from planting to harvesting (performed by men) to grinding grain (a hard women's job); activities such as needlework and handicraft making also required singing. Group singing was performed not only during collective laboring but also during calendar rituals: thus, there are specific singing traditions associated with Easter, summer solstice, St. Martin's Day (November 10), and Christmas. This tradition is strongest in the Džukija region of southern Lithuania, where the calendar cycle songs still survive. Indeed, even today the repertoires of the women who continue to carry on these traditions may consist of hundreds of songs. Some of these songs, especially those performed by professional singers at wedding parties, can be humorous or downright bawdy, playing on linguistic subtleties penetrable only by native speakers.

The smiles and laughter they elicit show that these singers, although they may be elderly, are no prudes.

Some folksong genres are quite specific, such as the uniquely Latvian *līgotnes*. Connected with the midsummer solstice celebration (June 23), the songs main feature is the refrain *līgo,* sung one or twice after each line.

Pār pļaviņu pāriedama
Līgo, līgo!
Pļavas dziesmu nodziedāju
Līgo, līgo!

Going across the meadow
Līgo, līgo!
I sang a meadow song
Līgo, līgo!

Estonian folksongs, called runic (*runo*) songs or runes, are derived from a different source than the Latvian and Lithuanian *dainas* and *raunos* and as a result have a somewhat different flavor. Estonian *runo* songs are similar to those of the neighboring Finns and, like Finnish and Karelian folksongs, are characterized by alliteration and parallelism. The earliest runes may go back as far as the first millennium B.C.E., making them much older than the folk music forms common in Latvia and Lithuania. Traditional Estonian folksongs consisted of eight-beat verses without end rhymes. By the nineteenth century, however, the traditional runic form was superseded by the new rhyming folksong (*vemmalvärs*), a development that likely owes much to several centuries of German influence. Yet Estonian folk music shares several characteristics with the traditional music of the Latvians and Lithuanians: it is the domain primarily of women, and its subjects are not epic in nature but are more typically concerned with love, domestic life, and work activities. Most of the oldest Estonian folksongs are monophonic, but polyphonic forms are common among the Setu people of southeastern Estonia (Setumaa), where recent years have witnessed a revival of Setu culture and dialect. Only in Setumaa can one still witness the death laments and rituals once common in other parts of Estonia.

Musicologists have drawn distinctions between two basic musical styles in the Estonian folk tradition: the recitative style and the lyrical style. The recitative style, consisting of only one or two lines (the second line being a variation on the first or an answer to it) was associated with work, calendar festivities, family celebrations, lullabies, and children's songs. Recitative *runo* songs might have as few as two notes, but rarely more than five. The lyrical style, on the other hand, is commonly associated with nonceremonial music and is characterized by a more developed melody and a wider melodic range. In either case, the performance of Estonian *runo* songs usually involved a leader alternating with a chorus, in which the chorus typically either repeated the leader's line or slightly modified it. In performance the singers commonly stood in a semicircle or moved together in a circle. While the Estonian *runo* songs were replaced by rhyming songs in the nineteenth century, some modern composers, most notably Veljo Tormis, look to the older runic forms for inspiration.

Folk Instruments

The folk instruments traditionally used by the ancestors of the Baltic peoples—as well as by Estonian, Latvian, and Lithuanian folk performers today—are quite similar. These have historically included a variety of wind instruments and zithers, played either with or without the accompaniment of vocalists. Wind instruments included animal horns, single-note wooden trumpets, flutes with only a few finger holes, reed instruments that sound roughly like clarinets, and whistles made of bark and clay. Folk percussion instruments include drums made from hollowed-out tree trunks, wooden bells, and tambourines. In ancient times the purpose of some of these instruments was more functional than recreational: for example, horns and whistles, like the bagpipes that began making their way into the region in the fourteenth century, were used for herding.

The most popular Baltic folk instrument is the board zither (psaltery), known as the *kannel* in Estonian, the *kokles* in Latvia, and the *kanklės* in Lithuania. At least 3,000 years old, the Baltic psaltery is similar to the Finns' *kantele* and other zithers of northeastern Europe. It has been noted that the Baltic names for the zither are derived from the proto-Baltic word *kāntles,* meaning "the singing tree." As the zither was traditionally seen as God's instrument, according to folk beliefs the tree for the instrument must be cut after someone has died but before he is buried.[4] Possessing no standard shape or size, the early *kannel-kokles-kanklės* was a five-stringed instrument that was played by placing it on a table or on the player's knees. Over time the number of strings—probably made of bronze, natural fibers, and later steel—increased, so that by the end of the nineteenth century the Estonian *kannel* had as many as 20 or 30 strings, including three bass strings. Some forms of the Baltic zither now contain as many as 50 strings.

The earlier zithers, possessing only a limited range, were played by plucking the open strings individually; however, with the addition of more strings it became possible to produce chords or even chords plus melody. Modern versions of the Estonian *kannel* (sometimes called *simmel*) are more complex still and are common throughout Estonia today, while the older *kannels* continue to persist in Setumaa and the Estonian islands. The 5-to-12-stringed *kanklės* remains common in Latgale and parts of Kurzeme in Latvia. Further modifications to the *kannel-kanklės-kokles* occurred during the Soviet period, which saw the creation of larger soprano, alto, tenor, and bass zithers.

A number of other instruments have been introduced into the region since the seventeenth century, including fiddles and violins, accordions, mandolins, and guitars. From the middle of the nineteenth century to the present day, folk ensembles typically include some combination of violinists, accordionists, zither players, and percussionists.

Song Festivals

Song festivals are a vital feature of cultural life in all three Baltic countries, continuing a tradition begun in 1869 when the first all-Estonian song festival was held in Tartu. Featuring more than 800 singers and presided over by a Baltic German pastor, the 1869 festival attracted an audience of 10,000 to 15,000 people. In recent decades the scale has grown dramatically as tens of thousands of singers and dancers have performed in front of audiences of more than 100,000 people (reportedly 300,000 were in attendance at Tallinn's festival in 1988) drawn from all over Estonia. The festival is always opened with Estonia's national anthem, *My Native Land,* written by Voldemar Jannsen (who borrowed heavily from the Swedish national anthem) and set to the music of Frederik Pacius.[5] While this was banned during the Soviet era, the Estonians' unofficial national anthem became *My Fatherland Is My Love,* a poem written for the first Estonian song festival by Lydia Koidula and set to music by Aleksander Kunileid-Saebelmann.[6] Choral works by Eduard Tubin, Mart Saar, and Veljo Tormis are still regularly featured at the Estonian festivals, which are held every five years.

Hardly less impressive are the Latvian song festivals, first held in 1873, and the Lithuanian festivals, held for the first time in 1924, after Lithuania gained its independence from the Russian Empire. As a tradition that began during the era of the Baltic national awakenings, the song festivals symbolized the heightened national consciousness and unity of the peoples that make up these nations. Despite the Soviet annexation of the Baltic states, the periodically held song festivals continued in each of the republics and eventually became a means of protesting against Soviet policies and demographic Russification. With the revival of interest in Baltic folk traditions in the 1970s the song festivals acquired even greater significance.

By 1987, a time when the Soviet Union was just beginning its experience with Gorbachev's policy of glasnost and the Baltic peoples had just begun to challenge the lie that had justified their absorption by the USSR, the Baltic republics started a tradition of holding a joint festival in rotation each summer. Today the Baltica International Folklore Festival remains the most significant cultural cooperation project among the Baltic countries, sponsoring the music, dance, and customs of each of the Baltic peoples. There are also regional folk festivals, including the Tartu Music Festival, held every spring, the Viljandi Folk Music Festival, and the triennial Setu Song Festival, held in the village of Värska in the Setumaa region. Here the Setu songs, known as the *leelo,* are performed in the distinctive Setu tradition by performers clad in their traditional costumes. In addition to its smaller folk music festivals in the provinces, each autumn Lithuania is host to a modern music festival as well, called Gaida, which features orchestral, jazz, choral, and chamber performances. Kaunas holds an International Jazz Festival for four days each April, an annual jazz festival is held in Klaipėda in June, and Vilnius hosts its own jazz festival in autumn. A popular summer event is the annual rock music festival, *Liepājas dzintars* (Amber of Liepāja), held in Liepāja, a western Latvian port city and the country's leading cultural center after Riga.

In addition Toronto, home to the world's largest Latvian population outside of Latvia, has been hosting Latvian song festivals for more than half a century. Song festivals have also taken place in New York, Cleveland, Chicago, Philadelphia, and Boston.

Modern Music

The development of modern and heavily foreign-influenced musical forms in Estonia and Latvia began in the seventeenth century during the era of Swedish rule. In cities such as Riga and Tartu there were concerts by professional orchestras, as well as opera and ballet performances. By the eighteenth century Jelgava (then known as Mitau), a modest Latvian city that was once the capital of the Duchy of Courland, had become an important center of Baroque classical music. Later the musical culture of Riga came to be associated with the name of the German composer Richard Wagner, who conducted more than 40 operas while living there in the late 1830s.

Latvia's organ culture, also imported from Western Europe, is a celebrated part of the country's musical history. In Latvia even the smallest churches often have their own organ. Tour guides in Riga always note that the city's Dome Cathedral—the largest cathedral in the Baltics and an architectural wonder—houses one of Latvia's great national treasures, a massive organ consisting of 6,768 pipes, grouped in 124 registers (or stops). When it was inaugurated in 1884 it was the largest pipe organ in the world.

The first form of professional music in which native Latvians and Estonians took an active part was the choral tradition. In Estonia the development of choral music was begun by the Moravian Brethren (see Chapter 2), who began to create choirs attached to their churches in the 1830s and 1840s. Although the melodies they sang were German, the words were Estonian. Eventually the repertory of these choirs expanded to include secular songs. Amateur choruses, heavily influenced by native folk traditions and consisting of thousands of singers, are have been a feature of Baltic song festivals since their beginning.

Since Lithuania was for so long subjected to Polish and then Russian cultural influences, the development of native Lithuanian art/professional music and theater were delayed. Since the fourteenth century Lithuanian kings had enjoyed their own court musicians, and Catholic churches in Lithuania featured organs and choirs; indeed, by the seventeenth century the Vilnius Jesuit Academy (later the Vilnius University) had developed a musical life that featured student choirs and orchestras. But professional music, such as the production of Italian operas, remained heavily foreign until well after Paris and Vienna had established themselves as the cultural capitals of Europe.

Among the first important Lithuanian composers was Vincas Kudirka (1858–99), who arranged folksongs for choirs and composed the words and music for the Lithuanian national anthem (1898). Česlovas Sasnauskas (1867–1916), Mikas Petrauskas (1873–1937), and Juozas Naujalis (1869–1934) also influenced the development of Lithuanian music in the early decades of the twentieth century. The organizer and conductor of Lithuania's first song festival in 1924, Naujalis, widely regarded as the "patriarch of Lithuanian professional music," was also the composer of a hymn titled *Beloved Lithuania,* which was banned during the Soviet era but began to be sung anyway at various events beginning in the mid-1960s.

No composer better represents the Lithuanian national renaissance than Mikalojus Konstantinas Čiurlionis (1875–1911), widely considered the greatest Lithuanian composer of his generation. Influenced by the Romanticism of the Polish composer and pianist Frédéric Chopin (1810–49), Čiurlionis studied at the conservatory of Warsaw, where he composed a series of piano pieces as well as his first symphony written for a full orchestra, the Wagnerian *In the Forest* (1900). This long composition reflects Čiurlionis's unique style, in which the Romantic tradition was enriched by folk rhythms and cadences. After studying in Leipzig, Čiurlionis turned to painting (see Chapter 8), yet he still found time to compose *The Sea* (1903–7), a moving, moody, majestic symphony that complemented his paintings of the period.

By the time Čiurlionis died at age the age of 35, Mikas Petrauskas had already established himself as a pioneer of Lithuanian opera, which became the focus of Lithuanian musical activity during the country's first period of independence. In 1906 Petrauskas presented the two-act *Birutė,* a work based on medieval Lithuanian history and the first attempt at a Lithuanian national opera. However, the first truly successful Lithuanian opera did not appear for another quarter century, when Jurgis Karnavičius (1884–1941) composed *Gražina* (1933). First presented at the Lithuanian Opera in Kaunas, the country's capital as well as its principal musical and cultural center during the interwar era, *Gražina* was set in medieval times when Lithuania was constantly threatened by German crusaders. Because of its anti-German themes the opera was instantly controversial and after 1940 was revised several times to meet the ideological requirements of the Soviet regime.

Karnavičius was part of an exceptional generation of talented composers who contributed significantly to the development of Lithuanian culture during the first era of independence. Like a number of other Lithuanian composers of this period—including Juozas Gruodis (1884–1948), Kazimieras Banaitis (1896–1963), Vladas Jakubėnas (1904–76), and Antanas Račiūnas (1905–84)—Karnavičius was trained in Russia, as were many of the leading Estonian and Latvian composers of the late nineteenth and twentieth centuries. Most received their musical training at the St. Petersburg Conservatory, where the Russian composer Nikolai Rimsky-Korsakov (1844–1908) taught for many years. Notable Estonian composers influenced by Rimsky-Korsakov include Miina Härma (1864–1941), Artur Kapp (1878–1952), Mikhel Lüdig (1880–1958), Peter Süda (1883–1920), and Juhan Aavik (1884–1982), who was the conductor at the Vanemuine Theater in Tartu from 1911 to 1923 and at the Estonia Theater in Tallinn from 1925 to 1933. Among the St. Petersburg–trained composers of this generation, Mart Saar (1882–1963) is distinguished by a body of work that drew much of its inspiration from Estonian folk music forms, while Rudolf Tobias (1873–1918), the composer of monumental symphonies as well as ballads, piano, and organ music, is considered by many to be the "father" of Estonian classical music and the country's greatest twentieth-century composer.

With the establishment of an independent state, aspiring Estonian musicians began to study at the Tallinn Conservatory of Music (founded in 1919). Evald Aav (1900–39) and Eduard Tubin (1905–82) were among the great Estonian composers who received their training at the Conservatory. Aav was the composer of the first Estonian opera, *The Vikings*, which premiered at the new Estonia Theatre in Tallinn in 1928, while Tubin, the composer of 10 symphonies between 1934 and 1973, was perhaps the best-known Estonian maestro of his day. One of Tubin's most beloved operas was *Barbara von Tisenhusen* (1968), a tragedy set in the sixteenth century concerning a noblewoman's ill-fated love for a commoner.

During the interwar era, Latvia's most distinguished composer was Jāzeps Vītols (1863–1948), who is widely regarded as the patriarch of Latvian orchestral music. A student of Nikolai Rimsky-Korsakov, whom he replaced at the St. Petersburg Conservatory, Vitols taught in Russia for more than 30 years. In 1919 he finally returned to Riga, where he immediately founded the Latvian Conservatory of Music and became involved in the Latvian national song festivals. Among his 850 compositions are 300 arrangements of Latvian folksongs. The Mediņš brothers were also among the leading Latvian composers of the interwar era: a music college has been named in honor of Jāzeps Mediņš (1887–1947), while Jānis Mediņš (1890–1966) was one of the founders of both Latvian opera and the national ballet.

Although Latvia produced fewer renowned instrumental composers during these years than its neighbors, choir music, because of its close connections with the traditions of Latvian folk music, played—and continues to play— a special role in the country's musical life. During the Romantic era Latvia's leading choral composers were Kārlis Baumanis (1834–1904), who also wrote the Latvian national anthem (1873), and Andrejs Jurjāns (1856–1922), who is credited with creating and defining the national style of Latvian professional music that was later perfected by Emilis Melngailis (1874–1954). The first attempt to create a Latvian national opera was J. Ozols's (1863–1902) *The Ghostly Hour,* performed in 1893, but cultural historians agree that the first real Latvian opera was *Baņuta* by the organist and composer Alfrēds Kalniņš (1879–1951). Set in pagan Latvia but with a tragic storyline reminiscent of *Romeo and Juliet,* it premiered at Riga's National Opera in 1920. Like the operas of Estonia and Lithuania, *Baņuta* and other early Latvian operas were based on pre-Christian mythology and history.

As in Estonia and Lithuania, the era of independence in Latvia gave birth to a series of national cultural institutions such as the National Opera (with at least eight new productions every year), the Riga Conservatory, and a permanent symphony orchestra. National control of these institutions ended in 1940 when the Baltic countries came under Soviet occupation, with consequences similar to those that temporarily obliterated the literary cultures of the new Soviet republics. Many leading musicians and composers fled to the West, while those who remained were subject to Party control, which emphasized Socialist Realism while endorsing certain "great masters" of the recent past. Although massive song and folk-dance festivals continued to be held, they acquired a distinctly Soviet flavor. However, by the 1960s the official controls over music had slackened and some real talents emerged from the generations that had been born during the era of independence or during the early years of Soviet rule.

One of the most original Lithuanian composers of recent decades is Osvaldas Balakauskas (b. 1937). Studying at the Kiev Conservatory in the late 1960s, Balakauskas, like Estonia's Arvo Pärt was part of a circle of students whose compositional styles broke with the prevailing socialist aesthetical norms. Balakauskas later went on to create his own technique, what he called "dode-catonic," with its own unique tonality.

By the 1970s a neo-Romantic trend emerged in Lithuania that was reflected in the folk-influenced compositions of Feliksas Bajoras (b. 1934) and Bronius Kutavičius (b. 1932), as well as in the compositions of Algirdas Martinaitis (b. 1950), whose most prominent early work, *The Book of Living Nature* (1979–83), echoed the growing ecological consciousness of his generation. The works of Martinaitis also reflected another trend that became evident during the 1970s: the writing of music for small chamber ensembles. The smaller scale of the new music can be heard in the earlier works of Mindaugas Urbaitis (b. 1952), which are clearly influenced by the compositions of the American minimalist Philip Glass.

In Estonia the compositions of Arvo Pärt (b. 1935) captured the new emphasis on simplicity. At the cutting edge of art music in the 1960s and early 1970s, Pärt was considered a radical by Soviet authorities for his experimen-tation with Western techniques. With his requests to travel abroad repeatedly denied, he applied for a permanent emigration permit and departed Estonia for Berlin in 1980. Drawing from medieval musical traditions and the spiri-tuality of Orthodoxy, Pärt's most famous compositions include *Tabula Rasa* (1977) and the haunting choral work *Magnificat* (1989). Some fans insist that listening to Pärt's music, which is frequently characterized by an ambient tranquility that gradually rises toward ecstasy, is nothing less than a religious experience.

Less well known internationally but of equal renown in Estonia is Veljo Tormis (b. 1930), a composer whose style differs significantly from that of Pärt. Where Pärt's music strains to be modern and aspires to the heavens, Tormis's works—mostly large-scale choral symphonies such as *Estonian Calendar Songs* (1967)—are heavily influenced by older, more earthly Baltic-Finnic folk traditions.

Choral music has always been one of the great Estonian traditions, and during the Soviet era no Estonian choir conductor (and composer) was bet-ter known than Gustav Ernesaks (1909–93). Ernesaks formed the Estonian National Male Choir in 1944 (it still performs 80 or so concerts each year) and conducted each of the Estonian Song Festivals during the Soviet occupa-tion. One of Ernesaks's most successful students is the charismatic Eri Klas (b. 1939). Although he is most famous as a conductor of choral and symphony orchestras, Klas was heavily influenced by jazz and has also conducted cham-ber orchestras, musicals, and ballets. Another celebrated conductor of the Soviet era was Klas's contemporary Neeme Järvi (b. 1937), an internationally recognized figure since the early 1970s whose interest in introducing Estonian composers to the West was thwarted by Moscow. Emigrating to Israel in 1979, Järvi has since conducted the Gothenburg Symphony Orchestra, the Scottish National Orchestra, and the Detroit Symphony, which he raised to the first rank.

Among the younger composers, Peeter Vähi (b. 1955) is perhaps the most eclectic, drawing inspiration from sources that range from Western rock and roll to the classical music of India. The composer of pop-rock, new-age music, and classical works, Vähi managed to combine all three of these genres in his *Pastoral of Computerized World* (1995), based on the four-note theme from "Shine On You Crazy Diamond," the first track on Pink Floyd's 1975 album *Wish You Were Here*. Another Estonian composer who earned international recognition during the 1990s was Erkki-Sven Tüür (b. 1959). Born and raised on the quiet Estonian island Hiiumaa, Tüür began his musical career in 1979 as a flautist and keyboard player with the art rock band *In Spe* (In Hope), which produced a genre of popular music that Tüür described as "chamber rock." Despite the burgeoning popularity of *In Spe,* in 1983 Tüür quit the band to continue his musical education at the Tallinn Conservatory. By the end of the decade he had emerged as a mature composer of orchestral, concert, and chamber music, and since the end of the Soviet era has earned an audience in Western countries as well as in his native Estonia. Among the youngest of Estonia's internationally renowned composers is Anu Tuli (b. 1972), who, along with her twin sister Kadri, founded the Estonian-Finnish Symphony Orchestra (now known as the Nordic Symphony Orchestra) in 1997.

In an effort to raise popular consciousness of classical music in Latvia, twice a year since 1999 the Riga Festival Orchestra, assembled from Latvia's most talented musicians, performs the great symphonic works of the twentieth century. Its conductor, Normunds Šnē (b. 1960), also plays baroque and early classical music as well as contemporary music with the Riga Chamber Players. Other Latvian composers who have earned international reputations in recent decades include Imants Zemzaris (b. 1951), who is especially noted for his contributions to theater music, and Maija Einfelde (b. 1939), best known for her chamber music and choral works. Perhaps the most famous Latvian composer today is Pēteris Vasks (b. 1946), whose works, which are often laced with elements of folk music, are often intimately connected with the tragic fate of Latvia. His place in Latvian musical culture is comparable to that of Arvo Pärt in Estonia: just as the emotional experience of Estonia can be captured by the ethereal music of Pärt, so, it is sometimes said, can Latvia be experienced through the string, brass, and piano music of Vasks.

Opera has also enjoyed a renaissance in Latvia as well as the other Baltic countries. In Latvia this is due in part to the recent renovation of the National Opera in Riga as well as the work of Andrejs Žagars, who has been its director since 1996. Lithuania's great opera tradition has received worldwide attention with the international success of Violeta Urmana (b. 1960 as Urmanavičiūtė), who left Lithuania in 1991 to become one of the world's most sought-after mezzo-sopranos.

Pop Music and Rock

Rock music has had social and political connotations almost everywhere, but this was especially true in a country—the USSR—where rock was viewed as a manifestation of Western decadence. Despite prohibitions on listening to foreign radio stations during the Soviet era, Western pop and rock trickled into the USSR and became an expression of counterculture in all three Baltic republics, as elsewhere in the Soviet Union, from the 1960s until the country's collapse. While bands such as *Blind, Vennaskond* (Brotherhood), and *Jäääär* (Ice Edge) drive the Estonian rock scene today, the country's most popular rock band in the 1970s and 1980s was *Ruja,* whose experimental music was influenced by British progressive rock bands such as King Crimson, Genesis, and Yes. Like these art rock bands, *Ruja's* 17-year career was also characterized by frequent personnel changes and constant stylistic evolution. By putting to music the poetry of young Estonians—notably, Ott Arder's "I Saw an Estonia Yesterday"—*Ruja's* music captured the ethos of a generation that saw rock as youth rebellion. Singing in Estonian and thus incurring the displeasure of Soviet authorities, the band was able to release only a handful of recordings.[7]

In Latvia the ethos of the rock star as musical rebel was embodied in the early career of Imants Kalniņš (b. 1941). A dissident and *enfant terrible* in the eyes of the Soviet authorities, in the 1960s Kalniņš led the Liepāja-based rock band *2xBBM.* In the 1970s he also founded the band *Menuets* (Minuet), whose members eventually went on to form *Pērkons,* a rock band that was as unpopular with the authorities as it was popular with young Latvians. Meanwhile, Imants, a classically trained musician, returned to composing symphonic music. His *Fourth Symphony* (1971) is considered by many to be an ode to freedom, but it was censored by Soviet authorities and was not performed in Latvia until 1997. The band *Līvi* also earned widespread popularity for its song "Mother Tongue," whose refrain "The language of my birth is my mother" struck a chord with young people during the turbulent glasnost era.

Although Latvian rock acts such as *Pērkons* and *Linga* have enjoyed local success since the late 1980s, international recognition eluded performers from Latvia until 1999, when *Prāta Vētra* (Brain Storm), one of Latvia's most popular bands in recent years, earned second place in the Eurovision Song Contest for its song "My Star." The song contest, which is typically viewed by more than 100 million Europeans on television, has also helped launch the international careers of Estonian artists such as Maarja-Liis Ilus and Ines (Eda-Ines Etti). The award finally went to Estonia in 2001 for the song "Everybody," performed by the duo Tanel Padar and Dave Benton (a 50-year-old black Aruba-born Dutchman residing in Estonia), backed by a popular Estonian boy band called *2XL*. With the contest shifting to Tallinn in 2002, the prize stayed in the Baltic states, as Marie N (Marija Naumova), a Russian singer representing Latvia, unexpectedly won the contest with the song "I Wanna." Estonians placed their hopes on the popular four-piece girl band Vanilla Ninja in the 2005 Eurovision Song Contest in Kiev, but despite their success in Europe (they actually represented Switzerland) the formerly kitschy but latterly "tough" blondes managed only eighth place.

While performers from the younger generation are able to enjoy this sort of international exposure, the most beloved of all of Latvia's musical entertainers is Raimonds Pauls (b. 1936), who, although little known outside Latvia and Russia, has been a dominant figure in the light pop music scene since the 1950s. A politician as well as a musical icon, Pauls held the post of Latvian Minister of Culture from 1988 to 1992. Despite his continued involvement in politics, Pauls remains an active composer, musician, and performer, composing countless hits for other performers in addition to writing the music for numerous films and theatrical productions.

Lithuania, in whose capital stands a memorial statue, erected in 1995, of the late avant-garde American rocker Frank Zappa, has also had its share of successful pop and rock acts. Kęstutis Antanėlis wrote the first Lithuanian rock opera, titled *Love and Death in Verona* (1982), which he later followed with *Peer Gynt* (1997). For more than a decade one of the country's most popular rock bands was *Foje* (The Lobby), which released 14 albums between 1983 and 1997. Its singer and leader, Andrius Mamontovas (b. 1967), has remained one of Lithuania's most famous singers, and since the late 1990s he has frequently headlined the country's pop and rock music festivals. Folk-country music is also popular in Lithuania; the most popular performers of this genre are Vytautas Babravičius (b. 1952) and the group *Jonis*. Virgis Stakėnas (b. 1953), Lithuania's most popular country singer, is known for stealing the tunes from American songs (e.g., Elvis Presley's "Love Me Tender") and replacing the lyrics with the texts of Lithuania's revered poets.[8] Other Lithuanian crowd-pleasers at the turn of the millennium were the pop band *Naktinės Personos,* the folk-rock group *Arija,* the hard rock band *Rebel Heart,* and the blues singer Arina.

While Baltic cities each have their own somewhat distinctive pop music scene (punk, heavy metal, techno, and so on), the reality is that youth-oriented musical culture is dominated less by native artists than by Western (i.e., British and American) and Russian pop musicians. Euro dance music and pop tunes of all kinds rule the airwaves, the nightlife, the shops, and the streets.

Nevertheless, jazz aficionados may find the Baltic capitals to be rewarding. Officially discouraged under Stalin and Khrushchev (a propaganda poster of the Khrushchev period bore the caption: "Today you're playing jazz; tomorrow you'll be selling your country"), by the 1960s modern jazz had become a staple of Lithuanian cultural life, especially in Vilnius.[9] In the 1970s the country's leading jazz artist was Viacheslav (Slava) Ganelin (b. 1944), a pianist who headed the free-jazz Ganelin Trio, which also included Vladimir Tarasov (saxophone) and Vladimir Chekasin (saxophone). A Russian Jew who also taught composition at the Vilnius State Conservatory for many years, Ganelin emigrated to Israel in 1987. Still active, Ganelin's body of work includes two operas that were produced by Moscow's Bolshoi Theater and the scores for more than 30 films. By the time Ganelin left Lithuania, a new generation of jazz musicians began to occupy center stage; among the best known of today's popular jazz artists are the pianist Gintautas Abarius and saxophonists Petras Vyšniauskas and Vytas Labutis. Since 1988 Vilnius has hosted an annual jazz festival, and every April since 1991 Kaunas has hosted its own jazz festival.

Although the jazz traditions of Estonia and Latvia are lesser known than those of their southern neighbor, every spring since the 1960s Tallinn has hosted its own *Jazzkaar* (Jazz Rainbow) Festival, which features prominent musicians from Estonia as well as from Russia and Western countries. Latvia has produced jazz talents as well, most notably the Māris Briežkalns Quartet, a post-bop and Latin–influenced band whose leader was recognized as one of the USSR's greatest jazz percussionists. Since 1997 Briežkalns has also run the Contemporary Music Center, a nongovernmental organization in Riga that is dedicated to training musicians in popular improvisational music.

THEATER

Early Theater

The deep roots of music and folklore stand in sharp contrast to the relatively recent development of theater in Estonia, Latvia, and Lithuania. While the improvised performance of the ancient *dainas* certainly contained elements of drama, the first formal theatrical performances in Estonia and Latvia took place only in the thirteenth century, when the region's new German conquerors attempted to bring Christianity to the pagan populace. This began a pattern in the region's cultural history that endured for most of the past 800 years whereby the existing authorities, as well as social and political rebels, used theater as a vehicle for the introduction of a new theology or political ideology. Having spent much of the modern era under the control of a foreign power, the Balts have only rarely enjoyed the freedom to pursue purely aesthetic goals in the arts. In recent years, however, theater and the performing arts in general have suffered from a lack of funding, which in the 1990s forced some professional theaters to shut their doors.

Despite its compromised artistic position throughout much of the twentieth century, stage performance has a rich tradition in all three Baltic countries. Until the national awakenings of the nineteenth century, however, most performance was in the languages spoken and read by the region's elites. Students who staged their morality plays at the Vilnius Jesuit Academy and similar educational institutions, beginning in the sixteenth century, did so in Latin, the language of humanist classical education throughout Europe. The early Italian influence on Lithuanian theater owes much not only to the Jesuits (many of whom were of Italian origin), but also to the Italian theatrical companies that performed in Lithuania as early as 1592. In the Latvian and Estonian lands, however, it was German theater that was more influential, for German was the language of the itinerant theatrical companies from Germany, composed exclusively of men, that toured the cities and courts of the Holy Roman Empire. Making their way to the Baltic seaports, they stayed in cities such as Riga for several weeks or months before moving on, typically performing at the estates of the local nobility as well as in the city streets and squares.

Only in the last decades of the eighteenth century did plays by local authors, in German of course, begin to be staged in the larger towns of Latvia and Estonia. In 1782 a permanent theater was finally erected in Riga; also used for fancy-dress balls and musical concerts, the Riga National Theater remained at the center of upper-class social life for nearly a century.[10] In 1784 a German nobleman named August von Kotzebue (1761–1819) founded an amateur theater company in Tallinn, but his plays, mostly comedies that he wrote for the amusement of the local nobility, are not noted for their high literary value. It was not until 1809 that a professional theater company was established with its own building in Tallinn. Although its repertoire was mostly German, plays in Russian and Estonian were performed there as well.

A watershed in the development of native Estonian culture was achieved in 1865, when the musical society Vanemuine—named after the old Estonian god of music and poetry—was established. Although it did not get its own professional repertory company for another 40 years, the Vanemuine Society's staging of Lydia Koidula's *The Cousin from Saaremaa* in 1870 marks the true birth of Estonian theater. The first truly Latvian drama was a play titled *Self-Tutored,* produced by Ādolfs Alunāns (1848–1912) in 1869. The director of the Riga Latvian Theater from 1870 to 1885, Alunāns was also a professional actor and playwright who wrote more than 20 plays for his company, ranging from historical tragedies to popular comedies. While the Baltic Germans' virtual monopoly on theater was broken, the Estonians and Latvians who were now writing and directing the plays for the new professional theaters were educated and trained in the theatrical arts by Germans.

Latvia's first great realist dramatist, and the country's best-known writer after Jānis Rainis, was Rūdolfs Blaumanis, whose turn-of-the-century comedies and dramas mainly reflected the conditions of rural life in his country. His comedy *A Tailor's Days in Silmeci* (1902), which features a sympathetic portrayal of Jews, remains a favorite at midsummer festivals. The leading romantic dramatist of this period was Elza Rozenberga, better known as Aspāzija (see Chapter 5). Laden with moral outrage at the injustices of a class-based society that repressed the rights of the Latvian people, the plays of Aspāzija and her husband Jānis Rainis—most notably Rainis's *Fire and Night* (1911)—reflected the values of many intellectuals of that era and demonstrate once again the Latvian pattern whereby theater has been used as an instrument for the dissemination of political ideas. This is not universally the case: some Latvian playwrights, such as Eduards Wulfs (1886–1919) and Jūlis Petersons (1880–1945), preferred to write popular comedies.

As the performing arts matured in Riga, several new theaters were established, including the Opera House (1863, rebuilt in 1887 after a fire), the Riga Russian Theater (1883), and the New Riga Theater (1908). The theater provided an important arena for talented and creative women in Latvia. Dace Akmentiņa (1858–1936) began her career at the Riga Latvian Theater in the late 1880s and became the most distinguished Latvian actress of the second half of the nineteenth century. This first generation of Latvian professional actors also included Berta Rūmniece, Jēkabs Duburs, Aleksis Mierlauks, and Jūlija Skaidrīte.

The leading patron of the theatrical arts in Estonia was the Vanemuine Society, which was headed by August Wiera (1853–1919) from 1878 to 1903, when its building went up in flames. As the tastes of Estonian audiences grew more refined, Wiera's amateur company was replaced by a professional Vanemuine company, and a new building was erected in 1906 to house it. Karl Menning (1874–1941) directed the Vanemuine for more than eight years, during which time he produced plays by Western (Henrik Ibsen, Gerhart Hauptmann), Russian (Maksim Gorky), and Estonian playwrights such as August Kitzberg (1855–1927), Oskar Luts (1887–1953), and Eduard Vilde. Like Latvia's Rūdolfs Blaumanis, Kitzberg was best known for his rural realism. *The Werewolf* (1912), whose central figure is a rebellious girl condemned as a witch, is considered his masterpiece. Eduard Vilde, also a writer of realist rural novels, found success as a playwright with plays such as *The Hobgoblin* (1914), which pokes fun at the Estonian literary establishment and the country's "nouveaux riches." By the time these plays hit the stage, the number of Estonian theatrical companies had expanded to include the German Theater (1906) and the Estonia Theater (1913) in Tallinn and the Endla (1911) in Pärnu. The buildings that housed them, all built in the Art Nouveau style (see Chapter 8), were destroyed in World War II; only the Estonia was restored to something resembling its former shape.

Because of the press ban in force from 1864 until 1904, the development of native-language theater in the Lithuanian provinces took place under considerably worse conditions than in Estonia or Latvia. Municipal theaters had functioned in Vilnius and Klaipėda (then known as Memel, in Prussian Lithuania Minor) since 1785, but the Vilnius Municipal Theater—the first professional theater company in Lithuania—suffered from the restrictions on the Lithuanian language that the tsarist regime imposed after the Polish-Lithuanian uprising of 1863. It was finally closed in 1880. To fill the void, Russian theater companies toured Lithuania and performed the works of Gogol, Tolstoy, Chekhov, Gorky, and Ostrovsky.

Since permission to stage plays in Lithuanian was difficult to obtain, the plays of (among others) Žemaitė and Gabrielė Petkevičaitė-Bitė (1861–1943), two of the country's leading female writers and social activists, were performed in secret, with barns, sheds, and private homes serving as makeshift theaters. Political liberalization followed the revolution of 1905, and in the years that followed amateur theatrical societies were established in Vilnius, Kaunas, Šiauliai, and other Lithuanian cities, where the plays of Gabrielius Žemkalnis (1852–1916), Vilius Storast (pseud. Vydūnas, 1868–1953), and Marcelinus Šikšnys (1874–1970) were staged.[11] At a time when Lithuanian nationalists were engaged in an open but nonviolent struggle with an oppressive regime, historical dramas were in especially great demand. The most significant play in this genre was Vincas Krėvė-Mickevičius's *Šarūnas* (1911), which depicted the unification of the various Lithuanian tribes in the Middle Ages.

By this time, a separate Jewish theater had also begun to develop in Vilnius, first in secret, and then openly after around 1908. The Vilna Troupe, established in 1916 or thereabouts, was composed of actors who spoke Yiddish in the Lithuanian dialect. Some Lithuanian theater scholars believe that Jewish theater in Vilnius during this era directly influenced the Vilnius puppet theater that developed decades later.

Theater since 1918

After declaring their independence from Russia in 1918, the Baltic states immediately created their own cultural institutions, including theaters and operas. In 1919 the National Theater was established in Riga and the city's

Daile (Art) Theater was founded at the end of 1920. Tallinn retained the Vanemuine and the Estonia, to which was added the Drama Studio, a theater school. In Lithuania, which lost Vilnius to Poland after the war, the main cultural center was Kaunas, where the Lithuanian State Theater was established in 1920; after 1931 it also had a branch in Šiauliai, which operated in Klaipėda for several years before World War II. Vilnius, which was not reattached to Lithuania until 1939, had its own state theaters under Polish administration.

In interwar Estonia no institution made a greater contribution to the development of the theatrical arts than the Drama Studio, as it was known from 1920 until 1933.[12] Its director, the charismatic Paul Sepp (1885–1943), introduced the principles of stage production and acting he had learned in Moscow, and its graduates became the actors, directors, and producers who shaped Estonian theater in the 1930s. By that time stage performances of translated world classics were being superseded by the original Estonian plays of Anton Tammsaare and Hugo Raudsepp (1883–1952), as well as the opera productions of Agu Lüüdik (1897–1949), which were staged at the Estonia. In Tartu the financially troubled Vanemuine, Estonia's first theater, favored operettas over dramas, while in Tallinn a Workers' Theater, which did not receive state subsidies, was established in 1925 for the benefit of workers and impoverished intellectuals; it staged plays that were mainly concerned with the class struggle.

Latvia also had its own Workers' Theater (1926–34), but it was the state-subsidized National Theater, under the direction of Jānis Rainis from 1921 to 1925, where the greatest Latvian actors of the independence era honed their craft, including Berta Rūmniece, Jānis Ģērmanis, and Lilija Ērika. It produced not only world classics but also the works of Rainis, Aspāzija, and new writers such as Andrejs Upīts, Vilis Lācis, and Mārtiņš Zīverts. The plays put on by the National Theater tended toward psychological realism, but the Daile Theater, founded and led by Eduards Smiļģis (1886–1966), rejected realism in favor of more metaphorical styles of expression. As Latvia's largest and most diverse city, Riga was also home to Polish, German, and Jewish theaters; however, professional theaters could also be found in smaller cities such as Liepāja, Jelgava, Valmiera, and Daugavpils.

Cultural life in interwar Lithuania centered on Kaunas, home of the Lithuanian State Theater and the Opera Theater. A number of outstanding plays were produced during this period, including a series of dramas by the country's leading realist playwright, Vincas Krėvė-Mickevičius. By the 1920s, however, realism had been largely superseded by a neo-Romantic trend that idealized Lithuania's past and reflected the rise of nationalism and political conservatism throughout the region. The coexistence of realist and neo-Romantic tendencies was also evident in Latvian and Estonian drama and literature during the interwar era, and all three Baltic countries were to some extent influenced by the theories and performance techniques of the avant-garde Russian theater artist Vsevolod Meyerhold (1875–1940), a revolutionary who sought to tear down the divide between performer and spectator.[13]

While all three Baltic states began to develop an operatic tradition in the 1920s and 1930s, Lithuanian opera was distinguished by its unusually high quality. Indeed, one of the outstanding events of Lithuanian cultural life was the premiere of Verdi's *La Traviata* on December 31, 1920 at the State Theater, which today is known as the Lithuanian National Opera and Ballet Theater. The performance featured the tenor Kipras Petrauskas (1885–1968), who along with Antanas Sodeika (1890–1979), Juozas Mazeika (1907–1976), and Juozas Bieliunas (1890–1955) were Lithuania's leading opera singers during the interwar era. In 1925 the State Theater broke new artistic ground in Lithuania by staging the country's first ballet performance, *Coppélia*.

Much of what had taken decades to build was destroyed during World War II. While the Estonia Theater was rebuilt under the Soviet regime in 1947, it took another 20 years before new buildings were erected for the Vanemuine and Endla companies. During the war Riga suffered less material damage than Tartu and the devastated "modern" section of Tallinn, and its main theaters stood intact. Eduards Smiļģis was able to return to the Daile Theater, while the National Theater was renamed the Drama Theater and was placed under the control of Alfrēds Amtmanis-Briedītis (1885–1966).

In Lithuania, the new cultural center and capital became the Vilnius, once the Jerusalem of the North but now tragically *judenrein*. The establishment in 1946 of the Russian Drama Theater (the capital of every Soviet republic had one), whose company was initially composed of actors from Russian theaters, reestablished Russian cultural hegemony. The neo-Classical buildings erected at the beginning of the century that housed the Vilnius Opera Theater and the Kaunas Musical Theater both survived the war and, like the Russian Drama Theater, still stand today. Meanwhile, the innovative Lithuanian Youth Theater was inaugurated in 1965 as an artistic alternative to the State Theater of Vilnius, and a new, modern State Opera and Ballet Theater was built in the capital seven years later.

Despite the strict ideological controls it was forced to endure, theater during the Soviet era suffered from no shortage of either resources or talent. By the time the USSR collapsed in 1991 Lithuania possessed 12 state theaters, all centrally funded by the Ministry of Culture, in five of its largest cities; Estonia and Latvia had 10 apiece. In addition, in each of the Soviet Baltic republics, as elsewhere in the USSR, hundreds of amateur groups were established in connection with existing cultural institutions (i.e., "houses of culture"), factories, or municipalities.

Theater occupied an important place in the Soviet state from the beginning; indeed, to the Bolsheviks the theater was a sort of spiritual surrogate for a church that had been suppressed.[14] Like literature, art, and film, theater was an instrument that the regime used to control its "flock" and to inculcate its ideology and values. Thus, during the first decade or so of Soviet rule, Estonian, Latvian, and Lithuanian directors and writers were told to avoid patriotic themes and to focus instead on the "class struggle." Socialist theater should focus on problems of mass production while refraining from any mention of the tragedies of mass deportations and collectivization.

Just as theater's content was subject to the ideological requirements of Moscow, so was its form. Aesthetically conservative and doggedly committed to "realism," Soviet theater rejected all forms of modernism as decadent. The only acceptable method was that of the Russian theater artist Konstantin Stanislavsky (1863–1938), whose influential system, first adopted by the Moscow Art Theater in the years before World War I, consisted of a series of techniques to help the actor convey the inner thoughts and emotions of his character. "Method acting," as it came to be called, demands that the actor shun imitation and unrealistic dramatic gestures; instead the actor's goal should be to *become* the character by completely identifying with the role.

The expectation of local compliance with Moscow's ideological and aesthetic demands was accompanied by a heavy influx of Russian dramatic literature, especially in heavily Russified Latvia. Even in Lithuania, the least Russified of the Baltic republics, the most frequently produced playwright during the Soviet era was the nineteenth-century Russian dramatist Aleksandr Ostrovsky. Indeed, most theater directors, especially in the early years of the occupation, concluded that it was safest to swim with the tide and model one's production on an officially approved example from Moscow or Leningrad. Despite such restrictions, theaters in the Baltic republics were packed throughout the Soviet era, and while most playwrights and directors complied with the regime's ideological requirements, many were able to speak indirectly about forbidden matters through the use of Aesopian language.

Baltic dramatists who fled to the freedom and safety of the West were allowed to write and to create as they wished, but few of their works were staged. Mārtiņš Zīverts, for example, found refuge in Sweden, where he lived and continued to write plays in exile for several more decades. For those who stayed behind, the choice was either to conform to the regime's ideological requirements—the model for which was Estonia's August Jakobson (1904–63), the leading Stalinist in Soviet Estonian drama—or become a "non-person," like the Lithuanian playwright Balys Sruoga, who was attacked on ideological grounds in 1946 and whose works were blacklisted. Deportation was the fate of the playwright Hugo Raudsepp, who left Estonia in 1951; like Sruoga, he died a year after he had become a "non-person." Theater artists such as Vera

Baļuna (1904–78), who worked at the Latvian Drama Theater from 1944 to 1956, applied the officially acceptable Stanislavsky method, which continues to be dominant in many theater training institutions today, especially in Lithuania.

Only after Stalin's death and Khrushchev's subsequent thaw was it possible to introduce new plays and new approaches to theater and the arts in general. While accusations of "bourgeois nationalism" continued to doom the careers of writers and politicians alike, the loosening of ideological controls that accompanied de-Stalinization gave theater artists somewhat greater freedom to explore once-forbidden themes. By the second half of the 1950s it was possible to stage plays by the exile playwright Mārtiņš Zīverts in Latvia. Under the new conditions Gunārs Priede (1928–2000), the most prolific Latvian dramatist, abandoned the theme of "class struggle" in favor of more realistic, and hence more gloomy, portrayals of daily life. Often out of favor with Soviet officialdom, who banned his *Mushrooms Are Fragrant* before it could even open, Priede sometimes had to "revise" his plays before they could be staged.

In Lithuania, where many theater artists agree that censorship was somewhat more lenient than in the other Soviet republics, the playwright Juozas Grušas (1901–86) embarked on his most creative period. Ill for many years after the war, Grušas rebounded after 1954 to write a series of significant psychological dramas, most notably, *Love, Jazz, and the Devil* (1967). Meanwhile, in his play *Mindaugas* (1968), about the harsh medieval ruler who unified his people against their external foes, Justinas Marcinkevičius explored Lithuanian history, and in particular the theme of power. Kazys Saja (b. 1932), Lithuania's most prolific and perhaps most popular playwright during the 1960s and 1970s, specialized in satirical comedies about everyday life; however, some of his plays, such as *The Holy Lake* (1970), dealt with more serious themes like ecology.

In general, Soviet playwrights and theater artists, while supported by the state and provided with ample resources, were largely cocooned. Only rarely during these five decades were the works of Baltic playwrights staged outside their home countries. For the aspiring non-Russian Soviet writer the route to international recognition lay through Russian translation. Despite the occasional appearance in the Baltic republics of international performers, only a relatively small number of Estonian, Latvian, or Lithuanian theater artists were able to travel even to Moscow to see Soviet Russian theater, while travel beyond the borders of the USSR was almost entirely forbidden. In fact, it was not until 1984, when the Vilnius State Youth Theater performed Eimuntas Nekrošius's play *Pirosmani, Pirosmani* at an international festival in Belgrade, that Lithuanian theater artists were allowed out of the USSR for the first time.

Still, eventhough the Baltic republics were almost entirely cut off from the West during the era of Soviet occupation, from the 1960s onward ideas and artistic trends seeped in as if by osmosis and turned Vilnius, Riga, and especially Tallinn into experimental centers for the performing arts inside the USSR. The performances of the French mime Marcel Marceau in Lithuania in 1956, part of a tour of the Soviet Union, catalyzed the subsequent creation of the Kaunas School of Mime. The first postwar production of works by Bertolt Brecht in the Soviet Union took place in Tallinn (in 1957–58), rather than in Moscow. Likewise, the Theater of the Absurd, popular in Western European countries as well as the Soviet-bloc countries Poland and Czechoslovakia (which enjoyed much greater access to Western intellectual trends), had its greatest impact in Estonia, where, only six months before his untimely death, Artur Alliksaar (1923–66) published the absurdist play *The Nameless Island,* an allegory of the Stalinist system.

The foremost practitioner of this style, and a member of an extraordinary generation of young Estonian writers and poets who emerged in the mid-1960s, was Paul-Eerik Rummo, whose multilayered play *The Cinderella Game* (1969) eschews the traditional storybook telling of the young girl and her Prince Charming in favor of an absurdist interpretation: after nine years of marriage, the Prince discovers that there is not one Cinderella but many, and they are all agents of her wheelchair-bound stepmother (the Mistress). The Prince's dialogues with the other characters portray how the characters try to understand what is happening in the very un-fairy tale-like world around them.[15]

Of the three Baltic republics, Estonia was the pioneer of the theatrical avante-garde. In the 1970s the young director Jaan Tooming (b. 1946) pumped new life into a series of Estonian classics by Kitzberg, Tammsaare, and Vilde, which were staged at the Vanemuine in Tooming's metaphorical style. When viewed against the Soviet background, Tooming's experiments with folk poetry and Eastern spiritual traditions are especially striking. Tooming's reputation extends well beyond Estonia: even during the Soviet era some of his productions were shown at international festivals in Western Europe.

Also significant for the development of Estonian drama were the directors Kaarel Ird (1909–86) and Voldemar Panso (1920–77). As leader of the Vanemuine for most of the period between 1944 and 1986, Ird gave free reign to Tooming and other experimental directors. And it was Panso who laid the foundations for academic theater education in Estonia in the 1950s and 1960s. In 1965 he founded the Estonian Youth Theater (now called the Tallinn City Theater), and from 1957 to 1977 he directed the Higher Drama School of the Estonian Academy of Music, which by now has produced several generations of professional actors and directors.

Since Panso's passing Estonian theatrical life has been dominated by Mati Unt, who in addition to writing numerous poems and novels has staged more than 100 plays since the early 1960s. Despite the financial difficulties experienced by theaters in the Baltic region since the collapse of the Soviet Union, Unt continues to stage the works of Ibsen, Chekhov, and Shakespeare at both the Estonian Drama Theater in Tallinn and the Vanemuine in Tartu, while at the same time continuing to publish his own novels and essays. Among leading Estonian directors today, Unt is joined by the Estonian Drama Theater's Priit Pedajas (b. 1954), a Panso student who since 1991 has staged most of the plays of the nuclear physicist *cum* playwright Madis Kõiv (b. 1929), and Elmo Nüganen, the director of the Tallinn City Theater since 1992. With the release of the film *Names Engraved in Marble* (2002), about Estonia's War of Independence in 1918, Nüganen has also established himself as one of the country's premier filmmakers (see Chapter 6).

Latvian and Lithuanian theater have managed to remain innovative despite Soviet-era political restrictions and post-Soviet financial challenges. The intellectual and director Pēteris Pētersons (b. 1923), director of the Daile in the 1960s and still active more than three decades later, was one of the inventors of Latvian poetic theater, which he launched in 1964 with his production of *The Motorcycle,* based on the poem by Imants Ziedonis. Ādolfs Šapiro (b. 1939), the only Latvian director to enjoy an international reputation, continued to develop Latvia's poetic-metaphoric tradition at the Youth Theater, where he staged works by Gorky, Chekhov, Ibsen, and Brecht. By the 1980s the genre of the rock opera had also become established on the Latvian stage. One of the most popular productions was the heroic Latvian epic *Lāčplēsis,* which was first staged in 1988 by Valdis Lūriņš (b. 1951). Latvia can also lay claim to having produced a national school of stage designers that includes the celebrated Ilmārs Blumbergs (b. 1943), Andris Freibergs (b. 1938), and Gūnars Zemgals.

In Lithuania Jonas Vaitkus (b. 1944) has produced dozens of plays in a variety of genres at practically every major theater in the country, most notably at the Kaunas Drama Theater, where he worked from 1975 to 1987. A master of the grotesque, his favorite themes are evil in its various guises (Camus's *Caligula*) and the conflict between the individual and society. Vaitkus is often mentioned in the same breath as Eimuntas Nekrošius (b. 1952), the longtime director of the Vilnius State Youth Theatre, which staged his plays from 1977 to 1991. Among Baltic theater directors Nekrošius is the best known internationally. Praised, like Vaitkus, for a directing style that is abstract, metaphorical, and poetic, Nekrošius has produced numerous innovative interpretations of various world classics by Gogol, Chekhov, Pushkin, and Shakespeare. Nekrošius's prestige as an artist has been matched by the financial success of his productions, which were the first to make a profit both abroad and at home in the troubled financial climate of post-Soviet Lithuania. However, despite this success (or perhaps because of it), Nekrošius has endured criticism from self-proclaimed patriots for his alleged failure to promote a genuinely "Lithuanian" theater.

While the new freedoms of the perestroika era allowed for unprecedented experiments such as the creation of a political puppet theater in Lithuania (called *Sepa*), dramatic productions suffered in the early 1990s. Many cultural figures became too involved in politics to produce anything of lasting significance, and the disintegration of the USSR heralded an economic catastrophe for the arts. In most of the former Soviet bloc countries popular interest in theater declined dramatically. The cause for this, however, was not entirely economic. While the collapse of censorship allowed for the appearance of hitherto "forbidden fruit" such as plays by Western and émigré authors, theater's purpose as a form of civil disobedience disappeared. As ticket sales declined, many theater artists were forced to seek additional or even alternative employment.

Since the nadir of the early 1990s, Estonian theater has enjoyed a modest recovery, and private theaters such as the Von Krahl and Theatrum were established in Tallinn. However, the heavily subsidized theaters of Latvia and Lithuania have experienced greater difficulties adjusting to market conditions. While the Latvian National Theater has remained quite popular and has been able to revive its tradition of psychological realism, most theaters in Latvia were forced to operate with sharply reduced budgets and staff. In the most unfortunate case, Latvia's innovative Youth Theater was forced to shut its doors in 1992. Despite the weight of crushing debt, the Opera House in Riga continues to operate, and several modest, mostly commercial, new theaters have sprung up in Latvia and Lithuania. Many fans of serious theater, who once made up theater's core audience in the Baltics, enjoy the productions staged at the New Riga Theater (1992), which focuses on a contemporary, modern repertory and has featured a number of highly praised productions by Māra Ķimele (b. 1943), Juris Rijnieks (b. 1958), and Alvis Hermanis (b. 1965), the theater's artistic director since 1997. Since it is subsidized by the Latvian state, the New Riga Theater can afford to ignore commercial considerations; many other theaters, however, have moved away from "serious" theater to stage more entertaining (i.e., commercially safer) productions.

DANCE

Folk Dance

Everywhere in northeastern Europe folk dancing is rooted in various festivals, rituals, and celebrations, and each nation or region has developed its own particular styles. The reserved nature of the Estonian national character can be seen in the country's traditional folk dances, which are slow, simple, repetitive, and marked by a certain dignity in their execution. Like the indigenous dances of the Finns, Slavs, and Balts, Estonian dances were performed in groups as line and, more often, circle dances. Often the dancers seemed to be walking rather than dancing, and traditionally they have rarely performed acrobatic feats or displayed much emotion.

For centuries these dances were intrinsic to the Estonians' rituals, celebrations, and games, and were accompanied by singing and the playing of music on traditional instruments. Latvian and Lithuanian dances, also performed in groups and led by women, can sometimes be nearly as slow and quiet as those of the Estonians. Some were dances for work; others were seasonal, ceremonial, and celebrational. They were marked by a certain restraint and, in many cases, surprising complexity. Only with the introduction of polkas, waltzes, and quadrilles from northern and Western Europe in the eighteenth and nineteenth centuries did couple dancing, in which men take the lead, become popular in the Baltic countries.

Assessing the authenticity of the dancing that is performed today at the various Baltic folk festivals is not a simple matter. While ethnographers of the late nineteenth century scoured the countryside of Estonia, Latvia, and Lithuania to collect folklore and folksongs, the traditional dances of the Baltic villages were overlooked. By the early decades of the twentieth century traditional folk dancing had begun to disappear, and only at this time—before World War I in Estonia, and only afterward in Latvia and Lithuania—were any serious attempts made to compile a record of the traditional dances of the villages. While there remained capable folk dancers in the countryside, they tended to be older and heavy-footed, perhaps making the dances seem even slower than they actually had been historically. Likewise, today the only people remaining who learned to dance in traditional village surroundings were born in the 1920s and 1930s; younger dancers learned from them or from people who had little or no personal connection to rural life. The Soviet era further distorted the "purity" of traditional dancing, for the heavy-handed Soviet attempts to provide the Baltic republics with the illusion of control over their own cultural lives accompanied a broader goal of assimilating the Balts; thus the complicated, mass choreographies of the Soviet-era song-and-dance ensembles (in Latvia these were disparagingly called "fake braid dances") added a distinctly Russian flavor to their performances that continues to distort the authenticity of today's folk dance performances.

Ballet and Modern Dance

With the best intentions and obvious enthusiasm, the women who dress in colorful peasant costumes and dance at the region's many folk festivals today are attempting to replicate for a primarily urban audience what they believe to be authentically Estonian, Latvian, and Lithuanian dance traditions. The ballets and modern dances that are performed today in concert halls and theater stages are an entirely other matter. Far from being an organic outgrowth of indigenous culture, modern artistic dances like ballet—although they may contain elements of folk dances—are wholly the result of foreign influences.

As early as the eighteenth century, touring companies were performing various kinds of dances before German-speaking audiences in Latvia and Estonia, and professional dancers are believed to have staged performances for Lithuanian magnates since the sixteenth century. While theatrical dancing was generally limited to discrete scenes in the operettas and dramas that began to be staged in the last decades of the nineteenth century, it was not until the twentieth century that theatrical dance began to develop in a more autonomous form in the Baltic countries. The two main influences on theatrical dancing in the region were Russian classical ballet and the "free" style of dancing to which the American dancer Isadora Duncan gave birth at the turn of the century. Although each of the Baltic countries has had its own standout performers and choreographers, their theatrical dance traditions share much in common.

Most significantly, from the beginning classical ballet developed under considerable Russian influence throughout the region. Former soloists of the Maryinsky (now Kirov) Theater in St. Petersburg laid the foundations for Estonian and Latvian ballet; Yevgeniya Litvinova opened a studio in Tallinn in 1918; while Aleksandra Fedorova (1884–1972) staged 18 ballets from the Russian classical repertory for the Riga Ballet as a dancer, choreographer, and coach from 1925 to 1937. In Lithuania the task of founding a national professional ballet fell to a Lithuanian, Olga Dubeneckienė (1891–1967), who staged the dances for the first productions of the State Opera Theater in Kaunas after its opening in 1920. However, it was a Russian choreographer, Pavel Petrov, who staged Lithuania's first professional ballet, Leo Delibes's *Coppélia,* on December 4, 1925, four years after the Russian choreographer Nikolai Sergeyev had staged Latvia's first full-length ballet, *La Fille mal gardée,* in Riga. During the Soviet era the Russian influence was obviously no less pronounced—most of the ballets were Russian classics such as *Swan Lake* and *The Nutcracker*—even if the leading directors and choreographers were native Balts.

Still, there was and remains such a thing as a "national" ballet in any of the Baltic countries. *The Goblin,* set to a score written by the composer Eduard Tubin, has been an Estonian favorite since it was first performed in 1943 at Tartu's Vanemuine Theater. Osvald Lēmanis, a ballet star in the 1930s and the first choreographer wholly educated in Latvia, staged the first classical ballets with Latvian national themes, including *The Triumph of Love* (1935), *Ilga*

(1937), *Autumn* (1938), and *The Nightingale and the Rose* (1938). Although the Russian choreographer Nikolai Zverev staged several one-act Lithuanian ballets in the early 1930s, it was the Lithuanian choreographer Bronius Kelbauskas who in 1941 staged the full-length national ballet *The Bride,* in which he blended classical dance with elements of Lithuanian folk dances.

As awful as the Soviet occupation was in many respects, in each of the Baltic republics it inaugurated, as *The Great Soviet Encyclopedia* notes, the "intensive development of the art of ballet." While Soviet propaganda consistently made similar claims about agriculture, industrial growth, the construction of urban housing, and achievements in nearly all areas of culture, in the case of ballet it is undeniably true. Indeed, on no other art did the USSR expend such lavish resources as the ballet, for no other form of art better highlighted the outstanding cultural achievements of the Soviet Russian people. The Baltic republics in no way lacked the talent to justify these efforts, and institutions such as Vilnius Ballet School (established in 1952) and the Riga Choreography School (1948), considered the third best in the USSR (after the Bolshoi and the Kirov), were built to train the young dancers who entered the USSR's numerous dancing companies. From the Western perspective, the Baltic region, and Riga in particular, was the door that opened up Europe to the holy grails of Russian ballet in Leningrad and Moscow.

While Mikhail Baryshnikov (b. 1948), who was born in Riga and trained at the Riga Choreography School, is the most famous ballet dancer from the region, any discussion of postwar ballet in Latvia must include the team of Elena Tangiyeva-Birzniece (1908–65) and Evgeny Čanga (b. 1921). Tangiyeva-Birzniece, after achieving considerable success as a ballet star in the 1930s, became a teacher and choreographer, leading the Riga Ballet from 1945 to 1965. The producer of a series of what might be called national ballets, one of her earliest successes was *Laima* (1947), which told the ideologically correct story about the joint struggle of the Latvians and Russians against the invading Germans in the thirteenth century. While Tangiyeva-Birzniece is associated with classical dance, Čanga, with whom she frequently collaborated, preferred a more dramatic and imaginative style.

Latvian star performers of the 1960s, 1970s, and 1980s included Māris Liepa, Zita Errsa, Inessa Dumpe, and Genadijs Gorbanovs, and the leading chorographer was Aleksandr Lembergs (1921–85). While heading the Riga Choreography School from 1968 until his death in 1985, Lembergs choreographed numerous classical ballets while also creating the first original Latvian ballets for children. The most influential figure in Latvian ballet today is Aivars Leimanis (b. 1958), the director of the Latvian National Ballet since 1998, and Latvia's top performers include Margarita Demjanoka and Viktorija Jansone. Since 1996 Riga has been home to the International Baltic

Ballet Festival, an annual event organized by the Latvian prima ballerina and choreographer Lita Beiris (b. 1952). The festival features both classical ballet ensembles and modern avant-garde performances by dancers and choreographers from Europe, Russia, and the United States.

For nearly two decades Soviet Lithuanian ballet's leading choreographer was Vytautas Grivickas (b. 1925), who staged numerous productions for the Opera and Ballet Theater in Vilnius in the 1950s and 1960s. *Eglė, the Queen of Grass-Snakes* (1960, 1969) starred the creative and precise Leokadija Aškelovičiūtė (b. 1939), a dancer whose three-decade career was highlighted by her performance as Aurora in *Sleeping Beauty.* Other leading Lithuanian ballet artists of the Soviet era were Loreta Bartusevičiūtė, who danced for the Lithuanian State Opera and Ballet Theater from 1976 to 1987, and Nelė Beredina, who has graced Lithuanian stages since 1975. The younger generation is represented by Vilnius Ballet School graduates Eglė Špokaitė and Edvardas Smalakys.

One of Estonia's most famous dancers and teachers was Helmi Puur (b. 1933), who made her debut in a performance of the Russian classic *Swan Lake.* However, nobody has done more to shape Estonian ballet than Mai-Ester Murdmaa (b. 1938), the Estonian National Ballet's artistic director and principal choreographer from 1974 to 2001, when she was succeeded by Tiit Härm, who had been a lead dancer for the company for nearly 20 years (1971–90). Blending classical ballet with modern dance, Murdmaa worked closely with Kaie Kõrb (b. 1961), who is perhaps the country's most famous dancer today. Better known outside Estonia are Toomas (Thomas) Edur and Age (Agnes) Oks, who since the early 1990s have been dancing as a couple with the English National Ballet.

Although forbidden as a Western evil during the Soviet era, modern dance was not unknown in Estonia in the 1920s. In 1924 Gerd Neggo (1891–1974) opened a studio based on the methods of the Hungarian dancer and Expressionist choreographer Rudolf von Laban (1879–1958), who is considered the intellectual father of modern European dance.[16] Ella Ilbak (b. 1895), one of Estonia's first professional dancers, was heavily influenced by Isadora Duncan, but with limited opportunities at home she performed mostly abroad. Only in the early 1990s, with the formation of the Nordic Star dance troupe, did modern dance begin to be staged in Estonia. In 1992 its five members founded the Fine 5 Dance Theater, and two years later they founded their own dance school.

Lithuania's modern dance tradition stretches back to 1939, when Danutė Nasvytytė, who trained in Berlin, operated a studio for several years in Kaunas. Although the Soviet regime frowned upon this sort of bourgeois decadence, in 1980 Birutė Letukaitė, who came under the influence of the

Duncanian tradition, was able to open the Aura Modern Dance Theater, which since 1989 has been organizing international festivals of modern dance in Kaunas.

NOTES

1. Karl Brambats, "The Vocal Drone in the Baltic Countries: Problems of Chronology and Provenance," *Journal of Baltic Studies,* 14, no. 1 (Spring 1983): 24–33.

2. All translations of traditional songs and verses are standard versions learned by the author.

3. Jonas Balys, "The Lithuanian Daina," *Lituanus,* 7, no. 1 (1961): 22.

4. Valdis Muktupāvels, "The Singing Tree," in *Insight Guide: Baltic States,* 2nd ed., ed. Roger Williams (Singapore: APA Publications, 2000), 85.

5. The Hamburg-born Pacius (1809–91) also composed the libretto for the first Finnish-language opera, *King Charles's Hunt.*

6. This unofficial national anthem was later set to a new musical score by Gustav Ernesaks.

7. Mel Huang, "Rock Estonian Style," *Central Europe Review,* 1, no. 19 (November 1, 1999) www.ce-review.org/99/19/huang19.html.

8. Artūras Tereškinas, "Between Soup and Soap: Iconic Nationality, Mass Media and Pop Culture in Contemporary Lithuania," *Lituanus* 46, no. 2 (Summer 2000): 14–17.

9. Vytautas Landsbergis, *Lithuania: Independent Again: The Autobiography of Vytautas Landsbergis* (Seattle: University of Washington Press, 2000), 43.

10. Heinrich Bosse, "The Establishment of the German Theater in Eighteenth Century Riga," *Journal of Baltic Studies,* 20, no. 3 (Fall 1989): 207–22.

11. Gabrielius Žemkalnis (the Lithuanian version of Landsbergis) was the grandfather of Vytautas Landsbergis, the leader of the mass movement for Lithuanian independence at the end of the Soviet era.

12. In 1937 the Drama Studio became the Estonian Drama Theater.

13. Meyerhold, a socialist dedicated to putting theater in the service of the people, imagined that theater "happened" when there was creative intercourse between the performer and the audience. In the decade before World War I he abolished the front curtain from his productions and emphasized the forestage, the locus of contact between performer and spectator. Stressing that it was primarily the actor upon whom the audience depended for its theatrical experience, Meyerhold encouraged his actors to make direct contact with the audience. His techniques proved too radical for the aesthetically conservative Stalinist regime and he was executed in 1940.

14. Anatoly Smeliansky, *The Russian Theatre after Stalin* (New York: Cambridge University Press, 1999), xx.

15. A member of the Estonian parliament (*Riigikogu*), since April 2003 Rummo has been the government's Minister for Population and Ethnic Affairs.

16. Labans was the creator of a system of notation to record body movement called Labanotation.

Selected Readings

Music

Brambats, Karl. "The Vocal Drone in the Baltic Countries: Problems of Chronology and Provenance." *Journal of Baltic Studies,* 14, no. 1 (Spring 1983): 24–33.

"Estonia," "Latvia," and "Lithuania." In *The New Grove Encyclopedia of Music and Musicians.* Vol. 19, ed. Stanley Sadie, 357–77. London: Macmillan, 1980.

Goertzen, Chris. "Lithuania." In *The Garland Encyclopedia of World Music.* Vol. 8, *Europe,* ed. James Porter and Timothy F. Rice, 509–15. New York: Garland, 2000.

Muktupāvels, Valdis. "Latvia." In *The Garland Encyclopedia of World Music.* Vol. 8, *Europe,* ed. James Porter and Timothy F. Rice, 499–507. New York: Garland, 2000.

———. "Musical Instruments in the Baltic Region: Historiography and Traditions," *The World of Music,* 44, no. 3 (2002): pp. 21–54.

Tall, Johannes. "Estonia." In *The Garland Encyclopedia of World Music.* Vol. 8, *Europe,* ed. James Porter and Timothy F. Rice, 491–98. New York: Garland, 2000.

Vīķis-Freibergs, Vaira, ed. *Linguistics and Poetics of Latvian Folk Songs.* Montreal: McGill-Queen's University Press, 1989.

Theater

Cakare, Valda. "The Ecology of Theater in Post-Soviet Latvia." In *Eastern European Theater after the Iron Curtain,* ed. Kalina Stefanova, 81–97. Amsterdam: Harwood Academic Publishers, 2000.

Carlson, Marvin. "Report from Estonia." *Slavic and East European Performance,* 19, no. 1 (Spring 1999): 62–65.

Marcinkeviciute, Ramune. "New Seasons of Hope and Crisis." In *Eastern European Theater after the Iron Curtain,* ed. Kalina Stefanova, 103–13. Amsterdam: Harwood Academic Publishers, 2000.

Popenhagen, Ludvika Apinytė. *Nekrošius and Lithuanian Theatre.* New York: Peter Lang, 1999.

Rouyer, Philippe and Peter Nagy, eds. *The World Encyclopedia of Contemporary Theatre.* Vol. 1: *Europe.* New York: Routledge, 1994.

Skendeliene, Ruta. "Lithuanian Theatre in the Last Ten Years: Directing, Acting, and New Forms of Expression." *Internet-Zeitschrift für Kulturwissenschaften,* no. 9 (May 2001). www.inst.at/trans/9Nr/skendeliene9.htm

Straumanis, Alfreds, ed. *Baltic Drama: A Handbook and Bibliography.* Prospect Heights, Ill.: Waveland Press, 1981.

Zeltiņa, Guna. "Latvian Theatre in the 90s: Trends, Repertoire, Personalities." *Slavic and East European Performance,* 17, no.1 (Spring 1997): 37–48.

Dance

International Encyclopedia of Dance. New York: Oxford University Press, 1998.

Other Sources and Websites

Central European Review, www.ce-review.org/archiveindex.html; Estonian Music
    Information Center, www.emic.kul.ee/InglE/; Information Centre of the
    Estonian Theatre Union, www.estoniantheatre.info/; Latvian National Opera,
    www.opera.lv/default.asp; The New Theatre Institute of Latvia, www.theatre.lv;
    Estonian Theatre Information Center, www.estoniantheatre.info/. The Lithu-
    anian Music and Publishing Center has links to numerous useful articles on
    Lithuanian music. www.mic.lt.

8

Architecture and Housing

To TRAVEL THROUGH the Baltic countries is to take a journey through time. In the "old" section of Tallinn the visitor sees one of the world's best-preserved architectural ensembles of the late Middle Ages. The secret of Vilnius's charm is its collection of Baroque style churches. For Art Nouveau architecture few cities of Eastern Europe can rival Riga. The Baltic countryside, too, retains an impressive architectural heritage: Estonia's 2,000 manor houses vary not only in size and elegance, but also represent a range of European styles, from neo-Baroque to neo-Classicist to Tudor.

Like the Gothic cathedrals that still stand in most cities of central Europe, medieval castles once abounded throughout the Baltic region. Some, like Bauska castle in central Latvia and, still more impressively, the Island Castle in Trakai, Lithuania, have been restored to their former glory, while others have been left in ruins or have disappeared altogether. In Latvia's picturesque town of Kuldīga, devastated by the Great Northern war of the early eighteenth century, only a small hill remains where the fortress of the pagan ruler Lamekins the Cour once stood. World War II destroyed entire cities, including parts of Inner Riga and nearly the entire architectural heritage of Narva in northeastern Estonia. The Great Synagogue of Vilnius, built in 1663, was heavily damaged when the Jewish ghetto was liquidated by the Nazis. Like the rest of the ghetto it was razed by the country's new Soviet occupiers.[1]

Despite these losses, a good portion of the region's architectural heritage has been preserved and can still be admired. While Estonian manor houses and the Art Nouveau buildings of Riga reveal the West European influence

Waterfall, Kuldīga, Latvia. The waterfall, reputedly Europe's longest, is located in Kuldīga, a picturesque town whose medieval castle was destroyed long ago. Once prosperous, Kuldīga has fallen on hard times as young people seek opportunities in Latvia's larger cities.

on Baltic architecture, the hundreds of wooden churches scattered around the Lithuanian countryside represent an intermediate link between folk and professional architecture. Many structures are neither old nor beautiful nor well preserved, as the usually bleak and shoddy residential housing constructed on the outskirts of every Baltic city attests. Nevertheless, in few places anywhere in the world can one see so many architectural styles peacefully coexisting in such a small area. Taken together or individually, the Baltic countries are truly an architecture lover's paradise.

MEDIEVAL ARCHITECTURE

The architectural landscape of Baltic cities has been shaped almost entirely by external, European influences. German styles can be seen in Hanseatic port cities like Riga and Tallinn (whose name means "Danish City" or "Danish Castle"), while Italian and Polish influences combine to give Vilnius its unique architectural ensemble. Russian influence—in the form of massive Orthodox cathedrals and modern Soviet constructions—is also evident in each of the Baltic capitals.

European architectural influences in the Baltic countries date to the thirteenth century, when German invaders introduced Romanesque and Gothic architecture to Estonia and Latvia as they constructed new churches, fortresses,

The modern parts of Tallinn were destroyed in World War II and were rebuilt in the Soviet style. "Old Tallinn" retains its medieval flavor.

and towns. Local resources determined the kind of building materials that were utilized; these in turn determined form. In northern and central Estonia, limestone was the main building material, and thus the structures there were simpler and heavier than in southern Estonia and Latvia, where red brick was more common. The Romanesque style, characterized by heavy stone vaults and round arches, was common at first, but it was quickly superseded by the Gothic style, whose main features included ribbed ceiling vaults, pointed arches, and more decorative exteriors.

The region's new German rulers quickly already created an architectural heritage that would last for centuries. Within 100 years the Livonian Order erected castles at Ventspils (then Windau), Jelgava (Mitau), Sigulda (Segewold), Cēsis (Wenden), and Riga, from which German-Latvian towns would later emerge. By the end of the Middle Ages Estonia had more than 50 stone castles, the best preserved of which is Kuressaare Castle (1338–80) on the island of Saaremaa. Lithuania's early wooden castles, built by Lithuanians rather than Germans, have not survived. By the fourteenth-century, brick castles, most of which were eventually equipped with tall Gothic towers, were built at Kaunas, Krėva,

Tallinn Town Square (Raekoja Plats). The squares in Baltic cities now typically feature beer gardens like this one. In the background, the towers of Toompea Castle and St. Olaf's Church (right) are seen.

Lyda, Medininkai, Trakai, and Vilnius; but these, too (with the exception of the Island Castle at Trakai, which was rebuilt in the 1950s), are in ruins.

When it comes to Gothic architecture, old Tallinn, which was constructed mainly between the thirteenth and sixteenth centuries, is the jewel of the Baltics. Had the city been more prosperous in the nineteenth century it would have gone the way of many other European cities, where much that was old was demolished to make way for the new and modern. Partly because of this quirk of history, Tallinn still possesses many of the region's oldest and most beautiful churches, many of which were expanded and altered over the centuries. For centuries the steeple of St. Olaf's (*Oleviste*) Church (1267) has been a major feature of the Tallinn skyline. Once among the tallest in Europe at 460 feet, the steeple was replaced by a smaller one (393 feet) after a fire in 1820. The Dome Church (*Toomkirk*), also called St. Mary's Cathedral, has also evolved since it was first built in the thirteenth century: once the main religious center for the city's leading German families, its steady enlargement included the addition of a Baroque spire in 1778.

Examples of Gothic civic architecture can still be seen in Tallinn in the area around the Town Hall Square. Now a tourist mecca full of restaurants and beer gardens, it was once the commercial center for Tallinn's German merchant class and the site for the floggings and executions of the town's ne'er-do-wells. The old Town Hall, built between 1371 and 1404, is Estonia's oldest intact late Gothic building. North from the Town Hall Square runs Long Street (*Pikk tänav*), on which stands the buildings of several old Tallinn guilds, including

Inner Riga. At the center of the picture is the Riga Dome Cathedral (*Rigas Doms*). Although its foundation stones were laid in 1211, the Baroque spire was added in 1776. The Daugava River flows through Riga.

the Great Guildhall (1407–17) and St. Olaf's (*Oleviste*) Guildhall (1422), as well as a number of merchants' houses from the era. These examples of late Gothic architecture feature relatively simple forms, austere façades, and deep portals.

Although Inner Riga suffered greater damage during World War II than did the historic section of Tallinn (the rest of Tallinn was flattened), some of the older structures managed to survive, albeit in significantly modified forms. Many of those modifications were made after the fires that would occasionally burn down half or even more of the city. St. Peter's Church, a Gothic structure that was built, burned down, and rebuilt in the thirteenth century, has been a frequent target of lightning strikes. Arson was the probable cause of a great fire in 1677 that destroyed its tower, but a new Baroque spire was added in 1690 that made St. Peter's the tallest wooden structure in Europe at the time. Destroyed once again by a lightning strike in 1721, the tower was rebuilt in 1746. Two centuries later, however, German bombs demolished the entire structure, leaving one of Riga's great symbols sitting in ruins until 1968, when its reconstruction finally began. This time the spire, completed in 1973, was built using metal construction, and an elevator and a viewing platform were also added to allow visitors to enjoy the magnificent view of the city.

The architectural history of St. Jacob's Cathedral tells a similar story: a brick building characteristic of the transitional period from Romanesque to Gothic architecture, St. Jacob's was built around 1225 and acquired a Baroque dome-like base in 1756. Its tower burned down in 1482 and, after being rebuilt, was struck by lightning in 1596. The Riga Dome (*Rigas Doms*), perhaps the most important sacral building in the Baltic countries, has also experienced an interesting architectural evolution since its foundation stones were laid in 1211. The high, arched windows of the church's wings marks the transition from the Romanesque to a Gothic architectural style; over time, however, the Dome's appearance acquired a Basilica form as new chapels and a Renaissance-style tower (1595) were added. The present-day Baroque spire was built in 1776, but at 295 feet in height (formerly 460 feet), it lost the competition with St. Peter's Church for the city's tallest structure.

While Riga possesses by far the country's greatest collection of old buildings, it by no means has a monopoly on medieval Gothic religious architecture in Latvia. Among the most significant Gothic structures outside Riga is St. John's Church in Cēsis, a city that was once the headquarters of the Livonian Order. Its original Gothic form was completed in 1287, and it has been altered through the centuries, most notably by the addition of towers in 1853. Indeed, because of alterations, fires, and reconstructions, there are no stylistically "pure" Gothic churches in Latvia today.

Lithuania's first masonry cathedral, built by Grand Duke Mindaugas at the time of his ostensible conversion to Christianity in the thirteenth century, was erected on the territory of the Lower Castle in Vilnius. Its foundations, unearthed in the 1970s, are located under the present Vilnius Cathedral and reveal brickwork that is similar to that of buildings being constructed around the same time in Riga. In 1419 Grand Duke Vytautas had a new Gothic cathedral built on the site, where his successors were ceremoniously crowned over the next 150 years. Over the centuries, however, fires and subsequent reconstructions transformed the Cathedral's appearance: once a combination of Gothic and Baroque styles, by the 1770s it had acquired a portico of six Doric columns and thus became, in the words of the Lithuanian writer Tomas Venclova, "the most monumental purely Classical building in the entire territory of the Commonwealth."[2]

While today's Vilnius Cathedral, used as a picture gallery and concert hall during most of the Soviet era and renovated in the 1990s, is a completely different structure than its medieval incarnation, other examples of early Gothic architecture in Lithuania have survived. The comparatively diminutive Church of St. Nicholas in Vilnius was first mentioned in written sources in 1387 but may date from as far back as 1320. This makes it the oldest intact church in the entire country. Gothic churches built in the era of Vytautas also survive in Trakai and Merkinė (each is known as the Church of the Assumption), as well as in Kaunas. The latter's Church of St. George, a spare structure erected in the early fifteenth century, fell into a state of disrepair during Soviet times and its tall lancet windows were bricked up. In considerably better condition is the mysterious Perkūnas House, whose name is derived from the discovery of a statue of the Lithuanian thunder god in one of its walls. Dating from the late fifteenth century, the Perkūnas House features more extravagant Gothic brickwork and is an excellent if rare example of the era's secular architecture. Also located in Kaunas is Lithuania's largest Gothic church, known simply as the Cathedral. Originally built early in the fifteenth century, the building has endured numerous fires and reconstructions, which explains the Renaissance and Baroque character of its interior.

Still more eclectic is the Church of St. John, which stands at the head of the 12-building complex that comprises Vilnius University. Founded in 1387—two centuries before the university arrived—and completed in 1426, the church was originally a Gothic structure, but in the eighteenth century it was reconstructed with a late Baroque-style façade. Its unique belfry has both Baroque and Renaissance features.

Of all of Lithuania's architectural monuments, the most celebrated is the Church of St. Anne, which was designed in 1495–1500 but completed only in 1581. A masterpiece of late Gothic architecture and somewhat smaller than the massive structures of an earlier era, its intricately ornamented façade is made from 33 different types of red brick. It is said that on seeing this gem Napoleon was so captivated by it that he declared his wish to take the church back to Paris with him.

RENAISSANCE AND BAROQUE ARCHITECTURE

Renaissance architecture arrived in the Baltic region in the first decades of the sixteenth century, but it left few traces in Lithuania. The building of Vilnius's defensive walls with its nine gates coincided with the arrival of this new architectural style, but these were almost entirely gone by at the end of the eighteenth century. Small portions of the wall have survived, as well as the Aušros (Dawn) Gate, which adjoins a chapel that houses the miracle-working icon *Madonna of the Aušros Gate*.[3]

As in Lithuania, the Renaissance's architectural impact in Estonia and Latvia was mostly limited to adding Renaissance ornamentation to existing buildings. In Tallinn the greatest architectural achievement of the period was the House of the Fraternity of Blackheads (1597), whose Renaissance façade

Art Nouveau architecture, Riga, Elizabetes Street 10b, designed by Mikhail Eistenstein (1903).

Last surviving medieval gate in Vilnius. Aušros ("dawn") Gate adjoins a chapel that houses the miracle-working icon Madonna of the Aušros Gate.

features the fraternity's coat of arms in carved stone plates on either side of the portico. Riga, too, has its own Blackheads' House, located in the architecturally eclectic Town Hall Square.[4] A medieval construction that dates to 1334, the Blackheads' House, which served as a social club for wealthy merchant bachelors (mostly Germans), was rebuilt in 1619–25 by Dutch builders in the Mannerist style that for a time supplanted Gothic architecture in Latvia.[5] Many additions over the centuries gave this building a distinctive appearance, but most of it was destroyed during World War II. Soviet authorities leveled the rest in 1948, but in the late 1990s the structure was rebuilt in grand fashion in anticipation of the city's 800th anniversary.

Several churches in the Mannerist style were built in Lithuania, but the only important surviving structure is the Church of the St. Archangel Michael (1604), which is located across the street from the Church of St. Anne in Vilnius. While the Renaissance style failed to leave a mark in Lithuania, Italian Baroque architecture flourished there in the seventeenth century and gave Vilnius its distinctive appearance.[6] This was due in part to the Jesuits' arrival to the Grand Duchy in 1569. Jesuits were responsible not only for establishing

Art Nouveau architecture, Riga, Strēlnieku Street 10b, designed by Mikhail Eistenstein (1905).

Art Nouveau architecture, Riga. Detail from Jauniela 25/29, designed by Wilhelm Bockslaff (1903).

Vilnius University, then known as the Vilnius Jesuit Academy but they also built Lithuania's first Baroque structure (1593), a church located in Nieśwież (now Nesvizh in Belarus) that was inspired by Il Gesù church in Rome. Il Gesù also served as the inspiration for the Church of St. Casimir (1604–16) in Vilnius. Its large, crowned cupola is unique in the entire region that once constituted the Grand Duchy of Lithuania. Turned into an Orthodox church after the 1830–31 uprising and converted into a Museum of Atheism in the 1960s, the church is once again in the hands of the Jesuits.

Among the most exquisite Baroque monuments in Lithuania is the Church of St. Peter and St. Paul in Vilnius (1668–76), which features a magnificent interior containing around 2,000 stucco statues. Also architecturally significant is the Pažaislis Monastery at the eastern edge of Kaunas. Designed by an Italian architect for the Camaldolese order (a Benedictine offshoot) and constructed during the last third of the seventeenth century, it is the only Baroque complex in Lithuania built according to axial principles.

Baroque styles were introduced to Tallinn in the 1630s, when it was under Swedish rule, but Dutch influences predominated in the seventeenth century. Narva, a city that is as old as Tallinn, once contained an impressive Baroque ensemble, but with the exception of the Town Hall (1671), these buildings were destroyed in World War II. In Pärnu the elegant Tallinn Gate (1690), called the King Carl Gustav Gate until Estonia came under Russian rule, is one of the last surviving seventeenth-century town-wall gates in the Baltics.[7] While its defensive function is now obsolete, it has recently acquired the equally significant function of serving intoxicating beverages to paying customers.

The changing face of Riga during the seventeenth century is best represented by the three famous medieval residential houses on Mazā Pils Street known as the Three Brothers: house no. 17, a Gothic structure built in the fifteenth century, is the oldest residential brick building in the city; house no. 19, which acquired its present exterior in 1646 and now houses the Riga Museum of Architecture, was a merchant house whose façade suggests the influence of Dutch Mannerism; house no. 21 was built in the late seventeenth century and features a Baroque-style roof.

Baroque styles began to arrive in Riga only late in the seventeenth century and soon spread throughout Latvia as the country began to be rebuilt following the devastation of the Great Northern War. At this time Latvian architecture began to lose its medieval characteristics. In Riga one of the most important examples of Baroque architecture is the Reitern (or Reutern) House (1685), an opulent dwelling house in the Dutch style that is distinguished by its large windows and a long wall that runs along the street. The symbolism of its façade, which depicts a Swedish lion battling a Russian bear, is lost on no one familiar with the city's tumultuous history.

In Latvia's Latgale region, which remained under Polish influence until 1772, examples of Italian Baroque survive in Pasiene and Krāslava, where churches were built in 1761 and 1763. However, the Baroque style is best exemplified by the grand palace and park ensembles located south of Riga in Rundāle and Jelgava (once the capital of the Duchy of Courland). Each of these palaces was built in two phases by the Italian-Russian architect Francesco Bartolomeo Rastrelli (1770–71) for Empress Anna Ioannovna's chief advisor Duke Ernst Johann von Bühren, while the court in St. Petersburg provided the funding. With a façade that stretches more than 200 meters, Jelgava Palace was designed to be imposing. Work on the palace was begun in 1738, but with the duke's arrest and subsequent exile in 1740, the interior was left unfinished until his return in the 1760s.[8] The Jelgava Palace—destroyed in 1919 and again in 1944—may be the larger of the two, yet the stylistically similar but even grander Rundāle Palace (near Bauska) is usually considered the most important Baroque style monument in Latvia. Begun in 1736, work on the 40-room palace was halted four years later for the same reason; thus the lavish Rococo interior was not completed until 1770.[9]

NEO-CLASSICAL AND RUSSIAN INFLUENCES

German, Dutch, and Italian influences are predominant in the architecture of Baltic cities, but influences from Russia are also hard to miss. The neo-Classical style favored by Empress Catherine II first appeared in Baltic cities in the 1780s but within a few decades was competing with several other architectural styles. The major center of Estonian neo-Classicist architecture is Tartu, a constant battleground where almost everything predating the eighteenth century has been destroyed by wars and fires.[10] Here the early neo-Classical style is represented by the Town Hall (1772–89), which features Dutch and Baroque elements, and several buildings in the surrounding square. At the heart of the town is Tartu University (1803–09), an excellent example of High Classicism. Its main building, which functions as an assembly and concert hall, was designed by the architect Johann Krause and with its Doric portico is the very symbol of Tartu. (It is depicted on the back of the 2EEK note.) In comparison to Tartu there are relatively few entirely neo-Classical buildings in the Estonian capital; more often this style appears as a new façade built onto what is often a partly medieval building. The most architecturally significant neo-Classicist structure in Tallinn is the pink Estonian Parliament (*Riigikogu*) building (1870, rebuilt in 1921), which is part of the Toompea Castle complex.

Neo-Classical forms are more common in the countryside of northern Estonia, which, thanks to the spendthrift ways of a local nobility eager to embrace European fashions, experienced an extraordinary construction boom in the late eighteenth and early nineteenth centuries. Among the many surviving neo-Classical structures are the estates in Hõreda, Pirgu, Kabala, Riisipere, Saku, and Roosna-Alliku. Although not exactly a neo-Classical structure (French, Dutch, and Italian influences are all evident), the Palmse mansion that was once owned by the von der Pahlen family is of particular interest. Begun in 1697 and restored in 1971–86, it is the largest manor house in Estonia.

In comparison to Estonia, neo-Classicism has not been very influential in Latvia and Lithuania. In both countries it is mainly evident in palaces and manor houses, as well as in a few churches. The best examples of neo-Classical architecture in Vilnius are the Cathedral and the Town Hall (1781–86), both rebuilt by Wawrzyniec Guciewicz (1753–98).[11] Another excellent example of neo-Classical (tinged with late Baroque) architecture from this period is Kaunas's remodeled Town Hall (1771–80), nicknamed the "White Swan" for its soaring tower. Also architecturally significant are the series of multistory houses designed by Riga's master builder Christoph Haberland (1750–1803). Examples of "burgher classicism," they are principally marked by their symmetrical, partially Baroque façades, and restrained ornamentation. Haberland also supervised the construction of the Peter and Paul Cathedral (1776–86), a Russian Orthodox church in Riga.

To the residents of the Baltic cities, the construction of new Russian Orthodox churches—as well as the conversion of older Catholic and Protestant churches into Orthodox houses of worship—was a constant reminder of the closeness of St. Petersburg. While the converted churches retain much of their earlier Gothic or Baroque appearance, those built during the nineteenth and early twentieth centuries are easily identifiable by their Byzantine cupolas. In Vilnius the most important Orthodox church is the Church of the Holy Spirit, which was originally built in the seventeenth century Baroque style. However, the Church of the Apparition of the Mother of God (1903) and the Church of St. Michael and St. Constantine (1913), both built in the traditional onion-dome style, are much more prominently located: the former was provocatively built on the same street (but at the opposite end) as Vilnius Cathedral, while the latter sits atop one of the city's highest points so that its garishly green cupolas might be seen from miles away. Likewise, the onion domes of Tallinn's Alexander Nevsky Cathedral (1894–1900) were designed to dominate the Tallinn skyline.[12] Although less obtrusive than the Alexander Nevsky Cathedral, the Russian Orthodox Church (1876–84) constructed just outside the Riga city center also served to underline the power of St. Petersburg. During the Soviet era it served as a planetarium but was recently restored to its former glory.

Russian architectural influence in the Baltics can also be seen in the relatively small number of structures built in the late Classical—or Empire—style favored by the tsars Alexander I and Nicholas I after the defeat of Napoleon in 1815. Intended to inspire awe, buildings constructed in the Empire style were conceived as imperial monuments and often featured soaring columns and massive façades. While these buildings are located mainly in St. Petersburg and Helsinki, modest versions of the Empire style can also be seen today in Krustpils, Latvia, where the Evangelical Lutheran Church was built in 1818, and in Vilnius, where the Tiškevičius (Tyszkiewicz in Polish) Palace was reconstructed in 1840. An excellent example of the Empire style is the monumental and solemn Presidential Palace in Vilnius. Originally built in the fourteenth century as a nobleman's residence, for most of its history (1543–1794) it was owned by the bishops of Vilnius; however in 1824–32 it was reconstructed as the headquarters for the Governor General of Vilnius. Today it is where the president of Lithuania performs his duties.

The period of Russian rule, especially after 1820, also coincided with the rise of historicist architecture. Involving the eclectic imitation of the architectural styles of the past, historicist principles were applied during both the restorations of damaged buildings and the constructions of new ones. Thus when St. Olaf's Church in Tallinn burned down in 1820, its restorers sought to rebuild the church in what they believed to be its ideal Gothic form. Likewise, the architect who designed the Alexander Nevsky

Cathedral in Tallinn based his design on seventeenth-century Muscovite churches. Throughout the Baltics buildings went up that sought to emulate the old Romanesque, Gothic, Renaissance, and Baroque architectural forms. While the Riga Stock Exchange (1852–55) was built in the Italian neo-Renaissance style, the city's Great Guild Hall was restored in the English Gothic style in 1854–58. In the Estonian countryside neo-Gothic architecture began to compete with the neo-Classicist style in the construction of manor houses.

NATIONAL ROMANTICISM, ART NOUVEAU, AND FUNCTIONALISM

During the second half of the nineteenth century the most active builders in Latvian and Estonian cities were architects of Baltic German or Russian descent, most of whom were trained at the Riga Polytechnicum. By the end of the century, however, this institute—now the University of Latvia—began to train the Latvian and Estonian architects who profoundly influenced the changing architectural landscape of Baltic urban centers. Of the latter, the most dynamic during the last decades of the nineteenth century was Riga, which by 1913 was the Russian Empire's fifth-largest city. With the demolition of its old walls and fortifications in 1857–63, the city's architectural landscape was quickly and dramatically transformed.

The makeover of Riga in the second half of the nineteenth century was largely the work of Jānis Baumanis (1834–91), the first professionally qualified Latvian architect. Focusing his attention principally on the new Riga boulevard area where the old fortress ramparts once stood, Baumanis designed more than 150 buildings in the city. Most were multistory neo-Renaissance and neo-Gothic style apartments, but Baumanis also constructed a number of public buildings in Riga as well as 17 Russian Orthodox churches in the Livland (eastern Latvia and southern Estonia) province. Several of the impressive public structures built—mostly by Baltic German architects—in the decades before World War I remain among the most important architectural and cultural landmarks in the city. They include: the Latvian National Opera (called the First City Theater when it was first built in 1860–63), which was reconstructed in the burgher Classicist style in 1887; the beautiful Latvian National Theater, built in the neo-Baroque style in 1899–1902; the Latvian Academy of Art, built in 1902–5 in the Gothic brick style; and the State Museum of Art, built in the neo-Baroque form in 1903–5.

Without a doubt Riga's most exciting architectural style during the years between 1898 and 1913 was Art Nouveau, which met both the living requirements of the city's rapidly growing middle class and the artistic need of architects who had grown weary of the prevailing historicist approach to the building arts. Developing originally in Germany (where it is called *Jugendstil*) and Belgium, Art Nouveau architecture reflected the era's neo-Romantic mood, whose supreme value was the depiction of universal beauty. Thus the buildings constructed in this style are flamboyant and exuberant, placing great emphasis on decorations and ornamentation. However, functional logic was never subordinated to aesthetics, for the architects who worked in this style were convinced that a building's exterior should be suited to its purpose. In the early period of Art Nouveau architecture (1898–1905), elaborately decorated façades featuring all manner of flora and fauna as well as fantastical creatures such as dragons were common. However, a distinctly Latvian National Romanticism emerged in the structures built in Riga after 1905: decorations became more subdued as naturalistic ornaments were supplanted by geometric forms. Although traditional Art Nouveau elements remained in place, the newer buildings were characterized by the use of natural building materials and their façades began to feature elements from Latvian folklore.

Most Art Nouveau buildings are located outside Riga's green belt—a series of small parks that divide the Old Town—and perhaps 40 percent were constructed by innovative young Latvian architects such as Eižens Laube (1880–1967) and Konstantīns Pēkšēns (1859–1928). While it was Pēkšēns, the designer of over 230 buildings in Riga alone, who did more than anyone to give central Riga its distinctive architectural character, the most famous architect to build in the Art Nouveau style was Mikhail Eisenstein (1867–1921), father of the famous Russian film director Sergei Eisenstein. Decorations on Eisenstein's buildings, several of which still stand along or near Elizabetes Street, tend to be dramatically expressive. An especially powerful example is the apartment building at 10b, whose Symbolist façade is breathtaking in its detail. Nearby Alberta Street features some of the city's most extravagant buildings in the Art Nouveau style, designed by various architects between 1900 and 1908 (including Eisenstein). A more rational interpretation of Art Nouveau can be seen in the National Romantic style apartment blocks on A. Čaka Street built a few years later by Eižens Laube. The sheer number and diversity of the buildings erected in the Art Nouveau style in Riga make it the preeminent center of Art Nouveau architecture in the Baltic states and among the most breathtaking in all of Europe.

In Estonia the National Romantic style, coinciding with and stimulated by the Art Nouveau architecture of Helsinki, that featured prominently in the construction of the country's theaters, clubs, and apartment houses during this period. The Finnish architect Armas Lindgren was involved in the design of both the Estonian Students' Society (1902) and the monumental Vanemuine Theater (1906) in Tartu. For a time the latter, described by a contemporary as "a magic castle emerged from the depths of the earth," was one of the country's most prominent national symbols, but it was destroyed in World War II.[13] Despite its distinct neo-Classicist features, the Estonia Theater, built by Lindgren and Wivi Lönn in 1909–13, is Tallinn's most impressive Art Nouveau building today; it too was destroyed in the war, but the building was later restored to more or less its original shape. Lost to history, however, is the structure that many regard as the greatest achievement of Estonian Romanticism, Karl Burman's (1882–1965) Kalev clubhouse (1912) in Pirita.

At a time when Art Nouveau and National Romantic styles were flourishing in Riga, Tallinn, and Tartu, construction in Vilnius and Kaunas stagnated. At the turn of the century Lithuanian architecture remained mostly traditional, characterized predominantly by an eclectic imitation of past styles. The massive Baroque and Gothic façade of the National Philharmonic Hall (1902) in Vilnius, for example, is a monument to eclecticism. A better guide to architectural development in Lithuania after World War I is Kaunas, the country's provisional capital, while Vilnius remained a neglected provincial city under Polish occupation. The Lithuanian Bank, the oldest commercial bank in Lithuania, was one of the capital's showpieces. Built in 1924–29 by Mykolas Songaila (1874–1941), the country's top architect during the interwar era, the bank's neo-Classical façade featured folk art motifs.

After World War I, a reaction against the historicist and eclectic approaches to architecture set in among younger architects and designers. This reaction was best captured by the ethos of the Bauhaus movement, which generally followed the principle that form must follow function. Emerging first in Germany and quickly becoming influential in Scandinavia, Functionalist architecture became the predominant style in the independent Republic of Estonia in the 1920s and 1930s. The Tallinn Art Hall, built by Edgar Johann Kuusik (1888–1974) and Anton Soans (1885–1966) is a masterpiece of Functionalist architecture and as the country's principal exhibition hall remains at the center of Estonian cultural life today. Among the country's loveliest Functionalist buildings from this era are those designed by Olev Siinmaa (1881–1948) in the resort town of Pärnu. The influence of Functionalism can also be seen in schoolhouses, industrial buildings, and the white villas that were built all over Estonia in the 1930s; despite the widespread destruction of World War II, a surprising number of these buildings have been preserved.

Modern, Bauhaus-inspired architecture arrived in Lithuania with the construction of Kaunas's Main Post Office (1932), which was designed by Feliksas Vizbaras. Vytautas Landsbergis-Žemkalnis (1893–1994) was another important Kaunas architect, but some of the capital's most important showpiece buildings were built by Vladimiras Dubeneckis (1888–1932), including the Vytautas Magnus War Museum (1929) and the Mikalojus Konstantinas

Čiurlionis Art Museum (1936); the latter is featured on the 20 Lt (*litu*) banknote today.[14] Characterized by a balance between functionality and aesthetics, such public buildings were intended to represent a distinct national architectural style in celebration of Lithuania's independence. However, since World War II Kaunas has occupied the position of Lithuania's second city, and the structures built since that time are generally of little architectural interest.

In Latvia, two of the most noteworthy architectural developments of the interwar era were the founding of the Open-Air Ethnographic Museum by Lake Jugla (on the outskirts of Riga) and the creation of Riga's Central Market. The fascinating Ethnographic Museum, founded in 1924, now covers 250 acres and, by including many objects of traditional peasant architecture, depicts the traditional Latvian way of life from the sixteenth through the nineteenth centuries.[15] Near the railway station and just outside the city center is the Central Market. Begun in 1924 and the second largest market in Europe when it was completed in 1930, it consists of five pavilions originally designed as zeppelin hangars and is one of the most identifiable features of Riga's architectural landscape today. Also hard to miss is the Freedom Monument (1935), which at 350 meters in height dominates the city center. Designed by Kārlis Zāle and dedicated on the seventeenth anniversary of Latvia's independence, the monument, which replaced an older monument to Peter the Great, consists of a tall granite column on top of which stands the figure of a westward-facing woman (popularly known as "Milda") who holds three golden stars over her head, representing Latvia's three cultural regions (Kurzeme, Vidzeme, and Latgale). At the monument's base are several sets of figures, each of which tells a story about the nation and its myths and history.

ARCHITECTURAL STYLES SINCE 1945

After the war ended in 1945, Soviet planners quickly drew up projects for the general layouts of the damaged Baltic cities, whose builders had little choice but to adopt the official architectural forms imposed by Moscow. As a result many Baltic cities acquired a somewhat Soviet appearance: Pärnu (Estonia), for example, has a Stalinist city center, while Šiauliai (Lithuania), which lost 80 percent of its buildings during World War II and later became a center for high-tech industries, is almost entirely Soviet in appearance. Among the few surviving monuments of Šiauliai's "old town" the most important is the late Renaissance-style cathedral (1617–34). Although Estonian and Lithuanian cities were not targeted for Soviet monumentalist architecture, a classic example of the Stalinist Gothic style can be seen in Riga, which was awarded a wedding-cake style skyscraper similar to those erected in Moscow and Warsaw after the war. Built as the Palace of Collective Farm Workers and completed in 1958, it now houses the Latvian Academy of Sciences.

Less ostentatious but more useful were the prefabricated apartment houses constructed in the residential areas located outside the city centers from the late 1950s onward. Mass-produced, cheap, and generally unattractive, these concrete panel apartment houses were built mostly to house the laborers from the Soviet interior who poured into Baltic cities to work in local industries. Rural areas were also given a new look with the construction of austere, strictly utilitarian buildings for the new collective and state farms. Hardly less severe in appearance were the new public buildings that were erected during the Soviet period. In many cities there was a tendency to construct Soviet modernist structures without taking into account the nearby architectural landscape. Among the most egregious examples of this is the black box next to Riga's House of Blackheads that now houses the Museum of the Occupation of Latvia.[16]

Yet the architectural legacy of the Soviet era is not entirely negative. Although cheaply built, the new structures clearly served a need. Indeed, as many as three times the number of buildings were erected during the 45 years of Soviet rule than in previous centuries. Moreover, after around 1955 architectural developments in the Baltic republics were no longer closed off to outside influences. While planners in Moscow attempted to homogenize Soviet cities, a number of dedicated young architects worked to preserve the architectural heritage of their cities while creating structures that would better blend into the surrounding environment. An excellent example of Estonian architectural creativity during the late 1950s is the Song Festival Amphitheater, the site of Estonia's national song festivals. Built in Tallinn by the Estonian architects Alar Kotli (1904–63) and Henno Sepmann (1925–85), the amphitheater is massive but does not overwhelm the surrounding landscape. Likewise, the Flower Pavilion (1960), built by Valve Pormeister (b. 1922) in nearby Pirita, is an example of organic architecture that also shows the influence of international modernism. On the other hand, there is the Viru Hotel, a 22-story monstrosity that brutalizes the capital's medieval architectural heritage. Originally built in the 1970s to seclude foreign visitors, it was renovated by its Finnish owners in the 1990s.

While Soviet modernist architecture—mostly in the form of massive, unoriginal apartment blocs in the city outskirts—remained the predominant style during the Brezhnev era, by the 1970s and 1980s it competed with the avant-garde "Tallinn School," whose practitioners advocated a return to the heritage of 1930s Functionalism and a greater connection with international architectural trends. Although the Soviet state's attempt to isolate the Tallinn School limited their influence mostly to the countryside, local architectural innovation was not entirely crushed. The USSR's last significant architectural legacy in Estonia, the massive National Library (1985–93) in Tallinn, is actually rather impressive: an eight-story building whose walls are made of dolomite limestone from Saaremaa, it is the largest library in the Baltic states.

Just as Estonian architects looked to Scandinavia, a Westward gaze persisted among the architects of Lithuania and Latvia during the Soviet era. Influential Lithuanian architects such as Vytautas Brėdikis (b. 1930) and Vytautas Čekanauskas (b. 1930) managed to insulate the center of Vilnius from the new industrially manufactured housing blocs of the 1960s. In an attempt to humanize Soviet modernism they looked to Finnish architecture, whose paramount principle was the accommodation of nature. Their success is evident in the terraced buildings that began going up in 1967 in the hills of Lazdynai, just a few kilometers from the center of Vilnius.[17] Čekanauskas also designed several public buildings in Vilnius, which, despite their size and purely functional design, are well integrated with the environment; the most notable of these is the Contemporary Art Center (1965–67). Also of some architectural interest is the television tower (1980) in Vilnius, which at 1,069 feet is Lithuania's tallest structure and the scene of a bloody confrontation between Lithuanians and the Soviet army in 1991.

In Latvia, an example of good modern architecture from the Soviet era is the television building (1987), a glass and steel skyscraper in Riga. Another local Soviet-era favorite is the television tower (1987) on Zaķu (Hare) Island outside the Riga city center, which at just over 1,200 feet is significantly taller than the Eiffel Tower. Less appreciated by most Latvians was the 27-story Hotel Latvijā, a Soviet-era eyesore that has dominated the skyline of Riga's New Town since 1979. However, many locals would agree that the complete renovation of the hotel in 2000–1 gave the building, which remains the tallest in the country, a more agreeable appearance.

With the emergence of a private commercial sector in the 1990s, new opportunities for architectural innovation appeared in Baltic cities, and especially in the capitals. In Vilnius, which is rapidly being transformed into a twenty-first century metropolis, glass and steel skyscrapers like the monolithic new 23-story city administration building and Audrius Ambrasas's split-cylinder Europa Tower—at 33 stories the tallest building in the Baltics—now loom over some of the city's historic structures. In Tallinn the Estonian Union Bank (*Eesti Ühispank*) building, a triangular shaped glass skyscraper designed by the immensely successful Estonian architect Raivo Puusepp, was completed in 1999. Its 24 stories are bested only by the Radisson SAS Hotel (2001), which at 25 stories is the tallest in Estonia. The commercial construction boom has been paralleled by architectural innovations in private housing, most notably in Estonian residential areas like Pärnu, where white neo-Functionalist villas are being built to meet the housing needs of the country's emerging middle class.

While new commercial buildings and private dwellings mushroom in and around the major Baltic cities, older structures have been undergoing expensive renovations that give the capitals a considerably fresher look than was the case during the Soviet era, when many old landmarks were neglected. This neglect still characterizes most of the provincial cities and towns of the Baltic countries. While the historic centers of Tallinn, Riga, and Vilnius have been designated UNESCO World Heritage sites and between them have thousands of protected monuments, just as many old structures in the towns and villages, including the 200-years-old wooden churches of Lithuania, remain at risk.

HOUSING

As is the case in nearly all countries, housing in the Baltic countries varies in quality and style, especially in the countryside. Whether they reside in Estonia, Latvia, or Lithuania, many rural inhabitants continue to live in individual small wooden houses in traditional villages, where they typically have gardens, sheds, and animals. Most city-dwellers, on the other hand, live in apartments designed by Soviet architects whose goal was to create mass, undifferentiated housing for the hundreds of thousands of country folk who were streaming to the cities in search of work in Soviet factories. In Baltic cities, preferential treatment was given to workers arriving from the Soviet interior; as a result of Soviet industrial and colonization policies, Russian speakers and their descendants form the majority of inhabitants in cities such as Riga, Daugavpils, and Narva.

The great boom in housing took place from the late 1950s through the early 1980s, when concrete-paneled prefabricated apartment buildings were hastily erected throughout the Soviet Union. While these apartments helped to ameliorate the housing crisis that plagued Baltic and other Soviet cities after World War II, they were built to last only a few decades and are generally of dubious quality. Most are located in suburbs that are easily reached by train or bus, but in only a few cases was much consideration given to the local environment and landscape. Indeed, the massive housing complexes of suburban Tallinn or Riga are nearly interchangeable with those of St. Petersburg or Minsk. The cheerless five-story *khrushchevki* (so-named after the Soviet leader Nikita Khrushchev) built in the 1950s and 1960s are in dilapidated condition everywhere they stand, while many of the pale Brezhnev-era high-rises—the ultimate in Soviet modernism—are also in poor condition. The stress on many of these buildings has been readily evident for years.

In Soviet times, families, such as newlywed couples, had to endure long waits on housing lists before the state awarded them individual apartments. Today these dwellings are typically the personal property of their inhabitants, although many apartments are rented as well. Reflecting the dearth of consumer choice in the Soviet era, there is little variety from one apartment to the next. A typical apartment has one, two, or perhaps three bedrooms (one of which usually doubles as a family room), a small bathroom (the toilet is located in a separate, adjoining room), and a tiny kitchen that is big enough for a small table and three or four stools at most. Closet space is the rarest of commodities: most families store their clothes in armoires. In most apartments it is the kitchen rather than the living room that is the focal point of activity. This is where people gather, eat, talk, and drink. While nearly all apartments have refrigerators and many now have microwave ovens, few are equipped with dishwashers or other modern amenities. Most also have balconies, which are typically used for storage.

Since the collapse of the USSR and the arrival of the market economy, new housing options have appeared that were unimaginable in Soviet times: while the affluent may buy downtown luxury apartments in new or renovated buildings, middle-class families often aspire to own a single-family home in a new subdivision. Country cottages of varying sizes and shapes, often with modern amenities, are also available to those who can afford to build or buy them, yet these are beyond the reach of most ordinary citizens living in the Baltic countries. Most people simply make do with the apartments in which they have lived since the days when they carried Soviet passports.

NOTES

1. There are now plans to rebuild parts of Vilnius's destroyed Jewish quarter and to reconstruct the Great Synagogue.

2. Tomas Venclova, *Vilnius: City Guide,* 3rd ed. (Vilnius: R. Paknys Publishing House, 2003), 80–83.

3. Historian Theodore Weeks pointed out that both the gate and the icon it houses have Polish origins. The Polish name of *Aušros Gate* was *Ostra Bama* (Sharp Gate) and its icon, a major pilgrimage site for Poles, was supposed to have won Polish, not Lithuanian, battles. Personal communication.

4. Once the city's administrative center, Town Hall Square is the largest in Inner Riga. Its size—1.2 hectares—is the product of the devastation of World War II.

5. Mannerism was a predominant style of painting, sculpture, and architecture in Italy from the 1520s until the end of the sixteenth century. A transitional style between the High Renaissance and the Baroque, Mannerism was characterized by its emotion and visual daring.

6. A style that sought to stimulate the senses, stressing complexity over simplicity, Baroque architecture emphasized grandeur, opulence, and decorativeness.

7. Another is the Swedish Gate in Riga.

8. In the interregnum, Rastrelli returned to Russia proper to build the magnificent Summer Palace (1741–44) in St. Petersburg, the Grand Palace at Peterhof (1747–52), and the palace at Tsarskoye Selo (1749–56).

9. The Rococo style emerged from the Baroque in France after 1715 and lasted through the 1770s. It was characterized by pastel shades and light, graceful interiors.

10. Restoration of Tartu's thirteenth-century St. John's Church—one of the most imposing Gothic buildings in the Baltic states—is scheduled for completion in 2005.

11. Begun in 1783, the Cathedral's reconstruction was not completed until 1801, after the architect's death.

12. The cathedral's name was significant, as Alexander Nevsky was a Russian prince who conquered part of Estonia during struggles with the German knights in the thirteenth century. A much less ostentatious Orthodox church is the Church of Our Lady of Kazan (1721), the oldest wooden structure in the city. Nineteenth century renovations gave the building a Classicist façade.

13. Liivi Künnapu, *Estonian Architecture: The Building of a Nation* (Helsinki: The Finnish Building Center, 1992), 17.

14. Originally opened in 1925 as the M. K. Čiurlionis Gallery, the museum was renamed the Vytautas Magnus Museum of Culture when its new building was finished in 1936; in 1944 it was named again after Čiurlionis.

15. Lithuania's best open-air museum is located in Rumšiškės. Established in 1966, it contains more than 150 buildings representing the country's four ethnographic regions. Its leading Estonian counterpart, located just outside Tallinn, first opened to the public in 1964 and now consists of more than 70 buildings.

16. The building originally housed the Riflemen Museum (1970), but it was closed in the early 1990s and reopened as the Occupation Museum in 1993.

17. John Vincent Maciuika, "Architecture and National Identity in Lithuania, 1945–1999: Looking West to Germany's New Federal States, France and Finland," www.humboldt-foundation.de/de/programme/stip_aus/doc/buka/berichte_98/maciuika.pdf.

SELECTED READINGS

Grosa, Silvija. *Art Nouveau in Riga.* Riga: Jumava, 2003.

Hallas, Karin, ed. *Twentieth Century Architecture in Tallinn: Architectural Guide.* Tallinn: The Museum of Estonian Architecture, 2000.

Jomantas, Alfredas. *Wooden Architecture in Lithuania.* Vilnius: Vaga, 2002.

Krastiņš, Jānis. *The Masters of Architecture of Riga.* Riga: Jumava, 2002.

Künnapu, Liivi. *Estonian Architecture: The Building of a Nation.* Helsinki: The Finnish Building Center, 1992.

Vaisvilaite, Irena, A. Sverdiolas, Tojana Raciunaite, and Vida Urbonaviciute. *Baroque in Lithuania.* Vilnius: Baltos lankos, 1996.

Venclova, Tomas. *Vilnius: City Guide,* 3rd ed. Vilnius: R. Paknys Publishing House, 2003.

Other Sources and Websites

"The Museum of Estonian Architecture," www.arhitektuurimuuseum.ee/eam/english/index.htm.

The Estonian Institute www.einst.ee/Ea/architecture/index.html.

9

Art

ANY ASSERTION THAT there is an art of "the Baltic region" would be a gross over-simplification, for despite their shared political history the Baltic countries are very different culturally. Yet the professional art of the Baltic countries does share one common characteristic: as with architecture, theater, and professional dance, the artistic heritage of the Baltics has been built on European foundations. Latvian cultural life, like that of Estonia, developed under the tutelage of the Baltic Germans, but by the nineteenth century Russian influences had become more pronounced in the Latvian lands. Estonia's cultural and artistic heritage is more closely linked to Scandinavia, while Lithuanian culture and art developed with a specifically Polish orientation. It is perhaps from these external influences that critics reflexively ascribe certain qualities to each country's art. While Latvian art is thought to be "monumental" and "classicist," Estonian art is reputedly "cool" and "rational"; "colorful" and "expressive" are the words most commonly used to describe Lithuanian art. These generalizations reflect a certain reality about the art of the Baltic countries, but a fuller appreciation of Baltic art requires a more flexible approach.

FOLK ART

Lithuania, Latvia, and Estonia all have ancient traditions of wood carving, weaving, knitting, leatherworking, metalworking, and ceramics. Although less outwardly complex than European-influenced professional art, the folk art that has flourished in the Baltic region for many centuries is of no less spiritual

Rural dwellings, Kleboniskes village, central Lithuania, part of the Daugyvene Cultural and Historic Museum.

Another rural dwelling from Kleboniskes village.

depth, and its makers have often possessed impressive technical skills. More-over, the unique patterns and spatial relationships evident in these ancient folk-art forms are often replicated in the fine arts of the Baltic countries today.

Estonia and Latvia have folk-art traditions that are several centuries old, but for variety and distinctiveness the folk art of Lithuania is second to none. Most of Lithuania's past folk-art masters, called *dievdirbiai* or "godmakers," are forgotten and many of the works they created before the nineteenth century are irretrievably lost. Yet some of these folk craftsmen are relatively well-known and their works are preserved in museums. The most notable of Lithuania's *dievdirbiai* was Vincas Svirskis (1835–1916), a wandering, self-taught carver of gigantic oak crosses and little wooden statues of Christ and saints. In the twentieth century the tradition was continued by woodcarvers such as Ipolitas Užkurnys (b. 1926) and Adolfas Viluckis (b. 1939).

Lithuania's figurative sculptural tradition began only in the seventeenth century, when people in the most remote parts of Lithuania, Europe's last pagan country, at last began to practice Christianity. Christian saints and holy figures have been among the most popular subjects of Lithuanian folk art; however, the most prevalent and perhaps finest form of Lithuanian folk sculpture is the cross, whose ubiquity has earned this heavily forested country

Lithuanian folk art, Couronian Spit, Lithuania. Wooden folk art can be found in the most unex-pected locations in Lithuania.

its reputation as a Land of Crosses. By the nineteenth century folk crosses became intrinsic to local culture as local customs began to be expressed in ways that were in line with official Church practices; thus older pagan motifs merged with Christian symbols to create uniquely Lithuanian folk-art forms. Iron graveyard crosses, for example, usually incorporate a sun, which is traditionally depicted as a circle surrounded by a six-pointed star, while the wooden crosses found outside farmsteads often feature a crucifix located within or atop a sun. The Hill of Crosses near Šiauliai features what is possibly the world's largest and most surreal collection of crosses, ranging in size from the miniscule to a height of five meters. (See illustration on page 60.)

But suns and crosses are not the only motifs of Lithuanian folk art: at crossroads, in cemeteries, and in village squares all over Lithuanian one still sees the wooden figures of saints and weathercocks, and depictions of the crucified Christ, the Virgin Mary, and the saints are found in chapels and shrines. The shrines (*koplytėlė*) themselves are of some significance: intended to commemorate an important event (such as a tragic death) or to express an appeal for God's protection, they could be located on the ground (as in Žemaitija), on a post, or in a tree (as was common in Aukštaitija); they were usually erected along roadsides, at homesteads, and in cemeteries. To this day

Shrine with cross, Lithuanian countryside. The intermingling of Christian and pagan symbols is common in Lithuanian folk art.

a traveler at a crossroad will occasionally find himself standing face to face with a "Man of Sorrows" (*Rūpintojėlis*), a pensive-looking Christ figure that developed from an earlier pagan form.[1] Another popular iconographic motif of Lithuanian wood carving is St. George, the mounted dragon-slaying warrior who was also the guardian of farm animals. Sculptures of St. Florian, too, served a protective function, as he guarded the homestead against fire.

Many of these sacral structures were destroyed in Soviet times, but surviving works are usually housed in museums or have come under state protection as cultural monuments; others can still be found in plain sight on the roads and in villages across Lithuania, mostly in Žemaitija and Aukštaitija. Most contemporary sculptures are monochromatic and made of untreated wood; subject to the elements, the outdoor sculptures are always weathered and cracked. This is no less true for Lithuanian folk architecture, such as the country's famous wooden churches, many of which date from the eighteenth century. Usually the natural ashen brown color of weathered wood, the exteriors of the old wooden churches are generally simple and unadorned. Their interiors, however, usually feature colorful altars and other objects. Likewise, the exteriors of Lithuania's traditional rural dwellings—preserved in national parks located in Žemaitija, Aukštaitija, and Dzūkija—are unremarkable except for the window frames, which are richly decorated with perforated carvings. These carvings often feature ancient pagan motifs, such as the sun and other celestial bodies that intermingle with Christian symbols.

EARLY PROFESSIONAL ART

Before the fifteenth century the leading art form in the Baltic region was sculpture, surviving examples of which are located in various churches. In Estonia and Latvia most art works from the Middle Ages were created by foreign masters, usually from Germany or the Low Countries, while Lithuanian art showed both Byzantine and Gothic influences until the eighteenth century. Some fragments of medieval Lithuanian art have been preserved, including several painted wooden Gothic statues, most notably a fifteenth-century Madonna from a church in Kretinga. On display at the Island Castle in Trakai is a fifteenth-century mural in the Byzantine style (which heavily influenced Russian art), while the vaults of the Vilnius Cathedral hold a Gothic-style fresco that dates back to the late fourteenth century.

Estonia's most important works of medieval art are housed in St. Nicholas's (*Niguliste*) Church in Tallinn, a thirteenth-century structure that was reconstructed as an art museum and concert hall after World War II. Among its most important artistic treasures is a series of sculpted altars, including the High Altar (1481) by the Lübeck master Hermen Rode and the Altar of St. Mary (1495). Also displayed at St. Nicholas's Church is Berndt Notke's famous fifteenth-century masterpiece *Danse Macabre*. Only one Estonia-born artist from this period stands out, and that is the great portrait painter Michel Sittow (1469–1525), who was also a painter of allegorical scenes and the first Estonian exponent of Renaissance art. The four saints depicted on the Altar of St. Anthony in St. Nicholas's Church are said to be his work.

While the art and architecture of Tallinn shows the influence of the Northern European Renaissance, the Italian influence can be seen in Vilnius, where Italian craftsmen created numerous altars, portals, and monuments. One of Lithuania's most famous artworks—indeed, many devout Catholics consider it to be miraculous—is *Blessed Virgin Mary, Mother of Mercy*, an icon in the Renaissance style that is located in the chapel of the Aušros Gate. The Italian style is also evident in the interiors of Vilnius's many Baroque-style churches. St. Casimir's Chapel in the Vilnius Cathedral, for example, was designed and decorated by Italian architects and sculptors. This extraordinary chapel also contains two large murals painted in 1692 by the portrait painter Michelangelo Palloni (1637–c.1705).

Only at the end of the eighteenth century did a recognizably native fine arts tradition begin to develop in Lithuania. The national art of Estonia and Latvia, where customary social divisions relegated ethnic Estonians and Latvians to the background of cultural life until the middle of the next century, developed somewhat later. In the meantime, departments for architecture (1793), drawing and painting (1797), sculpture (1803), and graphic art (1805) were set up at the Principal School of Lithuania (known as Vilnius University after 1803), which together made up the Vilnius Art School. In 1803 a drawing school was founded at Tartu University, but for more than half a century its students were overwhelmingly German, as was the language of instruction. By the middle of the century many of the Baltic region's leading artists trained at the St. Petersburg Academy of Art, and many others studied in the leading French and German academies. Thus, the national art of Estonia, Latvia, and Lithuania, as it finally began to emerge in the last decades of the nineteenth century, developed largely under the influence of European and Russian artistic movements and tendencies.

NATIONAL SCHOOLS OF ART

The modern art of the Baltic countries can be appreciated only in the context of the region's turbulent history. As the Baltic nations traveled the road from subjugation under foreign overlords to the establishment of national independence, their art, like the art of the other nations of Eastern Europe, tended to emphasize national individuality over universal themes. The assertion that the artists of Eastern Europe "responded variously to a public demand for expressions of national self-consciousness through which an emerging nation might stake its claim to membership in a modern world"[2] may be overstating the point, but it is certainly true that during the interwar era many artists and writers of Eastern Europe offered their talents in service to the nation as interpreters of its essence, its history, and its destiny. Thus, the art of the Baltic states, while developing during an era of national awakening and fertilized by the international exchanges of the modern era, ultimately retreated into a certain cultural narrow-mindedness as legions of modern artists became, in effect, state artists during the 1930s.

Lithuania

Pranciškus Smuglevičius (1745–1807) was the founder of modern Lithuanian art. Born in Warsaw of mixed Polish-Lithuanian ancestry, Smuglevičius (known in Poland as Franciszek Smuglewicz) became an exponent of eighteenth-century classicism while studying and living in Rome. Returning to Vilnius after two decades abroad, Smuglevičius became the first head of the drawing and painting school. Although most of his works use historical themes that reflected the classical ideals of the Enlightenment, he also painted some murals with folkloric themes as well as realistic images from everyday life (*Lithuanian Peasants*). His work can be found in some of Vilnius's beautiful churches: the Vilnius Cathedral holds *The Martyrdom of St. Stanislaus* as well as a complete series of paintings of the Apostles, while the altar of the Church of St. Peter and St. Paul holds *The Parting of St. Peter and St. Paul.*

Smuglevičius's role in the development of Lithuanian art also extended to his mentorship to a generation of artists who themselves went on to become teachers at Lithuanian drawing schools. His protégé Jonas Rustemas (1762–1835), an artist of Armenian descent, ran the Vilnius Art School until it was closed in 1832. Working in various styles, he was celebrated both for his neo-Classical portraits and his Romantic landscapes. Among Rustemas's greatest students was Kanutas Ruseckas (1801–60), another skilled portrait artist and landscape painter. A member of the Carbonari movement in Italy, Ruseckas's political idealism is evident in his painting *Women Reaping* (1843), which romanticizes the purity of the peasantry. A Ruseckas's most important pupils included the romantic painter Valentinas Vankavičius (Walenty Wánkowicz, 1799–1842) and Aleksandras Slendzinskis (1806–78), who in turn trained their own students.

Following the uprisings of 1830–31 the Vilnius Art School was closed, numerous paintings were confiscated, and a rigorous censorship was imposed on Lithuania. Conditions for artists grew still worse after the ill-fated 1863 rebellion, in which many established artists participated, including the Romantic painter Kazimieras Alchimavičius (1840–1916) and Mykolas

Elviras Andriolis (1836–93), who contributed 11 paintings for the Kaunas Cathedral. Some Polish and Lithuanian artists were exiled, while many others emigrated. Despite tsarist repression—and partly because of it—national life in Lithuania (as in Poland) regenerated in the last decades of the nineteenth century as the nation awakened. In 1907, just three years after the Lithuanian press ban was lifted, a group of young artists organized the first Lithuanian art exhibition in Vilnius; seven more followed in the years before World War I. Initiated by the young sculptor Petras Rimša (1881–1961), the first exhibition featured the works of the landscape painter and Devil Museum founder Antanas Žmuidzinavičius (1876–1966), the Symbolist Petras Kalpokas (1880–1945), and Lithuania's most cherished composer (see Chapter 7) and artist, Mikalojus Konstantinas Čiurlionis.

Although largely unknown outside Lithuania, Lithuanians regard Čiurlionis as a genius whose musical and artistic compositions reflect the spiritual and aesthetic mood of the era. His career as a painter was short, lasting only from 1903 to 1909, but it was explosive. Generally regarded as a Symbolist, Čiurlionis can equally be linked to Romanticism; however, the fact that some also regard him as a pioneer of abstraction or a precursor of the Futurists and Surrealists demonstrates the difficulty of assigning Čiurlionis to any particular school or set of artists. Influenced more by German art than by French Impressionism, Čiurlionis's favorite themes were the seasons (*Winter, Spring,* and *Summer* series, 1907–08), the cosmos (the *Zodiac* series, 1907) and fantastic architecture (*A Town,* 1908). *The Knight* (1909) shows Čiurlionis's fascination with Lithuanian folklore, while *The Crosses of Žemaitija* (1909) is an ode to the Lithuanian countryside. Often assigning titles to his paintings such as *Sonata, Prelude,* or *Fugue,* Čiurlionis tried to demonstrate that paintings may possess the same abstract aesthetic qualities as music; indeed, his uniquely complementary musical compositions and paintings may be considered to be two sides of the same coin. Nearly his entire painted output, consisting of some 300 works, is housed in the M. K. Čiurlionis Museum in Kaunas.

The most "Lithuanian" of Lithuania's cities, Kaunas became the new country's capital after the establishment of the new state, and thus the country's leading art institution, the School of Art, was founded there in 1922. The art of Lithuania was less daring than its literature during the 1920s, and the new developments in the art of Western Europe were almost unknown in the insular country. By the 1930s the artistic community was split along generational lines. The establishment in 1932 of the Lithuanian Artists' Society marked an attempt by older artists to consolidate a national art, while another group of younger artists known as *Ars*—which included the painter Antanas Gudaitis (1904–89), the graphic artist Vytautas Jonynas (1907–96), and sculptor Juozas Mikėnas (1901–64)—tried to renew Lithuanian art by breaking the barriers of conservatism and introducing a modern aesthetic. During the Soviet era, this group would be denounced as "formalist" and "bourgeois" and the prewar works of its members would be banned from museums until the early 1960s.

While art in Lithuania proper developed slowly during the interwar era, art in Vilnius—Wilno to its Polish administrators and inhabitants—developed more closely with European trends. At the same time, however, and despite official efforts to Polonize this ancient city, Vilnius remained an outpost of Lithuanian culture. Vytautas Kairiūkštis (1890–1961) was one of the few Lithuanian modernists to remain in Vilnius, where he cemented a local reputation as an avant-garde painter of Cubist compositions (self-portraits, landscapes, and still lifes) while working with the Polish artist Wladyslaw Strzemiński to organize the New Art Exhibition (1923), which marked the birth of the Polish avant-garde. Another important Vilnius-based artist during that period was Kairiūkštis's follower Vladas Drėma (1910–95), a painter of abstract landscapes (*Landscape,* 1928) who helped to realize a modern national style.

While a national style was being created in historic Lithuania, some artists raised in Lithuania prospered outside their homeland. Born near Minsk but brought up in a Lithuanian Jewish ghetto, the Expressionist painter Chaïm Soutine (1894–1944) trained at the Vilnius Academy before settling in Paris in 1911. While living in France he produced scores of landscapes, still lifes, and portraits, many of which are characterized by extreme distortion and a sense of suffering that reflected Soutine's own personal unhappiness. The Cubist sculptor Jacques Lipchitz (1891–1973), a Lithuanian Jew, also emigrated to Paris in 1909, where he thrived for more than 20 years before settling in the United States in 1941. Many of his works are housed in museums in Israel and at the Philadelphia Museum of Art.

Latvia

Nearly all of Latvia's most prominent painters were of German origin until the middle of the nineteenth century. By the time Riga's first art school was founded in 1873, professional artists of Latvian origin had begun to emerge, but the best of them were usually trained at the art institutions of St. Petersburg. Thus the art of Latvia developed largely under Russian influence. The works of Kārlis Hūns (1830–77), for example, show the influence of Karl Briullov's Romantic Classicism. A professor of painting at the Academy of Arts in St. Petersburg (1871–74), Hūns was also the first and only Latvian member of the Wanderers (*peredvizhniki*), a Russian movement of the 1870s whose artists were committed to raising the public's consciousness of art by touring the provinces and painting in a popularly accessible realistic style.

The influence of the Russian school of Latvian art may also be seen in the landscape paintings of Jūlijs Feders (1838–1909), whose studio in St. Petersburg became a meeting place for a younger generation of Latvian artists in the late 1880s. These younger artists included Ādams Alksnis (1864–97) and Jānis Rozentāls (1866–1916), as well as the landscape painters Vilhelms Purvītis (1872–1945) and Jānis Valters (1869–1932), all of whom were members of *Rūķis* (Gnome), a National Romantic school of Latvian art. Alksnis was its founder and leader, while the painter and graphic designer Jānis Rozentāls, who is usually considered the founder of Latvian painting, was the group's most eclectic artist. While his early works show the role of realism in the formative phase of Latvian art (*After the Service,* 1894), Rozentāls is most famous for his Impressionistic landscapes (*Sigulda in Spring,* 1913) and portraits. Rozentāls also wrote essays on art and architecture for several Latvian journals.

The opening of the Riga City Art Museum 1905 marked the true arrival of Latvian national art. By this time the modernist tendencies (Expressionism, Symbolism, post-Impressionism) of Europe were well established in Latvia. At the same time, however, artistic life in Latvia continued to be influenced by Russian artistic trends. The close links between Latvian and Russian art at this time is well illustrated by the short career of the Symbolist painter and art theorist Voldemārs Matvejs (1877–1914). Also known by the pseudonym Vladimir Markov, Matvejs was a leader of the Union of Youth (1910–14), a St. Petersburg art society that organized exhibitions of avant-garde paintings in St. Petersburg and Riga. Among the other prominent Latvian artists of the pre-World War I generation were the graphic artist and writer Jānis Jaunsudrabiņš, the set designer Jānis Kuga (1878–1968), and the painters Jēkabs Kazaks (1895–1920) and Jāzeps Grosvalds (1891–1920). The paintings of both Kazaks and Grosvalds—the latter was a member of one of the elite Latvian riflemen (*strēlnieki*) regiments that fought for the tsar for Latvia—portrayed the tragedy of the struggle in the Baltic; both died early deaths in 1920.

Latvian artistic and cultural life developed somewhat more independently of Russian influence—at least in institutional terms—after the establishment of a new Latvian state. In 1921 the state-sponsored Latvian Academy of Art opened in Riga under the direction (until 1934) of the Impressionist painter Vilhelms Purvītis, who was also placed in charge of the city art gallery. During this period a series of new art groups representing a variety of trends appeared in Latvia, including the Riga Artists' Group, the Association of Independent Artists, *Sadarbs* (Cooperation), *Zaļā Vārna* (Green Cow) and *Radigars* (Spirit). Leary of both Russian and German influences, many Latvian artists looked to France—the birthplace of Cubism (1908)—as a source of inspiration. The Cubistic approach can be seen in the paintings of Erasts Šveics (1895–1992) and Jānis Liepiņš (1894–1964), as well as in the granite and bronze sculptures of Marta Liepiņa-Skulme (1890–1962) and Emīls Melderis (1889–1979), whose works displayed a synthesis of the Cubist and Constructivist approaches.

The founder of Latvia's granite sculpture tradition was Teodors Zaļkalns (1876–1972), a Russia-trained sculptor. His works were characterized not only by their geometric abstraction, but also by the Baltic peasant traditions they often exemplified (*Sitting Woman,* 1916). Latvia's other leading avant-garde sculptor was Kārlis Zāle (1888–1942), a Constructivist whose art was decisively influenced by the two years he spent in Berlin in 1922–24, which at that time was a magnet for modern artists from Eastern Europe. Returning to Riga in 1924, Zāle built the sculptures representing the fallen Latvian soldiers of World War I in the Brothers' Cemetery (1924–38) as well as the Freedom Monument (1935) in the city center.[3]

The synthesis between modernist aesthetics and national cultural formation in Latvia is also evident in the art of Niklāvs Strunke (1894–1966) and Romans Suta (1896–1944), both of whom defy easy categorization as artists. Although known first as a painter, Suta was involved in costume and scenery design for the Latvian opera, theater, and ballet; he was also a leading porcelain designer (*Wedding,* 1928). Strunke's art was no less wide-ranging: while his paintings show the influence of Russian Constructivism and French Cubism, his poster art of the 1930s often married these modernist influences to Latvian folk influences. The graphic art of Sigismunds Vidbergs (1890–1970), who was also known for his interpretation of erotic themes, showed the influence of Art Deco. Art Deco elements also appeared in the set designs of Ludolfs Liberts (1895–1959), who was otherwise known as a prominent Constructivist painter.

Despite the innovations of the 1920s, political conditions in Latvia during the next decade grew less hospitable to inventiveness as the spirit of internationalism eroded throughout Europe and the global depression of the early 1930s devastated art sales. With exhibition opportunities limited and private patronage nearly nonexistent, Cubism and Constructivism gave way to more romantic subjects and conservative styles. By the second half of the 1930s the dictatorship of Kārlis Ulmanis attempted to set the tone of Latvian art by promoting a neorealistic trend, whose main theme appeared to be variations on Latvian boys and girls dressed in national costumes. The artistic uniformity fostered by the Ulmanis regime reached its logical conclusion with the incorporation of all existing Latvian art groups into the Latvian Society of Arts in 1938. Two years later Latvia was occupied by the USSR, thus ending free artistic development in that country for more than four decades.

Estonia

As in Latvia, artistic life in Estonia was monopolized by Baltic German masters until the nation's awakening in the second half of the nineteenth century. Yet ethnic Estonians and their milieu were not entirely absent from Estonian art: under the influence of the Romantic movement German artists such as August Georg Pezold (1795–1859) and Friedrich Siegmund Stern (1812–89) depicted scenes from folk life. Never far from German Europe, Estonia imported Georg Friedrich Schlater (1804–70), who liked to paint cityscapes of his adopted Tallinn, while it exported to Dresden the Estonia-born artist Gerhard von Kügelgen (1772–1820), a specialist in landscapes and portraiture.

While Estonia-born Baltic Germans such as Eduard von Gebhardt (1838–1925), Eugen Dücker (1841–1916), and August Weizenberg (1837–1921)—the founder of Estonian sculpture—secured international reputations in the second half of the nineteenth century, by that time ethnic Estonians such as the realist painter Johann Köler (1826–99) and the sculptor Amandus Adamson (1855–1929) had moved to the forefront of Estonian artistic life. The first truly great Estonian artist and the founder of the Estonian national school of painting, Johann Köler was born in rural poverty in Viljandi but spent the bulk of his time in St. Petersburg, where he attended and then taught at the Academy of Arts. In Russia he was best known for his portraits of royals and society people; during the summers, however, he returned home to Estonia, where he focused on Estonian themes in his historical paintings and landscapes (*Artist's Birthplace,* 1868).

The sculptor Amandus Adamson was also a product of and a teacher at the St. Petersburg Academy of Art. A precocious woodcarver in childhood, he later sculpted monuments in St. Petersburg, the Crimea, and Estonia. Among his most famous sculptures is the *Kalevipoeg* (1926) monument in Võru and the memorial to the 177 drowned sailors of the battleship *Russalka* (Mermaid) in Tallinn, which he completed in 1902.[4] Adamson's most important contemporary—or near-contemporary—was Kristjan Raud (1865–1943), a painter and graphic artist of the National Romantic tradition whose work consists mostly of pencil and charcoal drawings. Raud was best known for translating scenes from the folk epic *Kalevipoeg,* published in a special 100th anniversary edition in 1935, into visual language. Raud's twin brother, Paul (1865–1930), was also a famous portraitist and painter of historical and religious compositions.

While most artists of Estonian origin studied at art schools in cities such as St. Petersburg, Munich, and Paris, local artistic life began to bridge the gap with Europe with the founding of a series of new art Estonian institutions.

In 1903 the portrait and landscape artist Ants Laikmaa (1866–1942), known for his work in the National Romantic style, opened a studio school in Tallinn; in 1914 the Tallinn Arts and Crafts School was established; and five years later the Pallas Art School, where nearly all of Estonia's greatest painters of the era taught, was founded in Tartu.[5]

While few Estonian artists achieved international standing during the first third of the century, artistic life in Estonia was at least as dynamic as in the other Baltic countries. Artists of the century's first decade—especially those who had close personal connections with the *Noor-Eesti* (Young Estonia) group of writers (see Chapter 6)—were oriented mostly toward modernist European and especially Nordic art. The influence of German Expressionism can be seen in some of the works of Nikolai Triik (1884–1940) and the landscape painter Konrad Mägi (1878–1925), as well as in the sculptures of Jaan Koort (1883–1935), who is also known for his "Egyptian"-style monumental works.

Like Lithuania and Latvia, Estonia has never given birth to any single original art movement, but its artists have often incorporated strands from different artistic trends to create works that are not easily classifiable. At the dawn of the twentieth century Estonian artists were simultaneously cultivating numerous European trends: Impressionism, National Romanticism, and Art Nouveau were characteristic of the century's early years, while the experimental art of the 1910s and 1920s was dominated by Futurism (Ado Vabbe, 1892–1961), Expressionism (Peet Aren, 1889–1960), and Cubism-Constructivism (Jaan Vahtra, 1882–1947). Cubism and Constructivism were of particular interest to members of the Estonian Artists' Group (formed in 1923), which introduced a rational, intellectual conception of art. During the more conservative 1930s, however, these experimental trends were supplanted by late Impressionism (Adamson-Eric, 1902–68) and neo realism.

The best-known Estonian artist of the interwar period—and the only to achieve serious international recognition—was Eduard Wiiralt (1898–1954), a graphic artist who produced most of his works while living in Paris. An analyst of the human psyche, Wiiralt (or Viiralt) created a series of masterpieces in the early 1930s, including the surreal print *Cabaret* (1931) and the imaginative *Hell* (1930–32), a dark and rather unnerving print that features several dozen contorted human, animal, and mechanical heads. Also significant was the versatile Adamson-Eric, whose early paintings were in the German New Objectivity school; later he became better known for his innovations in applied arts such as ceramics, metalworking, and leather handicrafts. The neorealist movement of the 1930s, which appeared first in France and was paralleled in Latvia, can be seen in the granite sculptures of Anton Starkopf (1889–1966). By the late 1930s the political atmosphere in Estonia, as in

Latvia, was no longer conducive to experimentation, and a more conservative aesthetic prevailed under the dictatorship of Konstantin Päts.

ART SINCE 1945

"One may still paint an apple," lamented the writer Helmars Rudzītis in 1948, "but it must be a Soviet apple."[6] These words exemplify the state of artistic life under Soviet occupation during the late Stalin era. During the first decades of Soviet rule the dominant artistic mode was Socialist Realism, whose imposition in the Baltic republics was accompanied by a war on Western cultural influences. Less a creative style than a method of creation, Socialist Realism emphasized socialist political consciousness, heroic optimism, and the personality cult of the leader. For more than four decades creative life in the Baltic countries was regulated by Moscow and by the republican branches of the Union of Artists, which provided artists with material security and the means with which to pursue their artistic goals. While many artists fled to the West in 1944 and others chose silence rather than service, most artists, whatever their misgivings, implicitly accepted the terms that would allow them to exhibit their works in official venues.

Few artists who stayed behind were able to achieve artistic individuality in the early years of the Soviet occupation, when the assertion of one's creative independence usually resulted in prison, Siberian exile, or execution. After Stalin's death in 1953, however, controls on cultural life loosened. Alongside the official regime-sanctioned art there emerged what art historians in the West have called dissident or nonconformist art, encompassing many different styles. However, drawing a line between conformist and nonconformist art was always more difficult in the Baltic republics than in Moscow or Leningrad, since most Baltic artists were not interested in making a political statement or enlightening the authorities. (Ethnic Russian artists were also professionally active in the Baltic republics, but their contributions are usually overlooked.)

From 1965 onward, artistic developments in the Baltic world could be observed at the Vilnius Painting Triennial, which for more than two decades gave the clearest overview of the trends and tendencies in Estonian, Latvian, and Lithuanian painting. These exhibitions showed that despite the Soviet regime's attempts to quarantine its cultural life from the West, artists in the Baltic republics were not entirely isolated from European trends. Indeed, in many ways the Baltic republics, which enjoyed somewhat greater freedom of artistic expression than in other parts of the Soviet empire, remained an outpost of Western culture in the USSR. Today the Baltic artists of a younger generation, having had no experience of communist rule, are especially eager to participate in international trends. Some of their most innovative works, especially in the developing genres of installation art and digital media, are shown in exhibitions all over the world.

Painting and Graphic Art

Some of the artists who fled to the West in 1944 were able to resume their careers outside their homeland with some success. For example, the Lithuanian artist Vytautas Jonynas is best known for the sculptures and stained glass windows he created for churches in America, while the graphic artist, painter, and stage designer Adomas Galdikas (1893–1969) continued his work in Paris and Brooklyn. Somewhat younger artists from Lithuania, such as the painter Vytautas Kasiulis (1918–95) and the sculptor Elena Gaputytė (1927–92), also prospered abroad. Only a handful of artists of the older generation—among them the sculptor Bronius Pundzius (1907–59), the painter Antanas Gudaitis and stained glass maker Stasys Ušinskas (1905–74)—remained in Lithuania and were able to retain their artistic integrity. Many more submitted to the demands of the Soviet state. The painting *Establishing a Kolkhoz* (1950), by Vincas Dilka (1912–97), is a perfect example of a work that corresponded to the aesthetical and ideological requirements of Socialist Realism.

While the early representations of Soviet Latvian reality depicted by painters such as Aleksandrs Ziedris (1905–93) and Ārijs Skride (1906–87) met official expectations, other established Latvian artists such as Rūdolfs Pinnis (1902–92) and Kurts Fridrihsons (1911–91) were expelled from the Artists' Union for their earlier membership in foreign circles (in this case the "French group"). Numerous artists of the next generation, such as the Latvian painter Indulis Zariņš (1929–97), bolstered their careers by sustaining Socialist Realist aesthetics well after Stalin had passed from the scene. But it was not only Lithuanian artists who fled and Latvian artists who served: each of the Baltic countries lost many of their best artists to exile, arrest, or conformity; each produced artists of talent who continued to innovate despite the stifling conditions.

Nikita Khrushchev's thaw in the second half of the 1950s restored some freedom to Soviet artists, despite his famous tirade against abstract experimentation at the Manege exhibition hall in Moscow in 1962. By that time enough holes had been poked through the iron curtain for artistic life in the Baltics to once again begin taking its cues from progressive Western art. Nowhere were the cultural borders that separated the USSR from Europe more porous than in Estonia, which remains the Baltic region's leading center for abstract art today. Eager to experiment outside the boundaries of the officially sanctioned method of Socialist Realism, many progressive artists in Estonia were influenced by artistic developments in Czechoslovakia and Poland, where artistic controls were less stringent.

The first legend of Estonian nonconformist art was Ülo Sooster (1924–70), an artist of the prewar generation and a graduate of the Tartu Art Institute. Arrested during the 1949 sweep and exiled to a Siberian labor camp, Sooster returned to Moscow in 1955, where, despite close surveillance by the KGB, his apartment became a meeting place for liberal thinkers. Bluntly rejecting Socialist Realism, Sooster and his Tartu friends formed the first nonconformist art group. Sooster drew and painted in several different styles, from pure abstraction to Surrealism, Cubism, Expressionism, and realism. The sudden appearance of Surrealism in Soviet art around 1960 owes much to his influence.

Other members of Sooster's "Tartu group" included Valve Janov (b. 1921), Kaja Kärner (1920–98), Lüüdia Vallimäe-Mark (b. 1925), Silvia Jõgever (b. 1924), and Heldur Viires (b. 1927), an abstractionist and creator of collages. Most were former Pallas students, and they represented the first serious challenge to the reigning Socialist Realist orthodoxy. Although not a member of the Tartu group, Olav Maran (b. 1933), a collagist who worked in both the Surrealist and abstract styles, was influenced by the Swiss-born artist Paul Klee and was an important link between the older generation and Estonia's younger artists. The independent artist Lola Liivat Makarova (b. 1928), on the other hand, was indirectly influenced by the American artist Jackson Pollock. The only Estonian artist to work consistently in an expressive abstract style, Makarova mastered the technique of action painting in the early 1960s.

Abstraction emerged from underground with a youth exhibition in the Tallinn Art Hall in 1966, where a nonconformist group called *ANK 64* exhibited officially for the first time. This was one of three distinct artists' groups that formed in the 1960s; the others were *Visarid* (1967–72) in Tartu and *Soup '69* in Tallinn. The 10 original members of *ANK 64* were trained at the Estonian State Art Institute in Tallinn, the republic's leading art school in the postwar era. They included the abstract silk-screen artist and painter Raul Meel (b. 1941), the Surrealist painter Jüri Arrak (b. 1936), the pop artist Malle Leis (b. 1940), the "universal" artist Leonhard Lapin (b. 1947), and Tõnis Vint (b. 1942), who is widely regarded as the most influential avant-garde artist of his generation. Undergoing several stylistic phases during the late 1960s, Vint's art helped generate the 1970s movement of geometric and minimal abstraction.

Soup '69, whose name comes from Andy Warhol's famous Campbell soup can (a popular symbol of artistic freedom in Soviet Estonia), was inspired by American pop art. Organized by Leonhard Lapin—an architect, sculptor, poet, and an organizer of "happenings" and exhibitions—*Soup '69* borrowed from America the idea of using everyday subject matter and ready-made objects; the subject matter, however, was entirely local. The third significant art group of this era was *Visarid,* whose spiritual leader was Kaljo Põllu (b. 1934). Its most significant contribution to Estonian art was the dissemination of information on Western art—via Czech, Polish, Hungarian, and Finnish sources—and organizing exhibitions and seminars.

As the *Visarid* group's only professional artist, Põllu also helped revive printmaking in Estonian art. Graphic art, which had flourished in independent Estonia, experienced a boom in Estonia in the second half of the 1960s and the 1970s, thanks in part to the teachers and graduates of the Graphic Arts Workshop (1947) in Tallinn. The undisputed master of printmaking was Peeter Ulas (b. 1934), yet several important women innovators emerged in Soviet Estonia during this period, including Vive Tolli (b. 1928), whose work was notable for its blending of tradition and modernity, and Concordia Klar (b. 1938), who was the only printmaker in Estonia to experiment with color in the 1960s and 1970s.

Forming the nucleus of the movement of geometric and minimal abstraction, Tõnis Vint, Leonhard Lapin, and Raul Meel influenced a younger generation of artists including Sireje Runge (b. 1950), Siim-Tanel Annus (b. 1960), Ene Kull (b. 1953), and Mari Kurismaa (b. 1956). Some younger Estonian artists—notably Ando Keskküla (b. 1950), Jaan Elken (b. 1954), and Ilmar Kruusamae (b. 1957)—were inspired by photorealism (or, as it has also been called, hyperrealism or superrealism) in the 1970s and early 1980s, a style that eliminated any hint of individuality in the artist's work while challenging one to distinguish the original from a copy. Other artists searched for an altogether different originality. Kaljo Põllu, for example, became interested in Finno-Ugric themes, while Jüri Arrak is best known for his exploration of religious and mythical themes.

Although the art of Latvia generally does not exhibit the level of abstraction characteristic of Estonian art, contemporary Latvia has nevertheless produced a number of noteworthy abstract artists.[7] The watercolor painters Oļģerts Jaunarājs (b. 1907) and Kurts Fridrihsons, who in 1956 returned to Latvia after a long sentence in the gulag, were among the most important pioneers of abstract art in Soviet Latvia, as was the landscape artist Jānis Pauļuks (1906–84). While Ojārs Ābols (1922–83) was considered an establishment artist, he nevertheless was a supporter of unofficial aesthetics and openly exhibited his abstract oil paintings. On the other hand, Zenta Logina (1908–83), Latvia's most radical abstractionist, kept her work hidden until her death. Likewise, Aleksandrs Zviedris (1905–93), who began his career by painting industrial landscapes in the official Socialist Realist tradition, kept his later abstract compositions (*The Seagull,* 1972) hidden from the public eye. Contrary to once-popular beliefs about the uniformity of Soviet rule, the reality was that while Moscow tolerated the abstract art of Estonia, it showed somewhat less patience with nonconformist art in Latvia and Lithuania.

Despite these limitations, many Latvian artists were able to balance the system's insistent demand for obedience with their own personal desires for artistic freedom and experimentation. No Latvian artist blurred the boundaries that separated genres better than Ilmārs Blumbergs, who first gained public recognition for his stage designs in the early 1970s. Since then his creative impulses have found outlets in painting, printmaking, and ceramics. Although very different stylistically, Boriss Bērziņš (1930–2002) was one the most innovative Latvian artists of the Soviet era; his minimalist paintings are distinguished by their earthy colors. Latvian Surrealism debuted in the 1970s and can be seen in the etchings of Lolita Zikmane (b. 1941) and the paintings of Juris Ditimers (b. 1947). Surrealist elements can also be seen in the paintings of one of Latvia's most important women artists, the Expressionist Maija Tabaka (b. 1939).

While Jackson Pollack-style action painting never really caught on in Latvia, Jānis Pauļuks and Miķelis Golts (b. 1922) used the splatter technique in the 1960s and 1970s. The paintings of Birute Delle (b. 1944) often embraced the grotesque (*The King*, 1971). Like many artists in the USSR she was subjected to KGB surveillance (her husband was an informant) in the 1970s and 1980s. The abstraction of photorealist paintings by Bruno Vasiļevskis (1939–90), Miervaldis Polis (b. 1948), and Polis's wife Līga Purmale (b. 1948), also signified resistance to official aesthetics, but the style did not provoke the authorities—even if the content sometimes did. Many of the works that *did* provoke the Soviet government in the early years of Soviet rule—such as Indriķis Zeberiņš's *Kolkhoz Cow* (1951), which mocked the promised utopia of collectivized agriculture by outfitting comrade cow with two udders—have not survived.

The creative talents of a younger generation of Latvian painters were nurtured under markedly freer conditions in the late 1980s and 1990s. While some are attracted to the abstract art of northern Europe, others are oriented toward classical painting traditions. Dace Liela (b. 1957) is attracted to natural themes, especially the sea, while the monochrome paintings of Ritums Ivanovs (b. 1968) often seem to occupy the space between Impressionist painting and realist photography (*The Heat*, 1998). Ieva Jurjāne (b. 1972) began her career as an expressive painter (*Little Breast Holder*, 1999) but has found even greater success as a set and costume designer.

Lithuanian art during the Soviet era was influenced by the country's proximity to central Europe (and Poland in particular) and the Catholic Church. Even under Soviet rule Lithuanian artists retained their country's traditions of figurative realism and the use of bold, expressive colors. While Soviet authorities since the thaw tolerated Lithuanian expressionism, abstraction and surrealism were deemed unacceptable. Perhaps the most important constant in Lithuanian art has been its themes, which have most often included religion, suffering, and homeland.

The most important Lithuanian artist of the thaw generation was the Expressionist painter Jonas Švažas (1925–76). A Communist Party member after 1952, Švažas broke formal restrictions on style but satisfied party authorities by using acceptable motifs and subjects. The blurry line that separated official and nonconformist art was sometimes crossed by Silvestras Džiaukštas (b. 1928), a leader in Lithuanian figurative painting in the 1960s. With paintings like *Death of an Activist* (1967), Džiaukštas is considered a representative of "official" art, yet his expressive nudes were rejected by the authorities. Indeed, in the 1960s and 1970s only a few Lithuanian artists—Kazimiera Zimblytė (1933–99), Eugenijus Antanas Cukermanas (b. 1935), Vladislovas Žilius (b. 1939), and Linas Katinas (b. 1941)—were true nonconformists, as figurative realism and Expressionism continued to dominate Lithuanian painting and sculpture. While artists such as Antanas Gudaitis, who taught at the Vilnius Academy from the 1960s until the 1980s, upheld the prewar modernist traditions of the *Ars* group, artistic life in deeply Catholic Lithuania remained more conservative than in Latvia and Estonia.

The first Lithuanian to paint in an abstract manner openly was probably Vytautas Povilaitis (b. 1927), while the abstract works of artists such as Leonas Katinas (1907–84), Sarūnas Šimulynas (1930–99), Vytautas Šerys (b. 1931), and Eugenijus Cukermanas (b. 1935) remained hidden from view for many years. Indeed, it was not until 1990 that the works of Zimblytė and Cukermanas were exhibited at the Baltic Painting Triennial. Of this group, Cukermanas, whose use of dull colors contrasts with the bolder colors used by many Lithuanian painters, comes closest to pure abstraction. More "Lithuanian" in respect to coloring are the works of Gudaitis's student Jonas Čeponis (b. 1926), whose works are known for their bright coloring and emotionality, and the compositions of the abstract painters Raimundas Martinėnas (b. 1941) and Algirdas Petrulis (b. 1912).

Mythological and religious themes were popular among Lithuanian artists after the 1960s, exemplified in paintings and engravings of Vincas Kisarauskas (1934–88) and in the works of Leonardas Gutauskas (b. 1938), Sarūnas Sauka (b. 1958), and Jonas Gasiūnas (b. 1954). Kisarauskas's interest in human tragedies was manifested in paintings such as *After the War* (1965), which represented the maimed figure of an anti-Soviet resistance fighter. (It is hardly surprising that works such as this were not accepted for exhibition.) Likewise, paintings by Valentinas Antanavičius (b. 1936) often have at their center the human figure—"usually a peculiar, half human personage, with a greatly deformed anatomy."[8] Influenced by Expressionism and Surrealism as well as Lithuanian folk art, the paintings of Antanavičius attempt to show the beauty in "ugliness."

While painters such as Kisarauskas and Antanavičius focused on the human figure, some Lithuanian artists drew inspiration from the urban landscape. Aloyzas Stasiulevičius (b. 1931) is best known for his Vilnius cityscapes. An initiator of the collage technique in Lithuanian art, his works of the late 1960s focus more on separate fragments of the city. The 1970s paintings of Algimantas Kuras (b. 1940) focused on objects related to industry—bridge piers, railway junctions, electrical power stations, cranes, and so on. Rather than glorifying Soviet technological and industrial progress, his works, by focusing on the ugly, the discarded, and the banal, showed that even the unattractive aspects of one's environment are natural and beautiful. While Kuras focused on objects that represented "progress," the Expressionist painter Povilas Ričardas Vaitekūnas (b. 1940) was more interested in the objects one sees in an old Lithuanian village. Unlike Kuras, however, he was not interested in depicting the beauty of their ugliness. Rural themes were also present in the paintings of Leopoldas Surgailis (b. 1928), whose works sometimes showed the influence of Lithuanian folk sculpture, and in the works of Jonas Daniliauskas (b. 1950) in the 1980s.

One of the most popular Lithuanian artists today is Vygantas Paukštė (b. 1957), whose works are distinguished by their mythical character and subtle irony. In keeping with the Lithuanian tradition, he uses bold, expressive colors; however, his style is usually characterized as "postmodern," distinguished by the great variety and combination of expressive modes. The work of the popular Surrealist painter Petras Repšys (b. 1940) is also of interest, as it shows the influence of both folk art and Baroque graphic art. An ensemble of frescoes by Repšys, titled *The Seasons* (1976–85), decorates the interior of the Center of Lithuanian Studies at Vilnius University and features ethnographic and mythological themes. Among Lithuania's younger painters, the most noteworthy are Vilmantas Marckinkevičius (b. 1969), an expressive figure painter who enjoys mythological subjects, and Jurga Barilaitė (b. 1972), a painter and collagist.

Sculpture

The ubiquity of memorial culture in Baltic cities, and in Latvia and Lithuania in particular, is strinking. While the Balts prefer to erect memorial sculptures to their favorite writers and cultural figures, in the early years of Soviet rule the genre took on monumental proportions and was used for expressly political purposes. Nearly all of these works, such as the monument to Stalin that was built in Vilnius in 1949, or the monuments to Lenin that could be found in most Baltic cities, have been removed from public sight.[9] A number of Lithuania's Soviet-era monumental statues have been reassembled in the Soviet Sculpture Park in the Lithuanian hamlet of Grūtas—a haven of Soviet kitsch.[10]

While the Stalins, Lenins, and Marxes of the Baltic states have found new homes in sculpture parks and warehouses, a few works of Socialist Realist sculpture remain in place. Riga's most famous example of Soviet monumental sculpture is Valdis Albergs's monument to the *Latvian Riflemen* (1970) who defended Lenin's revolution. Today many Latvians would prefer to see the memorial removed from central Riga and replaced by something more politically neutral. The "Green Bridge" in Vilnius, reconstructed in 1950–52, is held in higher popular esteem. Featuring four sculptural groups—soldiers, workers, peasants, and students—in theatrical postures, the bridge is the last Socialist Realist monument in Vilnius. Other sculptural classics of the Soviet period in Lithuania include Petras Aleksandravičius's (1906–97) monument to the writer *Žemaitė* (1951) and works by Gediminas Jokūbonis's (b. 1927) such as *Mother* (1960), which stands in Pirčiupiai , and the granite monument to *Adam Mickiewicz* (or rather *Adomas Mickevičius*), which was unveiled near the church of St. Anne in Vilnius in 1984.

The influence of classical sculpture can be seen in the works of Lithuania's Petras Mazūras (b. 1949), which decorate the interior and exterior of numerous modern buildings. His statue *Elektra* (1994) stands atop the Lithuanian Energy Museum in Vilnius. The compositions of Stanislovas Kuzma (b. 1947) are often strongly influenced by realistic Renaissance sculpture. While Kuzma is best known for his church art and the restored statues of St. Stanislaus, St. Helen, and St. Casimir that stand atop the Vilnius Cathedral, his other significant monumental works include *Shooter* (1986) on Sundial Square in Šiauliai and *Feast of Muses* (1981), which looms over the entrance to the Lithuanian National Drama Theater in Vilnius.

Lithuania's most famous sculptor today may be Mindaugas Navakas (b. 1952), whose abstract sculptures are distinguished by their grand scale. Indeed, his giant metal constructions can be found all over Europe. At home Navakas organized the symposia of concrete sculptures in Aukštieji Paneriai (1985), in the courtyard of what is now the President's Office (1990, 1992), and in Santariškės (1991), thereby becoming the first Lithuanian artist to create nonfigurative and nondecorative sculptures for public spaces.

The Estonian sculptors Jaak Soans (b. 1943), Villu Jõgeva (b. 1940), and Kaarel Kurismaa (b. 1939) earned reputations as first-rate artists in the 1970s and 1980s. Soans's best-known monumental work is the bronze portrait of the novelist *Anton Tammsaare* (1978), which is a Tallinn landmark. One of the best-known sculptors of the younger generation is Tauno Kangro (b. 1966), who specializes in bronze sculptures with mythological themes. While staging exhibitions all over Europe, Kangro also built *Statue of an Aurochs* (2002) in Rakvere, one of Estonia's oldest towns. In general, however, the place of sculpture is less prominent in the art of Estonia than in that of Lithuania and Latvia. Indeed, with the departure of Soviet-era monuments in the early 1990s sculpture seems to have disappeared not only from exhibitions but from the cities as well. Lacking an outlet in the contemporary art scenes of Tallinn and Tartu, the more adaptable Estonian sculptors have moved toward performances, installations, and other media.

While sculpture has languished in Estonia, it thrives in neighboring Latvia, where sculptural quadrennials have taken place since 1972. The folklore revival movement of the 1970s did much to stimulate sculptural art in Latvia. Influenced by the earlier work of Teodors Zaļkalns, the sculptors who emerged in the 1970s broadened the relationship between sculpture and the Latvian landscape. The country's most significant landscape-inspired sculptural project is the Open-Air Art Museum at Pedvāle in western Latvia. Owned and directed by Ojārs Feldbergs (b. 1947), who founded it in the early 1990s, the museum displays Feldbergs's own stone, granite, and bronze compositions as well as the works of emerging artists. The guiding principle of all the exhibitions is their relationship with the hills and trees of rural Latvia. Another Latvian sculpture park, situated on Daina Hill (near Turaida Castle) in Sigulda, features 25 granite sculptures by Indulis Ranka (b. 1934). Inspired by the Latvian *dainas* collected by Krišjānis Barons, to whom the sculpture park was dedicated in 1985, these allegorical sculptures are intended to express the national ethos of the Latvian people.

Lithuania, too, has several open-air sculpture parks. The oldest and most famous of these is the Mažvydas Sculpture Park in Klaipėda. Modern sculptures are also scattered about the Youth Park in the small city of Alytus (the city's Museum of Ethnography also has a collection of wooden folk sculpture), located in Dzūkija. The statue *Angel of Freedom*, originally erected in Alytus's city center in 1928, is of some interest because of the way it echoes Lithuania's tragic and inspiring history: dedicated to the soldiers who fought for Lithuania's independence in 1918–20, the statue shattered in 1934 and was subsequently restored, only to be torn down by the Soviets in 1952. It was restored again in 1991.

Another interesting sculpture zone in Lithuania was the one created in 2002 in an industrial part of Kaunas. Built for the purpose of brightening up an otherwise dreary location, its layout keeps with the old Lithuanian tradition of roadside sculptures and features works by Algirdas Bosas (b. 1943) and Gediminas Akstinas (b. 1961). However, Lithuania's most ambitious sculpture park is Europas Parkas, founded in 1991 on the initiative of sculptor Gintaras Karosas (b. 1968). Located in a forest north of Vilnius at the precise spot where, according to the findings of the French National Geographic Institute, the center of Europe is located, Europas Parkas is a 55-hectare permanent exhibit of more than 70 works by internationally renowned sculptors. Karosas's most famous work is *LNK Infotree* (2000), a sculpture consisting of 6,000 broken television sets at the center of which is the figure of Lenin.

Photography, Installation, Performance, and Video Art

At a time when Baltic art institutions were starved for funds and public subsidies for art were disappearing, in the 1990s the Hungarian entrepreneur George Soros flooded Eastern Europe with money for the sustenance of contemporary art. For several years Estonia's Soros Center of Contemporary Art, founded in 1993, budgeted more money for art projects than the Estonian Ministry of Culture, although today the state has reclaimed its leading role and the Center operates without Soros.[11] In Lithuania the Soros Center for Contemporary Art operated from 1990 to 1999, while in Latvia the Soros Center was renamed the Latvian Center for Contemporary Art, and it continues to provide financial support for the creative activities of Latvian artists while organizing annual exhibitions. The principal beneficiaries of this largesse, especially in Estonia, have been artists employing nontraditional media. However, the shift away from the traditional art forms such as painting and sculpture toward photography and digital media, as well as installation and performance art, has been taking place for several decades, usually echoing trends that began first in Europe and America.

Like literature and just about all other forms of creativity, the art of photography, which only depicted places and locations in the independent Baltic republics in the 1920s and 1930s, belonged to the sphere of propaganda during the first decades of Soviet rule. Only in the 1960s did photography begin to achieve a certain creative independence in the Baltics. An early innovator was Lithuania's Povilas Karpavičius (b. 1909), who in 1953 staged an exhibition of color photographs made by means of the isopolychromic technology that he invented. Virgilius Sonta (1952–92) was best known for his landscapes of the 1970s and 1980s, while Antanas Sutkus (b. 1939) continues to add to his international reputation for excellence in human documentary photography. Among Lithuania's most prominent artistic photographers today is Romualdas Pozerskis (b. 1942), who chronicled the *Saąjūdis* period in 1988–91 and continues to work in many genres.

Estonia's most innovative photographer of the Soviet period was Peeter Tooming (1939–97), who in 1987 began to reconstruct various images of

Estonia that were collected in the 1930s by the photographer Carl Sarap. The result was a unique exhibition and book project titled *Fifty Years Later,* where the wordless comparison of "then" and "now" photos illuminated the changing Estonian landscape under socialism. Latvia's answer to Tooming was Egons Spuris (1931–90), who is remembered for his photographs of Riga's urban environment. Latvia's Atis Ieviņš (b. 1946) is one of the Baltic region's leading innovators of photo-based serigraphy, whereby photography's aesthetics are injected into other media, particularly silk screens.

By the 1990s photography had acquired a central position in the art of each of the Baltic countries, but perhaps nowhere more so than in Estonia. This is due in large part to the work of Peeter Linnaap (b. 1960), who is the spiritual leader of Tallinn's Center of Photography, and the *Destudio* team (Peeter-Maria Laurits and Kerkki-Erich Merila), whose photography has influenced advertising and fashion photography in Estonia since the early 1990s. Both the Tartu Art Museum and the Museum of Estonian Art have been actively purchasing photographic art for their collections, and numerous exhibitions of Estonian photographic art have been staged both in Estonia and abroad.

It was only toward the end of the Soviet era that performance and body art became popular in the Baltic countries. Among the early innovators was Andris Grīnbergs, who introduced these forms to Latvia at the end of the 1960s. His wedding—a two-day event titled *The Wedding of Jesus Christ* (1972)—was Latvia's first "happening." With his wife, Inta, Grīnbergs organized a series of hippie-like happenings in the following years, while also directing a series of short experimental films. The sexually provocative *Self-Portrait* (1972), for example, depicts the artist in protest against totalitarian ideology; it is part of a larger multimedia project of self-documentation that continues to the present day. The performances of Latvia's *Workshop for the Restoration of Nonexistent Sensations* (formed in 1982) echoed those organized by students at Tallinn's School of Architecture about a decade earlier. In the second half of the 1980s its artists—Juris Boiko (b. 1955), Hardijs Lediņš (b. 1955), Inguna Černova (b. 1962), and others—staged multimedia events in Riga comparable to those happening concurrently in New York's East Village. In recent years the performance art tradition has been continued by the cultural provocateur Miervaldis Polis, whose "Bronze Man" persona—part of an ongoing series of exercises in self-replication—was often seen on the streets of Riga in the late 1980s and 1990s.

While *Group T* (1986–96) established performance art in Estonia, one of the first performance art groups in Lithuania was the *Post Ars Group,* which formed in 1989 in Kaunas. Its talents included the sculptor Robertas Antinas, Jr. (b. 1946), the photorealist painter Aleksas Andriuškevičius (b. 1959), artist-musician Česlovas Lukenskas (b. 1959), and photographer Gintaras Zinkevicius.

From 1989 to 1993 the *Post Ars Group* organized as many as 50 actions, from simple exhibitions to complex performances involving scores of participants.

Installation art has been developing in the Baltics since the 1980s, when Latvia's Oļegs Tillbergs (b. 1956) and Ojārs Pētersons (b. 1956) came to the public's attention for their architectonic works. Among Pētersons's most famous installation projects is *Bridge across the Sea* (1990), which consisted of orange-colored sculptures in Riga and Finland (later Germany) that taken together formed a metaphorical bridge across the Finnish Bay. Jüri Okas (b. 1950) was one of Estonia's foremost installation and earth artists in the 1970s. However, by the 1990s he had turned to architecture, designing several large commercial buildings in Tallinn and Pärnu.

In Lithuania the leading video and installation artists of the younger generation include Giedrius Kumetaitis, Mindaugas Ratavičius, and Simonas Travydas, who together comprise the *Academic Training Group* (ATG). Producing their works jointly, the ATG artists have used installations combined with video images to explore themes related to war, politics, and culture. The works of Zilvinas Kempinas (b. 1969), Eglė Rakauskaitė (b. 1967), and Vita Zaman (b. 1976) have also attracted much attention in recent years. Many of these younger artists are accustomed to working in a variety of media. Dainis Liškevičius (b. 1970), who trained as a sculptor, today works mostly in sound and video, while Laura Stasiulytė (b. 1977) is not only a singer and performance artist, but is also a creator of videos and installations. Gintaras Makarevičius (b. 1965) is best known for his video works and visual art installations but has also worked as a stage designer. His most talked-about film to date is *The Pit* (2002), which depicts the everyday life of a family composed of three generations of gravediggers. As a counter to Soviet notions of progress, the film's intention was to recreate the rhythm and mood of the four seasons in a timeless Lithuanian village.[12]

Some of the most interesting developments in video art in recent years have taken place in Estonia. The career of Jaan Toomik (b. 1961) epitomizes the changes that have taken place in Estonian art in recent decades: once a painter of mythological themes—a popular motif in the 1980s—by the 1990s Toomik had evolved into a creator of land art and video installations. He first earned local notoriety for a piece titled *May 15th–31st, 1992,* in which he displayed cans of his own feces and the corresponding menu for that day. However, his best-known film internationally is *Dancing with Dad* (2003), a meditation on death that begins with its protagonist comically dancing on his father's grave to a guitar riff by Jimi Hendrix. Kai Kaljo (b. 1959) also earned international recognition for the unpleasant truths she revealed in her short film *Loser* (1997), in which she tells her entire life story in a few sentences, each of which is punctuated by a burst of canned laughter.

The development of video art in Estonia in recent years has been facilitated by the founding of the E-Media Center (within the Estonian Academy of Sciences), which instructs students on the use of technology in art. The top training center for young Latvian artists today is the Visual Communication Department of the Latvian Academy of Art, which is currently headed by Pētersons. Some of its recent graduates, having had no experience with social-ist artistic training, are now cutting-edge conceptual artists with strong inter-national connections. Dace Džerina, Anta and Dita Pences, and the members of the *F5* group that was formed in 1998 (including Mārtiņš Ratniks, Ieva Rubeze, and Līga Marcinkēviča), have all gained international recognition for their multimedia work. Likewise, Gints Gabrāns (b. 1970) earned national attention in 2001 for transforming Starix, a homeless person he discovered at the Riga rail station, into a nationally recognized media star. Working with Gabrāns, the artist Monica Pormale (b. 1974) created a project titled *Riga Dating Agency* (2001), another comment on media manipulation: it exhibits life-sized photo portraits of women from Riga who have responded to per-sonal ads placed by foreigners. Favoring digital video in particular, many of Latvia's young "lyrical technocrats" not only stage formal exhibitions of their work but also contribute their images to the local club and music scene.

NOTES

1. There has also been a "Man of Sorrows"—a suffering Christ—tradition in German painting since the fifteenth century. It is a common theme in Polish folk art as well.

2. S. A. Mansbach, *Modern Art in Eastern Europe: From the Baltic to the Balkans, ca. 1890–1939* (New York: Cambridge University Press, 1999), 4.

3. Zāle was also a participant in Lenin's Plan of Monumental Propaganda in the early years of the Soviet regime.

4. Another Kalevipoeg statue in Tartu, destroyed by the Soviets, has been restored recently.

5. The Pallas school was shut down by Soviet authorities in 1940 but continued after 1944 as the Tartu Art Institute. Also, during World War I the art collection housed by Tartu University was moved to Vorenezh in Russia, where these treasures remain.

6. Alla Rosenfeld and Norton T. Dodge, eds., *Art of the Baltics: The Struggle for Freedom of Artistic Expression under the Soviets, 1945–1991* (New Brunswick, N.J.: Rutgers University Press, 2002), 12.

7. Although he made his career in New York, Mark Rothko (1903–70) is the world's most famous Latvia-born artist. Born Marcus Rothkovich in what was then Dvinsk (now Daugavpils), Rothko and his family emigrated to the United States in 1913. His early years were spent in obscurity, experimenting with Surrealism and mythology. In the 1950s he achieved international fame for his pioneering work in Abstract Expressionism.

8. Raminta Jurėnaitė, ed., *100 Contemporary Lithuanian Artists* (Vilnius: R. Paknys Publishing House, 2000), 20.

9. The Lenin statue in the heavily Russian city of Narva was pulled down in December 1993, making it the last of the Lenin statues in the Baltics to be removed; however, it was immediately placed in the courtyard of Hermann Castle.

10. Reflecting the shift in the political environment, works such as Glebs Pantelejevs's *Monument to the Victims of the KGB* were erected in the 1990s.

11. In 1995 the Estonian Cultural Endowment was established to support the arts. Its income comes from taxes on alcohol, tobacco, and gambling.

12. One of the most provocative exhibitions by a Lithuanian artist in recent years was the "live art performance" of Ramune Mitrikevičiute (known by her pseudonym Gele) on April 24, 2005. Partner of the German performance artist Winfried Witt, Ramune Gele (flower) gave birth to her daughter before 30 live spectators at an art gallery in Berlin.

SELECTED READINGS

Gimbutas, Marija. *Ancient Symbolism in Lithuanian Folk Art.* Philadelphia: American Folklore Society, 1958.

Jurėnaitė, Raminta, ed. *100 Contemporary Lithuanian Artists.* Vilnius: R. Paknys Publishing House, 2000.

Ladjevardi, Hamid, and Barbara Crane. *Baltic Art: Contemporary Paintings and Sculptures.* Washington, D.C.: U.S.-Baltic Foundation, 2000.

Mansbach, S. A. *Modern Art in Eastern Europe: From the Baltic to the Balkans, ca. 1890–1939.* New York: Cambridge University Press, 1999.

Rosenfeld, Alla and Norton T. Dodge, eds. *Art of the Baltics: The Struggle for Freedom of Artistic Expression under the Soviets, 1945–1991.* New Brunswick, N.J.: Rutgers University Press, 2002.

Saliklis, Ruta T. Sacred Wood: *The Contemporary Lithuanian Woodcarving Revival.* Madison, Wis.: Elvehjem Museum of Art, 1998.

Other Sources and Websites

For more information on the folk art of Lithuania, see the Web sites "Folk Art" by Elena Počiulpaitė at ausis.gf.vu.lt/eka/art/art_c.html and "Lithuanian Folk Art" by Sister Ona Mikaila at javlb.org/bridges/iss999/folkart.html. For Lithuania's modern art, see the "Art Lithuania" Web site, www.culture.lt/Lietuva/en.html. An excellent resource for the art of Estonia is the Estonia Institute's Web site, www.einst.ee. Also see the Estonica website, www.estonica.org/. For recent trends in Latvian art, see "The 'Third Wave' in Latvia's New Art" by Helēna Demakova at www.kpp.lv/en/culture/texts_hd_1.php. A series of essays on contemporary art in the Baltic countries may be accessed from the Refleksija Web site, www.balticart.org/.

Glossary

Art Deco   an early twentieth-century movement in the decorative arts characterized by its opulence and the use of symmetrical geometric forms.

Art Nouveau   a movement in art, architecture and interior design from the 1880s to the 1910s, characterized by its eclecticism, exuberance, and high level of craftsmanship (also called Jugendstil).

Baroque   a period and a style that started around 1600; Baroque architecture was characterized by its boldness and ornamentation, while Baroque music emphasized polyphony and counterpoint.

belashi   a popular form of fast food in the Baltic countries, belashi are deep-fried dumplings filled with meat.

cepilin   a popular Lithuanian potato dish in the shape of a zeppelin.

classicism   in the arts refers to a reverence for the classical antiquity of the Greeks and Romans; it is characterized by its formalism and restraint.

constructivism   an art movement that began in Russia around 1914, constructivism was characterized by its geometric forms and use of industrial materials.

cubism   an early twentieth-century art movement in which the artist depicts the subject from multiple angles rather than from only one.

dainas   traditional Latvian folk songs, typically consisting of only four lines.

Deutschbalten (Baltic Germans) Germans who dominated the Baltic region since their arrival in the Middle Ages.

Dievs supreme deity of Latvian pagans (Dievas in Lithuanian).

Dievturība religion of Latvian neopagans.

Estland German name for northern Estonia during the eras of foreign (German, Danish, Swedish, and Russian) rule.

Expressionism a twentieth-century art form in which reality is distorted for emotional effect.

Finno-Ugric a subfamily of the Uralic languages that includes Estonian and Finnish.

Functionalism an architectural principle that the design of a building should be based on that building's purpose.

Futurism an early twentieth-century art movement that gave expressionism to the dynamism, speed, and energy of mechanical processes.

gira a Lithuanian nonalcoholic beverage made from fermented bread; in Latvia it is known as kvass.

glasnost the policy of "openness" that began in 1986 under Soviet leader Mikhail Gorbachev.

Gothic an architectural style associated with the cathedrals and churches built in Europe from the twelfth century onwards.

Impressionism a late nineteenth-century art movement that began in France and was characterized by visible brush strokes and the use of light, bright colors.

Jaunlatviesi (Young Latvians) Latvian intellectuals of the nineteenth century who chose not to assimilate into the dominant German culture and instead stimulated Latvia's "national awakening."

Jesuits Catholic clergymen who are members of the Society of Jesus; noted for their missionary and educational work and their intellectual contributions.

Kalevipoeg (Son of Kalev) Estonian national epic created by F. R. Kreutzwald in the mid-nineteenth century.

Karaites a small community of Turkic Jews in Lithuania (also known as Karaim).

kringel coffee cake of German origin.

Kūčios Lithuanian Christmas Eve celebration; in Latvia it is known as ķūķi.

kvass Latvian nonalcoholic beverage typically made from fermented rye bread and honey; in Latvia it is known as gira.

Lāčplēsis   (Bear Slayer) Latvian national epic published by Andrējs Pumpurs in 1882.

Laima   Baltic goddess of fate and happiness.

Latgale   region of southeastern Latvia distinguished by its distinctive dialect and traditions.

līgotnes   Latvian songs traditionally associated with the summer solstice.

Litvaks   Lithuanian Jews.

Livland   German name for the region made up of eastern Latvia and southern Estonia during era of foreign (German, Swedish, Russian) rule.

Mannerism   artistic and architectural style of the sixteenth century characterized by its emotion and visual daring; a transitional style between High Renaissance and Baroque.

Mardipäev   Estonian name for the St. Martin's Day (November 11); a holiday that is celebrated in a manner reminiscent of American Halloween.

National Awakenings   raising of national consciousness, led by Estonian, Latvian, and Lithuanian intellectuals, during the nineteenth century.

Noor-Eesti   literary group in early twentieth-century Estonia that sought greater contacts with the West.

perestroika   Soviet policy of "restructuring" that began in 1986.

Pērkons   Latvian thunder god (Perkūnas in Lithuanian).

photorealism   an art movement of the 1960s and 1970s dominated by painters who consciously created paintings that were barely distinguishable from photographs; also known as hyperrealism or superrealism.

pīrāgi   Latvian deep-fried dumplings, typically filled with bacon and onions.

Polonization   assimilation by Lithuanian elites by the dominant Polish culture.

Prussians   West Balts who were conquered by the Germans and who by the eighteenth century had been assimilated.

putra   Latvian porridge.

raudos   laments sung at funerals and weddings in Lithuania and parts of Latvia.

Riigikogu   Estonian parliament.

Romanesque   style of Western European architecture in the eleventh and twelfth centuries characterized by the use of round arches and vaults.

Romanticism   artistic and intellectual movement originating in the late eighteenth century that stressed emotion, nature, heroism, and the individual imagination.

Romuva   religion of Lithuanian neopagans.

Rūpintojėlis   "pensive Christ" figure that features prominently in Lithuanian folk sculpture.

Russification   Imperial Russian policy of culturally and linguistically assimilating the empire's non-Russians.

Rzecspospolita   once Europe's largest state, the Polish-Lithuanian Commonwealth was created by the union of the Polish and Lithuanian crowns in 1569 (Union of Lublin) and disappeared in 1795 following the third partition by Russia, Austria, and Prussia.

Saiema   Latvian parliament.

Seimas   Lithuanian parliament.

Setus   linguistically and culturally distinctive people living in the Setumaa region of Estonia.

Socialist Realism   realistic art form developed in the Soviet Union for the purpose of furthering the regime's ideological and political goals.

song festivals   Baltic tradition that began in 1869 in Tartu and features thousands of singers and performers.

Symbolism   late nineteenth-century art and literary movement that emphasized spirituality, the imagination, and dreams and was characterized by the use of symbols to express allegorical meaning.

Taara   high god of Estonian pagans.

Thaw   modest relaxation of political control over cultural life in the Soviet Union after Stalin's death in 1953.

verileib   Estonian fried blood bread.

Index

About the Author

KEVIN O'CONNOR is Assistant Professor of History at Gonzaga University, Spokane, Washington. He is also the author of *The History of the Baltic States* (Greenwood, 2003).